FILM AND COMIC BOOKS

EDITED BY

IAN GORDON

MARK JANCOVICH

MATTHEW P. MCALLISTER

FILM and

UNIVERSITY PRESS OF MISSISSIPPI / JACKSON

COMIC BOOKS

www.upress.state.ms.us

The University Press of Mississippi is a member of the
Association of American University Presses.

Copyright © 2007 by University Press of Mississippi
All rights reserved
Manufactured in the United States of America

First edition 2007

∞

Library of Congress Cataloging-in-Publication Data

Film and comic books / edited by Ian Gordon, Mark Jancovich, and Matthew P. McAllister.
— 1st ed.
   p. cm.
  Includes bibliographical references and index.
  ISBN-13: 978-1-57806-977-4 (cloth : alk. paper)
  ISBN-10: 1-57806-977-7 (cloth : alk. paper)
  ISBN-13: 978-1-57806-978-1 (pbk. : alk. paper)
  ISBN-10: 1-57806-978-5 (pbk. : alk. paper) 1. Comic strip characters in motion pictures.
I. Gordon, Ian, 1954– II. Jancovich, Mark. III. McAllister, Matthew P.
  PN1995.9.C36F55 2007
  791.43′657—dc22

                                           2006032675

British Library Cataloging-in-Publication Data available

CONTENTS

INTRODUCTION

Films based on comics are not a new or recent phenomenon. The association of film and comics dates back to the early years of both as forms of mass-distributed media. As early as 1906, Edwin S. Porter created a live-action adaptation of Winsor McCay's comic strip *Dreams of the Rarebit Fiend* and later McCay himself became a key innovator in film animation. In 1914 Charles H. France directed a short live-action film entitled *Buster Brown on the Care and Treatment of Goats* based on the comic strip character. Comic book characters such as Superman and Batman appeared in B movies and film serials long before the blockbuster adaptations of the 1970s and 1980s. Likewise Superman, Batman, Spider-Man, and the Hulk featured in low production value television series from the 1950s to the 1970s. The relationship between film and comics may also work in the other direction. Films have served as content fodder for comics since the silent-film era, including the creation of comic-strip or comic book versions of such movie icons as Charlie Chaplin, Fatty Arbuckle, Hopalong Cassidy, and Bob Hope.

In recent years filmmakers have adapted a plethora of comic books for the screen including Marvel's the X-Men, Spider-Man, Blade, and the Hulk, and from DC new film versions of Batman and Superman. Many of these have been wildly successful at the box office and are held up as the ideal model for the Hollywood blockbuster. In June 2006, the magazine *Entertainment Weekly* choose X-Men's Wolverine as "Hollywood's most dominant franchise character," over others such as James Bond and Harry Potter; Spider-Man was third (Stack, 2006). Producers have also tapped alternative comics such as *From Hell*, *American Splendor*, and *Ghost World* for cinemagraphic treatments. Production deals for comic book character-based movies have multiplied rapidly. It seems that more is at stake than a shift from low budget/status productions to blockbusters. Critical acclaim has flowed for many of the recent efforts, and respected directors such as Sam Mendes and Ang Lee have lent their talents to films based on comic books. At the same time, particularly since the success of *Maus*, comic books have gained increased critical respectability even attaining the dizzy heights of favorable reviews in the *New York Times* and the *New York Review of Books*, albeit accompanied by discussions of what constitutes a comic book and finely delineated distinctions between genuine artistic merit and dross.

In the modern blockbuster film era, which roughly dates from *Superman* (1978), and which forms a prime focus of this work, motion picture creative personnel use comic book texts and comic book authorial intention in an attempt to add authenticity to comic book films. Christian Bale, the actor who played Batman in the darker, more adult 2005 film *Batman Begins*, argued that his interpretation of Batman: "is what Bob Kane intended when he first created the character . . . I spoke with his wife, and she said that he was appalled when the (1960s) TV series spoofed what he had intended. But then you had the great revivals in the comic books" (Strauss U6). Movie studios may even court the approval of comic book superstars for endorsements, which, depending on the superstar, could be a tricky proposition. Rather than the Hollywood actors or best-selling novelists copping an attitude, it may be the comics' creators who become offended. Both *Entertainment Weekly* and the *New York Times* covered the feud between Alan Moore, the creator of the graphic novel *V for Vendetta*, and Warner Brother's, the studio behind the 2005 film version of the story. Moore apparently wanted to distance himself from the film version of V and was angry when a press conference about the film mentioned—or, from Moore's perspective, misrepresented—his excitement for the project (Itzkoff B1; Russo 26). And in perhaps the strongest signal of the symbiosis between film and comics to date, *Sin City* (2005) was co-directed by the creator of the comic book, Frank Miller, and the filmmakers designed the film to duplicate the specific look of the stylized comic, "as close to a frame-by-frame, panel-by-panel visual recreation of the comics as you could imagine . . . [t]he composition of the frames is the same;

the camera angles the same; and every line of dialogue, to the word, comes from the comics." (Leith ART4).

Comic book fans are often courted by the studios. Short rough-cut previews of films debut at comics conventions in an attempt to generate early buzz, such as an eighteen-minute version of *Constantine* at the 2004 San Diego Comic-Con International (in fact, seventeen other comics-related films were teased there) (Holson C2). The flap over the casting of Michael Keaton as Bruce Wayne/Batman for the 1989 Tim Burton-directed *Batman* underscored the importance of comic book fans to the success of films based on comics. In November 1988 the *Wall Street Journal* reported that fans were less than pleased about the casting, and fan publications such as the *Comics Buyer's Guide* had receiving hundreds of protest letters. Fans booed Warner representatives who attended comic conventions to promote the project (Hughes 1). In an interview with *Newsweek* in 1989 Jon Peters, *Batman*'s producer, recalled that the *Wall Street Journal* article had worried the financial community and a response became necessary.

> Months ahead of schedule, the filmmakers cut a trailer and persuaded Warners to screen it in Los Angeles. It was a hit, even among 300 Bat-fans who showed up for the late show. That, the filmmakers agree now, is what turned things around. When the trailer went into general release at Christmas, word of mouth spread among the fans and beyond. Retailers began to sense a bump in interest. Licensing Corp. of America, Warner's in-house merchandising arm, began to sprinkle just enough new movie-licensed goods into the marketplace—apparel, hats and pens—to freshen buyers' interest. "By the start of the year," says Rob Friedman, Warners president of worldwide advertising and publicity, "there was a feeding frenzy that we took advantage of, and to a certain extent fueled" (Barol 70)

The following year Walt Disney Pictures made sure to preview its film *Dick Tracy* to comic fans at the San Diego comic conference ("'Dick Tracy' Is Arresting Interest," 1989). As the *Newsweek* article attests the key to fans' involvement in comics-based films is the word of mouth they can generate and the resulting merchandising deals such word of mouth can generate, although in *Dick Tracy*'s case even positive fan reaction did not result in hefty profits from merchandising (Fabrikant D23).

Marvel and DC, the two major American comic book companies, have both spun off film adaptations of their characters, but each took a different approach. As part of Time Warner, DC's characters appeared in Warner Bros. films although not always under in-house production deals. Because of its corporate position outside a major media conglomerate, Marvel originally licensed its characters to a variety of studios. Gordon Hodge, a media analyst at Thomas Weisel Partners noted that this strategy involved not much risk, but also not "much opportunity for significant rewards." He added: "If you own the movie and handle the distribution all the way, soup to nuts, to home video and cable television, there's a lot better money to be made" (Gustines 8). But in April 2005 Marvel announced that it would start producing its own films. Harry Berkowitz noted in *Newsday* that "the venture opens up more opportunities not just for initial films, but also for the sequels, toys, video games, cartoons, clothing, and other merchandise that inevitably follow." Marvel and Paramount Pictures cut a deal in which Paramount will distribute the movies on a distribution fee basis resulting in Marvel not having to share merchandising revenue with the studio. According to Paramount chairman Brad Grey, the attraction of Marvel was that it had "become a marquee entertainment brand" and as Berkowitz implied would help Paramount attract a more youthful audience (Berkowitz A57).

Before the release of *Batman Begins* in 2005 DC's major comic book characters had been noticeable absent from the big screen since 1997's disastrous *Batman and Robin.* In 2003 the movie industry paper *Variety* reported that Thomas Weisel Partners had carried out an analysis of Warners and highlighted DC as a "hidden asset" whose value was waiting to be unlocked (Brodesser 7). Dennis O'Neill, a long time DC editor, in a clear expression of that value, called comics the "R & D division of the entertainment industry." Noting this comment the media scholar Henry Jenkins suggested, "Comic publishers are doing everything right—expanding creative rights for artists, tapping new global markets, reworking old genres to keep franchises alive and vital" (Jenkins "Will the Web Save Comics?"). Marvel's Bill Jemas took an opposing view stating that Marvel produced comic books for readers not in the hope of a director turning them into a film (Hanson 1E). Clearly though media corporations have increasingly created synergies between comics and films based on the concept of superhero characters as product to be sold across different media and merchandising forms.

Comics and films though are more than just product to be sold. As visual media both have aesthetic qualities and formal properties, such as frames and panels, which have important visual resemblance. Even in mainstream blockbuster movies, these visual parallels may lead to interesting aesthetic experiments, such as the "comics-look" attempted by such films as *Dick Tracy* and *Hulk*. In addition, both comics and films also fit within a certain type of narrative tradition, a point made by John Fell over thirty years ago. But these similarities are also accompanied by some distinct differences. Comics and films both have audiences, but comics have core audiences of fans that engage with characters over longer periods of time, and as noted above, these fans have distinct opinions on how characters should be adapted for film. Moreover different fans of the same comic character will have different views, and with a character such as Superman, who has been through numerous incarnations, competing expectations of different fans will further complicate the problems of adaptation. Fans then can be an asset to a film adapted from a comic, but also a liability particularly when taken for granted.

When comics are thought of as a product to be sold, generally comics are being defined as American superhero type comics. But the range of the form is greater than superheroes and always has been. Charles Hatfield's book *Alternative Comics* traces the development of a different sort of comic form in the United States from the undergrounds of the 1960s to the graphic novel. It is fair to say that many of these alternative comics deal with similar themes as superhero comics albeit with different storylines. Alienation and angst are particular favorites and of course the same could be said of novels, which lends support to Hatfield's argument for treating comics as literature. American alternative comics are but part of the range of the art form which in the United States alone also includes comic strips, and a range of comic books such as Archie, the Golden Key, Dell, and Harvey lines. The sustained presence of alternative comics and graphic novels have often combined with the "indie" film movement or modestly budgeted studio films to serve as an innovative counterbalance to the blockbuster superhero movie, offering aesthetically sophisticated critical reflections on such issues as youth alienation (*Ghost World*), violence (*A History of Violence*), or the nature of representation itself (*American Splendor*). In addition, comic art both as its own medium and as an influence on other media has a long history in other countries, and in this volume we offer some analysis of the relationship between comics and films in countries such as France, Germany, and Mexico and in the Malay-speaking areas and nations of Southeast Asia.

The first section of this volume examines problems of adaptation. Pascal Lefèvre argues that although films and comics are essentially visual media, both media differ significantly, not only in their material shape, but also in the way they are experienced and received by the public. For instance the visual ontology of a drawing creates problems for an adaptation from a comic book to a live-action movie. Every drawing is in its style a visual interpretation of the world. A photographic image has a completely different visual ontology. The more stylized or caricatured the drawing, the more likely the director of a movie will experience problems in finding a way to capture such a representation on film. The presence of sound in films also disturbs the mental world created by comic readers who fill in the silence with imagined aspects such as the sound of a character's voice. Michael Cohen pursues this line of enquiry through an analysis of Warren Beatty's *Dick Tracy*. Cohen explains that Beatty and his crew created an aesthetic of artifice that visually approached a replication of the comic form on film. Cohen argues that four aspects helped give *Dick Tracy* its distinct visual feel: production design, framing choices, the use of prosthetic makeup, and the combination of choices that placed Tracy as the heroic epicenter of the film, just as he is in the comic strip. The problems of adaptation of a comic into a film also hold true in reverse, an adaptation of a film into a comic. Kerry Gough reviews the processes through which Dark Horse Comics adapted the *Alien(s)* series of films to a successful comic book series. Just as with film adaptations the comic book producers had to make aesthetic choices and develop framing techniques to convey a sense of the original cultural artifact. Likewise they needed to be attuned to fan sensibilities. Gough also shows that movie studios are as anxious as major comic book companies to find ways to reap all financial dividends available to them through licensing their characters as a product. Treating characters as products, or as brands and subbrands, creates problems of keeping brand identity through a unity of form and content across different incarnations. Derek Johnson explores these issues through a study of Marvel's management of its *X-Men* franchise with a particular focus on the role and position of Wolverine. Johnson offers an account of Marvel's varying success in establishing a coherence for Wolverine while at the same time allowing for differentiation to attract different market segments, or audiences, such as adult and child readers.

The second section examines audience expectations, reception, and reaction to comic book films. If fans are important in shaping the production choices of moviemakers then the question arises about the manner in which comics fans view comic-based films, particularly in comparison with non-fans. Neil Rae and Jonathan Gray set out to answer this question through an ethnographical study of readers and non-readers and their responses to films. Mel Gibson traces the British press's response to the two *X-Men* films. She notes that the first film resulted in a wave of comments reminiscent of British cultural anxieties about Americanization in the 1950s and the essentially crass, low-class nature of comics, and by extension things American, in the eyes of the British middle class. The second film though saw a shift in tone that Gibson ties to a refusal of film critics to engage with comics at all and rather a preference to deal with the film as a summer blockbuster. The critics then refused to engage with the film outside their self-imposed genre constraints. Such a response echoed some comic book fans', and indeed even comics scholars', response to the M. Night Shyamalan film *Unbreakable*, which created some genre anxiety. Aldo J. Regalado unpacks the film and situates it firmly within the superhero genre and the fan culture that grew alongside such comic books. He suggests that *Unbreakable* is best understood by viewing it in conjunction with a reading of the 1933 science fiction short story "Reign of the Super-Man" by Superman creators Jerry Siegel and Joe Shuster.

The third and fourth sections of the volume look at specific themes and locales of film adaptations of comics. Martin Flanagan traces the teenage rite of passage to adulthood, a common comic book narrative theme, in *Spider-Man* and *Ghost World*. Despite their vastly different genres (superhero and alternative comics) and economics of production (blockbuster and art-house films), the films offered markedly similar coming-of-age narrative arcs marked by high-school graduations. Both films appealed to nostalgic memories: in *Spider-Man*'s case through a design aesthetic that evoked the 1960s or at least the original *Spider-Man* comic book artist Steve Ditko's representation of the 1960s, and in *Ghost World* through a satire of condescending adult attitudes to teenagers, which as Flanagan suggests has infinite appeal to aging baby boomers still living, or reliving, their own rebellion against their parents as some sort of halcyon age. Of all characters from comics Superman has surely appeared in more incarnations across different media forms and as licensed product. Rayna Denison takes two major instances of the Superman intertext, *Superman: The Movie* and the *Smallville* television series, as the subject for her study of genre in the comic book movie. She points to the reunification of action and melodrama as a single genre and the growing importance of production discourses, particularly through their increasing availability on DVD, to the construction of comic characters as cultural artifacts and product. If Spider-Man and Superman are the quintessential superheroes then Harvey Pekar is surely the comic book hero of everyday life. Pekar's self-referential comic book series *American Splendor* has documented the life of a character named Harvey Pekar, an ordinary Joe from Cleveland, for over twenty-five years. Craig Hight argues that in transforming this comic into a film, through a drama-documentary style, the filmmakers have produced a rich commentary on both forms of media and a statement of sorts on representations of reality in popular media.

Too often comics are associated with American comics, and comics-based films with Hollywood blockbusters. Filmmakers in many countries have drawn on comics for inspiration. For instance, the Australian director Bruce Beresford's first film was the 1972 production of *The Adventures of Barry McKenzie* based on the comic strip of the same name, which satirized beer-swilling Australians in London, and appeared in the British magazine *Private Eye*. David Wilt offers an account of one such character, El Santo, a superhero-wrestler whose career spanned forty-eight years in the ring, fifty films, and twenty-nine years as a comic book character. He was a unique example of synergy between professional sports, comic book publishing, and the motion picture industry. The combination of these three fields of endeavor made El Santo a national idol in his native Mexico, and an immensely popular and immediately recognizable figure around the world; for example in 2005 one of his films was included at a retrospective of comics films in Melbourne at the Australian Centre for the Moving Image. Paul Malone explores the complications of attempting to reach a popular German audience when translating, and by necessity transforming, a cartoony comic-book stylized frank depiction of both gay and straight sexuality for film. He studies the varying success of two movies based on Ralf König's popular graphic novels, *Der bewegte Mann* (*Maybe . . . Maybe Not*) and *Kondom des Grauens* (*Killer Condom*). Malone also reviews König's position on this transformation, as he himself, while making few concessions to self-censorship in the production of his comics, seems to have accepted constraints in film. Jan van der Putten and Timothy P. Barnard trace the transformation of Hang Tuah, a legendary figure from the fifteenth-century Melaka trading empire in Southeast Asia, in twentieth-century comics and films. The original tales, which focus on a brave warrior who served the sultan of Melaka without question, were presented to the community in an attempt to infuse loyalty towards the ruling dynasty. In the process these tales became the most famous pieces of oral (and written) literature in the region, thus making Hang Tuah the prototypical Malay hero. Interpretations and consciousness about these tales began to shift, however, following the rise of colonial rule and in particular when the prospects of independence swept through Malaya in the 1950s. This shift occurred as the story was reproduced and transmitted through newly developing media such as radio, film and comics, since these new idioms were in juxtaposition to the original narrative. Van der Putten and Barnard's analysis reveals the role of comics and film in shaping Malay identity in the process of decolonization. Finally, Sophie Geoffroy-Menoux offers a semiotic take on Enki Bilal's film *Immortel*. She argues that the film deconstructs the comics on which it is based. Bilal's view that globalization, eugenics, a cynical approach to money, a morbid fear of aging, the quest for eternal youth and sex have fueled progressive manipulations of all kinds, including the manipulation of visual images and their viewers; this argument finds form in the movie through Bilal's own manipulation of images. Reality is the key narrative theme in the film, which is ironically revealed by the very unreal, surreal, virtual aspect of the film.

Looking forward, with changes in industry structures, new digital production technologies and audience interactive venues (such as continued growth of the blogosphere), the relationship of film to comics is a dynamic and promising area for future research.

As noted earlier, Marvel, following in the footsteps of comics companies such as Dark Horse, will take a much more active role in the film productions involving its characters. Much of this activity would involve blockbuster-level theatrical production, but also include exploiting other media. Marvel's 2006 DVD animated release *Ultimate Avengers*, designed to keep the company's name in front of the public between blockbuster releases, is one such example. Such trends indicate a potentially fundamental change in industry identity and priorities. As comic-book companies see themselves more as film companies, to what extent does the cart drive the horse, with perhaps the development of comic-book readership, new characters and new talent being neglected.

The role of comics in the blockbuster film may also continue to affect the film industry, by placing more emphasis on digital special effects and costly production. *Spider-Man 3* (2007) is purported to have a production bill approaching $300 million (Kelly & Marr, 2006). Such figures reflect the economics of modern Hollywood given the spectacle element needed by superhero comics and the pressure to up the visual ante, siphoning resources to fewer and fewer films, and making the trend worthy of continued study.

Also worth tracking is other comics-related influences on film, especially with the long-term viability of more adult-oriented graphic novels that lend themselves to quieter, more thoughtful (and less-expensive) productions. Although *Art School Confidential* (2006), based upon a graphic novel story by Daniel Clowes, generated a modest U.S. box office, its relatively inexpensive production costs and potential "after-market" life on cable and DVD may offer its own economic benefits. The publicity generated by smaller-budgeted efforts may have beneficial effects on the sales and fandom of graphic novels, given the smaller numbers needed for a print title to be an economic success.

With digital graphics software and the distribution capabilities of the internet, the blurring of production and consumption will likely continue with all media, including comics. Graphics software make creation of graphic novels more viable, and websites make distribution more widespread for new talent. Fan communities via chat rooms and blogs make audience identity, feedback, and "buzz" a part of both the mainstream industry and labor-of-love efforts, and such trends may continue to influence production, marketing, and audience experiences.

It is hoped that the following chapters in this book will contribute to a foundation of future studies that chart the changing nature and social, cultural, and ideological implications of these two institutions.

The editors wish to thank Kevin Hagopian, Joanne Chia, and Kelvin Lawrence for advice and assistance with parts of this volume. Walter Biggins and Seetha Srinivasan at the University Press of Mississippi have supported this work from the outset and our thanks to them and the anonymous reviewer for expediting the initial review process. We also thank the contributors to the volume who have been uniformly good-natured, and quick to respond to us on all the matters that crop up in putting such a collection together. Ian Gordon's work on this volume has been helped by a research grant from the Faculty of Arts and Social Science at the National University of Singapore.

IAN GORDON
MARK JANCOVICH
MATTHEW P. MCALLISTER

FILM AND COMIC BOOKS

INCOMPATIBLE VISUAL ONTOLOGIES?

THE PROBLEMATIC ADAPTATION OF DRAWN IMAGES

— PASCAL LEFÈVRE

"Till today I haven't seen a cinematographic adaptation of a comic, which seems to add something to the original work, they have always been rehashes."[1]

The prominent French director Alain Resnais (Thomas 247) uttered this quite negative view on filmic adaptations of comics in 1990. Adaptations from comics seldom gain canonical recognition and they rarely figure in lists of best films of all times.[2] Not only do these adaptations seldom please the critics,[3] they seem to have little automatic appeal for comics readers.[4] Cinema critics and comics fans seem to agree that it is hard to make a good movie of a comic. The movie-going audience is less severe. Moreover, some adaptations from comics were real blockbusters including Richard Donner's *Superman* (1978), Tim Burton's *Batman* (1989), Barry Sonnenfeld's *Men in Black* (1997) and Sam Raimi's *Spider-Man* (2002).[5] That the comics the movies were based on were already a success does not explain completely the success of the filmic adaptations; the movies must have attracted viewers that rarely read comics. Moreover all these adaptations generated an offspring of sequels.

Adaptations of comics seem to be popular as well as controversial. While some analysts (Peeters[6]) recognize creative aspects of some adaptations, other critics (Fremion 166) state bluntly that adaptation is preferred by mediocre talents. Some comic artists are even opposed to the idea of a filmic adaptation. For instance, Art Spiegelman does not want to see his

Maus adapted as a live action movie, because he considers the metaphoric style of his storytelling essential and impossible to adapt outside the comics medium.[7]

Nevertheless it has been pointed out various times that there is a closer link between cinema and comics than between cinema and other visual arts (Christiansen 107, Costa 24). Films and comics are both media which tell stories by series of images: the spectator sees people act—while in a novel the actions must be verbally told. Showing is already narrating in cinema and comics, but while classical cinematic narratives situate the spectator at the centre of the diegetic space, comics on the other hand are rooted in a parodic tradition (Christiansen 118). Since the nineteenth century a majority of comics have used deformation, often caricatured, to various degrees as a major characteristic. Also the confrontation of texts and pictures and the fact that pictures are drawn reminds the reader of their artificial status. Moreover film and comics differ significantly not only in the way they are experienced and received by the public, but also in their material shape. This poses many problems for an adaptation from a comic to a live-action movie. In particular the visual ontology of a drawing seems to be a central issue, as will be developed in this essay. But in addition there is the problem of primacy: usually people prefer the first version of a story they encounter. When you read first a novel, you form a personal mental image of the fictive world and when you first read a comic, you have a kinetic visual idea as well. Any filmic adaptation has to deal with these first personal interpretations and images: it is extremely hard to exorcise those first impressions.[8]

In this article the term "adaptation" is used in a broad sense, including also films directly inspired by a certain comic or comic series.[9] Adaptations in animation format are not discussed. Animated adaptations deserve a proper analysis of their own, but most problems of live action adaptations will haunt animated version as well.

In contrast to the single and original artworks of painting and sculpture, only copies of films and comics are distributed and consumed.[10] Art philosopher Walter Benjamin argued that the aura of the work of art withered in the age of mechanical reproduction, because the reproduced object is detached from the domain of tradition.[11] Though they share a funda-

PASCAL LEFÈVRE

mental similarity (mass consumption) movies and comics still have some differences regarding their reception or consuming mode. The two main differences are the material shape of the images and the social aspects of reception. The difference in reception or consuming mode is individual activity (comic) versus group experience (cinema). While reading a comic is a solitary action, viewing a film in a theatre is largely a group experience: people gather in film theaters at precise moments to watch a film together.[12] A lot of moviegoers share emotions at the same time: they laugh and cry together. Reactions of other viewers may facilitate such emotional responses during a showing. Reading a comic, on the contrary, involves no direct emotional sharing with others. Only when the reading is completed, a comic reader can exchange his emotions with others. A film showing demands attention from the viewer, since the place is dark with only the screen light and often music plays loudly to lend aural atmosphere and to keep viewers attuned to the screen action. Reading a comic book, on the other hand, does not necessarily take place in such an undisturbed environment. Nevertheless a reader can seclude himself physically and mentally.

Not only does the reception of a comic and a film differ, but also their production. By necessity the production of a film implies a bigger organization and budget than the production of a comic. The creative part in film is done by a group of people (writer, photographer, director, actor, editor and the like), whereas drawing and writing a comic can be done by a small team or just one person. This essay, though, focuses on the visual differences of the two media. Despite their seeming concordance—at least when comparing films to novels—juxtapositioning their inherent visual ontologies highlights reasons why comics fans may literally "see" film adaptations as often unfaithful and even disrespectful.

There are four main problems in the adaptation of comics into film and three of them are related to the characteristics of the comics medium itself: panels are arranged on a page, panels are static drawings and a comic does not make noise or sound. Film is quite different. First, there is a screen frame, second, the film images are moving and photographic, third, film has a soundtrack. These characteristic differences of the two media become enacted as the four adaptation problems of (1) the deletion/addition process that occurs with rewriting primary comics texts for film; (2) the unique characteristics of page layout and film screen; and (3) the dilemmas of translating drawings to photography; and (4) the importance of sound in film compared to the "silence" of comics. Given these problems, perhaps the central question about filmic adaptation of comics is not, "how faithful/respectful to the comic the film will be," but rather, "how least dissimilar to the comic can the film be?"

The starting point for most adaptations is whether or not the scriptwriters will follow the storyline as presented in the comic itself, or will they take the existing material just as an interesting starting point to write a new story with a lot of new additions. Few adaptations respect meticulously the storyline of a particular comic. Every real artisan of cinema knows that this medium has its own laws and rules. A direct adaptation is seldom a good choice: some elements may work wonderfully in a comic, but cannot function in the context of a film. Usually a script writer for a movie has to leave out scenes, has to add others, and has to write out some principal characters or introduce new ones. For instance, the two police officers in the comic *From Hell* (Moore and Campbell) are combined in the film into one character. The necessity of such changes in large part is simply due to the different narrative-length norms of the two media. Since the comic book version of *From Hell* consists of hundreds of pages, not all the drawn sequences were shot. Thus, the original text is inevitably altered. *From Hell*'s creator Alan Moore (Mouchart 30) explains that he does not care too much about adaptations: "I force myself not to have an opinion [on the adaptations]. Those feature films do not resemble my books. If they are good films, it's the merit of the directors. It has nothing to do with me. Likewise if the films are mediocre. It interests me to see them, but since I don't like to work for Hollywood and cinema isn't one of my preferred media, I do not feel very implicated in those projects."[13]

Most comic creators (like Daniel Clowes, Stan Lee, Enki Bilal) understand that a film usually needs changes to the original material. Enki Bilal stresses that *Immortel* is not an adaptation of his *Nikopol* trilogy, but a rewriting ("réécriture"). He explains in an interview that it was important—amongst other things—to include some of the burning issues of today and forget about some other aspects (Bernière 12).

By contrast to the artists themselves, diehard fans of the original work rarely applaud such rewritings. For instance, the changes in costumes and the character motivations in the *X-Men* films dissatisfied some fans (Lee 2000). The organic webshooters of Spider-Man in the Sam Raimi film seem to pose a problem for some fans, because in the original comic book version the webshooters were a technological invention of the young scientist Peter Parker. When Kenneth Plume asked Stan Lee, the creator of *Spider-Man*, about this matter, he said that it worked out: "Maybe some purists who know the comics might feel, 'Oh, they didn't do it the way it was in the comics,' but the average person watching it would have no problem with the webs coming out of his hands that way" (Lee 2000). Some comics fans tend to consecrate the original work and scrutinize a filmic adaptation for so called errors or misinterpretations. Almost every attempt of adaptation becomes in their eyes some kind of betrayal. Moreover such filmic adaptations give superheroes fans a unique opportunity to show off their almost autistic-savant knowledge of a particular superhero comic book series. In the eyes of the large public and in particular of the cultural elite those superheroes fans do not have a high status: reading superheroes comic books is generally associated with childish behavior.

The dilemma is, then, that a film that too "faithfully" follows a comic will seldom be a good film. Since it is another medium with other characteristics and rules, the director has to modify the original work. Just as in a historical movie, there is no way to render the situations exactly as they were; it is therefore much more important to try to be truthful to the spirit of the original work. Of course, every decision is open to discussion, and not all the decisions of a director are necessarily good decisions.

The second problem relates to the transition from page layout to the image on a single screen. Whilst the images of a comic are mostly printed on paper, the images of a film are projected on a screen, typically wide screen in a film theatre or a television screen at home. The difference is important because the pages of a comic are in a closer range than the projected images of a film. It is the readers who have to leaf through a comic and they can choose their own reading speed. They can linger on a panel, scan the complete plate, and return to panels or whole sequences at free will. A film, though, obliges the viewer to follow the rhythm of the sequences.[14] In film the shots are put on a linear-time sequence; in comics the panels are not only placed in a linear sequence but also on a larger space, namely the page. In this sense comics are a more spatial medium than film. In cinema, filming and montage are two quite separate phases. In comics, the drawing of the panels and the combination of the panels on a page cannot be that easily separated: choices in one domain have consequences in the other domain (Groensteen, "Du 7ᵉ au 9ᵉ art" 28).¹⁵

In addition, the interplay of the various panels (their relative dimensions and their location) is a constitutive aspect of the comics medium. Cinema with its moving images and standardized screen formats is not well equipped to imitate the page layouts of comics, although attempts are made. Sometimes film directors use multiple-frame imagery or split-screens imagery; two or more different images, each with its own frame dimensions and shape, appear within the larger frame (Bordwell & Thompson 125). This device is used in various comics adaptations. The *Hulk* DVD contains a bonus feature in which editor Tim Squyres and ILM compositor Mark Casey explain they did not want to imitate a comic book page layout because it would not work in film, but they wanted to come up with some cinematic devices inspired by those dynamic pages. Since using multiple-frame imagery is still quite unusual¹⁶—especially when the split-screens themselves are moving on the screen as in *Hulk*—it tends to surprise the viewer and to make him or her more aware of the filmic code of framing. It then functions as a self-referential technique. Though multiple-frame imagery is closer to comics, it breaks the usual cinematographic illusion.

A third issue is the difference between drawn forms and photographic forms. Although both film and comics make use of flat images and similar shots (long, medium, and close-up),¹⁷ it is evident that the differences between the two media are more striking. A crucial and striking difference is that film functions with moving images,¹⁸ while comics use static images.¹⁹ This difference between moving and still images is of paramount importance. By and large normal moving images will give a greater impression of realism. A viewer of a still image will always be reminded of the fragmented and frozen time. Nevertheless such an unmoving picture can also look realistic and credible, especially when it is of photographical nature. Cinema is foremost a photographic medium: a camera registers what is in

PASCAL LEFÈVRE

front of the lens.[20] The photographic material fixates the bundles of light rays. As in daily life the brain of a spectator in a movie theater has to interpret the pattern of light intensities provided by a photographic picture in order to extract features such as edges. Therefore the British psychologist John Willats (128) calls it an optical denotation system: the picture elements denote features of the array of light reaching the eye or the camera, rather than physical features of the scene such as edges and contours.

By contrast to a photographic image a drawn panel from a comic usually offers clear edges. Generally the artist uses clear contour lines to denote the various objects in his pictures. Although such outlines in drawn pictures may be less analogous to the external world, they are not necessarily inferior in their capacity for grasping the essential aspects of a scene. Moreover, as art historian Philip Rawson (1979, 8–10) states, a well-developed language of marks can convey far more about what it represents than any mere copy of appearances. Good drawing always goes beyond appearances. A good portrait does not necessarily need a perfect imitation of all the individual traits, but rather the depiction of the essential aspects. Gestalt psychologist Rudolf Arnheim (149) claims that the better picture is one that leaves out unnecessary detail and chooses telling characteristics, but also that the relevant facts must be unambiguously conveyed to the eye. This outcome can be obtained by picture elements such as simplicity of shape, orderly grouping, distinction figure and ground, use of lighting and perspective and distortions.[21]

In addition a drawing offers many possibilities. A drawn image can more easily show impossible views (e.g. Escher) or combine various views (as in cubist art), and an artist will not be limited by budgets. Comic artists can choose their cast at will, imagine complete new worlds or civilizations; only their imagination and artistic skills pose restrictions on the creative act. The most fantastic scenes can simply be drawn in comics: people can fly in the air; whole cities can be destroyed and so on. In the past it was quite complicated and difficult to film such scenes, but with the coming of digital techniques special effects entered a new age. Thanks to the combination of computer animation with live-action filming the most fantastic and credible scenes can be created: ordinary looking people transform fluently into horrible monsters (e.g. *Hulk*), characters and objects fly in the sky (e.g. *The Matrix*), deformations and exaggerations are possible (e.g. *The Mask*). Such imaginings, though, while now possible in cinema, can still be a point of criticism in comics films when such effects do not live up to viewer/critic expectations of realism (such as, for example, criticism of the effects in early *Hulk* teaser trailers as cheesy). Also, of course, such effects remain quite expensive to do in that medium, especially when compared to the cost of a pencil as the necessary "special effects tool" for comic art.

Arnheim suggests that every successful work of art, no matter how stylized and remote from mechanical correctness it may be, conveys the full natural flavor of the object it represents. Rawson (1987, 78) tries to explain the richness of drawings: "Without precision in formulating the elements there can be no true variety; for it is only possible to recognize variety and variation if distinctions between the forms are made quite clear. And there can only be variety within an ordered structure, or else differences are simply chaos and not variation. Variation implies a substratum of norm-units which are varied." The "language" of the form creates its own reality and has a personal touch. In contrast to an average photographic image, a drawing is literally and figuratively "signed" (Groensteen, "Du 7ᵉ au 9ᵉ art" 23). "The structure of the artist's visual thought is what matters; and somehow or other it must be 'true,' i.e. have a functional relationship to what artist and spectator accept as truth." (Rawson, 1987, 23). A successful artistic solution is so compelling that it looks like the only possible realization of the subject (Arnheim 144). Hochberg and Brooks (382) even claim that comics approximate the ways in which people think of the visual world, which would be an explanation for their popularity.

An artist not only depicts something, but s/he expresses at the same time a philosophy, a vision—but one rather difficult to verbalize. Every drawing is by its style a visual interpretation of the world, in that it foregrounds the presence of an enunciator (Christiansen 115). The form of the drawing influences the manner the viewer will experience and interpret the drawing. A drawn image offers a specific view on reality and the creator's subjectivity of this reality is built into the work, and a fairly obvious part of this work. The viewer is obliged to share this figuratively view of the maker, and can not look at the object-in-picture from another visual point of view than the one the picture offers. The viewer, says film scholar Jan-Marie Peters (14), is invited to share the maker's mode of seeing, not only in the literal, but also in the figurative sense. Nevertheless the reader is not just a passive agent: he or she looks at images with prior knowledge and activates the images. The perspective and style of the particular artist also may foreground—as a medium—the human-constructedness of images in comics, even for realistic drawing styles. This may perhaps encourage speculation from readers and polysemic meanings. And, of course, the individual context is thus also of considerable importance in introducing variability in reader interpretation. So every drawing style implies a certain interpretation of the reality in visual terms, a particular visual ontology (Rawson, 1987:19).

A photographic image has, by its optic nature alone, a quite different visual ontology. Viewers do not react in the same way to a drawing as to a photographic image. Although photos can also be manipulated by using special software such as Photoshop, generally the viewer still accords more realism to a photo than to a stylized drawing. For instance, stylized drawings do not deliver a successful trompe l'oeuil, whereas an optic image can easily fool the eye and the mind of the viewer. That explains why a viewer more likely accepts violence in a drawn medium than in a photographic medium. If the violence of the *Tom and Jerry* animation series was not cartoonesque, but filmed with real-life cats and mice, the violence would probably seem much more difficult to digest. Viewers tend to accept more from a stylized medium than from a photographic medium.

The different visual ontology may also be the reason why it is extremely difficult to adapt a strongly stylized or caricatured drawing in a photographic image. The failure of the various filmic adaptations of Hergé's *Tintin* is exemplary, according to French writer and comics theorist Benoît Peeters: "Ambiguity is probably constitutive, because the work of Hergé balances between realism and caricature. The style of the artist—the famous 'clear line'—is the unifying element of the work that guarantees its coherence; when this is lost, confusion and incredulousness surface. On the whole, the Tintin-adaptations are an indirect demonstration of how strongly the qualities of Hergé's work are linked with the formal language of the comics medium."[22]

Also the Italian film scholar Antonio Costa (25) stresses the importance of the comics' figurative fascination: "Cinema can try to substitute this by complex operations of selection and stylization of its own expressive means."[23] As successful examples Costa mentions the art direction and photography of Tim Burton's *Batman* (1989) and Warren Beatty's *Dick Tracy* (1992). Elsewhere in this book Michael Cohen analyses in more detail what he calls *Dick Tracy*'s "aesthetic of artifice" in production design, framing, prosthetic makeup and other techniques. *Sin City* (2005, Robert Rodriguez and Frank Miller) and *Immortel*[24] (2004, Enki Bilal) are rare examples of comic artists as crafty (co)directors of films (see further in this book the analysis of *Immortels*). The mise-en-scene and the art direction are thus of paramount importance, because not only the characters, but also the decors are being defined by the visual style of the drawing. Real locations often look too ordinary and are not adjusted to the fictive and graphic world of a comic book.

Most filmic adaptations however do not succeed in grasping the stylization or mood of the original work as was achieved in *Sin City* or *Immortel*. If a film director does not find a way to transpose the visual style into photographic images, s/he can also develop an alternative, such as in *Annie* and *From Hell*. The deliberate choice for a clearly artificial, but credible world seems to work well.

When a comic is rendered in a more "realistic" style or in various styles, cinematographic adaptations seem to be less insuperable (e.g. *Superman*, *Spider-Men*, *X-Men*). Usually long-running comic book series do not have a unique defining style: such series can be drawn and told in very different ways, costumes and looks can change in time. Series like *Batman* or *Superman* were not only written by different scriptwriters, but also drawn by scores of artists. One cannot confuse the angular Dick Sprang Batman (from the 1940s and 50s) with the stylish Neal Adams Batman (of the early 1970s) or, the minimalistic and chunky Frank Miller Batman (of 1986) or, the photorealist painted Dave McKean Batman (of 1989)—these are only some of the scores of artists who worked on *Batman* since 1939. Because *Batman* is multifaced a reader of a certain period can have a particular idea about Batman that is not necessarily shared by readers from others periods, or even another contemporary reader. Moreover, as Bennett and Woollacott (1987:59) have demonstrated in their study of James Bond, there is no stable meaning of such a popular figure. Bond or Batman can not be abstracted from the shifting orders of intertextuality through which their actual functioning has been organized and reorganized. This is also the case for so called graphic novels. The various graphic treatments of the Harvey Pekar stories of *American Splendor* (since 1976) make a movie just another interpretation that fit in well with that series' visual eclecticism.

Finally the use of sound in films adds another layer of difference to the issue of adaptation. There was a time that the movies were more like comics. During the first decades of cinema the actors and the narrator only received a "voice" through written texts on intertitles. But the introduction of sound in the late 1920s changed the nature of cinema drastically. All films became "talkies"—except for some experimental films. Sound is a powerful film technique, because sound engages a distinct sense mode and sound can actively shape how the spectator perceives and interprets the image (Bordwell & Thompson 291–92).

Comics do not have a sound track: music, voices and noises can only be suggested by stilled and visible signs (text, ideograms, balloons . . .) printed on paper. It is possible to use similar techniques in film, but they do not function as well. Except for tongue-in-cheek approaches as in the *Batman* television series (1966–68), onomatopoeia in a cinematographic context looks rather strange.

The change from "silent" to "talkie" is fundamental. As in novels in comics a reader can never hear the sound of the characters' voices.[25] Of course, the written text can inform the reader about that aspect. Moreover in comics the visible appearance of the character and other ideograms can suggest the sound of a voice, but it remains largely an interpretation by the reader. It seems that at least some readers who imagine a particular sound of the characters voices are shocked by the way an actor speaks when playing that character.

Not only the sound of a voice is different but also the way the characters speak. The texts in speech balloons are generally not suited for film dialogue and they need some rewriting. Superhero comics, for example, often use very stylistic and bombastic dialogue; a literal screen translation may emphasize such dialogue's artificial nature to the point of unintentional camp. Stan Lee (2000) explains how Ken Johnson changed the texts in *The Incredible Hulk* television series (1978–1982): "He changed it quite a bit from the comic book, but every change he made, made sense. In the comics, when the Hulk talked—he'd go, 'Me Hulk! Me smash! Hulk kill!'

That type of thing. Well, that would have been corny as hell on the screen. He left that out . . . He didn't have the Hulk talk at all."

So the change from a "silent medium" to a "sound medium" poses also a lot of problems for the adaptation.

The starting point of this article was the debate on the value of filmic adaptations of comics. Such films may be popular, but they remain controversial, especially in the eyes of the cultural elite and the diehard comics fans. Although there are many similarities, the differences are still considerable. After a short look at the different reception and the production modes, four main problems were described at the creative level: first, to what extent has a scriptwriter for film to rewrite the story, second, how to go from page layout to a single, unchangeable screen frame, third, how to translate static drawings into moving and photographic images, and fourth, how to give the "silent world" an audible sound? These seem to be the crucial problems of filmic adaptations of comics. Although new computer technology facilitates the recreation of the comics' fantastic allures, cinematographic adaptations remain problematic; not the least because the reader of a comic constructs a mental image of the fictive world. Moreover, the reader adds elements that are not necessarily explicit in the comic, for instance the sound of the voices of the various characters. When an actor interprets a character from a comic, his/her voice does not always match the imagined voice by the reader.

Given these differences, perhaps we should not be too purist concerning adaptations and accept that a work may inspire a creator in another medium. If we look at an adaptation, we should forget—for a moment—about the original work and evaluate the newly created work on its own merits. Films such as *Annie, Dick Tracy, Batman, Ghost World, Hulk, American Splendor, Immortel* or *Sin City* should be judged as movies and not as successful or unsuccessful adaptations of comics. After all, Western spectators who watched and enjoyed the Korean film *Old Boy* (Chan-Wuk, 2004) usually did so without having read or even knowing about the original manga.

DICK TRACY

IN PURSUIT OF A COMIC BOOK AESTHETIC

— MICHAEL COHEN

"Reality was not our goal on this picture."
— Warren Beatty (Bonifer, *Dick Tracy: The Making of the Movie* 12)

When Warren Beatty's *Dick Tracy* arrived in 1990, it was the most meticulous effort to capture the aesthetic of a comic in a live-action film, and paved the way for the exploration of the visual correlations lying dormant between cinema and comics. Although there are ontological differences between cinema and comics, and it is not possible for a live-action film to replicate the formal properties of comics, *Dick Tracy* demonstrates how the cinema can adapt the conventions and characteristics of a comic. *Dick Tracy* is a fascinating film for boldly tackling the differences between these two media, and in doing so deploys a combination of an "aesthetic of artifice," "cartooning," framing of the hero, and "paneling," to create a cinematic comic aesthetic. The result is a film with eye-popping colors, a blatantly artificial diegesis, a bizarre mélange of villains, and a stalwart hero wearing a yellow hat and trench coat.

Comics do not possess a singular style, or a finite set of visual attributes, which are either inherent to the medium or historically stable. In his article, "Shaping *The Maxx*," Greg Smith explains that adapting material from different media "is necessarily a process of translation, since one cannot merely import forms from one medium to another" (32). Smith makes the point that characters, story, and iconography are easily transferred between media "because they appear to be the properties of a diegetic world and not characteristics distinct to a medium" (33). Chester Gould's "Dick Tracy" originated as a comic strip in 1931, and in the late thirties filmed serials were produced, as well as a number of films in the forties, either starring Ralph Byrd or Morgan Conway as the titular crime fighter. All it took to transfer these actors into the famed detective was a suit and a hat, and the basic iconography of the profession: a gun and badge. The "comic aesthetic," which distinguishes this latest version of *Dick Tracy* from many previous films based on comics, is the "transference" of the characters and their iconography from comics into cinema together with the "adaptation" of the conventions and characteristics of the comic medium.

There are four different aspects of *Dick Tracy* that combine to form a cohesive aesthetic: the fabrication of "Tracy Town" (Bonifer 42); the "cartooning" of props, characters, and behavior so they are excessive and implausible; the framing of Tracy (Warren Beatty); and finally, cinematic "panels." It is the incorporation of multiple elements that generates this "comic aesthetic," as Jon Landau, the production manager of *Dick Tracy*, explains: "It's not a building with green windows that makes a comic book. It's that same building with a Flattop character walking out of it, getting into the biggest, bluest limousine you've ever seen, and driving off on a red street into a matte painting. *That's* a comic book!" (Bonifer 12).

A number of exaggerated formal properties are associated with American crime fighter and superhero comics, and these are the visual tropes engaged by Beatty to depict "Tracy Town" as the world of a comic. As Scott McCloud explains in *Understanding Comics*, the garish coloring is the result of the four-color printing process that became the standard in comic book production (187), and "to stand out from the competition, costumed heroes were clad in bright, primary colors and fought in a bright primary world" (188). Crime fighting comic heroes belong on colored streets, chasing villains in a blur of motion lines. Such is Dick Tracy, with his chiseled features, wearing his yellow coat and hat, battling against Big Boy (Al Pacino), Flattop (William Forsythe), and the Brow (Chuck Hicks).

Warren Beatty and his film crew used the production design of *Dick Tracy* to turn a recognizable twentieth-century city into "Tracy Town." The spectator's attention is drawn to the overt artifice of Tracy's milieu through the use of studio sets, backlots, painted backdrops, and matte paintings in the production design. These are all old techniques, found in all genres of film, and are still prevalent in this age of digital technology. Used in combination with colored lighting reflecting off rain-soaked streets and primary colors painted directly onto *Dick Tracy*'s sets, "Tracy Town" is an implausible city proudly displaying the artifice of its fabrication.

The artifice of a comic's creation, consisting of hand-drawn images printed on paper, is an integral feature of its aesthetic, and affects the way the comic is received by the reader. Details such as backgrounds and facial features are difficult in comics as it is a very time-consuming process. Alan McKenzie notes, in *How to Draw and Sell Comic Strips for Newspapers and Comic Books!*, that too much detail often detracts from the story as many readers do not absorb dense visual material (80). Rather than challenge these facts, the trend in superhero comics has been towards exaggeration and not verisimilitude: artifice describes both the ontology of the media and the style of the genre. Cinema on the other hand is, potentially, an extremely realistic medium because the photographic process produces an accurate analogue of what is placed before it, and this grants the cinematographic image a level of plausibility not found in comics. Improvements in the quality and volume of special effects, particularly digital effects, contained in Hollywood features cast more doubt upon the validity of photographic reproductions. However, it remains that live-action Hollywood films contain recordings of real people in real spaces, and this ontology informs how photography is perceived and accepted. As André Bazin states: "The objective nature of photography confers on it a quality of credibility absent from all other picture-making" (*What Is Cinema*, Vol. 1, 13).

In their book, *Sets in Motion: Art Direction and Film Narrative*, Charles and Mirella Affron describe five different levels of production design, the fourth of which is relevant here: "artificial" sets. According to the Affrons, these sets "privilege their own artificiality. Prominently featured, consciously foregrounded, the set as artifice calls attention to itself as a consistently opaque object in pursuit of "the fiction effect." Design is rendered specific and legible through the invention of the patently unreal" (39). The Affrons refer to a distinction between the "reality effect" and the "fiction effect" (113), which is important for distinguishing between cinematic worlds that are plausible and *Dick Tracy*'s "Tracy Town" which is implausible. The "reality effect" keeps a film grounded in a world that is plausible beyond the fiction, whereas the "fiction effect" of the artificial production design does not. By increasing the level of fabrication in a film's diegesis, reality is left behind and the fiction of the artifice becomes "a primary focus of the narrative, challenging the force of plot and character" (Affron 39). However, the "comic aesthetic" does not challenge the plot and characters in *Dick Tracy*: because of their origin in a comic strip they are supported and enhanced by the "aesthetic of artifice."

The methods of fabricating a film's diegesis are often incorporated inconspicuously during film production so there is verisimilitude between the image and its referent. Verisimilitude and plausibility go hand in hand, and when these techniques are deployed in films, whether in genres such as westerns, *film noir*, and war films, or in comedies and melodrama, the effect is usually transparent so the fabrication of the diegesis is not deliberately brought to the spectator's attention. When deployed in fantastic or futuristic films, the methods of diegetic fabrication are still usually transparent even though the spectator's attention is drawn to the unfamiliarity of the diegesis.

The fully artificial production design in *Dick Tracy*, which eschews the plausibility of the "reality effect," enables this definition of a "comic aesthetic." "Tracy Town" is implausible because the "fiction effect" created by the "opaque" deployment of the production design is stylistically linked to the narrative focus on a comic character. The gritty urban settings of the claustrophobic city, bustling streets, and darkened alleys in *Dick Tracy* engages the milieu of the *film noir* and crime thriller genres as its narrative foundation, and it is the level of artifice subsequently applied to this generic trope that creates the implausible comic-style world policed by the crime fighter.

To effectively fabricate a city such as "Tracy Town" filmmakers need to control the environment, and this requires studio sets and backlots. The diegetic foundation of the city is never fully obscured; on the contrary, it is integral to creating a "comic aesthetic." Richard Sylbert, the production designer for *Dick Tracy*, explains: "If you're going to do *Dick Tracy* there's only one way to do it, and that's with icons, where a car is just a car and a building is just a building. A backlot is nothing but a series of icons—of a

Fig. 1. The production design is sparse and clean, devoid of realistic minutiae, to mimic the limitations of the comic strip, which cannot reproduce realistic details in a single panel.

city or a village or a town" (Bonifer 80). *Dick Tracy* illustrates how removing details in the set decoration and leaving only the necessary fixtures of a particular referent creates an uncluttered look to each environment (Bonifer 86). As Sylbert explains: "If it [the set design] became too realistic, too atmospheric, it wouldn't work. We started out with atmosphere, but we took it out. You couldn't have clouds and fog" (Bonifer 86). Because a "realistic" level of detail is not possible in a comic, particularly a small panel in a daily strip of "Dick Tracy," it creates a form of artifice in the medium, which the filmmakers of *Dick Tracy* have "translated" into the production design. The exteriors are noticeably clean and do not display the deterioration expected in a real environment, and the *mise-en-scène* of the interiors is also devoid of surplus details and decoration beyond the denotation of the basic set dressing.

Dick Tracy was shot on a studio backlot, and many exterior shots use matte paintings to extend the image or to replace conventional sets. The opening sequence of the film introduces this approach as the style for the rest of the film. As Harrison Ellenshaw, the visual effects supervisor on *Dick Tracy*, states: "The reason it was decided to make the first scene in the movie a matte shot was to get us immediately into *Tracy*'s environment . . . We're in a comic book. Boom. You're into the characters and the story, and it all meshes perfectly with that first thirty-second shot" (Bonifer 43). Traditionally, most shots involving matte paintings are unsophisticated and do not use camera movement. The matte painting used during the opening of *Dick Tracy* is more sophisticated in its integration of cel-animation, as well as its incorporation of complicated camera movements. This matte painting connects the opening shot of Tracy getting ready for work to another scene in an alley on the other side of town, which introduces the Kid (Charlie Korsmo), the young orphan who will become Tracy's sidekick.[1] A camera movement tracking up the outside of Tracy's apartment to the top of the building reveals the expanse of the city depicted in the matte painting. The camera then tracks left revealing more of the city in the distance as well as in foreground elements. The artifice of this shot is unmistakable: the setting sun casts a yellow-orange hue over the city of purple buildings, and the cel-animated elements, such as smoke stacks and trains, resemble cartoons. At the end of the film, Tracy drives off into the sunset heading into another matte painting as "The End" appears. As Ellenshaw claims: "In this movie the matte paintings *are* the reality" (Bonifer 43).

The combination of set design and matte paintings is elaborately enhanced by the use of colored lighting, as well as the application of colors directly on the sets. In some instances it is the choice of coloring that changes the set or a prop from being plausible to being completely unrealistic. In cinema and photography, objects and characters are made visible by the light shone on them. This lighting also shapes and defines their presence, and varieties of common lighting patterns are often used. Characters and objects in comics are not enabled and shaped by the reflection of light; therefore, parts of an image can be as dark or light as required, without affecting other areas. Black outlines define most graphic material on a page and within the panel, and the effect of lighting is actually determined by

MICHAEL COHEN

Fig. 2. The film is book-ended by matte paintings, creating an unmistakable cartoon-style opening and closing.

the lightness or darkness between demarcated fields of solid color, or black and white. This is enhanced with shape lines to give definition and volume to characters and objects. Solid color fields are a common stylistic feature of comics and are often used instead of drawing backgrounds in detail, which saves time, and heightens the dramatic context of the foreground.

In *Dick Tracy* colored lighting reflected off wet streets, particularly during night sequences, emulates the solid color fields of a comic. Single primary colors are used for costumes, sets, cars, and props. In some scenes the background coloring is strongly demarcated from the silhouette of a character in the foreground. To create the impression of solid color fields in the windows of buildings colored gels were used. However, the effect of creating colored fields similar to a comic is complicated by the variations that occur between the color, the material, and the lighting. A limited number of colors were used in the production design and costuming for *Dick Tracy* in an attempt to capture the limitation of the four-color printing process found in traditional comics. When discussing the limited number of colors used, the film's costume designer, Milena Canonero, explains, "with the way materials react to color and light, it may seem that there are nuances, but in fact there are just those ten [colors]. No browns, no midtones, no grays" (Bonifer 63). The loss of color on one object is usually made up for with the saturation of color on another object. For example, the colored lighting on the set causes Tracy's raincoat to lose the brightness of its yellow.

Sets, backlots, mattes, and models are actually unsophisticated staples of cinema, and improvements in technology are usually aimed at making them more transparent. However, *Dick Tracy* eschews the "reality effect" which comes so easily to cinema, and pursues a "fiction effect" through the "opaque" deployment of the common cinematic techniques outlined. The artifice of its diegetic fabrication does not make "Tracy Town" any less recognizable as a twentieth-century city; instead, it challenges its plausibility. The Affrons state: "All constructed movie sets are artificial, of course. . . . We reserve 'artifice' and 'artificial' for those that refuse to let us forget it" (114), and in *Dick Tracy* the artificial set refuses to let the spectator forget this film is based on a comic.

A strategy of "cartooning" in *Dick Tracy* makes the choreography of character actions and behavior implausible, and complements the "aesthetic of artifice" in the production design. Whether it is exaggerated filming effects, such as sped up footage, or the outrageous behavior of the characters themselves, "cartooning" transcends the communication of the story: the narrative referent becomes abstracted into a stylistic representation. "Cartooning" also includes the design of the villains using prosthetic makeup, and the design of their props and weapons, so that they all resemble the caricatures found in the pages of comics. Deployed in combination with an artificial production design, the result is a comic-style diegesis populated by outrageous characters, wielding farfetched weapons, whom look and behave as "cartoons."

Comics are the product of the relationship between hand and page and are inherently artificial. However, superhero comics are not only distinguished by the artifice of the graphic process. Typically, comics are excessive and flamboyant in their use of color, character proportion, and the choreography and depiction of action. To translate this artifice and excess into a cinematic form Warren Beatty and his creative team used a number of stylistic strategies that can be described as "cartooning," which is another way of elevating the "aesthetic of artifice" in *Dick Tracy*.

At first glance, any relationship between "cartooning" and live-action cinema is problematic, since cartoons are hand-drawn caricatures. In his article, "Delirious Inventions," Mike Atkinson states, "the relationship of both cartoons and comics to actuality has always been antagonistic" (12). "Cartoon" is also a common term for cel-animation of hand-drawn caricatures. As John Geipel explains in *The Cartoon: A Short History of Graphic Comedy and Satire*, "the popular use of the term 'cartoon' as a synonym of 'animated film' is long-established and probably indelible . . . later reinforced by the universal popularity of Mickey Mouse, Bugs Bunny, Popeye and other celluloid heroes" (150). This simplified explication of "cartooning" as being less than serious fails to take into account that many comics and animated cartoons can be humorous, dramatic, or horrific. However, the definition of "cartooning" applied to *Dick Tracy* mirrors both the continuing perception that comics and superheroes are childish or juvenile, and the stylistic approach of Beatty.

Will Eisner explains that the "cartoon is the result of exaggeration and simplification. Realism is adherence to most of the detail. The elimination of some of the detail in an image makes it easier to digest and adds to humor. Retention of detail begets believability because it is closest to what the reader actually sees" (*Comics and Sequential Art* 151). In *Dick Tracy* "cartooning" is used to preclude the plausibility of characters and their actions by either removing or countering the "realistic" detail recorded by the camera. Such strategies include speeding up footage and other techniques to draw attention to the fabrication of cinematic production. As Scott McCloud states: "By stripping down an image to its essential 'meaning,' an artist can amplify that meaning in a way that realistic art can't" (*Understanding Comics* 30). In this sense, "cartooning" is not necessarily a move closer to the ontology of comics; it is a move away from the potential "realism" of cinema, and towards abstraction and excess. "By de-emphasizing the appearance of the physical world in favor of the idea of form, the cartoon places itself in the world of concepts" (McCloud, *Understanding Comics* 41). The more abstracted the image becomes the more it represents concepts and ideas, and the less it represents its referent in the real world. McCloud claims, "when we abstract an image through cartooning, we're not so much eliminating details as we are focusing on specific details" (*Understanding Comics* 30).

In *Dick Tracy*, the use of bright and unrealistic coloring on sets and props emphasizes the concept or "idea" of the referent by exaggerating and simplifying it. The design of props in *Dick Tracy* operates similarly to the way the production design uses excessive artifice to add to the "fiction effect." Whether it is the exaggeration of proportions, or the application of coloring, the characters in *Dick Tracy* wield and handle an array of weapons and props that are farfetched and implausible. The villains themselves are covered in prosthetic makeup: a literal and metaphorical layer of artifice upon the actors. This definition of "cartooning" extends beyond Eisner and McCloud, to include the choreography of actions and behavior of characters, which is self-consciously "goofy" and incongruous with plausibility; it is embellished and enhanced beyond narrative justification.

"Cartooning" is established from the start of *Dick Tracy* when Flattop uses his Tommy gun to write the words EAT LEAD TRACY on the back wall of the garage, clearly linking the film with the animated television series, *The Dick Tracy Show* (1961), where characters would do the same. However, writing on a wall with a machine gun is not something in the original comic strip, and this is therefore an example of explicit "cartooning," rather than a reference to the comic strip.

When Tracy fights and arrests Steve the Tramp, he swings his arms around wide amplifying the motion of his punches. The film is sped up to further exaggerate the effect of the fight. This "cartooning" is carried over into a shot outside of the shack rocking back and forth, emphasizing the force of Tracy's attack on the thug. When Tracy utters the line, "maybe we should step outside," he punches the Tramp right through the side of the shack and onto the ground. This sequence is a demonstration of "cartooning" because Tracy does not have superpowers that would narratively explain the exaggerated depiction of the action.

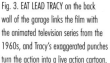

Fig. 3. EAT LEAD TRACY on the back wall of the garage links the film with the animated television series from the 1960s, and Tracy's exaggerated punches turn the action into a live action cartoon.

Dick Tracy has two *montage* sequences that demonstrate the artifice of "cartooning" in the depiction of action. In both sequences Breathless Mahoney, played by Madonna, sings songs describing narrative developments: "Sooner or Later (I always get my man)" and "Back in Business." In the first sequence, Tracy is able to foil Big Boy's crime operations by being on the scene in time to nab the criminals in the act. In the second sequence, Big Boy and his men launch a crime spree after Tracy has been framed and imprisoned. In both sequences, the action is abstracted from literal to "cartoon" representations. In one shot, Tracy punches out seven gangsters advancing on him with one punch, and in another shot he sends a gangster flying backwards through the air. During the crime spree the gangsters

Fig. 4. Two *montage* sequences demonstrate the artifice of "cartooning" in the exaggerated depiction of action, such as Tracy's knockout punches and the gangsters' looting and shakedowns.

throw their victims out of windows, and two gangsters literally shake a victim upside down causing coins fall out of his pockets onto the ground.

The functionality and plausibility of props in *Dick Tracy* is deemphasized using design and coloring, so they are abstracted into the denotation of their referents. Although film sets and props are often nonfunctioning they are usually designed to be perceived as functional. The spectator's suspension of disbelief is contingent upon the perception of a prop's functionality that is easily achieved using recognizable "real-world" designs. In *Dick Tracy*, the functionality and believability of the props is strictly limited to the denotation of the referent, and their implausible appearance is contingent and justified by the film's relationship with the comics. The design of these props has a cumulative effect with the fabrication of the artificial diegesis, as well as with the narrative context, which forms the "aes-

MICHAEL COHEN

thetic of artifice." In "Tracy Town," the outrageous props are only believable when in the hands of its crime fighter and its villains.

A sequence involving a boiler room in *Dick Tracy* demonstrates how the use of color lends implausibility to the props. The boiler is painted bright yellow with red pipes and handles to emphasize its artifice. Itchy (Ed O'Ross), one of Big Boy's henchmen, also wields a wrench in this scene which is painted bright red. As the boiler gets closer and closer to explosion, it begins to rock furiously and shake on its foundations, steam bursts from various pipe seams, and whistles blare. The "cartooning" of these props complements the outrageousness of Big Boy's plan to kill Tracy with the exploding boiler.

The abstraction of props extends to the use of generic labels so that the products, such as a can of chili Dick Tracy eats from, do not have the

Fig. 5. The abstraction of props extends to the use of generic labels, such "EXTRA" and "Daily Paper" to identify newspapers.

complicated design patterns that are usually found on commercial products, and they are colored in single primary colors. In addition, generic labels, such as "EXTRA" and "Daily Paper," identify newspapers.

In *Dick Tracy*, the transference of the villains and gangsters from the panels of the comic strip required complicated makeup and prosthetics, which abstracts and exaggerates a particular feature of each character. In this way literal names describe the character's facial features: Flattop has a flat head; The Brow has a strangely bulbous forehead; and so on with Little Face (Lawrence Steven Meyers), The Rodent (Neil Summers), and others. There is no exploration of the psychology or background of each villain because the prosthetic design creates the phrenology of a criminal. By abstracting the design of the villains the filmmakers "amplify" the evil nature of these caricatures, which places them "in the world of concepts" (McCloud, *Understanding Comics* 41).

Warren Beatty uses the design of props and characters, and the choreography of their actions and their behavior, to bridge the ontological gap between live action cinema and comics, albeit at a superficial level. As Atkinson explains, "[w]hen using actors and real settings . . . what results is perilously entangled in formal incongruities" (12). These "incongruities," these tropes of exaggeration are "cartooning," which is how Beatty has translated the aesthetic of cartoons into a live-action film. Taken in isolation these elements of "cartooning" might be considered aberrant. The suspension of disbelief required to accept the embellished behavior and

Fig. 6. Complicated makeup and prosthetics abstract and exaggerate a particular feature of each character, such as Flattop and The Brow.

actions and the bizarre collection of villains is contingent upon accepting their implausibility as a cinematic "translation" of a comic aesthetic.

Dick Tracy goes beyond simply transferring the character from the comic pages to the screen using elaborate costuming; the film illustrates the hero's iconic specificity through conspicuous framing and lighting. Tracy is introduced in shots that allow the spectator to fully contemplate the visual design of the character. The hero does not just pose for the camera, he pauses for a length of time which transcends the narrative moment, fulfilling the role of "the graphic center of narrative focus" ("The Aesthetics of the Comic Strip" 650) in comic panels, described by Robert Harvey.

The most popular comic book crime fighters and superheroes have entered into popular culture with an enormous impact. Their origins and their eternal battles with a gallery of arch nemeses are endlessly replayed across decades of comics, as well as cinema and television. The plot of *Dick Tracy* is inevitably a distillation of story elements from the character's comic history across different eras, to create a contemporary version. In "The Superhero with a Thousand Faces: Visual Narratives on Film and Paper," Luca Somigli claims, "[t]he development of comic book narratives over time can be characterized as sameness with difference, as a reshuffling of a number of narrative elements into new patterns" (289). This is how the most popular of characters remain fresh over their lifespan, even though some comic characters are more than half a century old. As Somigli states, "a comic book character is always already a remake" (286). This is true, yet wherever they go, wherever they are remade, they carry with them essential defining attributes and iconic designs for which they are famous, and this allows them to be instantly recognizable across various media.

Born of a visual medium, the most prominent feature of comic heroes is their appearance, and it is not surprising that films based on comics trade so heavily on the visual appearance of their characters. In *Dick Tracy* the iconic features of the hero's costume are a yellow hat and coat he wore in the colored Sunday comic strips. Despite slight alterations in the depiction of his facial features, Tracy has always had the same general visage, which conveniently suits the casting of Warren Beatty. Beatty's features are not quite as "chiseled" as Chester Gould's depiction; however, the costume is the primary icon defining the character. The opening shot of *Dick Tracy* is of Tracy's famous two-way watch-radio, his badge, and his gun all arranged neatly on the dresser. Tracy picks up these three icons of his profession, before the camera pans upwards to reveal the bright yellow hat hanging on a hook on the wall, which completes the character.

Comic characters do not move on the page: they are locked into the postures and poses selected for each panel. The frozen posture is the event of the panel, and often depicts an entire continuity of action. The depiction of motion by conventions in the artwork is complemented by the static nature of the image, which imbues it with a contemplative potential: even though the image might suggest or be part of a continuous motion, it can be scrutinized and savored in a way cinematic images cannot. When Tracy is leaving his apartment he pauses in the doorway, framed and lit in silhouette, to check his watch-radio. This is not the narrative act of a character establishing the time, but a posture to establish the hero based on the icons of his representation, his watch-radio, hat, and coat, which are very specific to the historical character of Dick Tracy. When Tracy does stop and pose the spectator can focus on the character's visual attributes and contemplate his presence within the frame.

During the "Sooner or Later (I always get my man)" *montage*, Tracy walks toward the camera firing his Tommy gun. The strong backlighting from a single source forms a halo of light around the character. The effect is the reverse of a comic image, where the background would be a light color or white and the character bordered by an outline of black. The outline of light in the film performs a similar function to a drawn border: it separates Tracy from his background. An important distinction between this shot and a comic is that the light simultaneously casts a shadow over Tracy's features, diminishing the detail of his face.

Fig. 7. Strong backlighting forms a halo of light around the character, which is the reverse of a comic image, where the background would be a light color or white and the character bordered by an outline of black

The stylistic deployment of Dick Tracy is an integral element of this definition of a "comic aesthetic" because it "translates" the privileged posturing and appearance of the hero upon the comic page. The very nature of a comic in the hands of a reader grants it the potential for contemplation at the reader's discretion. The page does not need to be turned and the next panel can wait while the reader appreciates the visual design of the character. Drawn in postures to accentuate the explosive potential and implications of an action, the comic character is a dynamic figure caught frozen upon the page. Freezing a character upon the screen for a lengthy period would be a dubious strategy: certainly possible, but narratively awkward as it has the potential to disrupt spectator engagement. Without freezing the image, the Tracy poses and the camera unobtrusively records him, whilst the spectator contemplates the heroic poise of the crime fighter during this narrative pause.

Describing a relationship between the mechanisms of cinema and comics is a more complicated proposition than attaining an ornate and colorful *mise-en-scène*, or costume design, or similarly developing a "cartooning" effect. Although cinema and comics use images in sequence, both utilize different mechanisms of narrative communication. "Paneling" is the use of framing and editing to adapt the paradigmatic arrangement of panels in a strip into a cinematic form and is the most complex of the strategies deployed in the creation of a "comic aesthetic" in *Dick Tracy*. It is possible to compare the functional and aesthetic equivalencies between *Dick Tracy* and the original comics, to determine the extent to which the "paneling" transcends the ontological differences between the media.

Francis Lacassin contends in his article, "The Comic Strip and Film Language," that the "language" of comics was developed before its equivalent in cinema, despite the intellectual and critical preference consistently granted to the cinema. As he develops his argument, Lacassin makes two bold claims: "The comic-strip page demonstrably corresponds to the film sequence," and "[t]he daily comic strip of three or four images is comparable to the cinematic scene" (11). These claims do not stand up to rigorous scrutiny because Lacassin simplifies the mechanism of both cinema and comics, and he does not provide a definition of either a film sequence or a cinematic scene. As with all narrative media, the boundaries determining the "sequence" or the "scene" are often arbitrary, whereas a page in a comic book or a tier in a comic strip are finite spaces. However, the goal in this article is not to reconcile the mechanistic differences between the two media, but rather to explain how the deployment of cinematographic frames and shots, in isolation and juxtaposition, can be compared with the aesthetic of panels in comics.

Both cinema and comics use images in sequence, yet the nature of the sequence is different: "each successive frame of a movie is projected on exactly the same space—the screen—while each frame of comics must occupy a different space" (McCloud, *Understanding Comics* 7). As Robert Harvey states, panels are always present with each other upon the page, and layout is a function in a comic for which there is no equivalent in cinema: "Only in the comics does layout assist in storytelling" (*Art of the Comic Book* 162). For this reason, Will Eisner explains there is a necessary level of cooperation on the part of the reader, that they will follow the narrative sequence instead of skipping ahead (*Comics and Sequential Art* 40). Control is taken out of the hands of the spectator in cinema, but is literally held in the hands of the comic book reader. As Greg Smith describes the process, the "comics readers first see the page as a whole before they then parse through the individual frames in narrative succession. The comics page is first understood as a unit, and then the reader fits the component frames into that overall structure" (44).

Even with the control afforded by video and DVD, cinema spectators cannot control and experience the juxtaposition of images in the same way they can with a comic. Although readers are guided by the traditional reading sequence and the artwork in a comic, they are able to read and reread the sequence in and out of order, and experience the spatial proximity of the panels as they read. As Harvey explains: "Simply by being chosen, [the piece of action] is captured and thus destined for longer contemplation than is possible for an equivalent action in a film" (*The Art of the Comic Book* 178). Striking and dramatic poses in comics are designed with this contemplation in mind. However, in "Comic Art: Characteristics and Potentialities of a Narrative Medium," Lawrence Abbott explains, "[s]everal minutes of picture contemplation would be out of the question because the story continuity would be broken. Each drawing on the comic strip/book page has its allotted reading time, without which narrative continuity would be severely hindered" (162).

The first place to begin a comparison of cinematic frames with comic panels is with the aspect ratios. In the original "Dick Tracy" comic strips there is consistency in the shapes and sizes of the panels due to the traditional comic strip layout established in newspaper publishing. In a daily strip, there are usually four panels with an aspect ratio of approximately 0.8:1, and in the Sunday color pages there are typically three tiers divided into four panels each with aspect ratios varying from 1.1:1 to 1.3:1,[2] which is very close to the original Academy ratio of 1.37:1.[3] These aspect ratios are all close to being square. In *Dick Tracy* the choice to use the narrower aspect ratio of 1.85:1 was made with direct reference to the panels of the original comic strip: "It was finally determined that a tighter frame, a standard aspect ratio of 1.85:1 . . . would come closer to duplicating the presentation of the original comic strip" (Bonifer 54–55). However, the choice of one frame ratio over the other in a film does not equate to the ontology of a comic. The 1.85:1 ratio does not resemble the size and shape of panels, and a cinematographic frame does not resemble the hand-drawn art, so a profitable comparison between cinema and comics requires more than a side-by-side inspection.

Individual panels are often called upon to be more than a single link in a sequence, and are used to depict the continuity of an action. Eisner refers to this as "encapsulation" (*Comics and Sequential Art* 39), where a single panel represents the "before" and "after" of an action. The panel does not freeze a moment in time; instead it has what Lacassin calls "dynamic time," which "represents the time span necessary for the unfolding of an action" (17). The panel's pictorial content embodies the preceding action and suggests the subsequent action through a number of conventional devices, such as character posture, motion lines, multiple images, as well as dialogue and narration. It is therefore a part of a temporal sequence of narrative: "In a panel selected from a series, the frozen posture tells its story—giving information about the before and after of the event" (Eisner, *Comics and Sequential Art* 105). Unlike cinema, the comic artist has to distill hundreds of movements comprising a simple gesture into one tableau: "The comic strip abbreviates movement, or rather relieves it of certain phases and contracts the time necessary for its execution" (Lacassin 18). This tableau has to support dialogue, story, emotion, and action.

In *Dick Tracy*, Warren Beatty chose to keep the action within stationary frames to "encapsulate" each narrative unit without moving the camera or relying on editing. According to cinematographer Vittorio Storaro, "we were trying to use elements from the original Chester Gould drawings. One of the elements is that the story is usually told in vignette. So what we tried to do is never move the camera at all. Never. Try to make everything work in the frame . . . Camera movement is normally your grammar

Fig. 8. These shots "encapsulate" the action of the two characters running and are functionally equivalent to comic panels and stylistically conspicuous.

in telling the story. In this case we were trying to use a camera that was steady all the time" (Bonifer 54).

This is certainly not the case throughout the whole film, as the camera does move frequently, with particularly elaborate shots incorporating matte paintings. However, there is a strategy to keep the camera motionless at very conspicuous moments where a moving, panning, or tracking shot would have been the norm.

When Tracy chases the Kid through the streets, the shots are framed in medium long shot, and the camera does not move. Each shot is framed to provide an image of great depth, which is compositionally reinforced by the use of perspective lines in the architecture, such as the side of a warehouse receding into the background. The action within each frame alternates between the characters running towards the camera and away from it, which makes the sequence dynamic without relying on camera movement or *montage*. The duration of the shots, and the deliberate lack of editing, except to depict transitions from location to location, draws attention to the deployment of these shots to "encapsulate" the action of the two characters running. These shots from *Dick Tracy* are both functionally equivalent to comic panels, and they are stylistically conspicuous. The superficial resemblance in the function of shots and panels does not translate into the same style of a comic, and adapting the cinematic form into "panels" requires more than recognizing the equation between shots and panels.

A conspicuous technique in *Dick Tracy* that produces a visual strategy of "paneling" within the frame is the repeated use of a diopter lens. Usually quite rare, this lens is used at least ten times during the film. The diopter lens allows the foreground and background characters and objects to be displayed in sharp focus, presenting a striking juxtaposition that defies the reality of their spatial position, and heightens their compositional proximity. The shortcoming of a diopter lens is a distinct blurred line down the center of the image, which divides the two focal planes.

In *Dick Tracy*, the diopter lens is used three times involving the Kid. In the first, he is in the background staring at Tracy's two-way wrist radio, which is in the extreme foreground. In the second, the Kid is about to escape out of a window in the background, and he stops to look back at Tracy's wallet, which is in the foreground. In the third, the woman from the orphanage has come to collect him and is walking up the corridor in the background, juxtaposed sharply beside the look of fear on the Kid's face in the foreground. The division between the focal planes is particularly evident in the first and second examples, as the line of blurred focus is not as well hidden as it is in the third example. In each shot, the juxtaposition within the frame heightens the relationship between the Kid and his situation or the props: the technology of the wrist radio fascinates him, the wallet tempts him, and he dreads the orphanage.

Warren Beatty's choice to use the diopter lens in *Dick Tracy* is the choice to move away from the language of "cinema" towards the language of "comics" in which the spatial arrangement articulates the narrative. Instead of using editing, camera movement, or rack focusing to create the juxtapo-

Fig. 9. The diopter lens is a move away from the language of "cinema" towards the language of "comics" in which the narrative dynamic unfolds within the single composition.

sition between subject and object in these scenes, which would therefore be syntagmatic and linear, the use of the diopter lens allows the narrative dynamic to unfold within the single composition. This is a simplistic summation of the mechanism of both cinema and comics, and overlooks the fact that the use of static framing and the diopter lens are privileged moments in a film that still relies on typical continuity editing. However, the conspicuousness of these cinematographic choices indicates the development of a style that explicitly alludes to comics through the paradigmatic juxtaposition of images.

The "comic aesthetic" in *Dick Tracy* is motivated by the presence of the hero. Costumed crime fighters and superheroes are natives of the comic medium, and this influences their formal appearance in a number of films:

they do not exist in a "real" world, they have extraordinary powers and abilities, they wear outrageous costumes, and they fight maniacal villains and foil their preposterous plots. The relationship between the comic medium and the heroes and villains that battle across its pages creates an aesthetic contingent upon their mutual artifice and implausibility. This distinct quality has guided the movement of Dick Tracy from the comic strips to the cinema screen.

According to Greg Smith, "[p]roducers adapting works from other media make choices about how to translate formal elements into their functional equivalents in the other medium" (32). The "comic aesthetic" in *Dick Tracy* does not transcend the ontology of cinema; it is an aesthetic translation of the characteristics and conventions from the comic medium by using the stylistic and functional equivalents in cinema. As Smith claims, "[w]hen a medium borrows an effect from other existing media, the borrowing medium often evolves and gains expressivity" (32).

The development of a "comic aesthetic" in *Dick Tracy*, through the adaptation of the conventions and characteristics of comics, has given cinema a new "expressivity." However, the "comic aesthetic" is contingent upon the hero himself: Dick Tracy's origin in comic strips motivates the combination of the "aesthetic of artifice," "cartooning," "paneling," and the heroic posturing of the crime fighter. There would be no "comic aesthetic" without Dick Tracy, and therefore the crime fighter is both the impetus and the limitation of the "comic aesthetic" as a unique cinematic style.

MICHAEL COHEN

TRANSLATION CREATIVITY AND ALIEN ECON(C)OMICS
FROM HOLLYWOOD BLOCKBUSTER TO DARK HORSE COMIC BOOK[1]

— KERRY GOUGH

Although the relationship between film and the comic book has had a long history (McAllister et. al.; Gordon, *Comic Strips* 84; Barker; Reitberger and Fuchs; Gifford; Waugh), the intermedia opportunities of comic book properties have been excessively plundered in recent years through the reciprocal relationship between Warner Bros. and DC, and Marvel's later synergistic relationships with Columbia Pictures and Twentieth Century Fox (Reitberger and Fuchs 156; Perry and Aldridge 242). As such the Hollywood comic book blockbuster movie has become a central and complementary part of both the comic book and the Hollywood film industries, in which the revenue generated can be staggering. At the beginning of 2006 *Spider-Man* was the most successful comic book movie, having earned a U.S. domestic box office of over $403 million and worldwide sales of over $821 million (Gordon, *Comic Strips*; Meehan 47–65; McAllister, "All-Time Domestic Blockbusters").

However, not only do the Hollywood studios take successful comic book characters and translate them into cinematic money-spinners, but those studios also seek to exploit existing, if apparently exhausted Hollywood successes, through their licensed translations into comic book properties. By branching out into alternative ancillary areas and markets, in effect these already existing and proven products "go large" in an effort to further maximize profit potential, as they break into the already established and lucrative market of the comic book (Barker, "News Reviews"; Bierbaum 24; Thompson, "The Spider Stratagem").

This chapter explores one such especially telling and successful comic book adaptation, that of the *Aliens* series by Dark Horse Comics. This series illustrates not only the economic potential of such activities, but also the creative possibilities that such adaptations facilitate. While economics have long been a factor in the production of cultural products, Eileen Meehan has identified how the "commercial intertext" itself is in fact a "response to economic conditions" and the expansionist rise of multimedia conglomerates (Meehan 47). However, in the particular case of the *Alien* film saga, we have the development of a conglomerate-produced cinematic product that did not originate in comics. Rather, Dark Horse Comics, in an effort to break into a previously untapped area of the comic book market, repackaged the Hollywood blockbuster action of the *Alien* film series as a branded, but still unique, pleasure for a comic book and fan audience. The film series, appropriately enough, in itself was also influenced by the visual arts, and built upon the branding of the *Aliens* franchise with the highly stylized artwork of H. R. Giger (Wyatt; Grainge 344–62). In this process of translation creativity, then—a process that culminated in both a striking visual style and extension of the original narrative worlds—this particular film property lent itself readily to the transformation process across into the comic book format.

Alien's adaptation into comic book art also denoted the relatively small Dark Horse Comics' elevated position as a direct challenger to its larger Marvel and DC competitors, including the cultivation of synergistic relationships between the less-well-known Dark Horse and the giant Twentieth Century Fox conglomerate. As a result, this project, through the creative nuances that it afforded, also breathed further longevity and financial incentive into the *Alien* franchise as a whole, thus benefiting the studio, the comics company, and the fans alike. In effect the nexus of productivity functioned around questions of innovation and re-creation, translation creativity, and franchisation, within a context of the growing strength of the multimedia conglomerates and multinational power (Wasko, *How Hollywood Works*; Hesmondhalgh).

In 1987, a full two years ahead of the release and crossover phenomenon of *Batman*, Dark Horse's *Aliens* series was a forerunner in a reverse of the by-now conventionalized process of translating comic books into films. The translation business itself was not new to Dark Horse at this point, and it became essential to its genesis and development as comic book publishers, as one Dark Horse Press release reveals, "At Dark Horse, we've been marrying movies to comics ever since our 1987 *Godzilla Special,* and we've never tried to justify the existence of one by its ties to the other. Instead we try to take what's best in movies and television shows and adapt them to achieve the same ends in comics (such as in the case of *Star Wars, Aliens, Godzilla,* etc.), or take comics that would work well as motion pictures (like *The Mask, Time Cop,* and . . . *Barb Wire*) and bring them to the screen" ("Press Release").

The primary function of the press release is self-serving, self-advertising rhetoric, but it does demonstrate Dark Horse's vision of itself as a home for creative film and comic book exchanges. Marvel Comics and DC Comics are frequently cited as the forefathers of the synergesis between the comic book and the contemporary comic book action movie; as McAllister argues, "The archetype of synergy in the comic book industry has traditionally been DC comics, whose parent company, Time Warner, is the largest communications conglomerate in the world. Its many holdings illustrate how a license—in this case a superhero character—can be moved across various media industries" (McAllister, "Ownership Concentration" 27). However Dark Horse's fit within the symbiosis of the comic book and the Hollywood film industries demonstrates the process of creative exchange that takes place within and across the industry, and particularly the potential connections that can be established between Hollywood and smaller comic book publishers.

Cofounded in 1986 by Mike Richardson and Randy Stradley, Dark Horse Comics, as a major independent comic book producer, went on to control 6 percent of the comic book market by 1997, outsold in direct market sales, to comic book shops and independent subscription services, by the comic book market leaders Marvel Comics at 33 percent and DC Comics with 28 percent (McAllister, "Ownership Concentration" 19; Henderson, "February

2005 Market Share"). This figure has remained comparatively constant and as of February 2005 Dark Horse's market share stood at 6.2 percent compared to 37.4 percent for Marvel and DC at 30.6 percent ("2004 Year in Review"). During this period Dark Horse's increased distribution figures have also nudged the company into third place ahead of Image Comics' 4.70 percent market share. However while Dark Horse's ranked position and market share has increased, in terms of reorders, or the rate at which older successful titles are reordered and stocked by comics retailers, by 2004 the margin between Dark Horse and the duopoly of Marvel and DC narrowed considerably with Dark Horse once more in third place at a significantly higher 9.9 percent compared to the relative stability of DC with 34.4 percent and Marvel's 23.1 percent ("2004 Year in Review"). Here Image Comics, Dark Horse's main competitor from the independent sector, had dropped back to fifth place behind both Tokyo Pop and Viz Llc, with Dark Horse building significantly upon sales of its back catalogue ("2004 Comics, Graphic Novel"; Henderson).

As a relatively independent comic book producer, Dark Horse Comics represents a successful example of how smaller competitors represent a challenge to the dominance of the major industry players. However, Dark Horse was not the first to develop a comic book series from a film franchise. Marvel had already produced the *Star Wars* comic series a decade before, producing 107 issues between 1977 and 1986. However, this series started out as a direct translation of the original *Star Wars* (1977) film, and while it did progress to explore and expand upon the original film, this expansion was largely restricted to the development of existing characters and storylines contained within that narrative arc, due to Lucas's protection of that property. During this period Marvel also went on to develop a four-part direct translation of *Return of the Jedi* (1983) in January 1985. However it was largely by 1992—after Dark Horse's purchase of the *Star Wars* license and publication of *Classic Star Wars #1*—that the comics' narratives were developed to encompass new and original storylines ("2004 Year in Review"). Dark Horse Comics' position as a relatively small, privately owned company granted it a degree of autonomy and freedom not ordinarily afforded within the ranks and hierarchies of Marvel and DC. Dark Horse's position, as a company less embedded in large-conglomerate power circles, permitted freedom in the process of that translation creativity.

Dark Horse's success is manifest not only in terms of its increasing market share as a comics, graphic novel, and magazine publisher, but also in the strength of its back catalogue, which represents the extensive outreach and longevity of its product when compared to other comic book publishers. Although comparatively small in relation to the Big Two, Dark Horse represents an important industry mainstay, and has had a significant number of films based upon its original comic book properties, such as *The Mask* (1994), *Barbwire* (1996), *Spawn* (1997), *Hellboy* (2004), *Aliens vs. Predator* (2004), *Sin City* (2005), as well as the scheduled development of *Concrete* (forthcoming) ("Comic Book Adaptation Figures").

Dark Horse, then, specialized in the development of these licenses, either in licensing its original products to other media, or in the cultivation of licensed comic books. In the mid-1980s, Dark Horse had begun the process of acquiring comic book licensing rights not only for *Aliens*, but also for *Flash Gordon*, *Godzilla*, *Tarzan*, *Terminator*, and *Star Wars* ("2004 Year in Review"). At the time of the release of the original six-part *Aliens* comic series, *The Terminator* comics series was the company's best selling title, however *Aliens* outsold *The Terminator* by thousands, with *Aliens #1* returning to press six times (Stradley, "Interview: Licensing the Franchise").

Licensing established products, of course, not only serves to generate revenue for the studio through the license itself, but simultaneously serves as an intertextual advertisement for other affiliated products (Meehan 56–57). Yet in the mid-1980s this concept was still underdeveloped as an industrial strategy. Randy Stradley, Senior Editor for Dark Horse Comics, and Editor of the original *Aliens* comic books, suggests that in 1988 "studios hadn't yet tumbled to the amount of money that could be made licensing their films. When we started, the licensing department at Twentieth Century Fox consisted of two people, so we had an easy relationship with them" (Stradley, "Re: Comic Book Chapter"; "2004 Year in Review"). Mike Richardson later reaffirmed this sentiment in an interview (Richardson, "Interview: Licensing the Franchise"). Getting in on the ground floor of such activities helped to establish and secure Dark Horse's position as an industry, even global, leader in the publication of licensed comics, and to attain their current ranking as the third largest U.S. comic book publisher ("2004 Year in Review"; "Dark Horse Comics Licenses"; "Company Overview"; "Dark Horse Services").

As fans of the *Alien* films themselves, and after the box-office success of both *Alien* (1979) and *Aliens* (1986), the editors of Dark Horse Comics approached Twentieth Century Fox with a view to purchasing the comics licensing rights to the *Aliens* property ("Comic Book Adaptation Figures"). The imperative was simultaneously to entertain the established adult fans of the films and to attract new audiences to the comic book series by developing the property. Recollecting the initial thought process surrounding the conception of the comic books, Randy Stradley said: "Well the films were the films, and everybody had already seen them. Who would want to read the same adventure over and over? We wanted to do the sequels to the films—to see how an encounter with the Aliens might affect different groups of characters in different settings and situations" (Stradley, "Re: Comic Book Chapter").

A central problem faced by Dark Horse in transferring and translating these cinematic products into a comic book language lay in establishing a unique vision while maintaining an "accurate" portrayal—striving for a degree of product differentiation, in an effort to generate newness and a degree of originality, while demonstrating an affinity with the series. Dark Horse had to negotiate an affinity of coherence across both an already established product and its readymade fan base.

Having secured the licensing rights to the *Alien* series, and with the necessity for coherence in mind, Dark Horse cofounders Stradley and Richardson approached the writer Mark Verheiden. They were already familiar with his work on *The American* in 1987, and, as will be argued, his style fitted neatly with the treatment they had in mind for the comic book series.

With such a visually striking property and given the visual emphasis of the comics medium, creating an effective look was central. Dark Horse sought to marry the visual tone of the accompanying comic book art with that of the original film product, which drew heavily on the artwork of H. R. Giger, the original creator of the Alien lifeform (Giger). These "biochemical, neuro-gynological, post-terrestrial" creations of Giger's original art for the film, as Timothy Leary described them, acted as the impetus and guiding inspiration for Dark Horse's progeny in the face of such an organic and sinuous, metallographic creation (Leary 4). In Giger's art, the alien xenomorph featured the contradictory enmeshing of the natural and the organic with the technological, of sinew and artifice with surface sheen, and the blending of contorted limbs with alien elegance. Giger's aliens both fascinate and disgust in their binaristic reductionism, and this was something that Dark Horse set out to emulate in its translation (see figure 1) (Haraway, 149–81). Armed with the bio-mechanical creations of Giger's art, Dark Horse's translation of the film into the comic book format aimed to build on the bio-mechanoidal origins of the film product, to create a new and original extension of the *Alien* film world through the comic books.

At the time of the publication of the original *Aliens* six-part comic book series in 1989, only Ridley Scott's *Alien* (1979) and James Cameron's *Aliens* (1986) had been released. With the already established visual sensi-

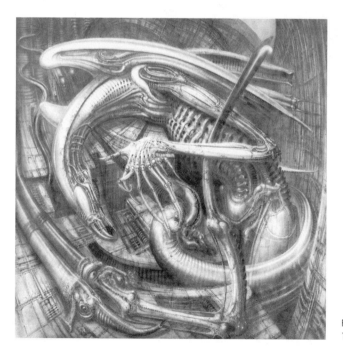

Fig. 1. H. R. Giger, *Alien Monster IV,* 140 x 140 cm.

bilities of the first two *Alien* films created, the artwork of Mark A. Nelson seemed an obvious selection for the translation of the film's visual style into comic book art. For editor Randy Stradley, it was Nelson's demonstration of a "real affinity for all things creepy and biological" that isolated him as the "hands-down choice" (Stradley, "Re: Comic Book Chapter"). Nelson's art work for the comics mirrored and embellished Giger's original conception of the alien's world and the alien xenomorph itself, in a complementary manner that extended the original premise and conceptualization of the first two films (see figures 1–4 for an illustrative comparison of Giger and Nelson's artwork).

With the creative personnel in place—publisher Mike Richardson, editor Randy Stradley, artist Mark Nelson and scriptwriter Mark Verheiden—the crew teamed together to produce the stories of the original series of six *Aliens* comic book issues (Brooker 260–61). In an effort to develop new and innovative storylines, the *Aliens* comic book series is set ten years after the events of the film *Aliens*, and focuses on the interplay of three (non-xenomorph) main characters. Two of these characters are from the Cameron film: Newt, who is now a young woman, and Corporal Hicks, injured and hideously scarred by acid at the end of the film, who is now recovered from his life-threatening injuries, but still physiologically scarred. The other central character is an original development within the comic series, Butler, an artificial being with whom Newt becomes attracted.

As an adaptation, the *Aliens* comic book series moved in two distinct, but ultimately complementary directions. Developing an innovative visual approach that demonstrated how comics can be faithful to a coherent but complex filmic style functioned as an important factor, not only in its attraction of fans of the film series, but also in its alleviation of the potential licensing concerns of Fox. As Pearson and Uricchio have identified elsewhere, it is this maintenance of a "uniformity of iconographic and narrative depictions . . . [that] prevents dilution of the trademark" (Pearson and Urichio 193). In tandem with this faithfulness and coherence to the visual style of the films, the narrative of the series significantly expanded the characterization and thematic possibilities, and as such pushed the boundaries of the original framework of the series. It was through this development of the original six-part *Aliens #1–#6* comics, that Dark Horse was successful in both its affinity with the Hollywood narrative and its extension of it beyond the confines of that set up by the film. The following sections detail the employment of these two adaptation strategies as they play out within the comic book extensions.

When it came to the translation of the *Aliens* film property into the comic book format, editor Stradley recognized the difficulties in the translation process, especially in visually capturing a film series that, at the time, existed as two separate texts:

> The problem, I think—at least from the film to comics end of the operation, stems from the fact that the people working on the comics forget that comics aren't film. When we began *Aliens*, it was decided (by Verheiden and Nelson) that the comic would have to rely more on the tension and mood of the first film rather than the full-tilt action of the sequel. Now don't get me wrong, James Cameron's film was, in my opinion, a brilliant sequel (and a perfect counterpoint) to the first film. But there's no way a black and white comic can capture the sound, or pacing, or movement that made *Aliens* (the movie) so exciting— and still fit a story into six 24-page issues. A conscious decision was made to utilize, and build the comic story around, devices and conventions of the comics medium (such as the ability to get "inside character's thoughts") instead of forcing a square peg into a round hole by trying to adapt film techniques to comics (Stradley, "Bug Hunt" 26)

Establishing a resonant visual mood, then, was crucial to the comic series and the concordance and compatibility of the two media was created and established through the visual unity of mood and atmosphere of Nelson's pencils. As Stradley maintains, "With our first series, we simply thought that Mark Nelson's art was so stunning in black and white (and fit so perfectly with the relatively subdued color schemes used in the first two films) that we felt it didn't require coloring" (Stradley, "Re: Comic Book Chapter"). The use of black and white thus became a stylistic choice that enabled a visual unity across the two media, and this coupled with the bricolage of visual contributions from the films themselves enabled an affinity between the comic book and filmic incarnations. Nelson's focus on atmosphere, mood, and tension replicated and melded together the tensions of the first film's suspense and the pace and freneticism of the second, through his ability to pencil in fine detail—both stillness and simplicity—and his simultaneous emphasis on the gritty realism of frantic action. The excerpt from *Aliens #1* (figure 2) highlights Nelson's attention to detail through the high key precision of his penciling, which echoes Scott's building of sus-

Fig. 2. *Aliens #1*, March 1989. Dark Horse Comics, p. 10.

pense and impending sense of doom, as the xenomorph is only partially revealed to us. In addition, Nelson develops the claustrophobic framing devices in the tightness of the cramped cells, as employed by both Scott and Cameron. In addition to his emulation of the suspense and tension created by Scott, Nelson also utilizes Cameron's dramatization and detailing of the alien. Here Nelson re-envisions Cameron's excessive use of violence in the graphic representation of cinematic spectacle, through the detailed and complex articulations of the xenomorph that served to gel with both Giger's origination of the alien, and Cameron's preference to reveal the xenomorph in all its metallographic beauty.

Echoes of the atmospheric intent and claustrophobia of the films can be found throughout these comic book translations (Barker, *Comics: Ideology*; Waugh). Within the splash panel of the alien xenomorph (figure 3), we have the coiled figure of the alien, looming in the foreground, filling the cramped cell and dwarfing the murky blackness of the ship, yet still retaining the high gloss of the xenomorph's exoskeleton (Brooker 260–61). Similarly, as the alien stalks the Dutton's crew, we have a match upon the claustrophobic framing utilized in the filmic representations within that of the comic book frames themselves. The dripping gore of the xenomorph's approach is in high key as the crew recoil into the gloom, emulating Scott's cinematic tension and Cameron's alien detailing, while the cramped, restrictive cells and stylized violent excess are evocative of both *Alien* and *Aliens* respectively (figures 2–4).

Throughout the *Aliens* comic book series, Nelson plays heavily upon the tight framing device within the comic strip, frequently positioning both the alien and the characters within the same cramped cell. This action not only relays the story in the minimum number of frames, which is necessary for the translation into the comic book format, but also adds to the momentum and tense pace of the narrative, through the condensed nature of that portrayal as evidenced in figures 2–4. The claustrophobia of the framing utilized by Nelson thus grants the comic translation of the film series an authenticity and legitimacy which stylistically is faithful to the tone and mood of the original films. Nelson's acute attention to detailing in the black and white pencils of the xenomorph itself permits an articulate and accurate translation of the alien in all its majesty, in which

Fig. 3. *Aliens #1*, March 1989. Dark Horse
Comics, p. 11.

every undulation is carved out in a manner that relays and maintains the
dripping gloss and mechanized gore of the creature of the original film series, along with the dank murk from which it emerges.

Nelson further demonstrates a continuity from the film property to
the comic book through the suggestion of action and movement in his detailing of the violence within the narrative. While the comic book format
does not lend itself easily to the suggestion of motion, Nelson's art conveys

KERRY GOUGH

a sense of the freneticism of the film series by his amorphous penciling of that movement, in the form of an ephemeral trace and a visually echoed disturbance of the action that is taking place. With the comic book representations in figures 2–4, we can see how that motion is expressed through character gesture, billowing disturbance, fracture and light within the explosion sequence, as well as the travel trajectory of the alien's drool as a causative factor in the visually turbulent excessive violence that it motivates. Through this suggestion of action and the attention to violent detail, the directional blood spatter of the wounded bodies is emphasized, and the sense of the frenzied violence of the alien's attack is maintained in the translation to comic book art. Regardless of the comic book's nature as a static form, motion is acutely highlighted and further reflected through the visual distortions, as implied through the flow patterns of hair and clothing.

Foreshadowing a later argument, while the translation into the comic book does provide us with a visual elaboration of the filmic, atmospheric stylization, the comic book representation also goes beyond the original conception of the film series. It does this through an elaboration upon the character development, which allows for a greater intimacy with the characters of the comic book narrative and enables Dark Horse to take the series in new directions. This feature is emphasized visually through the persistent use of close detailing and detours into the emotional state of the characters. The use of dialogue and narration allows detailed characterization and close attention to the mindset of the characters, with the comic strip frames themselves becoming a distorted reflection of the psychology surrounding character action and motivation. As such the comic book narrative form itself mirrors character psychology and motivation (Brooker 270–71).

In the case of *Aliens #1* we have a visual distortion or breaking of the actual comic strip frame featuring two key characters from the *Aliens* film, Corporal Hicks and Newt. Corporal Hicks recounts his horrific initial encounter with the aliens on LV-426 to another character, Doctor Orona, and again we have the fracturing of the comic cells, as we are guided through Newt's nightmare sequence. As Brooker notes, for the most part "layout and page design is 'neutral,' designed not to be noticed; our eyes flick easily from frame to frame, taking in the panel's content rather than its form.

Deviations from this strict grid . . . [where] the artwork escapes the panel borders, therefore help to convey a lack of order and reason through the very abnormality of the page design" (Brooker 270–71).

Nelson's artwork thus acts as a cohering force in the translation of the sensibilities of the film series into the comic book format, one which provided a close action match to the narrative and character psychology provided by Mark Verheiden. So for example where Verheiden writes of how "Sand and dust danced around the ship like some mocking, ethereal smoke," Nelson's art mimics the poetic imagery that Verheiden's words conjure, in a manner which affirms the narrational line (Verheiden and Nelson 19). Through Verheiden's scripts, the story is built upon detailed exposition and a careful layering of action to provide a strong narrative arc, with the slow building of tension and a gradual thickening of suspense. Verheiden envelopes either end with moments of complete stillness and frenetic action, both of which are reinforced visually through Nelson's art.

In much the same way as Nelson employs the fractured frame as a means of access to character psychology, the dialogue created by Verheiden and lettered by Willie Schubert also on occasion deviates from the conventionalized format of rounded speech bubbles to suggest the torment, anguish, and pain of characters through the jarred edges of the speech bubble and the application of stressed lettering (see figure 4). As such the art of Nelson, the script of Verheiden, and lettering of Schubert combine to provide a seamless intervention into the *Aliens* world. While Stradley reminds us of the difficulties of translating film sources into the comic book format, these problems are diminished through Nelson's mirroring of the subdued styles of the films, in his translation of them.

As a part of Dark Horse's development, this aspiration towards strong visuals became increasingly prevalent and featured as a part of the appeal in the translation of cinematic and comic book properties (Warner). These innovative visuals of the series were in turn complemented by a script in which Verheiden remains faithful and congruous to the origins of the series while developing it in new ways, both maintaining an affinity with the origins of the property, but also extending that property for new audiences (Parsons; Spigel and Jenkins; Rozanski; Gordon, "Superman on the Set"). Having established a strong visual style employed in the translation of the

|12|

Fig. 4. *Aliens #1*, March 1989. Dark Horse Comics, p. 12.

Aliens film property, the next section discusses the narrative development of the comic series that expanded the fictional world, and storytelling possibilities, of *Aliens*.

Commenting upon the translation of the film series into the comic book format, Stradley maintains that the series, once developed, "fit like a glove.

I don't recall any problems we had. One of the great aspects of the first two *Alien* films is that they don't reveal anything more about the world in which they take place than is necessary for the understanding of their stories. There's an old adage in writing science fiction that says, 'The more you define, the more you confine,' and it's absolutely true. We had a wide open field when we started—unlike, say *Star Wars*, where every writer has felt compelled to establish yet another 'fact' about the galaxy or the characters in it, until you can hardly say anything without contradicting something that has come before" (Stradley, "Re: Comic Book Chapter").

However, while Dark Horse was permitted a degree of creative control in its extension of the *Aliens* narrative, it was denied access to one of the most well-defined elements from the *Alien* films—that of Ripley herself (Stradley, "A Conversation"; Richardson, Stradley, and Gulacy). The terms of the initial licensing agreement of the *Alien* series with Twentieth Century Fox prevented Dark Horse from using the figure of Lt. Ellen Ripley in the comic book series. With the initial crossover, Fox was immensely protective of the *Aliens* property, ensuring that Ripley, as the most valuable aspect of that property, was protected and preserved as the domain of Twentieth Century Fox. As Stradley recollects, "The only specific restriction . . . was that we weren't allowed to use Ripley. But even that changed eventually . . . As long as we didn't interfere with the events from the films, we were free to explore—within the bounds of good taste, of course" (Stradley, "Re: Comic Book Chapter").

So with the initial transferal of 1988, and with the only direct demand made of Dark Horse being the omission of Ripley's character, Dark Horse was granted a degree of creative reign and little by way of restriction in terms of narrative content and character development. With the original *Aliens* six-part comic series, Dark Horse Comics sought to extend the film properties through an increased focus upon the characterization of Corporal Hicks and Newt as a young woman. So in denying Dark Horse the right to use Ripley in the initial series, as a result of their protection of the franchise, Twentieth Century Fox actually facilitated an enhanced creative drive on the part of Dark Horse, since without the heroic icon of the series, the team at Dark Horse was forced to work especially creatively to keep both Twentieth Century Fox and the fans happy with this next extension of the *Aliens* narrative. Verheiden's script succeeded on both counts, in extending Twentieth Century Fox's vision, but also in the widening of that world for fans—both with an expansion of the backstories of familiar characters, but also embellishing upon the original story enough for newcomers to the *Aliens* series to be able to engage with it as well.

In the narrative world of the original *Aliens* comics series, the story arc builds upon that of the films. Opening with the Bionational Corporation's captivity of an Alien Queen on Earth, Newt confined to a psychiatric ward, and Corporal Hicks incarcerated in a military cell on a drunk and disorderly charge, the comic book narrative essentially picks up where the *Aliens* film left off. Hicks, once freed from his cell for a mission to resolve a recent alien outbreak, rescues Newt, and the two become the main protagonists within the comic book extension.

On this return mission to Acheron Newt and Hicks are outrun by alien xenomorphs, and when Bionational's own marines jump the planet, Newt and Hicks are left for dead. However, just as all hope of survival appears to be lost, the "other" arrives. This creature (not unlike an elephantine version of the Predator), is explained, through the action, to be an arch enemy of the xenomorph, and as such serves to explain the existence of the original and mysterious corpse and "vessel" for the xenomorph in the first film. Within this comic book extension, the "other" has come to claim its revenge upon the aliens, and in the process inadvertently saves Newt, Hicks, and Butler.

In the meantime back on Earth, a cult group has discovered Bionational Corporation's captivity of the Alien Queen, and break into the Bionational Headquarters in order to offer themselves up as incubus for the alien spawn. Newt, Hicks, and Butler then arrive back on Earth to find the alien seed has spread across the globe, and just in time to find the Bionational evacuating Earth, leaving the planet to the xenomorphs. They hijack a ride on one of the company's automated supply ships, heading out for deep space on a cargo ship laden with livestock. So, rather than a simple repetition and stagnation of the *Aliens* property, here we have renewed creative drive and initiative, which expands the *Aliens* universe for fans, whilst simultaneously expanding the profit margins.

While the original *Aliens* comic series expands upon the film characters, Newt and Hicks, the successful development of the comic series on Earth and the investigation of other communities such as the cult and the "other" become an extension of the original property through Dark Horse's treatment of adult content. Further to this, in maintaining a commitment to the *Aliens* pursuit narrative format, Verheiden embellishes a sensitivity in the development of both Newt's and Hicks's character psychology. Hicks is physically scarred by his encounter with the aliens with his acid burnt face, while Newt's scars are mental. This sensitivity is pursued further as Newt falls in love and becomes sexually involved with Butler, and here a strange triangle ensues in which the relationship between Newt and Hicks is tested, as he tries to keep her away from Butler. However, what at once seems to be jealous possessiveness is later revealed to be the warmth of paternal protection as we learn, along with Newt, that the marines on board *The Benedict*, Butler included, were synthetically produced for the mission. It is not until Butler becomes severed at the waist and learns of his own artificiality, however, that Newt follows her heart and the two are reunited. Through this development of Newt and Hicks's relationship and the introduction of the new character, Butler, Dark Horse were able to address more adult content and be thematically persistent with the themes of protection and parenthood in the Cameron film (Bierbaum 24). Other adult-orientated themes within this series included extreme violence, alcoholism, and prostitution. It was in this position as an independent comic book publisher that Dark Horse was granted this degree of creative license in its development of the *Aliens* narrative.

In addition to the legitimating presence of Hicks and Newt, their extended characterization and narrativization, coupled with the increasingly adult-themed content of the series, another narrative development that Verheiden pursues is the presence of the aliens on Earth (Jenkins, *Textual Poachers*). Verheiden's translation enabled a successful extension of Dan O'Bannon's original film story, maintained an affinity with the original film property, yet also recognized the fans' desires for the exploration of new alien narratives and worlds and the arrival of the aliens on Earth. As well as expanding the *Aliens* universe, Verheiden's narrative also performs an illustrational function for those aspects that were left unexplained within the initial filmic versions of *Alien* and *Aliens*.

It is in these extensions of the original property that Dark Horse is at its most creative as comic book producers. Verheiden's narrative has Hicks, Newt, and Butler trapped aboard *The Benedict*, which is being outrun by the alien xenomorphs. It is through the arrival of another life form which intercepts, killing the aliens, and thus freeing Newt and Hicks to destroy the alien hive on Acheron, that Verheiden not only provides explanation for the existence of the original alien corpse aboard the derelict ship in the film *Alien*, but in addition develops the backstory of the "other" entity. Through Verheiden's narrative, we learn that this is not an entirely benevolent action, as the "Other" reveals in a vision to Newt the intentions of its species to later colonize the Earth as its own.

Developments within the series include Alien adventures on other worlds, with the introduction of further characters and through encounters with alternative established comic book properties in the numerous crossovers that developed. For example *Aliens: Book II* extends the first *Aliens* comic series, with Newt and Hicks discovering that the organic cargo they are carrying is that of the xenomorphs themselves, as they arrive on an isolated military installation under the command of General Spears who attempts to train a xenomorph army in vain, resulting in the death of numerous terraformers. Aliens narratives have also been set on a space station in Earth's orbit (*Tribes*), at the site of a toxic waste dump (*Colonial Marines*), the Pluto moon, Charon (*Rogue*), Celeste, the pleasure planet (*Kidnapped*), a cargo ship (*Salvation*), 1950s small town America (*Earth Angel*), atop an active volcano (*Mondo Heat*), and on a planet of religious fundamentalists (*Alchemy*). *Stalker* travels back in time to have the Viking warrior Rainulf hunt the alien in a narrative that is not unsimilar to that of the *Alien v. Predator* (2004) film. Besides the numerous narratives in which crazy scientists and military leaders inadvertently, or deliberately, release alien hell, *Labyrinth* examines questions of animal vivisection, incest and bestiality, and *Colonial Marines* traces the company's plan to interbreed humans with the xenomorph. The *Berserker* narrative examines the defensive strategy against the xenomorph in the form of Max, a Mobile Assault eXo-warrior which contains a human host, while in *Pig*, pirates send a nuclear-loaded piglet into an alien hive in order to raid a crashed spaceship. *Kidnapped* traces the impregnation of a media star and the development of an alien airborne virus, and in *Survival* we have the bizarre twist of humans bursting from the chests of aliens. As such the breadth and scale of the Dark Horse *Aliens* comics series as a whole is far-reaching in aims and outlook, with the two-part *Alien Resurrection* comic book released in

1997 to coincide with the release of the film, and providing the only direct cinematic translation of the series.

In addition a number of crossovers have also ensued, including those integrating another film series species, the predators; *Alien vs. Predator* (1989–90), *Aliens vs. Predator: Eternal* (1998), *AVP: Xenogenesis* (1999–00), *AVP: Deadliest of the Species* (1993–95), *AVP: Duel* (1995), and *AVP: War* (1995), as well as a number of crossovers with other properties including *Superman vs. Aliens* (1995), *Batman vs. Aliens* (1997), *Aliens vs. Predator vs. Terminator* (2000), *Green Lantern vs. Aliens* (2000), *Witchblade vs. Aliens vs. Darkness vs. Predator: Mindhunter* (2000–01), *Superman vs. Aliens: Godwar* (2002), and *Judge Dredd vs. Aliens: Incubus* (2003). Dark Horse's ownership of the comic book licenses for *Aliens, Alien vs. Predator, Terminator*, and *Judge Dredd* made for easy negotiation, while the others were the result of comic book industry crossover productions. To date there are now in excess of two hundred *Alien*-affiliated comic book properties in the Dark Horse catalogue (and still counting), and as such the longevity of the *Aliens* comics is impressive for a series that originated outside of comics (Stradley, "Re: Comic Book Chapter"; Stradley, "Interview: Licensing the Franchise").

While ultimately answerable to the licensor of the comic book rights, Dark Horse was permitted a degree of creative reign, freed from the stifling constraints of the major comic producers and their need to regulate output. Dark Horse Comics' relationship with Twentieth Century Fox was a seemingly comfortable one, in which once it had proved its mettle and faithfulness to the *Aliens* franchise, the studio granted a degree of creative control, albeit one which was bound up in the cultural-legal hold of the licensing agreement, in which Twentieth Century Fox had ultimate veto control.

For fans it was the coherence across the film properties, the comic book narrative, and the accompanying art work that served as a marker of authenticity and ensured the comic book's place as a worthy product in the continuation of the series (Hunt; Jenkins, *Textual Poachers*; Lovell). Part of this authenticity could arguably be seen as a direct result of the more "creator driven" projects that were emphasized at this time, with the *Aliens* comic book series itself being produced by members of that very same group that consumed them, the fans (Brooker 249–308; Jones & Jacobs 63). At the same time, the *Aliens* comics' success could be seen as a result of its emergence within a period in which the institutional shifts in the comic book industry had moved towards "direct sales," whereby the emphasis upon specialist comic book dealers and outlets facilitated in the more speedy distribution of comic book titles and carved out a cultural space in which comic book fans could congregate and share in their fandom (Biochel 16; Brooker 260–61). The increased development of fan communities and participation created a space in which comic book creators and industry workers were increasingly becoming recognized for their role in the artistic creation of those fan products. As such they were rewarded through the move towards royalty payments, whereby works that were valued would in turn have higher sales and generate higher royalty payments for the creators of the more successful titles (Biochel 6; Brooker 260–61).

Within the letters pages of these comics, fan discourse surrounding the *Aliens* film property circulated around the merits of the work, and here artistic creation was frequently the topic of debate. Letter writer Kevin Mathews praised the team for their translation of the *Aliens* property: "Mark Verheiden has actually improved on the basic premise supplied by the two films. Thought-provoking and nerve-tingling, his vision of Dan O'Bannon's creations is sheer blinding brilliance . . . Mark A. Nelson's art— words fail me! He has brought a new dimension to the black and white art. The aliens never looked better" (Matthews). So, at least for this one fan, the real affinity and compatibility then, is one through which the elements specific to the original film series were successfully transfigured to its comic book incarnation.

Frequently fans identified Mark Nelson's art as a key binding force in the translation of the film into comic book. However not only were fans particularly protective of the comic book manifestation of the *Aliens* series, but they also demonstrated a particular desire to recognize and maintain its origins as a "film" property. For fan, John De la Cruz, it is through this affinity that the *Aliens* comic marks out its space as a viable extension of the film series: "At first I thought this was the comic book adaptation of the film . . . Then I realized this story actually carried on from where

Aliens (the movie) ended. Now, I think *Aliens* is one of the best sequels I've ever seen. Although it had a different director, it remained faithful to the characters and events in the first film and developed its themes in a different but believable way. Usually sequels are just a moneymaking rehash of the original. Now *Aliens* (the comic) has continued with the good work" (De la Cruz).

For Cruz, it was this ability to maintain an affinity with the original product that marked out its success from a fan perspective. It is important to recognize the instrumental part that fan discourse and debate played in the genesis of the comic book narrativization and one that is acknowledged by Stradley as a key factor in Dark Horse's devising these adaptations (Stradley, "Re: Comic Book Chapter"). Fan discourse surrounding the *Aliens* film property was fierce, centering on plot anomalies, the original film's liberal "borrowing" from other texts, its selective use of science fiction and horror formats, and unexplained phenomenon occurring within the films. Dark Horse made a knowing bid to build upon these fan mediations, acknowledging their desires in order to create original stories and conceptions that would be both palatable and welcomed in the convergence of *Alien* film fans and comic book audiences alike (Jenkins, *Textual Poachers*; Hunt).

Notwithstanding Dark Horse's creative impetus, the decision to publish an *Aliens* comic book series had an economic motive and one that paid dividends. Stradley notes that *Aliens #1* sold in excess of 250,000 copies and was reprinted on six occasions, while Mike Richardson confirms that the series in its entirety sold millions of copies, and at the time of its release outsold all the Marvel and DC Comics lines that were running (Stradley, "Interview: Licensing the Franchise"; Henderson). The *Aliens* comic series thus proved to be an extremely lucrative conception which not only continues to generate revenue through the reorder market, but has an extended life through the recent release of a new *Alien vs. Predator* comic book on the back of the film release.

For Twentieth Century Fox, on the other hand, the development of yet another *Aliens* product represented not only a direct increase in revenue in the form of the license fee paid by Dark Horse, but also an advertisement for other *Aliens* properties and ancillary products. However, while Dark Horse was granted a generous degree of autonomy in its development of the *Aliens* license, this is not to say that licenses were granted capriciously by Twentieth Century Fox. Rather, Fox was fiercely protective of the *Aliens* license. During the creative process, the Twentieth Century Fox licensing department reviewed the comic book scripts, art work, and completed pages in order to ensure that the franchise would not be unduly damaged by the licensed products created by Dark Horse. Stradley maintains that Twentieth Century Fox acted "Just like any licensor would, . . . mainly looking to make sure we didn't do anything disrespectful or stupid with the characters, and that we didn't step over any lines which would result in the studio receiving bad press, etc." (Stradley, "Re: Comic Book Chapter"). However, as a whole, the licensing process surrounding *Aliens* worked to the mutual benefit of both Twentieth Century Fox and Dark Horse Comics. Twentieth Century Fox benefited through Dark Horse's resurrection and innovative extension of the *Aliens* franchise, which in turn developed further awareness of Fox's other *Aliens* properties, ancillary products, and licenses, as well as the additional revenue generated in terms of the license itself, with Dark Horse paying a royalty on every comic issue sold (Brooker 270–71; Henderson). Further to this, the comics released by Dark Horse throughout the eighties and nineties have also served to regenerate interest in future installments of the later film releases of the franchise.

For Dark Horse Comics, the purchase of the *Aliens* comics license allowed it to pick up the already proven and successful film franchise, develop this in new ways, and build upon an already established market of film fans. That fandom also extended to include the comic book format, simultaneously functioning to attract the already established comic book audience and its willingness to buy into other similar series. Indeed Stradley contends that in Dark Horse's initial foray into the *Aliens* series, its intent was to attract "Anybody who liked the films" whilst simultaneously recognizing that "There have been very few films whose characters and subject matter can make the jump to comics and still hold their original audience" (Stradley, "Re: Comic Book Chapter"). Indeed the repetitious and bastardizing nature of the comic book action movie has often been cited and lamented in the press, as John Sutherland writing in *The Guardian* maintains: "Like the comic books that inspire them, Action Comic Book Movies are, by nature, series. They repeat themselves with small variations until the well runs dry" (Sutherland).

However it is important to recognize here that Dark Horse's comic book series, in its revisualization of an original film property, rather than a narratively reductive rehashing of comic book storylines for the big screen, represented an innovative approach to the recycling of materials. Largely through the result of a media-savvy maneuver in the buying up of comic book licensing rights, Dark Horse Comics has secured its place in the development of the adult comic book narrativization of the comic book action movie. In this way Dark Horse Comics posed, and continues to pose, a direct challenge, albeit small, to the duopoly of DC and Marvel.

Dark Horse has been credited with the successful translation of the *Aliens* franchise into the comic book format and can arguably be regarded as having marked out something of a precursor for the current revisiting of presumably exhausted film properties, in an economically inspired effort to squeeze additional revenue and longevity from the archives. The original six-part series concluded in 1989; however as a result of its success, numerous spinoff projects resulted. As Stradley maintains, through the economic regeneration of the original *Aliens* comics series, "Dark Horse made a tidy sum off of *Aliens*—especially the early issues, which we kept reprinting and reprinting every time they'd sell out. At the time we ceased publication of the *Aliens* comics, it was clear that the situations and characters were getting 'tired,' and that it was time for them to ride off into the sunset" (Stradley, "Re: Comic Book Chapter").

However while Dark Horse was instrumental in its realization of the potential for the conversion of archive materials into comic book projects and began the process of buying up the licensing rights and translating successful films into comic books, Fox has since realized the commercial viability of such ventures. On the reverse of this, Fox has concentrated its efforts further upon the multidisciplinary, multimarket, and multiplatformed approach to selling these franchises, with each new retail avenue building upon the successes of those that have gone before. With the cinematic release of *Alien vs. Predator* (2004), there was a decidedly marked shift in terms of how, and indeed which, audiences were targeted with the PG-13 film classification in the U.S. and 15 in the U.K. respectively (Anderson 23). So while Twentieth Century Fox released the film, this was at the expense of the deep-layered stylization that fans had come to expect. Fans felt let down by the cinematic release of *AVP*, and although they had enjoyed the comic book variants of the *Aliens vs. Predator* narrative, the Fox film release was received with suspicion. Instead fans complained of its "manufactured, 'factory-made' artificiality," tiring of Hollywood pandering to the "lowest common denominator" and "taking advantage of the die-hard fans" (Ron; Clegg).

In effect Hollywood had repackaged a particularly successful fan product in an effort to regenerate it as a mainstream Hollywood blockbuster. Much of this suspicion and dissatisfaction on the newsgroups and message boards circulated around the films recutting and reclassification as a PG-13 (Anderson 23). Elsewhere Brooker has raised issue with the ways in which fan product is frequently given over to those with an investment in that product, in an effort to ensure commercial success in the attraction of non-fans (Brooker 280, 288–89). In the case of *AVP*, this reclassification could be seen as a direct result of the studio's desire to keep that audience as wide as possible, rather than restricting access to the adult market alone (Anderson 23). It is this exploitation of the commercial market that transcends the concerns of fandom instead to appeal to the larger non-fan potential audience, and it is at these points of disjuncture that conflict between fans and the multinational conglomerates surfaces in the ever-increasing necessity to make a profit (Brooker 385–86). What Dark Horse did, then, is function as a bridge and mediator between the fans and mainstream commercial Hollywood, providing an innovative, reenergized re-working of an already established cinematic success, from its relatively autonomous position as an independent comic book producer. As such Dark Horse operates in such a way that enables it to pose a direct challenge to DC and Marvel, albeit a small one, in its ownership and extension of these licensed properties.

While Dark Horse may have begun the plundering of the archives for the purposes of regenerating the franchise for a fan audience, Twentieth Century Fox, in the face of this success, has since taken a very specific and instructive move towards the licensing of the comics which extended beyond the success of the initial 1988–89 *Aliens* series. This is also reflected in the current range of materials in circulation on multiple platforms surrounding the most recent intervention into the franchise, with the film release of *AVP: Alien vs. Predator* in 2004.

With the release of *AVP: Alien vs. Predator*, grossing over $80 million in the U.S. and £5 million in the U.K., the licensing spiral continues with the two latest AVP comic book releases and a whole new range of Todd McFarlane collectible figures, plush characters, and toys available to collect ("Alien Vs Predator Snatches $38.3 Million"; "Box Office Figures," *Variety*; Dawson). As well as the usual range of DVD, VHS, and soundtrack releases, there are also Alien and Predator busts and statues, plush figures of the various incarnations of the Alien and Predator, AVP collector's plates, Alien Egg and Predator cookie jars, Alien and Predator bookends and trading cards, as well as a Collector's Alien vs. Predator Battle Chess Set.

Through this process of regeneration and recycling, and building upon the original *Aliens vs. Predator* (1989) comic book series, which came off the presses only four months after the concluding issue of the successful *Aliens* six comic series, Dark Horse Comics in association with Twentieth Century Fox, later rereleased the comic book series as a Classic Reprint in February 1997 prior to the release of *Alien Resurrection* film (1997). This coupled with the release of the *Alien vs. Predator* computer game in 1999 functioned not only to reenergize interest in the comic books once more, but also served to stir up interest for a cinematic release of the venture off the back of its success, with the cinematic version of *AVP* later entering production in September 2003 (McIntee, "Prepare for Battle").

Through its partnership with Twentieth Century Fox, Dark Horse was able to compete with the leading comic book publishers. Through the translation of Hollywood blockbusters into the comic book format it carved a niche in the market. In an increasingly conglomerate-dominated market Dark Horse Comics is a glimmering light for the independent comic book sector. Dark Horse Comics seeks to meet its competitors on their own ground through multimedia presentations of licensed products. Herein lies the problem between innovation and re-creation, translation creativity and franchization.

While the tangential and reciprocal undercurrent relationship between creativity and economics can be identified through the synergistic relationship between Dark Horse Comics and Twentieth Century Fox, what becomes apparent is how Hollywood, having discovered the infinite transferability of comic book heroes and villains, is now turning its attention to archived properties in order to squeeze every last ounce of revenue from its established products. Why go to the lengths of marketing and promoting a new product, when you can repackage an old one at a fraction of the cost? New and improved, and cheap at half the price.

WILL THE REAL WOLVERINE PLEASE STAND UP?

MARVEL'S MUTATION FROM
MONTHLIES TO MOVIES

— DEREK JOHNSON

While media conventions of any sort tend to foster crossover interest in genre and media form, the dominance of Hollywood film and television projects at the 2003 San Diego Comic-Con, a convention purportedly designed to promote the comic book form, is still surprising. The San Diego Comic-Con is the most prestigious and important of such annual summits devoted to comic book culture, yet even its official website acknowledges the dearth of content actually devoted to the comic book. To introduce the 2003 event, the site hoped to legitimize the comic convention amid an onslaught of tertiary or otherwise tangential content, claiming that with "287 programs in the daytime hours of Comic-Con, comic fans can count on 167 of them having *something* to do with the comics medium."[1] But while 167 of these panel discussions did focus on comic books in *some* way, this number did not take into account the numerous panels among them in which comics were only a secondary consideration, merely the source material for a feature film, television, or video game adaptation. Individual Comic-Con panels in 2003 explored the role of Hollywood in bringing a comic title to the big screen, offered seminars in designing characters with film in mind, and explicated the license negotiation process.

As cultural critic Matthew Pustz has argued, the interactions between fans and industry personnel at these conventions create distinct boundaries that construct a specific comic book culture and the reading communities within it (158, 205). In the case of the 2003 San Diego convention, the program offerings worked to construct comic book culture as one that cannot be conceived of separate from tie-in synergies with film, television, and video games. While the Comic-Con does putatively enlarge the boundaries of comic book culture, it does so at the expense of the comic book itself. In the Comic-Con discussions and programming, the comic book appears to have somehow been lost, unable to stand alone, replaced in comic book culture by the tie-in adaptation.

This dissolution here of the comic book's autonomy as a cultural text, however, may stem at least in part from the economic realities of the comic book industry—especially in relation to those of the film industry. While comic book publishing seems to have recovered from the overspeculation, sales busts, and bankruptcies of the mid-1990s,[2] it still has not regained—and may not ever—the same sales strength that it enjoyed prior. While comic book publishing pulled in sales of $850 million at its peak in 1993, that number dropped to only $425 million in 1997 (McAllister 17). Finding accurate data for the industry's more recent annual performances is more difficult, but the industry has slowly begun to improve; dealer orders from Diamond Comics, the monopolistic distributor for both Marvel and DC Comics, increased by 7 percent in 2002 from the previous year.[3] However, this growth has been both small and slow, spread out amongst a total North American readership that has been estimated to be made up of only 500,000 regular comic book readers (McCloud 97). While this estimate seems shockingly small, it seems to be authenticated by recent sales figures; *Batman*, the top selling comic in July 2003, sold only 146,601 issues.[4] Moreover, in March 2001, that month's top selling comic, *Ultimate X-Men*, sold a mere 97,985 copies—calling the validity of the comic book form as "popular" culture into serious question.[5]

The comic book's inability to reach a mainstream audience has not, however, been duplicated by film and television shows based upon these same properties. The most successful publisher of comic books in 2003, Marvel Enterprises (née Marvel Comics) appeared poised that year to become an important Hollywood player. In particular, films based upon Marvel properties—including *X-Men*, *Daredevil*, *Hulk*, and *Spider-Man*—have together been enormously profitable for both Marvel and the studios distributing the films. While none of the multiple *X-Men* comic books published in 2003, including *Uncanny X-Men*, *New X-Men*, *X-Treme X-Men*, and *Ultimate X-Men*, regularly sold significantly more than 100,000 issues a month, the *X2* film that same year made $85.6 million at the box office in its first weekend alone, the fourth-highest opening weekend gross at that point in history. *X2* would ultimately go on to make over $213 million in its first ten weeks. Even though the *Hulk* film was less enthusiastically received, it made over $129.5 million in ticket sales that same summer 2003 season. Of course, neither of these films comes close to matching the success of *Spider-Man* in 2002. Still holding in 2005 the record for the best opening weekend box office gross in history, *Spider-Man* started its run with $114.8 million before ultimately earning $403.7 million, making it the sixth highest domestic grossing film of all time. The sequel, *Spider-Man 2*, performed similarly in 2004 with a domestic gross of $373.5 million.[6]

As popular texts, a clear discrepancy exists between the cultural status of comic books and their filmic counterparts, one that certainly contributes to the subordination of the former at the industrial level. On one hand, it makes sense that Marvel would choose to emphasize its filmic efforts to filmgoers at an event like the San Diego Comic-Con, rather than limiting its marketing efforts to the much smaller audience of comic book readers. At another level, however, the subordination of the comic book to more profitable media raises questions about the role of a corporate entity like Marvel Enterprises in setting the boundaries of comic book culture. This study will explore those discrepancies by focusing on Marvel and its recent attempts to rebrand itself not as a comic book publisher, but as a repository of licensable superhero characters with synergistic potential in other media. Because these industrial practices determine to a certain extent the field in which the comic book and its surrounding culture can function, central to this study will be an examination of the relationship between the comic book and its adapted counterparts that explores the ways in which the boundaries and relational hierarchies between texts are shifted and blurred. This chapter will argue that these overlapping and amorphous boundaries between comic books and their adaptations problematize their textual coherences and continuities—both as a brand and as a basis for comic book culture. I will suggest that Marvel's attempts beginning in 2000 to rebrand itself through a new focus on the adaptation

DEREK JOHNSON

of comic books into other media first required the elimination of difference between the comic and audiovisual versions of its character properties. At the same time, however, the need for clarity between the subbrands in each media created a second tension between exigencies of standardization and product differentiation. It is this tension that Marvel struggled (and continues to struggle) with in its rebranding efforts, resulting in the fragmentation of individual comic book texts, films, and the larger continuities between them.

This study will tackle these issues in three parts. First, I will situate my analysis of Marvel Comics by looking at the ways that previous scholarship has considered the comic book in relation to industrial strategies. Second, through the examination of primary documents and trade sources, this paper aims to demarcate the strategies of Marvel within the contemporary comic book industry, contrasting them to past strategies and likening them to other attempts to establish character-based licensing brands. Finally, this study will track these strategies through the texts themselves, examining their boundaries and the implications for one Marvel character brand. By looking at *X-Men*'s Wolverine and tracing his function between 2000 and 2004 within Marvel's synergistic strategies as a comic book, a film franchise, and a video game license, this paper will illustrate the ways in which the reorganization of characters into brands and subbrands has erased and rebuilt the boundaries among and between comic book and comic book-derived texts. It should be emphasized, however, that my study applies only to the dominant superhero genre in mainstream comics, and not to the independent titles that are affected by these phenomena in different ways. In the end, the goal will be to provide a theoretical basis with which to consider and question these comic books as cohesive texts in relation to their adaptations in audiovisual media.

While Thomas Inge has argued that film and comic books have historically followed "mutually supportive paths of development in America" (142), many scholars have since questioned the tenuous relationship between comic books and audiovisual media. Matthew McAllister sees the comic book as a microcosm of the effects of concentration and conglomeration on culture industries. He focuses on both Marvel and DC comics, the "Big Two" comic publishers, comparing and contrasting their ability as corporations to capitalize on licensing and synergy. Unlike Marvel,

DC Comics benefits from horizontal integration with the Warner Brothers film studio owned by the parent company of both, Time Warner. Marvel, on the other hand, has no built-in film outlet for their intellectual property, and thus cannot duplicate the successes of DC's synergies by utilizing the same strategies. McAllister writes that actual comic book publishing has become less crucial to Marvel as a business as more licensing deals are made that extend its properties into other media (29). This perceived transition from publishing to multimedia is viewed optimistically by comic author, artist, and theorist Scott McCloud, who explains this growing connection between comics and audiovisual media by suggesting that the latter are a more suitable venue for the power fantasies of the superhero genre so dominant in the comic world (118). Suggesting that digital media forms outmatch the superhero-saturated mainstream comic industry, McCloud offers an economic rationale for the translation of once-successful comic properties into filmic or televisual formats, welcoming the adaptation and potential exodus of superhero characters into audiovisual media as a means of making room in comics for experimentation in new styles and genres. Roger Sabin disagrees with McCloud's prognosis, questioning the technological determinism that assumes new media to be the next natural step in the evolution of comics (54). But McCloud is not alone in attributing change to the power of new media; Glen Norcliffe and Olivero Rendace share this trust, writing that through digital technology, comic production has been decentralized and given way to new geographies of cultural work. Norcliffe and Rendace see a vertically disintegrated, diverse comics industry that is no longer sales driven, but focused on niche marketing, driven by new technologies that enable new modes of production to replace older forms of the comic medium (243–44). If, as these authors suggest, the superhero comic may be phased out by the economics of new media and by competition from the power fantasies of superhero films and video games, what will become of a mainstream comic book industry and a mainstream comic culture dependent on such texts? Dan Raviv's journalistic inquiry into Marvel's recovery from bankruptcy suggests that the comic book publisher perceives exactly such a threat to its superhero-based business. To survive, Marvel believes it essential to transition its comic book characters into film, television, and other media. While pre-bankruptcy Marvel may have seen film production as a potential liability,

DEREK JOHNSON

as too risky an investment, Raviv characterizes the reborn comics company as one deeply committed to film production, believed to be "the best way to promote superheroes" (8). The work of Dan Raviv is also important as the only work to focus solely on the industrial culture of Marvel Comics, offering another starting point with which to consider Marvel.

Many of these authors have suggested that Marvel's main strategy for negotiating these threats to its publishing interests has been an attempt to rebrand itself not as a comic book publisher, but as a licensor of characters. Thus, it becomes crucial to understand the logic behind the branding strategies that Marvel has employed—especially if we want to understand the effect that rebranding will have on comics both as a business and in their reception. Laurence Vincent offers a how-to for the advertising executive, describing the ways in which a troubled brand like Marvel might redefine itself by nurturing the cultures surrounding its brands (188–89). Similarly, David Aaker provides a basis for us to understand the relationship between Marvel, its comic characters, and their incarnations in multiple product lines across varying media. Aaker posits a relationship between corporate brands, product brands, and subbrands, showing how each of these works together as a brand system that provides a "clarity of product offerings" (241–42). As we will see, this need for a clear, consistent brand identity informs many of Marvel's industrial strategies—many of which are identical to those used by corporate megaconglomerates like Disney. In equating the success of the Disney brand to its "self-contained universe which presents consistently recognizable values through recurring characters and repetitive, familiar themes," Janet Wasko, like Aaker, argues that successful leveraging of a brand depends upon its cohesiveness as a carefully controlled and constructed set of texts (3). Thus, while Disney and Marvel occupy very different positions of power in the entertainment industry, Wasko's look at the Disney phenomenon and its manufacture as a brand will provide an interesting point of comparison with Marvel's attempts to brand its own characters.

Pustz too suggests that comic books are "themselves becoming less important to the publishing companies. Today, Marvel and DC can make more money from the licensing of their characters than they can from the apparently finite number of comic books they can sell" (16). In his study of the cultures surrounding comic texts, Pustz finds that the niche market of comic book readers is being replaced by a larger, mainstream blockbuster audience. Ultimately, Pustz argues that the boundaries of comic book culture have isolated the comic book from mainstream American popular culture (209). As those boundaries change, this study will ask whether this isolation persists, whether it is eliminated by the mainstream acceptance of comic book heroes, or if it is made irrelevant by the dissolution of the comic book as a discrete entity.

The last decade of the twentieth century was certainly a time of great transition for Marvel Comics. After purchasing Marvel in 1989, corporate raider and junk bond king Ron Perelman set upon the dream of turning Marvel into a major conglomerate. Buoyed by a speculator's market in comic book publishing, the increasingly profitable and powerful Marvel diversified its holdings in order to capitalize on the popularity of its comics and extend that into other media. The company's stock price quadrupled in this early 1990s boom period, and its market share of the comic book publishing industry reached 70 percent (Croal 50; Lauro 3–4). Encouraged by this success, Marvel bought up companies like Topps and Fleer to begin moving its comic characters into the trading card business. The goal of Perelman's Marvel, in transitioning (and overextending) itself into the role of the conglomerate, was to become a kind of "mini-Disney" (Lott 68; Raviv 40). Marvel's strategy in the 1990s was one of duplication, of trying to restructure the corporation along the lines of a conglomerate like Disney, or of rival comic book publisher DC Comics. Because DC was part of the Time Warner media conglomerate, its comic book characters boasted a potential for synergy and profit-making that Marvel's could not match. With a single character or property, Time Warner could release a comic book through DC, a film through Warner Brothers, a novelization through Warner Books, or a television program through the WB network. As McAllister has shown, this synergistic strategy "cuts down on development time (one license can provide content for several subsidiaries), allows internal control of licensing use, and maximizes potential profits from licenses" (27).

By 1996, however, the speculation that fueled Marvel's publishing fortunes came to an end; along with boycotts by fans who perceived a decrease in the quality of Marvel titles, these industrial changes resulted in

Marvel's market share dropping to 25 percent, down by almost two-thirds from just years earlier (Raviv 71). In 1996, Marvel declared bankruptcy, and in 1998, it came under the control of Toy Biz, a toy-making company that had been dependent in large part on its licensing deals with Marvel. The old Marvel's attempts to duplicate strategies of conglomeration and synergy had faltered, so a new strategy was needed to facilitate the comic book publisher's recovery. But while expansion strategies had failed, the fact remained that in the perception of Marvel and the industry as a whole, "comic books had become . . . the outmoded 'buggy whip' of entertainment" (54). Marvel found itself in a position where it could not expand yet its primary output—comic books—offered little hope for a recovery. Not only was the company in danger, but the comic industry as a whole also seemed to be in need of translation into a new media.

Writing at the end of the speculation boom, scholar Jeffrey Brown argued that the comic book industry and "[t]he future of comic culture is almost assuredly destined to focus around the talents of individual creators rather than anonymously produced characters" (26). While an emphasis on auteurism might have been a means by which Marvel could have attempted to rebrand itself, the reborn company ended up taking the route least suspected by Brown. In the new Marvel strategy of the twenty-first century, every emphasis was placed on character. Although individual creators like Grant Morrison and Joe Casey were signed to Marvel titles like *New X-Men* and *Uncanny X-Men* and given highly publicized debuts, these marketing strategies were subordinate to the larger emphasis on character that guided editorial decisions and lasted after these individual creators had finished their runs. In fact, while its overly ambitious 1990s strategies failed to duplicate the *corporate* structure of Disney or Time Warner, Marvel's new approach settled for the *creative* structure of a "mini-Disney." As Wasko has argued, Disney's synergistic strategies are based upon its characters; each character is a wheel whose spokes each represent a product revolving around that brand (71). Marvel, while no longer pursuing the conglomerate dimension of the Disney model, began to refocus its efforts to mirror the character-centeredness of the world's "most powerful licensing force" (49). In a 2002 radio interview, Bill Jemas, then-President of Marvel publishing, articulated the company's approach without making reference to Disney, but by describing an identical model. "Each character is sort of the center of a wheel," Jemas explained as if he had just come from a Disney strategy seminar, "so Spider-Man will show up as a T-shirt, as comic books, as electronic games, as movies, and soon, as a television show. So the heart of Marvel is the characters" ("All Things"). Marvel thus transitioned from the production of comic books to the creation of characters; its primary product was no longer printed volumes of superhero adventures, but the intellectual property of the superhero itself.

The conscious remaking of Marvel into an intellectual property production company was well documented by both trade and popular sources (Lauro 3–4). Journalists also noted that this new emphasis on creating characters, rather than the products derived from them, enabled licensing agreements that spared Marvel from having to risk massive capital investments of its own—the very kinds of ventures that left Marvel overextended after the bottom fell out of the 1990s speculation market (Brownstein 25; Croal 50). In a business model based in licensing, profits had to be split, with the distributors that licensed Marvel characters receiving the lion's share. At the same time, however, Marvel earned a new lease on life by extending its characters out of the perceived-to-be-doomed comic book industry and into a popular culture that was a little more popular—film. While it did not own its films outright, the licensing fees alone proved quite profitable for Marvel. Over 26 percent of the company's 2002 revenue came from licensing deals in nonprint media (Lauro 3–4). Moreover, Marvel developed a strategy to use its past licensing successes to demand increasingly larger sums from its licensees. While Marvel sold the rights to the first *X-Men* film to Twentieth Century Fox for only a few hundred thousand dollars, Avi Arad (the former Toy Biz executive whose role in the new Marvel organization was to oversee all film and television licenses) hoped to parlay the success of Marvel's first films into better deals in future negotiations (Raviv 57, 257). This strategy paid off, as Sony Pictures gave Marvel a $10 million down payment for the rights to make the first *Spider-Man* film in addition to agreeing to a first-dollar participation deal (271). This means that Marvel received a certain percentage of each ticket sold to the licensed film—regardless of how much the studio spent to produce the movie and whether or not the film actually earned a profit.

Clearly then, while Marvel's licensing model does lack the neat conglomerate synergy of Disney or DC under Time Warner, this kind of

DEREK JOHNSON

character-based licensing synergy does have its advantages. In fact, in the 2000–2004 motion picture market for comic book characters, DC could arguably have been held at a disadvantage. Exploiting the full potential of synergistic tie-ins demanded that Time Warner make every film and television show based on its comics in-house. Whereas Marvel could solicit its licenses to any Hollywood studio or production company, DC tended to funnel all of its properties solely through Warner Brothers and its subsidiaries to maximize profits. In the rare cases when some of DC's properties, like *League of Extraordinary Gentlemen,* were farmed out to film studios like Fox, the potential for corporate synergies was dampened. Time Warner was understandably reluctant to let go of its properties, so some remained "hidden assets" buried within the bureaucracy of the conglomerate; farming out its licenses, Marvel could therefore release more comic book films than its competitor DC (Brodesser 7). In an industry based in trends and fads, Time Warner was largely on its own, forced to work quickly before superhero films became passé. Additionally, Warner subsidiary New Line Cinema also developed several Marvel products (the *Blade* trilogy, for example), helping to keep afloat DC's main competitor in the comic publishing industry. At the same time, however, the conglomerate nature of Time Warner did insulate and protect DC in a way unknown to the more independent Marvel. While Time Warner hurried to take advantage of a synergistic opportunity, Marvel's financial security depended upon these films as key spokes in the wheels of its character-based and revenue-sustaining brands.

This dependency on other studios may have been partially responsible for Marvel's continued interest in purchasing its own motion picture production company. While this endeavor seemed to be a throwback to its conglomeration strategy in the 1990s, Marvel consciously adapted its strategies to avoid similar failures. Instead of duplicating the organizational structure of Time Warner, Marvel pursued potential means to supplement its licensing model while slowly allowing it to bring in greater profits. While Marvel did try in the 1990s to become a corporate titan that could finance its own movies, in the early 2000s it toyed with the idea of purchasing a small studio, like Artisan, that would allow Marvel to take on the production responsibilities for bringing smaller properties to the screen and tighten its grasp on box office and home video revenues

(Moreels 7/2/03). While licensing deals remained lucrative, Marvel would not have minded a larger ownership stake in its licensed products. Nevertheless, it also understood the risk of film production, and sought a studio like Artisan so that it could capitalize on the projects that require the least investment and the smallest budget—while leaving the major studios to put up the big money and take the big risks. Moreover, industry analysts also suggested that Marvel would have been glad to become a horizontally integrated arm of another larger conglomerate (Raviv 278).

Thus, Marvel's plan involved not just character licensing, but also taking advantage of the synergy between licenses—even if it did not profit from product ownership like the horizontally integrated Time Warner. Moreover, while Marvel extended itself beyond the weakened comic book publishing industry, its approach did reserve a place for comics as a key spoke in the character wheel. While Marvel's licensing revenues continued to increase, so too did its publishing income, still accounting for 21 percent of its 2002 revenues. Still far from its peak in the early 1990s, Marvel's market share of the comic book publishing industry also steadily increased to 43 percent by 2003 (Lauro 3–4). Both Marvel and industry analysts credited the success of the company's comic book movies with sparking the renewed popularity of its comic books (Krantz B.1; Flores D.16). Marvel Studios chief Avi Arad stressed the licensing synergy at work here when he described the films as "a significant product to support our core businesses," comic book publishing and toy making (Moreels 11/13/03). To make these synergies as strong as possible, however, Marvel used its new character-based strategy not just to create a brand for itself at the movies, but to rebrand itself in publishing as well.

Marvel's twenty-first-century strategies shifted focus away from direct sales in order to target new audiences, widening the customer base away from the insulated comic book shop and more towards the general audience that sees its films. One initiative undertaken by Marvel in its publishing operations was a shift in publishing emphasis to trade paperback and hardcover books—compilations and anthologies of previously released material—rather than emphasizing the monthly periodicals (Wolk 32). Crucially, Marvel stepped up its paperback release schedule, aiming to have the same comic stories released in book format only several weeks after a storyline has been completed in the "traditional" periodical format.

Marvel also expanded its distribution of these books into general bookstores like Barnes and Noble (to whom Marvel has provided a number of exclusive editions) where they could reach new audiences. In fact, general bookstores like these were estimated to account for almost half—$50 million of a total projected market of $120 million—of all trade paperback and hardcover sales of comics in 2003. These nonspecialty stores had become "the fastest-growing retail venues for book-format comics" (Wolk and Reid 27). Cross promotion and synergy with the films, however, can be seen in the kinds of books emphasized in these general bookstore sales. The most successful paperbacks were those that shared tie-in connections with the films. According to one trade source in 2003, "[m]ovie tie-ins are definitely driving Marvel's sales in the bookstore market" (MacDonald 30). Marvel chose to publicize and release those books that could both promote and benefit from the concurrent run of one of its licensed films.

These new models allowed Marvel to make available to a general audience the recent reimaginings, restructurings, and relaunches of its comic book titles. Of the major changes and overhauls to the Marvel line of comic books, the first and arguably largest restructuring of the Marvel Universe came in 2001, some months after the first *X-Men* film's successful run in 2000. Spearheaded by Marvel executive Bill Jemas, the relaunch "in concert with the development of films and tie-in merchandise, was intended to reposition the franchises. The program increased publishing revenue and consumer awareness of Marvel's characters" (Brownstein 25). One major adjustment to Marvel's titles came in the addition of a new, parallel "Ultimate" universe to exist alongside the familiar, forty-year-old "classic" universe.[7] The titles that comprised the Ultimate line were "most like the movies," rolling back the characters to their origins and attempting to tell their old stories in a new way; they were "designed specifically as starting points for new readers and promoted through a program of free samples" (Wolk 28, 6/17/02). At the same time, the old continuity of the "classic" Marvel universe was revamped, with many titles either scrapped or redesigned. As my examination of a single character brand will show, the revamped "classic" Marvel universe featured more mature, adult storylines, while the Ultimate line targeted younger, teen and preteen audiences. This bifurcation served Marvel's goal of appealing to a younger audience of "intelligent twelve-year-olds" while at the same time keeping the continuity of the texts older fans had grown to love more-or-less intact ("Morning Edition"). Marvel's 2001 publishing relaunch mirrored the logic by which many of its films were targeting audiences. Comic book films were " 'tent-pole' pictures—that big summer release aimed primarily at kids, but with hopes that adults will go see it too" (Ramin 16). Because the older fans were no longer Marvel's primary target audience, Bill Jemas's restructuring of the Marvel universe emphasized the new directions of the Ultimate line, the product line most congruent with its motion picture analogue.

Interestingly enough, Bill Jemas was pulled from his role as President of Publishing in 2003 and assigned a less prominent role in the organizational structure of Marvel. Some reports have suggested that the reason for Jemas's removal was that Marvel Studios head Avi Arad had considered "some of the initiatives spearheaded by Jemas as an obstacle when it came to marketing [Marvel] properties in Hollywood" (Moreels 9/9/03). This move seems contradictory at first, as we have seen how Jemas's relaunch efforts were instrumental in allowing Marvel to take advantage of the synergy between the multiple product lines encircling each of its character wheels. At the same time, looking more closely at the way in which all of these strategies of licensing and synergy functioned to establish Marvel and its characters as *brands* will demonstrate the way in which Jemas's efforts may have been insufficient to maximize and capitalize upon the corporate and character identities being constructed.

Like Disney, a company that revived its character brands in the '70s by harkening back to "traditional Disney" while simultaneously modernizing them (Wasko 34), Marvel the "mini-Disney" recalled the origins of its superhero characters while at the same time reworking them for modern youth audiences. Like Disney, Marvel too had to be conscious of the need to maintain a particular degree of control over a brand. Aaker argues that brands depend both upon a constant, core identity, as well as an extended identity that includes "brand identity elements, organized into cohesive and meaningful groupings that provide texture and completeness" (68–69). A brand must therefore maintain a consistency of meaning and message over time in order to succeed as a cohesive identity for a corporation or its products. Aaker writes that the goal of a brand system is to clarify a range of product offerings, making clear distinctions between corporate brands, range brands, and subbrands (241). Thus, the problem that arose for Marvel in its own rebranding emerged from the lack of cohesiveness found in its character wheel. Unlike Disney, Marvel's postbankruptcy characters did not have a standard cohesiveness that lent them to immediate product differentiation and identification. A range brand like the Spider-Man character had toys, comics, and television shows all based upon it, but if each synergistic aspect of the character presented Peter Parker/Spider-Man in a different way, there was no way for "Spider-Man" as a brand to cohere into any one single identity. Because a subbrand character like *Ultimate Spider-Man*'s Peter Parker, a teenager, existed alongside the Peter Parker from the "classic" continuity—then a divorced school teacher—"Spider-Man" as a (range) brand remained discontinuous and nebulous. Thus, to profit most readily from the licensed synergies within its stable of over 4,700 characters and transform them into more viable brands, Marvel found it necessary to eliminate the inconsistencies and contradictions between incarnations of its characters. Keeping this argument in mind, we now turn to a single Marvel character—one of its brands—and look at the way in which its rebranding impacted its coherence both as a brand and as a cultural text.

A fast-healing, clawed mutant with an adamantium-laced skeleton, Wolverine (a.k.a. James Logan, a.k.a. Weapon X) has become one of Marvel's most popular and profitable character brands, second perhaps only to Spider-Man. While Spider-Man may have been more recognizable (and apparently, more profitable at the box office), as a member of Professor Charles Xavier's X-Men, Wolverine was perhaps the most prolific brand in the Marvel stable of characters between 2000 and 2004. In the "classic" Marvel Universe continuity in 2003, Wolverine starred in *New X-Men* and made regular appearances in *X-Treme X-Men, Uncanny X-Men*, and *X-Force/X-Statix*. In the parallel "Ultimate" universe, Wolverine also lead the cast of *Ultimate X-Men*. Add to that his very own solo series, *Wolverine*, and one can see that this character was anything but underexposed in the comic world—and that is not even counting miniseries, discontinued titles, or past guest spots in other books. Expanding into filmed entertainment, Wolverine added to his earlier 1990s appearances in the animated *X-Men* and *Spider-Man* television series a starring role in the *X-Men: Evolution* cartoon. Moreover, the 2000 and 2003 live action *X-Men* features not just included Wolverine, but also gave him the lead role. Add to this several video games, including *X2: Wolverine's Revenge* and *X-Men Legends* and one can see that Wolverine had built a sizable mutant resume for himself as one of Marvel's most important brands.

But, as I have already suggested, these brands were heterogeneous and disharmonious ones. While each of the above texts indeed focused on Wolverine, it is impossible to say that any one of them featured the "real" Wolverine. Moreover, the exact number of Wolverines filling the above roles is unclear. Some Wolverines were constructed unlike any other, while some appeared to be hybrid composites of several competing interpretations. The point is that Wolverine as a Marvel brand, unlike the carefully constructed and controlled Mickey Mouse for Disney, seemed untenable for supporting an overall brand identity, lacking coordination across organizational units, media, and markets (Aaker 340). But with the rebranding, restructuring, and relaunching strategies employed by Marvel in this period, the hope was that this could change.

As the overall tendencies of Marvel's licensing and synergy strategies might suggest, the Wolverine given priority by Marvel was the Wolverine of the motion picture franchise, the Wolverine portrayed by actor Hugh Jackman. This Wolverine was different from the comic book character that came before in many ways, particularly at the level of appearance—and not just because he was not pencil and inked. While focusing on the appearance of Wolverine seems like a shallow level at which to examine the character's major differences, I situate my analysis of the character brand in this way for three reasons. First, because comics are a visual medium, the appearance of the character, rather than his manner of speaking, acting, or moving, assumes a particular primacy. Second, because brands perform the iconic role of immediately conveying a meaningful product identity, the character's appearance can be considered in the same way a logo might be. Third, I focus on these surface details because they are very important to the cultures surrounding such a character, both in terms of locating the character within particular continuities and identifying the artist behind the image. At the same time, the following arguments must be tempered by the fact that in the production of mainstream series like Marvel's, a single title sees frequent turnover between new artists and new writers. So, while Jackman's Wolverine represented a departure, it cannot be said that the two-dimensional depictions of Wolverine that had come before—even throughout a single comic book title—had been consistent.

Still, even accounting for artist variation, certain generalizations can be made. Unlike the comic book Wolverine of the "classic" continuity, consistently drawn as short, stocky, scruffy, and ugly (or at least unattractive), Jackman's Wolverine was tall, trim (but muscular), and handsome. In the films, Wolverine's body was objectified and idealized. Jackman was frequently shown bare-chested, whether fighting in a cage match, lying on an exam table, or walking around Professor Xavier's mansion. Jackman's toned, relatively hairless body stood in contrast to the way in which the frequently shirtless Wolverine of the comics was often drawn as hairy and animal-like, muscular but bulky. But most shocking to some fans were the costumes chosen for Wolverine and the rest of the movie X-Men: black leather uniforms rather than the colorful, individual costumes each character wore in the comics. Of course, none of these changes alone should have been surprising or particularly noteworthy, as no adaptation can be expected to translate its source material to a new medium without bringing in new elements or interpretations.

Nevertheless, what is noteworthy is the way that this new Jackman Wolverine became a template for the construction of brand identity during the relaunch of 2001—not solely in the new Ultimate line, but more subtly in the "classic" continuity. At the visual level, the retitled and revamped *New X-Men* #114 saw the end of the individual hero's costume. Gone was Wolverine's signature yellow and blue cowl; instead each member of the X-Men sported matching black leather uniforms. While they were not identical to those worn in the films, the design was certainly reminiscent. In addition, the title inherited a roster of characters that paralleled the casting of the first *X-Men* film. Of the five X-Men featured prominently in the film, Wolverine, Cyclops, Jean Grey, and Professor Xavier were all kept together in *New X-Men*, while Storm was made leader of the new *X-Treme X-Men* team. Due to his popularity, Wolverine also played a starring role in the concurrent relaunch of *Uncanny X-Men*, bringing with him in issue #394 the same standardized uniforms. Also injected into this issue was a romantic subplot suggestive of the *X-Men* film that heightened the sexual tension between Wolverine and Jean Grey. While Wolverine had always pined for Jean in the comics, his love remained an unrequited one;

despite knowledge of Wolverine's feelings, Jean remained faithful to her fiancé/husband, Cyclops, prior to 2001. The film continuity, on the other hand, left open and endorsed the romantic possibilities between Jean and Jackman's handsome Wolverine.[8] That the cover of *Uncanny X-Men* #394 (the first issue of this "classic" title after the relaunch) featured the two passionately kissing, with Wolverine groping Jean as she wraps her body around his, suggests two things. First, narrative threads suggested by the first film were now also being explored (or at the least, exploited as marketing ploys) by the comics. Second, the issue's sexual tone suggests that the aforementioned bifurcation of Marvel into "classic" Marvel and "Ultimate" universes had truly rendered the former a more mature, less kid-friendly place.[9]

While it is possible that some these visual and narrative changes to the comics may have been coincidental, and not a specific corporate response to the success of the Wolverine character in the first *X-Men* film, further evidence suggests that in the interim before *X2* in 2003, Marvel did indeed work editorially to blend all the various Wolverines into a single, uniform entity more like the Hugh Jackman Wolverine. Darick Robertson, artist on the revamped *Wolverine* comic book timed to debut with the release of *X2*, stated on his website that he was given a directive from Marvel "to bring [Wolverine] more in line with his big screen counterpart" (quoted in Moreels 6/2/03). This directive applied not just to the character's solo title, but across the entire *X-Men* line. Although Robertson later revealed that Marvel was not looking for the character to appear "spot on Jackman," he admitted that he was required to make him less short and ugly. Robertson later framed this directive as a corporate miscommunication, but the requested change still served to cultivate a generalized all-purpose Wolverine, rather than relying on individual artist interpretation, to strengthen the character's potential as a brand.

This new, generalized conception of Wolverine across the range of Marvel comics and products was what Aaker might call a "silver bullet," a subbrand that is used to either change or support the image of a parent brand (261). In being close to Jackman, but not "spot on," the made-over Wolverine of the solo comic series became similar enough that it could support a parent brand—a cohesive, general conception of Wolverine as a character—that in turn could logically contain both a comic book Wol-

DEREK JOHNSON

verine and a cinematic Wolverine. Simply put, the differences between the two characters were minimized and the similarities emphasized so that both could be thought of as subbrands of the same overarching brand identity. Because Marvel's rebranding focused on character, the subbrands all had to work together for that character to have a single discernible identity. Wolverine could not be tall and handsome, short and ugly. So Marvel choose the most profitable Wolverine—the one involved in increased licensing revenues and trade paperback sales—and tried to make him the model for its silver bullet.

The drive for a streamlined Wolverine also emerged in but was complicated by Marvel's subsequent "spring cleaning" practices. Before the opening of *X2* in 2003, Editor-in-Chief of Marvel Comics Joe Quesada believed it might be time once again for another restructuring, similar to the one that accompanied the relaunch of 2001. Sending several more titles to the chopping block, Quesada believed, would trim down the *X-Men* line in order to clarify the definitions and differences between the various titles (Moreels 9/9/02). While Jackman's Wolverine and Robertson's Wolverine had to be similar as subbrands of "Wolverine" the brand/character, paradoxically here they also had to be differentiated from one another in a way that allowed for distinctions between the two subbrands. Thus, it was imperative to give each Wolverine in the *X-Men* line of comics—"classic," Ultimate, and film adaptations—a clear, defined identity as a separate subbrand subordinate to the overall Wolverine character/range brand. Nevertheless, this model of product differentiation may only have been a stop-gap measure in the overall Marvel rebranding process. Quesada admits that "Marvel has also strived to [combine] the various [Wolverine] designs into a single one to appease licensees . . . When it comes to your commercial icons like Spider-Man, Wolverine, and Hulk, you need consistency. So working with the animators and [*Ultimate X-Men* artist] Andy Kubert, we came up with a look that was similar across all fields" (Moreels 10/21/02). Thus, a plan was in play, and the adjustments made to Wolverine(s) can indeed be attributed to the need to conceive of the character as a singular brand.

However, while my aim here is to set out Marvel's strategies in negotiating the tension between brand consistency and differentiation, the success with which the company met its goals is another matter. Though Marvel had worked to construct a definitive Wolverine, by early 2003 it did not yet appear that they had been successful in doing so, even at the level of appearance. Due to the sheer number of titles in which the character appeared and the number of artists working on them—artists accustomed to bringing their own interpretations to the character—Marvel's rebranding of Wolverine necessitated a slow, gradual, embattled process of bringing the character under control. A comparison of the covers of *X-Treme X-Men* #27, *Uncanny X-Men* #423, and *Ultimate X-Men* #33—all released during the same summer as *X2*—gives us a glimpse of the progress being made nevertheless at the level of icon and brand image. While the artists designing the pages inside still offered their own interpretations of the character, cover designs across continuities took on a much more homogeneous look. While the Wolverine on each of these covers did not match his appearances within the issues, they did match across the character brand—even though they were each drawn by a different artist and represented characters in separate continuities. This singular Wolverine wore an unmasked uniform similar to that worn previously in the *Ultimate* series that nevertheless had yellow "tiger" stripes and a red "X" logo like the costume worn in the "classic" continuity during the 1980s and 1990s. Simultaneously, he was much leaner, much taller, and less hulking than previous incarnations, more like the Wolverine of the film franchise. This new iteration of the character hoped to encompass and amalgamate all the Wolverines of the present and past. Thus, while the brand had not solidified, progress was being made, if only initially at the level of the cover. This seems like a logical place to have started, since it was the cover that could attract new readers recognizing the Wolverine brand across product lines. In addition to comic book covers, this iconic, free floating Wolverine logo, unattached to any one continuity, could be found on lunch boxes, candy, and other *X-Men*-themed products, and would shortly be adopted as the new character design for the *Ultimate* comic series and the *X-Men: Evolution* cartoon. But at the same time as this amalgam emerged, alternate iterations persisted, including the uniquely suave and satirical Wolverine envisioned by Mike Allred and Peter Milligan in their contemporaneous *X-Statix* crossover issues.

The 2003 video game, *X2: Wolverine's Revenge* evidenced the challenges of bringing such a polysemous character under tighter brand control. Rather than a testament to Marvel's successful solidification of Wolverine into a cohesive character brand, its patchwork union of a variety of incompatible would-be subbrands instead revealed the difficulties that Marvel faced in its character branding strategies. The video game presented a mélange of different Wolverines and narrative elements from several of the Marvel universes. Released to coincide with *X2*, the game sold itself first as an adaptation of the film, bearing no markers of the Wolverine amalgam brand being deployed simultaneously. Sitting on the retailer's shelf, *Revenge* boasted both the signature bluish-silver *X2* logo as well as a glamour shot of Hugh Jackman in the film uniform. Once the player entered the virtual space of the game, however, the cinematic Wolverine used to market the game vanished. At the player's control was not Jackman, but a Wolverine much more akin to the "classic" comic book incarnation: bulky, hunched over, animalistic. Yet instead of settling into the role of the comic book Wolverine and attributing the game's cover art to sneaky promotional tactics, the player encountered the voice of Patrick Stewart, the actor who portrays Professor Xavier in the feature films. So while the Jackman Wolverine was notably absent, the conventions and iconography of *X2* did make their presence known in the game. Disorienting the brand identity even further, the uniform worn by the video game avatar was not a singular, distinct one; it was neither the film uniform featured on the cover, nor a general, amalgamated one, nor a new generic one created especially for the game. Instead, as the player progressed through the game, he or she could unlock and choose from the various costumes of several incarnations of Wolverine: from the black leather to the blue and yellow spandex.

As a whole then, the Wolverine presented by *Wolverine's Revenge* was not one with a cohesive, singular brand identity. The producers of the game acknowledged the competing incarnations, but instead of creating or reinforcing a unique subbrand, they illustrated the character/brand's lack of cohesion and blurred differentiation between subbrands. Nevertheless, the game did represent an attempt by Marvel, if an unsuccessful one, to square away the inconsistencies and posit each of the Wolverine subbrands as compatible facets of the overall character brand. Comparing *Wolverine's Revenge* to 2004's hit *X-Men Legends*, one sees that Marvel had made greater progress in creating a cohesive brand identity for its video game incarnations of Wolverine. The latter game faced similar challenges and impediments to brand cohesion, trying to incorporate the youthful design of the *Ultimate X-Men* characters while making references to past events within the classic *X-Men* comic continuity and once again bringing back the films' Patrick Stewart to voice Xavier. But instead of presenting an unorganized mix of *X-Men* elements, *Legends* subsumed each of the narrative elements it borrowed under a new continuity, marked off by the same brand-aware character designs that began unifying Marvel comic covers and ancillary products in 2003. Instead of fragmenting continuities, *Legends* offered a new continuity that encompassed each of the subbrands within the range brand, incorporating advantageous elements from each of Wolverine and the rest of the X-Men's multiple pasts. Thus, the Wolverine that appeared in this game hailed not from the "Ultimate," "classic," or filmic universes, but from the marketing universe.

In the 2001 relaunch of the "classic" Marvel universe, the new narratives introduced the idea of a "secondary mutation"—genetic growth spurts that would grant new superpowers to the same old mutant characters. While these new abilities made comprehensible the new looks the writers wanted to give some of the characters, no secondary mutation was ascribed to Wolverine.[10] Yet, in the revisions and reimaginings of Marvel's rebranding strategies between 2001 and 2004, the Wolverine character continued to mutate. His efficacy as a brand fluctuated somewhere in between the cohesion necessary for overall brand identity and the distinct multiplicity needed for product differentiation among subbrands. The many iterations of Wolverine—not just the multiple comic book characters, but also the film, television, and video game versions—were at once disjointed but inseparable. The character had been differentiated in some ways and homogenized in others, resulting in a fragmentation that made the boundaries between Wolverines and between texts impossible to tack down. As a brand, Wolverine was emblematic not of the unbridled success with which Marvel has pursued its rebranding strategies, but rather of the contradictions and struggles that it faced in the process. As the company continued to transition itself from publisher of comic books to licensor of transmedia characters, Marvel's characters continued to be reshaped and molded into new configurations. In the end, Wolverine will continue mutating until he provides the "clarity of product offerings" so crucial to Marvel's brand strategies (Aaker 141–42).

While future research will need to track Marvel's progression towards its goals, the licensor's more recent moves indicate that the company will continue to grapple with the fragmentations and contradictions in its branding strategies. Another relaunch occured in May 2004, this time entitled "Marvel ReLoad," once again revamping *X-Men* titles, and to the delight of many fans, bringing back individual character costumes. But with television writer Joss Whedon committed to a twelve-issue run on the new *Astonishing X-Men* title, and Bryan Singer, director of the first two *X-Men* films, at one time signed to take over production duties on *Ultimate X-Men*, Marvel's continuing plan to groom these characters for a transmediated marketplace proceeded uninterrupted in this "ReLoad."[11] Today Marvel maintains the pursuit of an audiovisual foundation on which its characters can be rebuilt as brands and subbrands for the exploitation of licenses. In further attempts to realign comics to corporate strategies (like 2005's continuity-altering *House of M* crossover miniseries), Marvel characters may likely be reimagined in ways that further obfuscate the continuities between texts. However, as Matt Hills argues, fan cultures and the reading formations they contain depend on the unity, coherence, and "ontological security" of texts (138). While further research needs to be done to determine the continued impact Marvel's emphasis on licensing will have on comic culture, it is unlikely that its fragmentary effects on characters like Wolverine will reinforce its cohesiveness. Pustz reminds us that boundaries "have helped to create comic book culture and the specific reading communities within it" (205). As these boundaries are redrawn, comic book culture is redrawn with it; as these boundaries are eliminated, the clarity with which readers make sense and make use of a character like Wolverine will be similarly confused.

WHEN GEN-X MET THE X-MEN

RETEXTUALIZING COMIC BOOK FILM RECEPTION

— NEIL RAE AND JONATHAN GRAY

While comic book adaptations such as *Spider-Man* and *X-Men* have grossed up to $820 million, and attracted millions of viewers worldwide, it is unusual for the global sales of the most popular American superhero comic books to rise above 150,000. At the time of writing, for instance, according to listed trade sales, *Superman/Batman #12* was the number one selling comic for September 2004, having sold in 139,516 units to comics retailers ("Comics Economics" 54). If we are to examine adaptations and their audiences, therefore, we must realize that although comic book readers are the most knowledgeable of audiences, they are very much a minority within the total number of viewers for comic book movies. Consequently, this chapter seeks to answer a question that is often overlooked in reception studies focusing solely on fans: how do viewers read and make sense of comic book movies differently when they have and have not read the original material being adapted? Through analyzing qualitative audience research conducted with both comic readers and non-readers, we argue that comic book movie reception requires all viewers to struggle somewhat with intertextual networks of knowledge and precedence, ultimately creating two very different textualities for the film, with significant tension between the two types. As a result, while comic readers and non-readers may well see the same film, they experience two starkly different modes of textuality.

To inquire into the reception of film adaptations of comic books is, fundamentally, to inquire into the machinations of contemporary media intertextuality. An adaptation is, by its very nature, an intertextual outgrowth or extension of the comic book, and so we could understandably expect an audience's reaction to and interpretation of the film to be in part precoded and inflected, if not largely predetermined, by that audience's reaction to and interpretation of the comic book. Certainly, Camille Bacon-Smith with Tyrone Yarborough's and Martin Barker and Kate Brooks's respective studies of the reception of Tim Burton's *Batman* and of *Judge Dredd*, both confirm this hypothesis, as do related studies by Bertha Chin and Johnathan Gray into the reception of the *Lord of the Rings* films, and by Will Brooker into original *Star Wars* fans' reaction to the recent prequel trilogy. To begin with, all of these studies chart significant *fear*, on behalf of fans of the original text preparing to see the film, of how bad the film might be. Thus, for instance, Barker and Brooks write that "one of the recurrent features of very many of our interviews was, if you like, getting ready to be disappointed," and yet, "Nowhere was this stronger than among the *2000AD* readers" (59). Similarly, a woman in Bacon-Smith with Yarborough's study "expected the movie to be terrible" (99), while a Tolkien fan in Chin and Gray's study wrote of the film that, "I can't help but feel that it's going to be screwed up and wrong. And be a total veggie effort" (n.p). In all these instances, the fear is clearly of symbolic violence being perpetrated on the beloved story and its characters by a botched, "Hollywood-ized" translation. To be scared of this outcome, then, is to have a sense of what the text should be and should look like before watching it, based largely on one's experience of the original material.

The viewers in these studies talk of "tactically lowering their expectations" (Barker and Brooks 59), and they even go to considerable lengths to explain away the perceived violence perpetrated against their beloved story before it occurs. For instance, Chin and Gray found Tolkien fans "understanding" that no film could fairly be expected to capture all the nuances of plot, history, and thematics in Tolkien's writing. Brooker's *Star Wars* fans discuss the "eyes of a child" defense, which states that cynical viewers of the contemporary trilogy have lost the ability to watch the films' more silly and juvenile moments as a child, as they once did in the seventies and eighties. Bacon-Smith with Yarborough notes that "When the product falls short of fulfilling the fans' need, viewers make use of an extreme form of traditional fill-in-the-blanks interpretation," so as to "impute to the creators of the film conscious motivations for the unsatisfying direction of the film" (105). However, for an audience member even to try to recoup a film, or to go into the theater actively trying to like it, reflects a heightened degree of attachment. This attachment is afforded by the love for the original text. Much, then, as we might show greater kindness to a family member or a close friend, whether out of a belief in common genetics or merely to honor our relationship with the friend, these studies suggest that viewers of adapted material frequently allow similar degrees of leniency to the adapted film.

When we treat a film as a "family member" of a favorite text, though, we ascribe to it certain qualities of another text; or, if we merely show it kindness out of faith to another text, once again we are engaged in an intricately intertextual process of decoding. Rather than take the film as a solitary text, and "at face value," we come to it prepared for certain readings, looking out for others, and even hypersensitive to yet other meanings. In short, we have subjugated its textuality to another text's, becoming, as Chin and Gray argue, "viewers *between* texts, anticipating one *with* the other, already reaching to one *by way of* the other" (n.p, original emphasis). Whereas most models of mediated communication somewhat commmonsensically look for reactions to a text only *following* textual consumption, through intertextuality, the semiotics of adaptation allow for and frequently encourage us to start decoding the new text before we have even purchased a ticket and bought our popcorn. Effectively, the film becomes part of a series, not a full text in and of itself.

A useful analogy here is to the textuality of episodic television programs. Such texts must be pieced together over time, and thus any one episode will be made sense of in light of previous episodes. Indeed, as will be elaborated upon later, this is also the textuality of comic books: "Spider-Man" cannot be found, per se, in one comic book, since he exists across multiple texts. As Tony Bennett notes of Batman, and of James Bond (Bennett and Woollacott), texts that exist in such series, or in episodic form, present the hero, the text, and other characters more broadly, as "shifting signifiers," that are "subject to a constant process of definition" (viii). At one level, all texts are constantly open to redefinition and redecoding (see

Bakhtin, Kuhn), but episodic texts never rest, and thus whereas, at any one point in time, most viewers will treat a non-episodic text (such as most films or books) as a text, episodic texts rarely experience such comfortable stasis. Meanwhile, as has been illustrated by Henry Jenkins in particular, not all episodes are created equal. Fans often dispute moves by creators, and both individually and communally will decide upon various hierarchies of "authenticity," whereby some episodes are rendered canonic, while others are spurned and rejected. Jenkins focuses his work more prominently on television fans, but Brooker sees an active discussion and debate over a *Star Wars* canon, and Bacon-Smith with Yarborough concludes that many Batman comic readers refuse to consider the film a part of Batman's "ongoing macrotext" (112).

This means that the viewer's experience of a film that has been adapted from a favorite comic book will involve, and rely upon, significantly more intertextual ties and connections here to that comic, and to its own phenomenological existence for the viewer than it would for a non-comic-book-reader, who is more likely to approach the text as an individual text, not as a number in a series. Admittedly, some non-comic-book-readers will "episodize" the film in other ways, so that, for instance, *Spider-Man* viewers may construct or work with intertextual networks of Tobey Maguire fandom, or so forth. Our stark division here between comic book readers as experiencing an episodic text and non-readers experiencing a more hermetically sealed text should thus be regarded as a discursive move alone, designed to hold certain variables in place. However, accepting this division, herein lies the dilemma for understanding the reception of comic book movies. One group of viewers, it would appear, are intertextually "rich," yet likely a minority in a theater audience, while another group are intertextually "poor," yet likely the majority, and hence the dominant viewing group who have the ability to determine the dominant reading and interpretation.

To further analyze this apparent division, and to inquire into differences in reception, in the summer of 2004, we interviewed fifteen individuals about their experiences with and interpretations of comic book films. All but one of the interviewees were in their twenties or early thirties (the exception being forty), middle class, and living in Los Angeles or Berkeley, California, where the interviews took place. While seven subjects were interviewed alone, the rest were interviewed in pairs, one comprised of two comic book readers, and three with one reader and one non-reader. By no means could this group be considered representative, but our interest lay not in exhausting the possibilities of reception or in finding common practices, but in hearing a sample of how both comic readers and non-readers talk of adaptations. Furthermore, given the size of our sample, any attempt to correlate responses to interview setting (two readers, mixed, or individual) would be perilous, and thus we structured interviews this way solely to provide opportunities for different types of discussion to emerge. All interviewee pairs knew each other beforehand and were solicited through a "snowball" approach (Hermes). In the interests of disclosure, it should also be noted that both interviewers fall into the same age and class demographic as the interviewees, and one read comics as a teen, and the other remains an avid reader.

Discussion with and amongst the comic readers followed many of the patterns observed by Bacon-Smith with Yarborough, Barker and Brooks, Chin and Gray, and Brooker. More often than not, prior knowledge of the comic translated into great hopes, mixed with a realistic-cum-pessimistic sense of fear that these hopes would be dashed by numerous changes to characters, their motivations, and plotlines seen as unnecessary or nonsensical. Kristof,[1] for instance, noted that "I always hope for the best but expect the worst"; Ethan stated that "You just need to prepare for it to suck. . . . That way, if you see *Catwoman*, so what? But when you get *X-Men* or *Spider-Man 2*, you're rewarded, unexpectedly"; and Clarence observed, "I have to see these films, you know, but I'm never expecting to see something great." Why these movies "suck" often had to do centrally with being poor adaptations, or even poorly conceived adaptations. Of the latter, for example, Rory noted that "*Tank Girl* was really bad because it shouldn't have been a movie. It was just a comic book that didn't lend itself to adaptation. They tried to force a story into something that wasn't there." Meanwhile, though, Adam voiced a common comic reader complaint, that "Unnecessary changes bother me." Or, offering a more detailed discussion of poor translation and "unnecessary" and ill-conceived changes, Richard stated of *Daredevil*:

One of my big issues with it was, in order to, they tried to make some character growth for the movie, they take this character who, [in the comics,] as Matt Murdock and as Daredevil, believes in the law. Granted, as Daredevil he's got more latitude, but he never, like, what I'm familiar with as far as Daredevil, there's never a case where suddenly, he's going to go breaking the laws, as far as like killing people or, you know, doing things that, that are, you know, way outside of the [law], he believes in the system, but it's, it's, I guess it needs some extra help, is my impression of it. . . . In the movie they make him somebody who's killing people, as I recall, in the movie he lets several people die, or kills them himself, then, when he meets the *most irredeemable character of all*, Bullseye, "No, I think I should let him live." What!? [. . .] I thought it was just dumb.

Knowledge of the comics clearly formed an essential part of the evaluation process for comic readers when viewing or discussing these films, and the films were often dreaded in advance, then watched, and later derided, for careless deviation from the comic, and for enacting what Jenkins's *Star Trek* fans call "character rape" (*Textual Poachers*), a term that in itself shows the degree of symbolic violence some fans feel is perpetrated when characters and plots are "messed with." As Rory insisted, "the character should be the character from the comic, it should have the same, you know, issues and problems. . . . Not just some guy in a suit, you know, doing whatever some screenwriter wants him to do, that doesn't know the character." However, to say that the readers expected absolute fealty to the comics would be incorrect. After all, if the films were to be evaluated solely based on whether they met up to comic standards, viewing would equate to little more than policing a character or plot. Rather, amidst expressions of fear and despair, most readers were actively excited by the prospects of a film, as is evident in Bob's conflicted commentary that, "I have such low expectations when a movie comes out. [Adam laughs] I really do! It's not like I'm expecting them, it's going to be very different than the comic book. [But,] I just think it's cool that they've depicted it on film, even if it's a bad movie, it's got good moments." Fealty, then, wasn't wholly required. As Kristof noted, "I do care about keeping it true, but to a point. Like I said, you don't have to throw it all in there to make it successful." Similarly, Richard stated that, "I do care if it [the movie] is true to the comic, but I don't think it has to be a slave to the comic," and Peter agreed that "Comic books aren't, it's not like they're holy texts, they're not. They're not sacred books."

Certainly, some of the readers' comments, taken out of context, could sound as if they had attributed holiness to the comics. Hence, for instance, a common concern was that no filmmaker could seemingly replicate the comics' tone. As Bob noted, "You say, well, they have the source material, why did they change it? But then, you expect it to be changed. You know it's not going to be the comic book. Just like you knew that the *Lord of the Rings* movie isn't going to be the book." But leeway was given not (only) because the comic was seen as unreplicatable, but because readers realized a difference in medium required shifts in characterization, "look," and style. Readers understood that films and comics are, as Brian offered, "such different mediums," and that the production and format are not the same. This became most apparent in discussing the question of how a comic book movie should look. The general response from comic readers was that the movie should *not* look like the comic. The process of accepting the *interpretation* of the characters and stories as portrayed in the movie adaptation is not a simple translation of reading pleasure from one medium (comics in this instance) to another for readers of both formats, but a question of negotiating the differences between the texts, taking into account the expressive rules and potential of the new medium.

Many comic readers enjoy and appreciate film as much as comics, and value and critique both media equally. Or, as Clarence noted, "Okay, so you've got a movie that copies the comic exactly. So what? Who gives a damn, if it's a crappy flick." When asked if he was concerned about "loyalty" to the comic, he continued: "Well . . . I withhold the right to say they butchered the story or killed my favorite characters or parts, but a good movie offers the characters and the story more than a bad one does, and perhaps you, uh, need to make *some* changes, and each director's got his own vision, right? So, make a super film, and it honors the character. Heck, it may even get people interested in reading the comics."

Changes were allowable, as such, particularly when the lack of change would cause a clunky translation. As Peter noted of a film's look, for instance, "it has to adhere to, you know, the logic of film, I mean it has to be

NEIL RAE AND JONATHAN GRAY

somewhat . . . rooted in the real world, unless you're doing something animated or CGI." Or, likewise, a change generally accepted by fans was the decision to use alternative costumes for the characters in the *X-Men* movie. As Kristof noted about the costume change for Wolverine, "that's all acceptable because you can't be running around in yellow spandex."

Comic readers have a repertoire of knowledge about specific characters and plots that is drawn on in interpreting the movie text itself, but this competency and experience of reading comics also translates to a familiarity with the different expressive limits of each medium. Adam stated, for example, that, "I think comics are a unique medium in that I think there are comic book stories that you couldn't tell on the big screen, but I don't think there's any big screen story that you couldn't do in comic book form," whereas Rory asserted that, "A static visual doesn't always translate to a moving visual." This does not necessarily translate to mean "comics are better than films," but shows a belief in the power of the comic medium to display the unbelievable or intangible in a way that can prove difficult on screen through the bounds of "movie-believability."

Nevertheless, if comics could offer favorite characters something that films could not, the films were also seen as carrying great potential to offer the characters something themselves. When a film "got it right," it could humanize the characters and give them flesh and a third dimension. Kristof stated, "What *Spider-Man* and what *X-Men* did was they actually made the characters human, and not larger than life; you actually knew they had faults and that they were vulnerable as people, even though they were, they had all these, you know, fantastic powers, and things like that." Moreover, a common critique of poorly made films was that they had no "vision," but in saying this, the readers displayed an active interest in films and filmmakers who could "add" something to a character or story, and could approach the character from an interesting angle. Thus, while Adam criticized Joel Schumacher's directorial leadership of *Batman and Robin*, saying, "I don't think his vision was very well defined apart from butt shots and nipple costumes," Peter offered that, "If you're going to be a filmmaker and you're going to adapt something, I think in a lot of ways it has to be your vision, it has to be true to the original, but it has to be . . . it also has to be true to you as a filmmaker."

Gary, in particular, elaborated upon this idea, suggesting that really good comic book films, with substantial vision, could reinterpret characters and plots, and thus add to his understanding, appreciation, and enjoyment of a character. "Some films blow," he noted, "because they're bad films, some blow because they focus on what I think is a stupid part of the character, [but] some make me think about them in new ways. Not much, but enough." He also added:

> Let's be clear—many of these characters exist in hundreds, maybe even thousands of comics. I think some of them are really dumb. Take Spidey, for instance: [. . . .] Some Spidey fans hate some of the titles. And then you get the graphic novels, which might give a nice edge to the story, or might do something totally retarded with it. I guess my point is that comics aren't novels—you don't just get one person creating the character. The character is used in different ways across time, and by writers with different attitudes and interests.

Therefore, while Gary felt that many comic book films were bad, he linked this evaluation to the episodic nature of comics, posing that while "comic readers get really pissed at bad movies, the way I look at it is that the same people get just as pissed at bad comics with their favorite characters." Gary saw each comic book as either adding to or failing to add to his understanding, appreciation, and enjoyment of a character, and any film was regarded in the same light. Effectively, to Gary and to the other comic readers, a comic book film could be in some ways like a new episode or graphic novel of the comic, in that it might be poorly done and add little if anything to the mythos of the character, it might even "butcher" a character, or it might add to the "macrotext."

However, fundamental differences between a new comic and a film existed in the readers' relative levels of trust in the creative personnel behind them, and in the degree to which they felt as though filmmakers were actually addressing them at all. Although compelled to see these movies, comic readers occupy the position of "floating voters," as defined by Tulloch and Jenkins, with regard to the movie-going experience. That is to say, although they have the greatest amount of textual knowledge invested in the property developed for the big screen, they are powerless to affect the way

NEIL RAE AND JONATHAN GRAY

it is reinterpreted. Ethan stated, for instance, that, producers "try to convince fans they're making it for you, but they're not. So if something that means a lot to you doesn't to them, and if their 'industry savvy' tells them to dump it, they will. So don't expect much." Kristof similarly voiced that, "I um, just blame it on the directors and the producers because, you know, they've either got too much pressure from someone above who's putting the money down, or the director never read it a day in his life, and didn't care about the characters and had no idea what he was doing." To examine further how audiences are invited to participate in, and how they interpret comic adaptations, we will therefore shortly turn to those who comic readers felt were being addressed: the everyday, non-readers.

First, though, and before crossing the "divide" between readers and non-readers, a word should be said about the division. After all, in the interview process, we asked respondents if they were readers or not, and their self-identification as belonging to one or the other category is worth interrogation. Some "readers" of a few issues, for instance, may have felt free to call themselves either readers or non-readers, and it seems particularly likely that some "readers" may claim the title so as to give themselves and their opinions an air of authority. In one way, such a ploy would highlight how meaningful and how value-loaded the division can prove to film viewers, and would illustrate that, as alienated from the Hollywood-ification process as readers feel, the very position of being an intertextually "well-equipped" viewer is still regarded by some as discursively more authoritative. That said, we heard little evidence of position "fudging" in our respondents. Besides, as we will now discuss, the irony of such a ploy would be that the non-readers we talked to showed themselves to be fairly indifferent to intertextual equipment. Instead, they were an equally competent viewing group who had developed their own equally involved and complex viewing strategy, albeit one that brought them into contact with a starkly different mode of textuality.

While the readers clearly saw the film as a link in an intertextual chain, and often as a potentially weak link at that, non-readers often saw no chain, or resented the remnants or suggestions of one. As we will discuss later, some non-readers were interested in readers' interpretations and viewing experiences, but only after the fact. At the point of viewing, and in evaluating the film, they cared solely of the film as a structural whole. Without the same repertoire of comic knowledge to draw on, non-comic-readers could not place the movie into the same intertextual field as comic readers when viewing and discussing these movies. In other words, they are forced to take the movies at "face value" in reading and evaluating them as texts. As such, "back story" was almost irrelevant, as was any notion of fidelity or fealty to an "original." Clarisse, for instance, felt that "way too much emphasis is being put on tracing back the roots, showing where these people came from," noting further that, "I don't have to know how it is that he [the supervillain] became who he is, what he is today. Have him do some really crazy stuff and we'll have the superhero guy stop him, and have it be done in a really creative, fun kind of way and I'm happy." As such, she continued, "I've never read a *Superman* comic, [so] if you told me that no, no, no, what happened in the first Christopher Reeve movie isn't what happened at all, I wouldn't know otherwise and I certainly wouldn't have been offended, because that, to me, was the story." Or, as Roderick spelt out, "For me, what matters first, foremost, *only* is the strength of the thing as a film. Does it look good? Is the acting good? Do I care about the people in it? Is it fun to watch?"

With both Clarisse and Roderick, we see not only an insistence that films be judged on their merits as films alone, but both clearly resent the idea that a back story *should* matter. Meanwhile, Naomi spoke of feeling "clueless" while watching some adaptations, an experience that clearly detracted from her enjoyment. Not being privy to the back story, non-readers would of course be regarded as "clueless," deficient, or ill-equipped viewers if intertextual history mattered, and certainly, fans can and will often look down upon non-fans as lesser, even more facile viewers of intertextual outgrowths of beloved material (see Barker and Brooks, Chin and Gray). Thus, Clarisse and Roderick in particular had to assert their "legitimacy" as viewers by pronouncing the near irrelevance of intertextuality and the primacy—"first, foremost, *only*"—of the text at hand.

While stated with less vehemence than either of these two viewers, all of the non-readers echoed in other ways Clarisse and Roderick's rejection of the comics as highly pertinent. For instance, while being interviewed with Richard, a reader, Kirk noted of *Daredevil*, "I think it was just awful. I mean from a movie standpoint, I wouldn't base that comic book wise, but

NEIL RAE AND JONATHAN GRAY

from a movie point of view, it was just awful. I couldn't get through it." He and Richard then discussed numerous flaws of the film before he declared simply, "I just thought it did *completely not* work." Again, then, after framing his viewing as based solely "from a movie point of view," he was able to assert that it did "*completely not* work," a judgment that, while perhaps rhetorically overemphasized, still declares the absolute importance of a film working "from a movie point of view." Similarly, although reasoned very differently, Naomi drew on her experiences as an editor who adapts comics and novels from Japanese to English, to state that "all the fans want it to be authentic, and true to its original form, but you have to understand, like, especially with novels, that you can't, you can't do exactly what was in the original, it can not just be a translation, like it has to be its own thing in order for it to work, you know?" Here, then, Naomi discussed the process of production to declare that true adaptation can never work anyway, the suggestion therefore being that viewers should, or at least could, abandon hopes of intertextuality, and learn to take the new text as "its own thing."

Another key difference between readers and non-readers became evident in how they discussed "reality." To the readers, good adaptations were usually those that performed an adept intertextual feat by transferring the humanity of the characters to the screen, and reality—in the form of psychological integrity and coherence—was seen to already exist in the comics. For non-readers, by comparison, both a good movie and reality were achieved when a filmmaker handled the effects well and made superpowers seem believable. Kirk, for example, commented that he liked the second *X-Men* movie better than the first *Spider-Man* movie because the CGI in *Spider-Man* looked computer generated, not "real," whereas, with the opening scene with Nightcrawler in *X2*, "it's not even that believable that somebody disappears like that, but it worked, you know, . . . I mean obviously you know it's from fantasy, someone disappearing like that, but they made it believable, and that's what I loved about it." Or Seth noted that comic book films seem to be getting better, since filmmakers are finally adding more realism. As he stated, with the current films, "you get a real sense of what moves them and how they must feel. They seem very realistic, in a bizarre way." When asked how they were "bizarre," he responded, "Bizarre because it's totally outrageous—these things don't happen, unless you've taken over your daily fill of drugs. But the movies pull you in, make you believe. Smart stuff." Interestingly, then, non-readers seemed to see realism as something that good filmmakers *added* to the stories, almost working against the inherent "unbelievability" of "totally outrageous" comics—in which "it's not that believable that somebody disappears like that"—and breaking from the movie's intertextual baggage so as to, as Roderick stated, "really flesh out the psychology and to *add* to the tale" (emphasis added).

As we have quoted them so far, the non-readers may appear to be quite hostile to comics, but this was by no means the case. None appeared to stigmatize either comics or their readers as lesser beings. Nor did they feel comics or readers were *wholly* irrelevant to their own consumption, as most spoke of being interested in discussing the comic with readers after viewing the film. Even Bob, a reader, noted that "people who aren't fans, I find that they always want to know what it was like in the original. You know, not that they ever, most of the time they'll never pick up the original, but they'll want to know how it's been changed." Roderick, in particular, insisted that, "I'm really interested to hear from comic fans about how true the thing is to the comic, and I love talking with people who can tell me." When asked why, he commented: "I think it's 'cause I love knowing about films. You know, what other films an actor has done, what the director was trying to do—I absolutely love directors' commentaries. And, so, knowing what the comic was all about adds into that: it's more info, more background. Not background I'll ever read myself: I won't buy the comic or anything, but it kind of makes the film more, lets me appreciate other parts of it."

At first sight, this might seem to contradict the idea that non-readers resent back story, but Roderick is only saying he wants back story *outside of the film*, not in the film itself. The film must be able to stand on its own, in other words, but he will then explore background information. Effectively, to him, the comics are little more than interesting sidebars, and having read them is akin to knowing "what other films an actor has done." He was also adamant that comic readers' readings wouldn't *replace* his, and he insisted, "I'm never going to change my mind about liking a scene or thinking it's dumb just because that's not what happened in episode 34, page 13." Rather, it seems that information gained from readers is a way to deepen the postviewing experience. If the comic is still conceived as part of the film's intertextual chain, it is wholly subjugated to the film in both importance and status. After all, if non-readers truly cared about the film as an episodic entity, they would most likely be moved by good films to buy and read the comics, yet all showed little to no interest in doing so.

In asking comic readers and non-readers about their experiences with adaptations, we were inquiring into their experiences with textuality, and we found two disparate experiences. Non-readers could watch the films as films, and largely as distinct texts. They occasionally had to work at excluding the film's intertextual history, or, rather, at welcoming it only on their terms, but they therefore reduced it to the status of cast biography: interesting, yet peripheral background. By contrast, readers, predictably, looked at any adaptation as part of an episodic text. If the film failed to contribute to their vision of that macrotext, it could be brushed off and/or denigrated as an unworthy link in the intertextual chain, but even if it succeeded, it became no more than another link. Thus, our research suggests the existence of complex hierarchies of intertextuality that will differ from interpretive community to interpretive community. Furthermore, though, while interpretive community theory (Fish, Lindlof) and much recent theory on reception suggests that different audiences may interpret a text differently, our research suggests that they may even be interacting with an entirely different *textuality*. What is a fairly static text to one group may be an intertext and an episode to another. Thus, while significant work has been conducted into the differences between media (Ellis, Levinson, McLuhan, Meyrowitz), the case of the reception of adaptations adds the complexity of the growing pains of "adapting" textuality itself.

These growing pains are also felt by some viewers more than others, as we saw. The comic readers in our research struggled with the conversion of their favorite characters and episodic texts into filmic texts, and felt excluded by the whole production process, and by the "Hollywood-ification" that they believed offered the text to non-readers more than it did to them. Indeed, it is noteworthy that many of the readers' favorite comic films were those, such as *Spider-Man* and *X-Men*, that announced themselves as sequel hungry from the outset, or in other words, those that were more episodic by nature. It is also interesting to note that the sales of *Spider-Man* comic series have not been greatly increased by the release of the second movie. According to *Comics International* ("Comics Economics" 54), the highest placing Spider-Man title in the top 100 among the comics retail trade for September 2004 was *Ultimate Spider-Man #65*, with just under 100,000 issues sold two months after the release of the movie *Spider-Man 2*. In other words, non-comics-readers have generally not found the need to engage with the film text in its regular serialized comic book format.

Meanwhile, despite comic readers' frustrations at being shut out of the retextualization process, and their feelings of being turned into lesser viewers, our research also points to an interesting link between a text's textuality and how much it welcomes fans. Episodic texts, after all, encourage fan involvement: in the spaces between episodes. Fans keep the texts alive through play, discussion, creative fan practices (Jenkins, *Textual Poachers*), and so forth. Fans may even feel more able to communicate desires and dislikes to producers, through letter writing, petitions, or purchase decisions. Episodic texts promise fans a certain degree of agency. By contrast, non-episodic texts offer less crevices for fans to inhabit, and the glossy veneer of a solitary text can leave little if any traction for fans to grapple onto (Hills 134). While our research shows that comic book readers still found or made space for themselves within this new textual environment, it is ultimately the shift in textuality more than the mere retelling of a story, that renders certain audience behavior and certain practices of textual interaction more difficult.

NEIL RAE AND JONATHAN GRAY

"WHAM! BAM! THE X-MEN ARE HERE"

THE BRITISH BROADSHEET PRESS AND
THE X-MEN FILMS AND COMIC

— MEL GIBSON

In July and August 2000 the first *X-Men* film opened in Britain and America to considerable press attention. In analyzing a range of articles on the film, I was struck in particular by the way in which those in the British press, and especially broadsheets[1] such as the *Times, Telegraph, Independent, Guardian,* and their Sunday equivalents including the *Independent on Sunday* and the *Observer* (as well as the electronic versions of these papers) often articulated concerns, indeed, fears, about comics. The writers in the broadsheets often discussed the comics, rather than the film, and in doing so made clear the historical perceptions and underlying tensions around comics in general in Britain, in addition, often articulating emotional responses to comics in a way untypical of broadsheet articles. These articles demonstrate a history of middle-class fears about the popular. These reviews and articles then continue the largely negative assumptions about comics that have dogged the medium almost constantly since it began. Moreover they represent a culturally specific British perspective on comics. In comparison, articles about *X-Men 2* (2003) primarily focus on the film, suggesting that the discussion of comics that emerged in articles about the first film may have had a cathartic function in relation to discussions of the comic as medium in Britain.

My focus is on articles that went beyond simple reviews of the films. In relation to the first film, the vast majority of items in British newspapers, whether broadsheet or tabloid, concentrated on plot outline and star rating, rather than giving any commentary. The brevity of these items was in itself indicative of a rather dismissive attitude towards the film. This situation may have arisen because the film was not only based on a comic, but also seen as a film for younger viewers and part of a genre deemed a minority interest. In contrast, more extensive attention was given to *Bridget Jones's Diary* (2001). In addition, the differences between the two films in terms of press attention could be partly due to the source of *Bridget Jones's Diary* being considered "respectable" literature rather than "disreputable" comics. Further, the overwhelming interest in the film of *Bridget Jones's Diary* in Britain was based on its British source material, something that suggests a cultural nationalism that also underpinned some of the articles about *X-Men*.

In what ways then, was the first film discussed? The most important aspect of the articles, as I suggest above, was that the film was often only relevant to them in a minor way. The articles and reviews consistently hearkened back to the comics, considering the film primarily as an extension of them, which, whilst perfectly valid, shifted discussion away from film and onto the comic medium.[2] The educational and class background of the writer and assumptions about the social class to which the readers belonged were also woven into these articles and linked to assumed perceptions of comics. The newspaper audience, as seen through the articles, was middle class, predominantly male, educated via grammar or public school and saw the medium as trivial or dangerous. In addition, these middle-class writers addressing a middle-class audience perceived the readers' values as including a dismissal of popular culture (even when the writers themselves espoused it). Further, the overall political perspectives that the papers espoused also had an impact on the tone of the articles. In general, the traditionally more liberal and leftist *Guardian* contained more sympathetic readings of the film and comics whilst the more conservative *Telegraph* took a debased "mass culture" viewpoint. The *Guardian* chose to emphasize the complexity and depth of comics. For instance, Xan Brooks in the *Guardian Unlimited* of 18 August 2000 said that the film " . . . doesn't take big liberties with the Marvel Comics material" and went on to argue that Marvel has "always offered darker, more complex tales than your standard cartoon fodder." In conclusion, Brooks stated, "Singer's film evolves into a rich and unusual oddity: a blockbuster that dreamed it was an indie angst movie. In the end, it's a bit of a mutant itself." In contrast, the *Telegraph* tended to take a tone that was trivializing or scathing, depending on the writer's understanding of comics. Thus, whilst these texts were nominally about the film they were much more revealing about middle-class perspectives on comics (as refracted through left or right wing discourses) at the turn of the twenty-first century.

As I suggest above, there was often an apologetic tone from writers who took the first film, or the comics, seriously.[3] For instance, writing in the *Independent* of 14 July 2000 (a newspaper that can be characterized as left leaning and liberal and so has some common ground with the *Guardian*), David Thompson ended his article by saying, "David Thompson is a freelance writer who has spent far too much time reading comics" (12). It is also possible, for instance, to read the "jokey" tone in Peter Bradshaw's article in the *Guardian* of 18 August as a distancing technique masking genuine engagement. Bradshaw's article can be read in this way because, although maintaining a light tone, he identifies the film as, in part, a social commentary. This use of distancing techniques and apologetic tones suggests that the writers believe their positive viewpoint to be somehow improper and culturally unacceptable. The writers seem to anticipate that their readers will respond to the film and the comic in a "properly" middle-class manner: that being to treat them as "fun" or largely dismiss them. In contrast, the writers reveal themselves to be serious about comics, and so, potentially, to be labeled as fans, or as childish, or not properly middle class, and thus vulnerable to all of the value judgments that such labels might bring.[4] Where articles were complimentary, then (largely in left wing papers), they were hedged with qualifications, emphasizing both writers' fears about their own status as adults and professionals, and the low position that comics hold in the journalists' imagined British hierarchy of arts.

The emotional, engaged, and personal nature of some of the first set of articles went beyond the need for a journalistic "peg" on which to hang a piece. This aspect of the articles could also be seen as very different from the emotional context for a typical "broadsheet" item. In effect, the more measured and depersonalized discourse about the film as film, central to the second set of articles, is a more "normal" tone in relation to broadsheet writing. The contrast between the two emphasizes that the first set of articles offer both an untypical discourse within broadsheets, which is then hidden, removed, and denied, in a discursive shift to more distanced discourses about class and culture. That there is a preexisting history of comics that have become films and have been reviewed suggests that the emotional and comic-based response in this set of articles is not related to comics becoming films in general. Rather, I would argue that it means that the focus on comics in the reviews of the first film is about a specific generation of comic readers, predominantly in their thirties and forties and Marvel readers as children, if no longer, acknowledging themselves as having been comics readers and recognizing the emotional role of comics in their lives for the first time.

In contrast to those articles that took comics seriously, a very different and culturally dominant set of definition of comics in Britain emerged in other articles, suggesting that all the articles were engaged with questions of defining the medium. This exercise can be characterized by the frequent use of the term "fun" and reminders that the basis of the film was "only a comic." For instance, Matthew Bond's article in the *Telegraph* of 18 August 2000 was entitled "Fun Was Never Such Work." Further, the headline was followed by an assertion that the film "takes itself too seriously for its own good" arguing that a film of the comic should "know its place" and not aspire to be serious. Bond's perception of the film was entirely based on his value judgment of comics. He felt the film was enjoyable when it was about "good versus bad mutants" but not otherwise (8). Bond, therefore, only celebrates those parts of the film that reflect his definition of comics.

The definition of comics as "fun" is tied to British understandings of comics as primarily a vehicle for humor. Such a perception of comics derives from classic British titles such as *The Beano*, which resemble more the American comic strips of the early twentieth century than say comic books. As a result of this cultural construction of the comic, the first *X-Men* film was read as a failure in not being funny. For instance, in Philip French's review in the *Observer* of 20 August 2000 he states that "*X-Men* lacks the humor that made the similar, but more ambiguous, *Men in Black* [1997] such a delight" (13). With regard to tone, that of Bradshaw's article in the 18 August *Guardian* showed the impact of this definition of comics, even for a comic fan, in being largely "jokey" and using slang. For ex-

ample, Bradshaw describes Cyclops's powers as " . . . a bit rubbish, really—
if he loses his Ray-Bans behind the sofa, he is stuffed" (4).

This definition of the comic as centered on humor was also typically
related to an assumption that the comic as a medium solely addresses children (thus linking constructions of the comic and of the child). Given that
classic British comic *The Beano* consists of short gag-based, often slap-
stick, stories and is targeted at a child audience under ten years old, the
assumption that texts like *X-Men* are only of interest to children is not
a wholly surprising one. Further, that the first film gained an age twelve
exhibition certificate was used to reinforce perceptions in a number of
articles that comics were solely for children. This cultural positioning of
comics in Britain is tied to The Children & Young Persons Harmful Publications Act (1955) which banned importation of American crime and horror comics.[5] The very title of the act shows how comics were defined in
terms of assumptions about their audience. The campaign that led to the
act, organized by the Comics Campaign Council (CCC), constantly reiter-
ated that these were texts for children, or at the very least, texts that children were attracted to and could access. The articles on the *X-Men*, then, in
the slippage between comic and film partly reflect the inheritance of perspectives on comics generated in Britain in the 1950s.

Another of the major themes in the articles linked to this culturally
dominant definition of comics as for children and containing humor concerned the opening scenes of the first film. Bond, for instance, argued that,
"The best we can say about this sequence is that it is over quickly . . . [t]he
worst is that exploiting this universally recognized image of real horror to
make some cheap point about a fantasy world where all-in wrestlers have
knuckles that sprout razor-sharp knives and shape-shifting women cover
their bits with old tyre treads is grotesque. And before the comic-buffs
write, I neither know nor care whether this is faithful to the original. It's
still crass" (8).

This attitude dismisses any attempts to take on serious issues or discuss morality in such texts. It also demonstrates the continued slippage
between the comics and the first film. Bond refuses to accept that comics may explore, or reflect, social issues, insisting that they are fantasy and
that fantasy is, in effect, exploitative, or an insult to "the real." In labeling
the comic trivial, fantastical, and parasitical, the high ground, as it were, is

maintained as an arena for other forms of more "acceptable" cultural engagement.

Bradshaw, in contrast, describes the opening sequence rather differently, seeing it as "a moment of sheer audacity, which if managed with any less deadpan bravado would certainly be offensive. And even as it is, it is right out there on an edge of provocation undreamt of by other mainstream Hollywood movies." He then links that sequence with the Ellis Island finale in a reading of the film as a "toweringly sarcastic denunciation of the US as a cradle of pluralism and tolerance" (4). This article emerges as one of only a few which sees the text as worthy of serious consideration, and, further, is one of even fewer to locate the film and comics in a culturally specific context. Responses to the introduction of the film, then, depended on the writer's perceptions of comics. For some, the dominant definition of comics as "fun" and for children meant that the opening sequence was unacceptable. When arguing that the film belittled real events, definitions of comics were invariably the means through which the writers judged the film.

Comments about the acting in the film, and the dialogue, also reflected definitions of comics. For instance, Bond argued that "at times the dialogue is a little too close to the comic-book original" (8) implying that all comic book dialogue is inherently simplistic and crude. In terms of acting, "comic-book" remained shorthand for wooden or shallow performances. The female performers, in particular, were described in this way, or as secondary or "silly." Sean Macaulay in the 17 July 2000 *Times* for instance, states that "[Berry plays] uber-weather girl Storm with all the swirling fury of a light mist. Cleavage would have been a more suitable sobriquet" (24). In addition, most of the reviews assumed that the lack of female characters (and where they did appear, the emphasis on their cleavage, as described above) was also derived from comics. Hence, the cliché of the female character in comics informed how the film was interpreted, even when, as is the case with the *X-Men*, such comics, have been known for depictions of strong female characters that take central roles.

The tensions in the articles created by the various definitions of comics were often further exacerbated by the choice of title. Sensitive or serious writing was frequently undermined by humorous or sound effect-based titles. Such was the case with the 6 August 2000 *Independent on*

Sunday article "Wham! Bam! The X-Men Are Here," which prefaced an article in which Ekow Eshun described his experience of being a black British child in the 1970s. Eshun addressed what the *X-Men* comics had meant to him as a child and in so doing produced an article supposedly about the film but, once more, dominated by comics. In addition, he contextualizes an American text in relation to a British readership. Eshun stated, "I used to read *The X-Men* as escapism. But often the world felt more real than the world around me. Here were outsiders, mistrusted by a bigoted majority, who had learnt early about the capricious unkindness of life. It all seemed achingly familiar" (1). In this article, the writer shows that an American comic may be a tool that can be used to address issues about British identity, class, race, and childhood. Although readers may be tied to culturally specific ways of understanding any given text (rather than being free to make any meanings they choose), Eshun's article suggests how readers might make meanings that are personally relevant. Where the text originates from is less important here than how it is used. As Eshun concludes: "And I actually felt a rush of nostalgia [when watching the film]. Not for my actual childhood. But for how, through reading *The X-Men*, I imagined it might be" (1).

Both this article and Bond's shared a reflection on childhood experiences of comics.[6] Whilst Eshun's reading was both lyrical and emotional, Bond took a dismissive approach, stating, "I did, I confess, have a brief Marvel comics period. They were excellent boyhood reading on long train journeys, had the considerable bonus of earning strong parental disapproval ("but they're American, darling"), and only came to an end when I discovered something more interesting. Girls or horses, I forget which" (8).

In this case where the comic came from had a distinct impact upon how it was understood and used, in direct contrast with Eshun's reading, which acknowledges cultural specificity but sees certain themes as crossing cultures. In Bond's article, the definition of the comic in Britain is shown as one that developed in the late twentieth century in relation to other comics and one that has, at its heart, a nationalistic element. This sentiment too had an impact upon the responses to the first film.

Working with a model of American comics as offensive (and so useful as a tool for his child self in suggesting rebellion against parental values),

Bond flags an historical fear of American culture in Britain and the equally historical perceived need for reinforcing British culture (here through an insistence on the British definition of the comic). He identifies American comics as having, in the past, represented an alien, and threatening, "other," particularly to middle-class adults. Such attitudes were a factor in the approach of the Comics Campaign Council (CCC) in the 1950s. As Martin Barker (*Haunt of Fears*) explains, the CCC was initially marked by anti-Americanism. This took several forms, ranging from seeing comics in a highly political way as part of a policy of cultural imperialism by America, to a generalized feeling about maintaining a specifically British culture. Barker says that this anti-Americanism was replaced, as the campaign developed, by "a moralised, depoliticised version of the old theme" (29) that described the comics as degrading. An undercurrent of anti-Americanism remained in British attitudes to comics after the campaign ended. This is exemplified in the use of the term "American-type," in George H. Pumphrey's 1964 *What Children Think of Their Comics*, to describe what he considered the very worst kind of comics. It is this undercurrent, although representing middle-class unease rather than outright hostility, which, I believe, was revealed in the articles about the *X-Men* film.

The articles suggest a continuing correlation in Britain between American culture, cultural imperialism, the popular, and "dumbing down." This notion of the film of the comic as representing cultural threat appeared in various guises. For instance, there were notions of a completed cultural invasion in the headline "The X-Men Are Here" (Eshun). This opinion could also be seen in the differences between the first round of reviews in British broadsheets, usually in response to the U.S. opening, which were fairly positive about the film, and the more ambiguous reviews that accompanied British openings. Films from comics then were an acceptable text in an American context, but less so in a British one. Such a response suggests that the comic book culture the film represented, a culture seen as specifically American, was one that could only be dealt with by British commentators through their having a literal, physical distance on it as well as distancing it mentally.

Such perceptions of the film of the comic as a representative of American culture and as alien to Britain also found a space in other articles. Some, for instance, identified the entire project (which was seen as otherwise irredeemable) as being "saved" by the involvement of the Royal Shake-speare Company (RSC) trained Sir Ian McKellen and Patrick Stewart.[7] In these articles what was specifically American about the film was marked as lesser. What such articles simultaneously did was claim that the success of the film was entirely due to this British input (implied to be inherently superior) and therefore the film itself was seen as a British success, reveal-ing that the flip side of rejection was appropriation.[8] Hence, Hiscock in the 4 August 2000 *Telegraph* offered the headline "Cartoon Mutants—RSC Trained" (8). The insistence on seeing the film through the British contri-bution was also apparent when searching for the term *X-Men* on British search engines. Such searches offered very little, whilst searches on McKel-len and Stewart immediately led to *X-Men* reviews. I see this as a clear in-dication of how the "British connection" became an attempt at appropri-ating the text.

The tensions around the *X-Men* film and its "parent" comic book text in all of these articles can, then, be explained as a reflection of the way that the comic remains, for many of these writers, part of what could be described as a specifically British middle-class "mass culture" discourse. These perspectives on the part of some critics, then, remain as a fallback position when faced with what they identify as problematic culture. A high/low culture perspective remains firmly in place (despite the supposed encroachment of postmodernism) as part of a naturalized and "common-sense" approach to the comic medium. Thus, it is possible to extend David Lusted's (1998) argument about television, to comics. Lusted suggests that anti-Americanism is not merely an elite fear with regard to the American-ization of popular culture, but also reflective of a hostility to its popu-lism and its adoption by the non-elite in Britain (178). The tension around America, comics, and popular culture in these articles is, then, a tension around class in Britain.

The views expressed about both the *X-Men* film and comic could be seen as an echo of the "culture and civilization" tradition as initiated by Matthew Arnold.[9] The way that these articles interpret popular culture can be traced back to Arnold, through the influence of Cambridge academic F. R. Leavis on education in Britain.[10] Leavis's impact upon the educational curriculum in English in general, from the 1930s and onward, was im-mense. Leavis proposed direct intervention in schools to develop students' critical skills in ways that would ensure that they resisted mass culture. Such critical skills would, of course, also value and maintain what was considered high culture and particularly that in the keeping of British cultural authority. Bond's article demonstrates this sensibility of being part of a cultural elite that acts as a barrier or resistance to mass culture, implying a cultural or national stronghold under attack from without.

The intervention Leavis proposed took the form of forceful educational politics represented in a range of texts including the 1933 practical handbook *Culture and Environment* written by Leavis with Denys Thompson, and Thompson's journal for English teachers, *The Use of English.* Leavisism was in turn a considerable influence upon pupils, particularly through teachers' use of the practical exercises for students offered in these texts.[11] In addition, the seductive notion of being a member of a discriminating elite may also have played a part. The appeal to the reader of the middle-class medium of the broadsheet newspaper in Britain, then, is very much along these lines. The way that the reader is positioned (through the way that the paper positions itself) is as part of an elite, with the paper (and by extension the reader) "protecting" an elite culture within its pages.[12] Hence, such newspapers report on some forms of popular culture, especially those that the *X-Men* film represents, through a filter of "mass culture" discourse.

Such concern about comics and mass culture is not limited to a conservative middle class. These articles also echo the threat felt by Richard Hoggart, one of the founding fathers of British Cultural Studies, from American culture. Hoggart both shared and challenged some the assumptions of Leavis[13] (once more emphasizing the importance of Leavis in the mediation of mass media texts in Britain). Whilst Hoggart rarely touched on American comics, he does mention them in his 1957 work *The Uses of Literacy.* In particular, Hoggart described the popularity of comics as dangerous, depicting that danger in sexual and educational terms. He stated: "for page after page big-thighed and big-bosomed girls from Mars step out of their space-machines, and gangsters' molls scream away in high powered sedans. Anyone who sees something of Servicemen's reading, of the popularity of American and English comics (with the cruder English boys' comics serving their turn where the supply of hotter material runs out), knows something of all this. The process continues, for a substantial number of adolescents especially; a passive visual taking-on of bad mass-art geared to a very low mental age" (201).

Hoggart also links the comic with fragmentation, passive consumption, and what he saw as purely American commercialism, all of which he felt undermined British working-class culture (something typically not flagged up in other accounts of the comic) and particularly the young, revealing concerns about the developing popular teenage culture. Here too, concerns about the suitability of these texts for a child audience, echoed in the way that the articles on the *X-Men* film focus on "fun" and humor as part of a definition of the comic book medium, may also have their roots.

The broadsheet press's response to the first film reveals a continuance of the hostility and ambiguity that has traditionally marked middle-class, and particularly educational, discourses about comics in Britain. Ignoring the film in pursuit of making points about the "parent" texts implies that comics continue to be an "uncomfortable" medium within that culture. In particular, the perspectives on "mass culture" and education, developed by Leavis and others in the 1930s and onwards, mediated perceptions of comics over several generations, as commentators' understandings of the medium filtered through to parents and teachers.

The culturally specific, Leavisite educational position on popular culture, then, continues to have an impact on British cultural attitudes, particularly those of the middle classes. The ideological construction of the "commonsense" approach to understanding popular culture retains its "mass culture" overtones. For all that educationalists and media critics, both of whom are involved with the analysis of these texts, might insist that popular culture is no longer considered in this light, the articles on the first *X-Men* film suggest otherwise. This approach remains a British cultural "default setting," as it were. Such middle-class attitudes continue to have an impact not only on specific texts like the first *X-Men* film, and not only on specific media, such as the comic book, but on British understandings of most popular culture.

There are, then, some interesting shifts revealed in relation to the responses in the broadsheets to *X-Men 2* (*X2*) (2003) in that the tone in the majority of the articles and reviews is much more subdued and even. The extremes of opinion and the deep-lying attitudes revealed in responses in 2000 to the first film are no longer there, even among the same authors.

This development suggests that the first film provided, perhaps, a cathartic moment in which British cultural assumptions about popular culture erupted, before being either moved beyond or, more likely, reburied. It also suggests that film franchises based on comic books are no longer a cultural flashpoint.

What are notable, in the articles about *X-Men 2*, are the absences. One such absence is the emphasis on "fun" in the language used to discuss the film, although there is an underlying theme that still ties the comic book form (and so the film) to childhood. For instance, an article by Charlotte O'Sullivan in the 2 May 2003 *Independent* mentions that, "children stand around in playgrounds, trying to decide which superhero they'd most like to be." This, however, is a dim echo of the constant infantalization of the medium with regard to the first *X-Men* film.

There are also other dramatic shifts, in that the comic book and memories of comics are rarely present. Thus, the articles on the second film are much less personal, and much less part of a criticism of a medium, or an articulation of class. There are no apologies about having enjoyed comics, and neither are there justifications of the medium as an art or an inspiration. Again, this could be seen as emphasizing a new respectability with regards to the franchise, in part derived on its profitability and also, perhaps, from the higher and largely positive profile of some graphic novels in the broadsheet press (the *Guardian*, in particular, periodically reviews graphic novels). In addition, whilst many of the articles and reviews of the second film are negative, this negativity is focused on the film itself. For instance, Barbara Ellen in the 1 May 2003 *Times* describes "a whiff of stale franchise in the air" (12).

The use of language in the articles is also different. Whilst those addressing the first film typically had titles that instantly referred the reader back to the comics, these titles, for instance, "X Misses the Spot," tend to avoid such a focus. Indeed, the comics are rarely mentioned in the body of the articles, whilst it was central to most pieces in the case of the first film. Of the few that do flag that this is a franchise based on comics, such as the article by O'Sullivan in the *Independent*, most do so as a side issue, or to set the scene using only a brief descriptive sentence. The articles and reviews for the first film spent much more time on emphasizing its comic roots. This development could suggest an assumption on the part of the writers that the narrative and the medium need little introduction, showing how film franchises based on comics are more in the foreground, an accepted part of the cultural landscape rather than a blot upon it, or could reflect a flight away from discussing what proved, in the previous case, to be a very emotive discussion of a medium.

Fandom remains a problematic area, however, although with a change of emphasis. For instance, O'Sullivan argues that "*X-Men 2* is a snobby creature, geared to fans who know *X-Men* backwards and are already dizzy with excitement about *X-Men 3*." Here, the appeal of *X-Men 2* is seen as to insiders, following the notion of the "fanboy." However, the statement is applied only to knowledge of the films, not the comics. Again, it is an emphasis on silence around comics that dominates the articles. This could be seen as a dead issue, but the tone of some of the articles, notably that by O'Sullivan, do retain an edge, belittling the film for being both too simplistic and too confusing, too much summer blockbuster and too conformist (with the emphasis on Nightcrawler's faith being a key factor). The hostility remains, then, but has shifted into a more medium-specific form, whilst still being indirectly critical of the underlying comics.

There is generally a relocation of the *X-Men* films in these articles away from superhero comics as a genre, another key absence. Overall, these articles analyze the film more as a film, rather than as a representative from another medium. As a consequence, *X-Men 2* is compared, not even to other films based on comics, but to films seen as blockbusters, or special effects films, or films for younger audiences. In addition, it is also relocated as science fiction. For example, Ellen (2003) describes the costumes worn by the female characters as having come from "a Star Trek garage sale" (12) thus neatly trading one set of clichés for another, but clearly indicating a change of perception of the franchise.

Further, the reviewers also see it as a film that slips across genres, rather than being seen as representing a hybrid genre. Nicholas Barber in the 4 May 2003 *Independent* for instance, sees the failure of the film as centered on the lack of action scenes, in its emphasis on character, seeing it as a film that does not stay in genre as a blockbuster (one of the few writers to address both films, Barber still retains an enthusiasm for the franchise). There is, then, a problem for these writers in locating and labeling *X-Men 2*. In effect, the reviewers are either unsure about how to explain the film or inconsistent in placing it in any specific genre. In doing so, they reveal an ambivalence in their reviews that corresponds with their reluctance, or confidence, about the necessity to mention comics. However, the frequency of these gaps suggests a continued tension around the medium, a reluctance to reopen the debates that the first did.

Of all the articles mentioned here, only two locate *X-Men 2* as comic book based. That by Barber compares *X-Men 2* to other comic-based film franchises (and, in addition, also partly shifts the franchise across genre by mentioning *Star Wars*) only indirectly referring to comics. Here again, we see a distancing from the original medium. That the references are to other films is telling, showing how a body of work, either the *X-Men* films themselves, or a group of films inspired by comics, exists that can be considered with reference to each other, rather than with reference to the original texts, reflecting the growth of this type of film, but also moves the writers away from discussing comics altogether.

The only variation on this use (or lack of use) of comics comes from Cosmo Landesman in the 4 May 2003 *Sunday Times*, who uses the history of the comics, or more specifically, a perception of their roots in 1960s civil rights movements, as a way of interrogating the notion of tolerance, which he says lies at the heart of the film, and which he sees as a dated concept (C8). From there, he too refocuses on the film franchise, comparing it to *Star Wars*, again, shifting it across genre.

In contrast to Landesman, most of the articles refer to the sociopolitical themes with a degree of enthusiasm, although O'Sullivan argues that the philosophy and so the plot, is too muddled and criticizes the notion of the *X-Men* as representing any oppressed minority. In contrast, Tim Robey, in the *Telegraph* argues that "Singer, lest we forget, managed to conjure an illusion of sense out of *The Usual Suspects*, and has no real problems flicking back and forth here between plot, counterplot, and other related bits of business." In addition, he sees the theme of oppression as well handled with some "deftly written" scenes.

However, whilst the focus on comics is generally minimal, the power of comics is occasionally acknowledged. O'Sullivan argues that "Singer knows how potent comic book allegories can be—*X-Men*, which hurled us straight into scenes from a Nazi concentration camp, left a real bruise. His take on paranoid, post–September 11 America has none of the same poke."

So, whilst seeing the film as a failure, O'Sullivan also sees, in retrospect, the first film as significant and comics as a medium which can engage with serious themes. Note however, that the film and comic are collapsed together here, but that it is the film that is the dominant form.

So, one can conclude that the construction of comics has shifted, in this second set of articles, to one which is both profoundly visible through the films and yet almost invisible. The absence of the comic, on the one hand, shows the films being seen as capable of standing alone. On the other hand, this could be seen as a refusal to engage with the comic.

There is a sharp contrast between the two sets of articles in that there is little revelation about class or perceptions of culture in the second. This may indicate the way that comics can be seen as a flashpoint around taste, and that by avoiding them, one may avoid that discussion. However, the tensions around the notion of the summer blockbuster, itself a term that can be seen as critical, and some of the more pejorative comments about the plot do suggest the continuing hierarchy within culture.

Whilst it was possible to see the judgments about culture and class in relation to the former film very clearly, these later articles are much more guarded. The writers offer no scope for that, effectively shutting down the debates and revelations about medium and genre that the first opened up, simply by refusing to engage with the comic at all. Instead there is a desire to relabel the franchise as belonging to another genre, and, alongside that this set of absences that are all connected with the comic book medium itself.

UNBREAKABLE AND THE LIMITS OF TRANSGRESSION

—ALDO J. REGALADO

In the year 2000, filmmaker M. Night Shyamalan followed up his highly acclaimed and commercially successful *The Sixth Sense* with *Unbreakable*, a misleadingly marketed film that presented unsuspecting American moviegoers with a story about comic books and superheroes. In this story, the seemingly ordinary and unfulfilled central character (David Dunne, played by Bruce Willis) gradually comes to believe that he is in fact a superhero. His conviction is simultaneously triggered by a horrific train accident and the insistence of another character (Elijah Price, played by Samuel L. Jackson), who, as it turns out, has purposefully arranged the accident—and others—in attempting to uncover a real-world manifestation of superhero fiction. Although in one sense *Unbreakable* boils down to a typical superhero tale, Shyamalan tells this story in an atypical fashion, largely stripping the genre of spandex, capes, death rays, over-the-top action scenes, and the rest of its more flamboyant conventions. Focusing instead on psychologically realistic issues related to marriage, work, childrearing, illness, racism, and social identity, Shyamalan challenges his audience to take superhero fiction seriously.

Although by no means a failure, mixed reviews and relatively modest box office returns indicate that audiences found Shyamalan's treatment only partially convincing. Musing on the fact that *Unbreakable* "grossed less than a third of *The Sixth Sense*'s take," Shyamalan notes that the film seemed to "split" audiences into two camps, one that considers *Unbreak-able* his best film, and another that wonders "what happened to him?" (Shyamalan, "Question"; Shyamalan, "Chair"; Shyamalan, "Vision"). Al-though Shyamalan expresses surprise and disappointment when interview-ers ask about the film's reception, perhaps no other response was possible from American moviegoers ("Question"; "Chair"; "Vision"). The film itself suggests as much. More than just a superhero origin story, *Unbreakable* is about the American public and the various ways in which it interacts with the idea of the superhero. By placing this cultural conversation about super-heroes at the center of his narrative Shyamalan deals with societal ten-sions that exist in the appreciation of superhero comic books. These ten-sions revolve around the marginal status that superheroes, comic books, and their fans hold in America. Showcasing the way in which superhero and non-superhero fans speak to one another, however, Shyamalan also re-veals how this marginality moves beyond "geek" culture to address the at-omizing dislocations of American modernity more broadly, as well as the ways in which popular culture might serve to resist the oppressive nature of modern systems. Examining *Unbreakable* with an eye towards explor-ing the nature of these comic book centered cultural conversations, there-fore, offers us a promising avenue for understanding the deeper cultural and historical meanings of the superhero in American culture.

In exploring the nature of these conversations as they appear in the film, however, one should be mindful of the fact that these conversations are rooted in actual comic book related discourse. Indeed, the critical dialogue surrounding *Unbreakable* reveals this fact and underscores the marginality of superheroes in America. This is especially evident in the negative criti-cism of the film. Many of those who disliked *Unbreakable* walked away from the film disappointed, grumbling that the plot was silly and not as plausible as that of a young boy who can see dead people. For them, super-heroes are "patently ridiculous," and notions that such fictional charac-ters possess a link to "ancient hieroglyphs" or embody a "near-Shakespear-ean encapsulation of the human condition" are "farfetched," "ponderous," "boneheaded," "fanciful" and laughable at best (Butler; Rea; Radford). One such critic complained of both *Unbreakable* and Tim Burton's 1989

Batman that "When pop culture broods, it just looks silly—it loses the immediacy, that jolt of energy, which is its only advantage over the other kind" (Mars-Jones).

Some superhero fans, along with many mainstream audience members, agreed with this comment, finding the movie dull when compared to more action-oriented superhero films. Others, however, rejected the film due to their fears that the character of Elijah vilified comic book subculture. One fan, for instance, expressed that he was "extremely worried that the general public, after watching this movie, would conclude that people who like comics all wear bright purple suits!" Recalling psychologist Frederic Wertham's 1950s anti-comics crusade, he also expressed concern over the political consequences of the film, adding, "It's *Seduction of the Innocent* all over again!!! Help!" (Boyd). Other fans voiced similar concerns in less alarmist tones, arguing that *Unbreakable* perpetuated the "masses stereotype that comics are for geeks and only contain superhero stories" (Dan). Some academics reject the film on similar grounds, arguing that the commercial linkage of sequential art to superheroes and film undermines appreciation and acceptance of the medium. Exemplifying this point of view, one scholar recently shared his "wish that movie makers would stay the hell away from comics," since "movies derived from comics" don't do "comics any good whatsoever." "I also think," he continued, "that since now movies can use CGI, there is no need for comics to have superheroes in them" (Brooks, "Re: Shyamalan").

Most superhero fans, however, seemed to enjoy the film, appreciating what they perceived as Shyamalan's attempts to ground superheroes in the real world and hence grant them legitimacy (Ramirez). One fan typically commented that *Unbreakable* was "a realistic, human approach to superheroes," that couldn't have touched him more (Gondek). Another stated that "*Donnie Darko* and *Unbreakable* are the only superhero movies that can be defined as great that aren't tacky or silly" (Andrew). Likewise, many scholars respond to their less enthusiastic peers by citing the ways in which *Unbreakable* engages various important cultural and structural issues, including Shyamalan's exploration of the myth of the hero, his construction of the nemesis, and his attempts to translate the conventions of sequential art onto film (Robbins; Pellitteri; Tondro).

Whatever his intentions were, Shyamalan tapped into this rich cultural debate about comic books, making it central to his narrative. Like audience members, the characters in the film all engage superhero comics from various critical perspectives. By dismissing, embracing, appropriating, or aggressively rejecting the concept of the superhero, the characters in *Unbreakable* find meaning for themselves and uncover roads for navigating the world around them, articulating deeply held notions steeped in the realities of race, class, and gender in modern (or postmodern) America along the way. Considered in this fashion, the previously described critical responses to the film, along with the cultural politics they embody, become the subject, rather than merely the product, of the movie. Indeed, by artistically recreating cultural conversations about superheroes and then placing these conversations at the center of his story without privileging one over the other, Shyamalan perhaps unwittingly employed what Mikhail Bakhtin referred to as the dialogic imagination. Specifically, Shyamalan seems to accept the notion that social and cultural meaning is not discovered in isolation, but rather depends on the interaction between speech and response. The truth about superheroes in both the real world and in *Unbreakable*, for instance, is not objectively evident or individually discerned, but rather depends upon and emerges from the interaction of multiple perspectives and the cultural or even psychological responses these interactions elicit. Furthermore, Bakhtin posits that words and images capture and preserve the voices of those who shaped their meanings, transmitting them through space and time to new audiences who continue the cultural conversation (*Dialogic Imagination*; *Rabelais and His World*). As an active listener of these cultural conversations as they pertain to superhero comic books, Shyamalan successfully uncovered the historical forces that led to their creation, forces dealing with the potentially oppressive realities of modern systems and with the human need to finds strategies for transgressing these realities in attempts to reaffirm human existence. Analyzing *Unbreakable*, therefore, provides us with an opportunity to examine the origins and continued cultural significance of superheroes, as well as the broader dynamics of American popular culture.

If one accepts Bakhtin's notion of words and images preserving historical voices, then understanding *Unbreakable* benefits from examining the historical meanings of superhero fiction that served as Shyamalan's inspiration for the film. No character is more evocative of those meanings and hence more worthy of study than Jerry Siegel and Joe Shuster's Superman. Indeed, not only did Superman propel the comic book industry to new heights of market success when DC Comics published his first adventure in 1938, but he also established the superhero genre, setting examples and themes that creators aped and continue to ape in comics, radio, advertising, television, and film. Superman, therefore, embodies the essence of superhero fiction, and Shyamalan mined it in his own unique exploration of the genre and the society from which it sprung.

Superman, however, seems somewhat at odds with the world and characters that Shyamalan presents in *Unbreakable*. Despite his superpowers Shyamalan's superhero, David Dunne, is firmly chained by daily routines, systems, and societal expectations that govern his choices and render his life unsatisfying. Superman is, by contrast, otherworldly. Born on the planet Krypton, his parents rocketed him to Earth in a spacecraft, saving him from the planetary disaster that left him both an orphan and his home world's last surviving son. Possessed of an "advanced physical structure" he manifested super powers as a child, and upon reaching maturity he discovered that "he could easily leap one eight of a mile; hurdle a twenty-story building . . . raise tremendous weights . . . run faster than an express train . . . and that nothing less than a bursting shell could penetrate his skin" (Siegel and Shuster, *Archives* 1). Thus prepared, he made the easy decision to "turn his titanic strength into channels that would benefit mankind" (Siegel and Shuster, *Archives* 1). Calling himself Superman he became the "champion of the oppressed, the physical marvel who had sworn to devote his existence to helping those in need!" (Siegel and Shuster, *Archives* 1). Triumphal, ebullient, optimistic, and self-assured, the brightly clad caped crusader seems to share little with Shyamalan's sullen, despairing Dunne, yet Shyamalan imagined Dunne by tapping into the deep-seeded social and historical meanings of superhero fiction, thus creating a character that illuminates the darker, anxious realities that gave impetus to Superman and the countless superheroes inspired by his market success.

With regards to the superhero, these darker realities date back to the Great Depression of the 1930s, when markets crashed and misery reigned. Initially it seemed that the cold financial realities of the business world mattered more than human suffering. State and federal governments, following the example and policy set by President Herbert Hoover's administration, failed to curb human suffering, believing that business should regulate itself, and that people had a moral responsibility to lift themselves up from economic ruin through character, pluck, and determination (Gartner 290). As documented in Studs Terkel's *Hard Times* and elsewhere, many felt trapped in a world beyond their control and searched frantically for ways of breaking the chains of their despair.

Such was the case for Superman creators Jerry Siegel and Joe Shuster, whose hometown of Cleveland, Ohio, suffered major losses in business and industry even before the stock market crash of 1929. By 1931 Cleveland's unemployment rate rose to 35.1 percent, and the social framework of the city collapsed into chaos (Gartner 290). As Jews living in an ethnically segregated neighborhood with less access to already limited relief monies, Siegel and Shuster, along with the rest of their community, suffered the privations of the Great Depression even more intensely (Gartner 290—93). So it was that Jerry Siegel and Joe Shuster experienced a world where breadlines, homelessness, violence, political upheaval, hopelessness, and despair were commonplace, and where their own possibilities for partaking in the "American Dream" were curtailed by both ethnic prejudice and the systemic limitations of an apparently failing capitalism. Creatively responding to their condition, Siegel and Shuster created the first incarnation of the Man of Steel—one with lineaments unfamiliar to most casual readers of the now iconic character. Glossed over by most fan historians, this version of the character is nevertheless vitally important to understanding the cultural and social roots of the superhero, capturing as it does the voices of Jerry Siegel and Joe Shuster before they were reshaped by the dictates of the marketplace.

Written by Siegel and illustrated by Shuster, this version of Superman appeared in "Reign of the Super-Man," a piece of short fiction produced in January of 1933 for Siegel's self-published fanzine, *Science Fiction*.[1] The story's first line grounds the tale in its Great Depression roots. "The bread-line," it begins, "Its row of downcast, disillusioned men; unlucky creatures who have found that life holds nothing but bitterness for them. The bread-line! Last resort of the starving vagrant" (Shuster, "Reign"

1). Here, among this row of "wretched unfortunates" we meet Bill Dunn, the "raggedly-dressed person" that becomes the story's Super-Man (Shuster, "Reign" 1).

Dunn, however, does not possess the wherewithal to master his environment or his life. Instead, he is propelled into his super-activity through the actions of a chemist identified only as Professor Smalley. Siegel heavy handedly establishes Smalley as a member of the wealthy elite, describing him as one "who had come of rich parents and had never been forced to face the rigors of life" (Shuster, "Reign" 1). To Smalley, as well as to more than a few policymakers insensitive to the plight of those who suffered during the Great Depression, the "miserableness" of those in the breadlines "seemed deserved," especially since "if they had the slightest ambition at all they could easily lift themselves from their terrible rut" (Shuster, "Reign" 1). Driven by a worldview that understands poverty as stemming from an innate moral inferiority, as well as by the dictates of a scientific mind that quests for power over the natural and human worlds through empirical observation and rational calculation, Smalley hatches a nefarious scheme apropos of the genre of pulp science fiction. Possessed of an unidentified meteoric substance, he designs to explore its properties by selecting a test subject from the jobless masses and then exposing this person to the strange mineral. Barely stopping to consider the crowd of potential victims, Smalley randomly selects Bill Dunn.

Initially suspicious, Bill Dunn's hunger and despair win over and he accepts Smalley's vaguely articulated business proposal. Later, while supping at the Professor's home, he unknowingly ingests the powdered fragments of Smalley's meteoric ore. Although initially collapsing from its effects, Dunn manages to escape his captor's clutches and disappears into the city. A short while later, he finds himself possessed of both a sharpened mind and the preternatural ability to hear thoughts. Using his newfound powers, he penetrates the hidden life of the city and deciphers its secrets. Prying into the private dramas of those around him, he experiences the fear, hatred, anger, and cruelty of his fellow man. More importantly, he comes to understand how these forces are arrayed against him, and this knowledge allows him to navigate around the otherwise insurmountable systems of modern life. Further developing the abilities of mind control and future sight, the once vagrant Bill Dunn appropriates the power once possessed by the wealthy Smalley, and employs it to penetrate and survive in the modern urban city.

Although Siegel and Shuster seem to delight in exploring the transgressive possibilities of Dunn's newfound abilities, this first incarnation Super-Man was not a superhero. Overcome by a sense of class hatred fueled by envy and a desire for power, Dunn uses his powers for personal and material gain, cheating at the racetrack, investing in the stock market, and coercing wealthy individuals to sign over their money to him (Shuster, "Reign" 3—4).

Ultimately, Dunn's lust for wealth and power escalates to the point where he dreams of global and even cosmic domination. After returning to and killing Smalley, who planned on becoming a second Super-Man by ingesting what remained of the meteoric substance, Dunn turns his attentions to the International Conciliatory Council, a fictional gathering of all the world's nations that had resulted in peace accords promising to join all races into "one tremendous, everlasting fraternity" (Shuster, "Reign" 8). Using his vast mental powers, Dunn disrupts this peace accord by projecting feelings of intense hatred into the minds of the diplomats in attendance. Then, summoning a newspaper reporter to bear witness to the final stages of his plot, he prepares to "send the armies of the world to total annihilation against each other" (Shuster, "Reign" 9). However, before he can do so, Dunn receives a vision of his immediate future. He sees himself sleeping in the park once more, the effects of the meteor fragments having worn off. Dejected and disillusioned, he turns to the captive reporter, sharing his final regrets in the following passage. " 'I see, now, how wrong I was. If I had worked for the good of humanity, my name would have gone down in history with a blessing—instead of a curse.' . . . 'In fifteen minutes you will be automatically released and I—' he grinned wryly, 'I shall be— back in the bread-line!' " (Shuster, "Reign" 9).

By thus developing the character of Bill Dunn, Siegel and Shuster revealed their middle-class sensibilities. While they clearly sympathized with the plight of those abandoned and preyed upon by the immorality of "laissez-faire" capitalism, they also worried about the more drastic alternatives that manifested in the class struggles of the late 1920s and early 1930s. Caught between the vested political and economic power of American big business on one side, and the potential for revolutionary politics championed by communists, socialists, and millions of increasingly disaffected Americans on the other, Siegel and Shuster took a middle ground, warning that power corrupts, regardless of the victor, and hinting at the catastrophic social implications of continued class conflict. Despite their vague musings on the desirability of peace between nations and races and their more emphatic acknowledgement of the social inequities inherent in modern urban systems, Siegel and Shuster refrain from offering concrete solutions to the problems of the modern world. Instead, the story seems paralyzed, ill at ease with self-serving ambition and the privations caused by established power, and yet equally uncomfortable with the notion of dismantling established social systems and surrendering power to an angry working class. These were logical sensibilities for two young men who, despite the hardships of the Great Depression, maintained optimistic hopes of successfully engaging American professional life as entrepreneurs.

This youthful optimism, combined with an innate understanding of what was marketable in America, led Siegel and Shuster to willfully recast the Super-Man with the hopes that he might succeed in the then nascent and somewhat disreputable comic book industry. Reminiscing about their decision to refashion their protagonist, Siegel commented: "Obviously, having him a hero would be infinitely more commercial than having him a villain. I understand that the comic strip Dr. Fu Manchu ran into all sorts of difficulties because the main character was a villain. And with the example before us of Tarzan and other action heroes of fiction who were very successful, mainly because people admired them and looked up to them, it seemed the sensible thing to do to make The Superman a hero" (Siegel, Shuster, and Siegel, "Of Superman and Kids").

And so it was that Siegel and Shuster obscured the more despairing motivations behind their character, choosing instead to craft a more ebullient figure who affirmed the possibility that the American Dream could somehow be maintained, a character who would tweak the inequities of an inhumane system, ensuring that it worked for the people, rather than against them. Leaping over menacing skylines, tearing through barriers, and ignoring police, politicians, and other representatives of official authority, Superman redistributed wealth, reformed city and federal governments, effected urban reform, protected small businesses, and otherwise promoted a more equitable America.

Superman also transgressed traditional definitions of race in America, thus helping Siegel and Shuster overcome the psychologically limiting realities they faced as Jews. Although the nature of this transgression might not seem evident to twenty-first-century Americans who perceive whiteness as a relatively broad category that includes a diversity of ethnic and national groups, nineteenth- and early-twentieth-century notions of race in America were more rigid and hinged on Anglo-Saxon genetic purity. Non-Anglo-Saxons were marginalized regardless of their skin color. This was true even in popular heroic fiction, where explicitly Anglo-Saxon heroes, like Edgar Rice Burroughs's Tarzan, served as the preeminent heroic paradigms for generations of Americans. Siegel and Shuster's Superman is, by contrast, a culturally white hero that is not genetically Anglo-Saxon. Hence, Superman fictively and subtly broadened definitions of American whiteness, basing them more on color than on blood and suggesting that the foreign born could become white and hence be included in the promise of America (Regalado 1–15). Clad in patriotic colors, this metaphor for the New Immigrant dismissed the limitations of modern America, joyfully affirming for his readers that the nation offered boundless possibilities rather than hopelessness, that the essence of American liberal capitalism was good and worth fighting for.

And yet the social alienation that originally produced Superman and launched the genre of superhero fiction never truly disappeared, a fact that accounts, perhaps, for the continued resonance of the superhero in American culture. The privations of the Great Depression did give way to suburban affluence in the years after World War II, but the move to suburbia resulted in abandoned city centers throughout the nation, leaving nonwhite communities to fend for themselves against rising levels of unemployment and poverty. Furthermore, as Elaine Tyler May argues in *Homeward Bound: American Families in the Cold War Era*, suburbanites had to face the realities of Cold War America, with its own unique ways of trapping individuals into rigid patterns and systems of behavior. Linked concerns over nuclear annihilation and domestic subversion by Soviet inspired "deviants" led to an increasingly conformist culture that stymied personal expression by reifying the nuclear family, narrowing the definition of gender roles, and upholding the role of government and business over that of the individual. Confronted with these cultural imperatives Americans were expected to conform or face the consequences.

Those consequences proved harsh for Siegel and Shuster. Upon returning from serving his country in World War II, Jerry Siegel found that DC Comics had, in his estimation, all but hijacked Superman as well as several other characters and concepts. Joined by a reluctant Shuster, whose deteriorating eyesight was making it increasingly difficult for him to make a living as an artist, Siegel sued DC Comics for control over the character. Legally and financially outgunned by the company, Siegel and Shuster lost their court battle, which meant that they would never capitalize on the millions of dollars generated by their creation and that they would eventually fade into obscurity. Although Superman embodied his creators' desire to transform (or perhaps deny) the uncaring and dehumanizing aspects of capitalistic business and finance, the realities of these systems ultimately caught up with them and destroyed their careers. Both would have died as penniless nonentities if not for the efforts of fellow creators and fans who organized more than thirty years later, pressuring DC Comics to grant them recognition and a modest stipend to carry them through their final years.

Most readers of superhero comic books, however, experienced the dislocations of American modernity more subtly that Siegel and Shuster. Mostly suburban male youths, these readers felt stifled by the conformity of Cold War America. Many of them found the unwavering insistence on productivity and professionalism morally and spiritually unsatisfying, the rigidity of the nuclear family oppressive, the high culture of educational institutions stagnant, and much of the mass culture bombarding them through television mind-numbing. Superhero fanzine writers from the period evidence this fact, often railing against what they refer to as the "normal, typical, All-American moron mentality" and express concerns about a "tired, weary world" of grown-ups, rife with "ulcer-ridden businessmen" and terrifying news about "war casualties, or the testing of more powerful annihilation weapons" (Gambaccini "Listen"; Kyle; Decklinger). One fan articulated these sentiments most strikingly when he wrote that his "know-it-all" parents, "created a world" for him to "revolt against" (Glassman). Consequently, fans such as these searched the world around them for alternate avenues for self-expression and they found one through comics. More accurately, they used superhero comic books as a vehicle for reinventing both community and the self.

Comic book fandom stands as the most extreme expression of these acts of reinvention. Starting in the mid-1960s readers of superhero comic books began talking with one another through the letter columns that appeared as regular features of their favorite superhero magazines, and since comic book publishers included return addresses for their respondents, many fans began corresponding directly with one another. These initially unorganized relationships rapidly grew into full-blown fan communities. These fan communities pulled together largely male audiences of varying ages without regard for the physical and cultural boundaries of the suburban family. Collectively, these fans produced a great deal of material, including artwork, fiction, historical articles, and biography, most of which appeared in self-published fanzines, which were then circulated to the community more broadly. They created officer-led fan associations, staged their own conventions, instituted their own awards ceremonies, and otherwise honed their professional, creative, and interpersonal skills. Comic book fans, therefore, had a work ethic, but organized as they were around the flamboyant, fantastic, and nonsensical characters appearing in so-called "four-color" comics, their productive activities presented playful challenges to an official culture that looked askew at both homosocial interaction and unproductive leisure activity. Even Frederic Wertham, the self-proclaimed leader of the 1950s anti-comics crusade, observed in his *The World of Fanzines: A Special Forum of Communication* that fanzines were "a vivid and vital" medium for the "interchange of thoughts and opinions" and that they showed "a combination of independence and responsibility not easily found elsewhere in our culture." Fanzines, he continued, carried the potential to counter "the noise and haste" of modern society, which had the "tendency" to "reduce people to statistics," and which made "for the slipshod, the shallow and the mechanical."

The triumph of fandom over America's official culture, however, was about as partial as Superman's victory over the oppressive power of modern systems. Despite their sometimes defiant tone, fan publications also reveal the marginality and loneliness that often results from the outright rejection of mainstream values. Aware that most Americans were either condescending or "just plain mean" when it came to characterizing fandom, many fans began to internalize mainstream perceptions (Gambaccini "Listen"). One fanzine writer felt the need to assert that while he collected comic books, he still had a "regular life," which included "golf, a genuine-type Italian-grandmother and a love for pizza, lasagna, and spaghetti," as well as riding his bicycle, reading respectable literature, and listening to "music, violin concertos, piano, Ferrante, Teicher, Roy Orbison, Peter-Paul-and-Mary, Leonard Bernstein, the Beatles, and the Staples High School Choir" (Gambaccini "Teenage"). Another fan admitted to his fellows his belief that comics are "childish insults to the intelligence," the majority of which are "written for a mental age of fourteen and under," while another stated that "the main thing wrong with comics is that they are a mass media," and hence "subject to the same faults that plague television, radio, movies, 'popular' books, and 'popular music.'" That is, "they do not call upon the reader/listener/viewer's intelligence," but rather on a "person's ability to sit in front of the television watching 'Gilligan's Island'" (Kuhfeld; Weingroff). However, rather than abandon fandom and the genre that spawned it, most of these fans remained participants, thus contending with the lonely reality that their pastime, and to some extent their values and their sense of self, were somehow marginal and shameful as far as mainstream America was concerned.

Most superhero movies ignore these fundamental elements of loneliness and despair, which serve as important cornerstones for both the superhero genre and superhero fandom. Instead, their makers understandably choose to perpetuate the escapist fantasies and optimistic mythologies of American heroic individualism, which continue to generate millions for the business interests traditionally involved in producing superhero fiction. M. Night Shyamalan, however, put the more despairing undercurrents of fandom and superhero fiction at the center of *Unbreakable*, which becomes evident upon considering the similarities between Shyamalan's film and the Shuster and Siegel's original "Reign of the Super-Man."

Although Shyamalan has never, to my knowledge, specifically cited "Reign of the Super-Man" as a source, the parallels are striking enough to suggest that he read and was directly inspired by the short story. Most of the similarities lie in the general lineaments of Shyamalan's main characters, protagonist David Dunne and antagonist Elijah Price, as well as in the general tone of the movie. David Dunne, of course, carries a surname strikingly close to that of Siegel's Bill Dunn. He also bears a striking physical resemblance to Siegel's character, as Bruce Willis's shaved pate and shambling demeanor in the movie compare pretty closely to the more serene portrayals of Bill Dunn that Shuster provided for Siegel's original narrative. Mostly, however, David Dunne is, like his 1930s counterpart, trapped by modern systems that keep him from achieving personal spiritual fulfillment.

These systems are, however, different for David Dunne than they are for Bill Dunn. Whereas Bill Dunn is trapped by the privations caused by capitalism in the throes of possible collapse, David Dunne is trapped by the realities of a stable modern capitalism, with social mores firmly locked in place. In this sense, David Dunne's angst is far more akin to the angst faced by the first generation of organized comic book fans than by the first generation of comic book creators. Indeed, David Dunn is doing everything that baby boomers were told to do in order to secure happiness for themselves and their families. A hard worker, David dutifully engages his 9-to-5 job as a security officer at a local sports stadium in an attempt to provide for his wife and child. Hardly a maverick, he observes the rules of the workplace and of the home, suppressing any acts that might transgress social or domestic norms. For David, this suppression appears to be highly gendered, manifesting as a crisis in masculinity.

This is most evident through his relationship with his wife, Audrey, and his son, Joseph. Audrey, a physical therapist by profession, presents a consistent indictment against aggressive, violent, and competitive acts, including sports, schoolyard fights, and other activities that many would consider typical of masculine behavior. She reveals as much while serving as Elijah Price's physical therapist. "My husband was a star athlete in college," she tells the antagonist. "Our car flipped on an icy road, and we were both injured, and he couldn't play football anymore. If that hadn't happened," she continues: "we wouldn't have been together. I couldn't spend my life with someone who played football, it's pretty much that simple. I don't hate the game. I admire the amount of skill it involved and, like everyone else, I was in awe of the way he played it, but football in many ways is the opposite of what I do. You're rewarded the more you punish your opponent, it's too much about violence, and I don't want violence in my life."

David's relationship with Audrey, therefore, is based on David's apparent inability to perform the type of masculine activity that is typically celebrated in American culture. Furthermore, Audrey maintains a vigilant eye on the ways in which this violent culture might intrude on her son's life. She chastises David when Joseph, following his father's advice, physically confronts bullies at school. She frowns upon her son playing sports with his friends, and she adamantly forbids any further contact between her son and Elijah Price when her son starts taking seriously the latter's talk of his father being a real-world manifestation of comic book superheroes. The fact that Joseph desperately yearns for his father to fulfill societal definitions of heroic masculinity makes matters worse, and seems to add strain to the stability of the Dunne family. Indeed, when we first meet them Audrey and David are on the verge of divorce.

The system that confines David Dunne, however, is far broader than marriage or the traditional family. Indeed, towards the end of the film it is revealed through a flashback that due to his super powers David is more than capable of pursuing his former career as a football star. Although he and Audrey did suffer a car accident before their marriage, David emerged from the wreckage unscathed. Rather than suffering a life-altering injury he chose to feign one as a means of building a new life with Audrey. We could explain this decision away as one motivated by "true love," but such a clichéd answer does not play well when dealing with Shyamalan's subtle, nuanced, and well-conceived narratives. If such was the case, David could have easily reaffirmed his natural talents once his relationship with Audrey began to wear thin.

A more plausible explanation is that David felt trapped even before he met Audrey. Although highly successful, he too felt unfulfilled by the competitive lifestyle of professional sports. He remains true to this throughout the movie. When his son insists that David could "lick" an up and coming football player who happens to be tossing the ball around with the neighborhood kids, David appears genuinely uninterested. Entering into a relationship with Audrey, therefore, was a willful turning away from the values of competitive aggression celebrated by professional sports. Given his talents and the realities of the sports industry in America, David's rejection of professional sports is also a rejection of great wealth, fame, and material success. By rejecting sports, therefore, David turns away from the type of success valued in America's capitalist consumer culture, choosing instead to live a simpler life, with a spouse who shares values similar to his own. More comfortable with protecting than punishing his neighbor, he enters into his modest career as a security guard.

Denying his natural talents, however, is not at all satisfying for David, and we meet him at the beginning of the movie as a lost soul. In the moments before the train accident that reveals his powers of invulnerability, we find out that he is searching for a new job away from Philadelphia, and that he is willing to consider marital infidelity. As directed by Shyamalan and acted by Bruce Willis, however, all of these options are contemplated with a quiet desperation that seems to rule out self-fulfillment of any sort. Like Bill Dunn, therefore, David Dunne is first seen by the audience stumbling through life, trying to escape the social and cultural forces that bind him, blindly searching for viable avenues towards self-fulfillment.

Whereas Bill Dunn finds his answers through the actions of the unscrupulous Professor Smalley, David Dunne is shepherded towards his answer by the equally unscrupulous, though far more thoughtfully developed, Elijah Price. Like Smalley, Elijah purports to be a man of science, but while Smalley is a physical scientist, Elijah claims to be a social scientist, albeit an unorthodox one. Specifically, Elijah is a successful collector of comic book art, who owns a gallery in the city where David lives. For Elijah, however, superhero comic books are far more than a hobby, or even an art form. Instead, he believes, that superhero comic books are "a last link to an ancient way of passing on history. The Egyptians drew on walls. Countries all over the world still pass on knowledge through pictorial forms. I believe comics are a form of history that someone, somewhere felt, or experienced. Then of course those experiences and that history got chewed up by the commercial machine, got jazzed up, made titillating, cartooned for the sale rack."

Superhero comic books for Elijah, therefore, are windows pointing towards historical wisdom and forgotten truths, and like Smalley he is ruthless in his search for a real world super-man. Reasoning that such a being would be blessed with physical invulnerability, he arranges for a series of catastrophic "accidents" resulting in the deaths of hundreds, hoping to eventually find that one survivor that would prove his theories correct. Once he finds this being in David, he manipulates him into fulfilling the role of the comic book hero.

Elijah, however, is not driven by mere scientific curiosity. Like Professor Smalley, his passion is fueled by a very personal need, albeit a more psychologically nuanced one. Whereas Smalley craves absolute power and world domination, Elijah's passion seems fueled by a desperate need to establish legitimacy for the art form that helped him overcome his prodigious physical and social handicaps. Although Shyamalan never dwells overtly on Elijah's ethnicity, the fact that he is an African American of modest urban origins serves to underscore Elijah's marginal status. More importantly, however, Elijah suffers from osteogenesis imperfecta, a genetic condition that renders his bones painfully fragile and subject to fracture at the slightest jostle or bump. As such, Elijah spent his early years terrified of the outside world, and unwilling to leave the confines of his home. His mother, however, helps him to overcome his fear by leaving a brightly gift-wrapped box on a park bench across the street from their apartment. Drawn to the gift, Elijah makes his way to the package and opens it to find a superhero comic book waiting for him. Noting his pleasure and wonderment, his mother promises him a continual supply of comics as long as he continues to venture outside the home. And so it is that Elijah finds the courage to survive, a marginal individual turning to a marginal subculture as a means of navigating the contours of the world he faces.

In many ways it is Elijah's particular engagement with superhero comic books, rather than the superhero story itself, that is the subject of *Unbreakable*. If "Reign of the Super-Man" imbues a mysterious meteoric substance with the potential to grant individuals with power enough to transgress oppressive systems and ideologies, *Unbreakable* does the same with comic books. True, David Dunne's superpowers exist independently from Elijah's comic books. In addition to physical invulnerability and an undetermined measure of enhanced physical strength, David is possessed of an extrasensory perception that allows him to sense acts of evil, both past and present, upon touching a guilty individual. Despite possessing these powers, however, David is paralyzed about what to do with them, and comics provide him with a satisfying framework for focusing his talents and needs into action. Guided by Elijah's insanity, he dons the guise of a costumed superhero and steps outside the confines of the systems and expectations that so carefully order his life, saving two children from the clutches of a serial murderer who has already killed the children's parents. By doing so, David employs his masculine prowess towards selfless ends, driven by compassion and a desire to help and protect, rather than by competitive aggression. Only by doing so does David find deeper spiritual fulfillment, a fact demonstrated in the last scene with the Dunne family, which shows them happier and their relationships on the mend.

It should be noted, however, that David's choice to become a real world manifestation of the superhero does not prove Elijah right in any objective sense. Beyond existing, David's powers are never convincingly tied to any historical manifestation of the superhero by any empirical evidence. Rather, Elijah seems to tailor his theories to the "reality" of David's powers in order to make them work. When David finds that he is susceptible to drowning, for instance, Elijah deftly employs the genre convention of a Kryptonite susceptibility or an Achilles Heel to explain away this wrinkle in his theory. Furthermore, David explores other plausible resources that might have explained or focused his abilities just as easily. One such resource appears in a scene not shown in theaters, but included in the film's DVD release. In this scene, David turns to a priest, searching for a divine explanation for the miracle of his surviving the train wreck. Overcome with his own crisis in faith, however, the priest responds negatively, thus shutting off the possibility of David finding direction through the more mainstream avenue of religion. Left without further recourse, David ultimately accepts the explanation offered by Elijah, and patterns himself accordingly.

Unbreakable, therefore, argues that superhero comic books (and, by implication, mass media more broadly) are cultural productions that do more than merely entertain audiences or reflect cultural realities. Instead, they are dynamic forms of cultural expression that individuals actively employ to shape and give meaning to individual as well as social existence. Despite their presence on the "sales rack" they can serve the function of a temple, as they do for ultimate fans like Elijah. Their rendition of masculinity can similarly serve to inspire lost souls such as David, who searches for direction and transgression, or Joseph, who yearns for a male role model. Furthermore, the film suggests that the work performed by comics is as varied as the truths that individuals imbue them with.

One critical mode evidenced by several of the characters in the film can be characterized by an attitude of dismissal, exemplified in the character of a nameless customer, who attempts to purchase an original piece of artwork from Elijah's gallery. After patiently listening with passive disinterest to one of Elijah's lectures on the aesthetics of superhero comics, the customer unintentionally offends Elijah by revealing that he hopes to make a gift of the masterpiece to his four-year-old son. By relegating superheroes to the realm of mere children's fiction, he allows them to fly under his critical radar and hence fails to even consider that they might be culturally and socially significant. By reducing Elijah's treasure to the level of crass commercialism, the nameless customer also embodies the worldview that celebrates ownership and material possession over deeper spiritual significance.

If the unnamed customer is critically dismissive of superhero fiction, there is evidence to suggest that Audrey might bear the genre some measure of active hostility. Although she never addresses the issue directly and allows her son to play with superhero action figures, her feelings about violence are probably strong enough that she would reject superhero comics were she to give them a moment of serious thought. This inference about her probable inability to accept the superhero in concept is further reinforced by David's decision to keep his heroic deeds a secret from her, despite the renewed intimacy of their relationship.

Shyamalan, therefore, allows that comic books legitimately serve all of the above functions. As cartoons, they serve as juvenile fiction, as collectibles; they enable conspicuous consumption. As violent adventure stories, they make legitimate targets for all who reject such modes of behavior. Overwhelmingly, however, Shyamalan is concerned with the ways in which comic books enable individuals who desire to use them as a means of transgressing the confining, oppressive, and atomizing aspects of modern American society. Comic books in *Unbreakable*, therefore, emerge as cultural tools that present audiences with new alternatives, allowing them to shape and reshape otherwise unsatisfying realities. In short, comic books are presented as one of many possible sets of building blocks for constructing or reconstructing identity.

Shyamalan, however, complicates his pro-comic-book argument in the last scene of *Unbreakable*, when the now mended and purposeful David Dunne shakes Elijah Price's hand, thus making physical contact with him for the first time in the film. Triggering David Dunne's extrasensory powers, this act reveals Elijah's insane machinations and true motivations to both David and the movie audience. Like David, Elijah too is questing for his own place in the world, but the superhero comic books that shape his worldview also tell him that he is ill suited to fulfill the role of superhero. With a skeletal structure as fragile as David's is invulnerable, Elijah fails to match up to the masculine physicality celebrated on the four-color page. It stands to reason, therefore, that Elijah is the natural opposite of the superhero—the supervillain. Finding David, therefore, is an act of rounding out his own identity and finding his place in the world.

This last scene also asks us to consider other ways in which Elijah might feel marginalized by superhero fiction. Whether by accident or by design, Shyamalan's casting African American Samuel L. Jackson as Elijah Price forces us to reflect on the role that race might play in the film, in real-world superhero fiction, in the minds of audiences, and in society more broadly. Indeed, when creating the optimistic and exuberant character of Superman, Siegel and Shuster were addressing the problems of race in America. Faced with the realities of anti-Semitism, they created a new type of superhero— a non-Anglo-Saxon immigrant that transgressed the strict racial classifications of late-nineteenth- and early-twentieth-century America to create a more inclusive definition of whiteness based more strictly on phenotype and allegiance to country, and less on biological or genetic purity. This new white hero, however, still excluded Asians, Native Americans, and African Americans, who were phenotypically precluded from passing for white, and were often rendered as fiendishly monstrous villains by early comic book artists.

While Shyamalan presents superhero fiction as a potential vehicle for social transgression, however, he does not present it as an all-terrain vehicle, capable of breaking all boundaries. Comic books themselves are molded and shaped by the systems that produce them, in this case racially constructed notions of American masculinity. The white heroes on the comic book page offer the physically able and Caucasian David Dunn an avenue for channeling his own life in constructive ways. While they also channel Elijah Price's, they do so by telling him that he is marginal. Black, disabled, fragile, intellectual, he is relegated to the level of the "monstrous," the "evil," and the "Other." For all their transgressive potential, therefore, comic books in *Unbreakable* perpetuate the social, cultural, and psychological chains of race and gender inequities in America.

Given its intricacies and nuances Shyamalan's *Unbreakable* is perhaps the most clever and artful treatment of superheroes and comic books. Using the medium of film, Shyamalan is able to distance the iconic figure of the superhero from the more familiar environs of the comic book page, and through this distance explore and rediscover the essence of anxiety and despair for modern systems that created both the superhero and the fan culture that evolved around it. His filmic treatment simultaneously places the superhero in both the realms of fantasy and the real world, examining the connections between the two and the utility of fiction to construct identity, to order social and cultural life, and to navigate modernity. Perhaps more significantly, however, he leaves us with questions regarding the possibilities and limitations of transgression through popular culture. While entertaining the notion that despairing souls might always find unlikely avenues towards self-fulfillment, the film's last moments poignantly deem the cultural and social systems that limit our potential for transgression as truly unbreakable.

TEEN TRAJECTORIES IN
SPIDER-MAN AND *GHOST WORLD*

— MARTIN FLANAGAN

The core ideological business of the teen "coming of age" narrative is to present spectators with a fiction that hinges on a promise of transformation, the move from adolescent "abjection" to adult "agency," as John Stephens puts it (124). Reflecting views that maturity is "first and foremost a social phenomenon and only secondarily a biological one" (Hine 46), genres and subgenres representing or aimed at teen audiences are implicated in this social construction of maturity and the passage into adulthood. Many genres and texts play their part in the process by which young consumers are placed "within a limited range of options which have already been incorporated into the cultural hegemony" (Brooks 2). Yet, many contemporary teen texts formally incorporate discourses of critical, playful contempt for this project, blurring or qualifying their own complicity in the production of "normal" adult identities and satirizing their own cooptation within dominant, corporate worldviews. This heavily ironicized and self-reflexive approach to the depiction of adolescent development seems to be disproportionately applied to the representation of teen girls, with exemplary texts including *Clueless* (Amy Heckerling, 1995), *The Opposite of Sex* (Don Roos, 1998) and *Mean Girls* (Mark S. Waters, 2004). Male adolescent trajectories tend to be approached in a more formulaic way, and are more easily resolved in the populist vein of teen movie culture that encompasses sports, college, and sex comedies such as *Varsity Blues* (Brian Robbins, 1999), *American Pie* (Paul Weitz, 1999) and *Road Trip*

(Todd Phillips, 2000). Teen horror films may represent a more radical and complex case, although it is widely recognized that the development and assertion of young female sexuality prompts societal anxiety in that particular genre (Clover; Linda Williams).

Recently, U.S. box office charts have been dominated by another subgenre that is centrally concerned with how the (usually male) adolescent ego develops into a flexible, mature, and socially viable adult identity: the superhero narrative. Following a classic arc within American culture where the attainment of agency is linked to the assumption of power, self-mastery, and the acceptance of a singular heroic destiny (most evocatively seen in the Western genre), contemporary superhero films view the process of maturation as an emotionally and physically complex and dangerous phase, yet one that must be surmounted if the heroes are to quell their own chronic doubts about their place in the world, or resolve a diffuse identity. Texts in the recent cycle of comic adaptations, including *Spider-Man* (Sam Raimi, 2002) and its sequel (2004), *X-Men* (Bryan Singer, 2000), *X2* (Singer, 2003), *Daredevil* (Mark Steven Johnson, 2003), and on television, *Smallville* (2001–), as well as the Summer 2005 features *Fantastic Four* (Tim Story, 2005) and *Batman Begins* (Chris Nolan, 2005), tend to skew towards youth in one or both of two ways: firstly, via the provision of numerous points of identification for teen viewers of both genders; and secondly, in their marketing and demographic orientation. For example, the prominent inclusion in *Daredevil* of a song by the goth rock act Evanescence, cross-marketed with the film, helped to build the career of the band in the U.K. While in the realm of comics fandom, age groups are demonstrably becoming more splintered and stratified,[1] the diverse audience sought by comic book movies would seem to stretch from the very young to the adult audiences apparently courted by Ang Lee's self-consciously arty *Hulk* (2003) and the R-rated *Punisher* (Jonathan Hensleigh, 2004). Most films in the cycle deliberately try not to exclude any sectors, if at all possible, which obviously has implications for the degree to which violence, so integral a part of the superhero world, can be graphically presented.

The narrative of growth and development embodied in the recent wave of films stands in contrast to the established adult hero archetype featured in the popular texts of the previous wave of comic adaptations— *Superman* (Richard Donner, 1978), *Batman* (Tim Burton, 1989) and ABC-TV's

Wonder Woman (1976–79)—with the new films appropriating the adolescent experience as a central symbolic motif. Even recent comic-inspired narratives that do not explicitly feature teen characters are recognizably preoccupied with issues of identity, belonging and ascension to the symbolic order or negotiation of Oedipal problems of succession, as in *Hulk*, *Daredevil*, and *Blade* (Stephen Norrington, 1998). This chapter will examine the incorporation of the teen "rite of passage" narrative in *Spider-Man*, exploring its implications for the film's overall rhetoric of power and destiny. As an instructive companion piece to this activity in the superhero subgenre I will consider the version of female adolescent passage presented in *Ghost World* (Terry Zwigoff, 2001). This film, derived from a non-superhero "underground" comic by Daniel Clowes, and relatable in cinematic style to the culturally critical, postmodern slant of independent filmmakers like David Lynch, Richard Linklater, and Todd Solondz, bridges the gap between the comic adaptation movie and the "straight" teen genre, parodying and ironically citing the clichés of both the teen film and the more general narrative of heroic destiny found in mainstream Hollywood productions and the modes of identification which they exploit. Although markedly different in terms of approach, style and subgenre (*Spider-Man* the blockbuster superhero adaptation, *Ghost World* the indie adaptation of an underground comic), the two films explored here each demonstrate the intimate connection between comic narratives and the trajectory from teenage to adulthood.

Both films privilege their heroes' nascent struggles with their own subjectivity and feature high school graduation as a key marker. Ultimately, Peter Parker (Tobey Maguire) accepts his "unique" identity and destiny and integrates into society as its servant and protector; conversely, *Ghost World*'s narrative sees Enid Coleslaw (Thora Birch) painfully recognize her own *lack* of uniqueness and choose to leave society rather than conform like her friends Seymour (Steve Buscemi) and Rebecca (Scarlett Johansson). *Spider-Man* thus appears to sincerely replay the popular comic trope of the "origin" story, while *Ghost World* indicts the coming-of-age process, as familiarly shaped by movie and comic book wisdom, as yet another form of "interpellation" within late capitalist commodity culture. Louis Althusser's concept of interpellation—the moment in which culture "hails" us and, acting on our recognition as the subject of the hailing, inserts us into its symbolic design—will be used intermittently throughout this essay in support of the notion (prevalent in *Ghost World*) that cultural choice is illusory and that processes like growing up take place within ideological bounds, despite societal attempts to camouflage them as purely spiritual or biological markers (Althusser 299–303).

This divergence (*Spider-Man* as sincere origin tale, *Ghost World* as ironic indictment of the typical routes into adulthood posited by pop culture) indicates ideological variations in the narrative and generic agendas of the two films which the following discussion will seek to bring out. However, despite emerging from different institutional backgrounds, both films operate in relation to received ideas about youth and adulthood that ultimately reinforce a familiar hierarchy of values, with teenage being associated with vulnerability and insecurity but also freedom from responsibility, and adulthood representing compromise, sacrifice of individuality, and the attainment of deadening bourgeois respectability. As a result, the way in which values of age and cultural positioning are mobilized in the films can appear problematic in relation to the distinction between projected audiences and real ones. Thus, *Spider-Man*, an early summer, PG-13 blockbuster sporting tie-ins to burger chains and a ubiquitous line of child-oriented merchandising, nevertheless references the hallowed 1960s in crucial elements like production design, and by incorporating symbols and narrative devices that have become fixed as standard images of the American adolescent experience and which transparently target their appeal beyond contemporary teens and children (for instance, Peter appears to have no interest in contemporary fashion or music; although a science geek, he is not associated with computers; and his rival for the affections of Mary Jane [Kirsten Dunst] is sports car-owning "jock" Flash Thompson [Joe Manganiello]). Such elements, coupled with the inbuilt nostalgic popularity of the character across forty years of "remediation" in various forms of text (comic, syndicated newspaper strip, Saturday morning cartoon, live-action TV show), serve to underline the film's sense of its own generational appeal, which stretches from the baby boomers (initial consumers of the early 1960s comics) onwards, through many subsequent waves of fandom. In a similarly complex and perhaps compromised way, *Ghost World* stakes a position that purports to examine the emotional turmoil of lower middle-class American females at the threshold of high school graduation no earlier than the 1990s, yet the author of the adapted comic and the director of the film are both middle-aged men who would be classically defined as part of the boomer generation, while the idiom of the text is strictly that of the postmodern arthouse movie familiar since at least the early 1980s.

The two films, then, are instructive in terms of the contributions they make to a recent stock of popular images of youth, as will be discussed later; yet they have to be understood within a cultural context where such images support an ideology of youthfulness that is a desired (and ruthlessly commodified) quality coveted by much older cultural consumers and producers. This context, indeed, is synonymous with what Thomas Frank has identified as the prevailing climate of American capitalism since the 1960s, the decade when concepts associated with youthfulness came to structure and define the lexicon of consumerism, with youth itself transforming into "an attractive consuming attitude, not an age" (118). Clearly, American movies are not exempt from such a blurring of age categories; "high concept" blockbusters like *Spider-Man*, as stated above, address diverse audiences with their "modular" aesthetic (Smith 12–13), while independent film strives to establish itself as "hip," clued-up, and irreverent by appealing to a hierarchy of taste in which its values oppose those of the blockbuster. In the complex process of what Sarah Thornton refers to as the "cultural organization of youth" (5), care must be taken that mediated versions of youth are recognized as "symbolic rather than . . . material," expressive of a "market fantasy . . . rather than accounting for the ways in which in the real world children still become adults" (Frith 382).

Initially, it will be necessary to offer some general comments about the archetype of the modern comic hero before moving on to look in detail at the protagonists of the two films, and at certain specific sequences which foreground ideas of transformation, interpellation and identity.

A traditional function of American comics has been to express childhood and teen anxieties, mirroring and processing the experiences of their adolescent readers; this was especially true of the pre-1980s superhero comics sector, which blurred the lines of address between adult and child readers far more than the sharply differentiated market of today. Commentators such as Gerard Jones argue that, in their popular cultural representations of teen traumas and identity issues, comics essay a social function that works against conservative governmental and educational critiques of their pernicious influence (Jones *passim*). This function has tended to crystalize around issues of identification, leading to the development of heroes like Bucky (young partner to Captain America) and Robin in the 1940s and, later, the introduction of the likes of Johnny Storm and Iceman to the Marvel universe. These teen characters would frequently be paired up with older mentor figures (Captain America, Batman, Reed Richards, Professor X); others like Spider-Man would be forever defined in later life by the truncation or disturbance of their Oedipal narratives.

Superheroes, whether in comics or movies, derive much of their power from the sense of archetypicality that they project. Although there is undoubtedly a degree of variation within the classic DC/Marvel postwar superhero, the archetype tends to split into two fairly distinct subtypes. The first is the all-powerful, omnipresent, invulnerable and often emotionally imperturbable hero (Superman is the iconic figure here, with other examples including Marvel's Thor, Silver Surfer, and The Vision). Like Superman, orphan of Krypton, such heroes may harbor deep emotional scars, but refuse to indulge their own losses so that they may better function as instruments of a natural, unquestionable justice. For these heroes, secret identities are either magically secure (Superman) or unnecessary (Silver Surfer, the latter day version of Thor); with affairs concerning identity rarely at issue, their stories do not particularly foreground elements of melodrama or soap opera.

Conversely, tales featuring the second category of hero are often aligned with those subgenres. This brand of hero, crystalized in Stan Lee's 1960s Marvel work (Spider-Man, Hulk, X-Men, the Thing) but indisputably foreshadowed decades earlier in Bob Kane's Batman, tends to feature character traits of self-doubt, self-destructiveness, awareness of their own "dark side," and (in the Marvel characters especially) a profound sense of irony regarding their own powers, or the perception of those gifts as a curse or unbearable responsibility. Their adventures usually transpire in more "realistic" and often squalid surroundings (Gotham City, Hell's Kitchen) and are interlaced with the hero's domestic and emotional struggles with family, relationships, secret identities, and money. They may shade towards vigilantism and thus sometimes find themselves ambiguously positioned with regard to the law (Punisher, Batman) or even unjustly pursued by the police (Spider-Man). Even more frequently, such characters' motivations for donning their masked personas (or, in the case of the Hulk, their expressions of internal rage) stem from traumatic episodes in their pasts: the deaths of loved ones, whether parents (Daredevil, Batman, Ang Lee's version of the Hulk) or parent surrogates (Spider-Man) figure regularly. This strand of flawed, introspective, and sometimes outright antisocial hero finds its apotheosis in the post-1980s wave of graphic novels and limited series that deconstruct/reconstruct classic origin tales or form new heroes via ironic reworkings of archetypal myths and characters.[2]

With heroes such as these, concerns with identity, purpose and the hero's place in the social fabric coalesce around an Oedipal narrative which is an ubiquitous structural presence in the modern superhero mythos. This is especially the case with the more neurotically flawed "outsider heroes" Spider-Man, the Hulk, and Daredevil, who were defined by their creators within the terms of a continual clash with patriarchal order and authority.[3] Foreshadowing the countercultural direction that superhero comics would take later in the 1960s (for instance, in Dennis O'Neil and Neal Adams's famous *Green Lantern/Green Arrow* run of 1970–72), this Oedipal trope allegorically worked through the struggle for recognition from a deeply suspicious establishment that the entire comics industry had faced with the Wertham campaign of the 1950s.[4] In their contemporary cinematic makeovers, *Spider-Man* and *Daredevil* trace the development of the heroic persona explicitly from their protagonists' truncated Oedipal passages (the death of Uncle Ben for Peter Parker; the death of Jack Murdock for Matt Murdock). The death scene of Jack Murdock (David Keith) in *Daredevil* could hardly make this point any more overtly. As the teenaged Matt stands numbly by his father's corpse, Ben Affleck in voiceover as the adult hero opines: "I waited outside the Olympic [theatre] for my father . . . in some ways, I'm still waiting." The sequence ends as the camera tilts up into the night sky, briefly revealing a billboard bearing a slogan that sums up the symbolic power of this primal scene: "What Legends are Made of." A comparable sequence is found in *Spider-Man*, and the scene occurs yet again, albeit with a matriarchal twist, in *Hulk*. *X2* suspends its heroes in the struggle for mutant "hearts and minds" between Charles Xavier's benign, nurturing patriarch and Magneto's rebelliously attractive "bad father." Even the vampire hunter Blade (Wesley Snipes), only tangentially superheroic (the character originated in Marvel's 1970s *Tomb of Dracula*), is marked by the early disappearance of his mother and later experiences the apparent death of a surrogate father figure (*Blade*, 1998).

The assumption of a superheroic destiny is inevitably marked as Oedipal, though it is not necessarily limited to an exclusively masculine trajectory; nevertheless, in recent adaptations only Elektra (Jennifer Garner) in *Daredevil* stands out as taking virtually the same route to a heroic identity as her male counterparts. However, the development of the characters of Rogue (Anna Paquin) and Jean Grey (Famke Janssen) in the *X-Men* movies strongly foregrounds issues of identity and power; excessively instinctual and powerful abilities that severely test the heroines' self-control are associated with both figures. The *X* films themselves notably incorporate soap opera/teen movie dynamics, especially in terms of the emotional triangle that is set up involving Wolverine (Hugh Jackman), Jean Grey, and Cyclops (James Marsden), and the budding but physically awkward romance between the teenaged pair Rogue and Iceman (Shawn Ashmore). Indeed, although her character falls beyond the scope of the present essay, Rogue stands as a paradigmatic example of the figure of the scarily powerful and emotional teen that will be discussed shortly. Moreover, in her detachment from (biological) family, profound sense of herself as a misfit, and her opportunistic attraction to Wolverine, an older mentor figure who seems to share her nonconformist worldview, Rogue makes an interestingly close parallel to Enid in *Ghost World*. Perhaps Rogue is the kind of superhero that Enid imagines herself being when she dons a Catwoman-style leather mask, purchased in a local adult store, to amuse and "gross out" Rebecca (an episode that is the most explicit reference to superhero culture in Zwigoff's film).

If superhero comics and their associated films see the involuntary loss of one's parents as a singularly traumatic and influential event, purposeful abandonment *by* one's parents is also seen to have severe repercussions on the development of the protagonist. This is the case in the darkly comic opening scenes of *Batman Returns* (1992), when a "penguin boy" is washed down the Gotham sewer—an event that justifies the malcontent worldview of the Penguin (Danny DeVito), a villainous character nevertheless seen sympathetically by Tim Burton's film. Similarly, Enid in *Ghost World* appears to have lost her mother (although the film text does not specify whether this is through death or parental break-up), resulting in a family unit consisting of Enid and her well-meaning but utterly suburban and conformist (unnamed) father (Bob Balaban). In the long-running Spider-Man comic mythology, Peter's parents Richard and Mary died as "secret agents [. . .] in the service of America" (Fingeroth 73), although this sensational element of the origin story is usually downplayed to strengthen the orphan angle (and is completely absent from Raimi's films, perhaps in deference to the most widely remembered incarnations of the hero from Saturday morning cartoons and newspaper strips).

Adventure and superhero comics paradigmatically deal with the orientation of the hero towards and within their world; although frequently displaced by fantasy/genre landscapes, a violent, harsh environment is more or less a given, especially in the Marvel comics tradition. What is notable about these worlds is that often, the young defenders of society are simultaneously the victims of some of its blackest deeds and betrayals; the young hero fills the roles of persecuted, savior, and threat all at once. This tendency explains the longevity of the device of the secret identity and is used to justify various narratives that deal with the assumption of new identities, new heroic guises, or the temporary rejection of the hero identity; the latter plot is seen in both *Superman II* (Richard Lester, 1981) and *Spider-Man 2*. For the post-1960s breed of superhero, identity is a puzzle, various mad paternal interlopers block succession, and the society one fights for quite often reacts with hostility to displays of power. Comics, like their associated film subgenres of action-adventure and melodrama, focus the social universes they depict through the prism of the emotional subjectivities and struggles for selfhood of their protagonists. For all its clear generic differences, *Ghost World* employs this method as much as does the more obviously individualist *Spider-Man*, to the dismay of commentators like Henry A. Giroux, who bemoan the former film's resulting lack of "historical, political and social" perspective (299).

Comics have long had the capacity to harness a powerful repertoire of images around adolescence, growth and the assumption of responsibility in a form that communicates with and reassures a juvenile readership but also, crucially, addresses other audience sectors with an investment in how cultural representations of youth and growing up are organized. Clearly the factor of adult readers problematizses the notion that superhero comics speak in a perpetual present tense to an exclusive audience of the young. Bradford W. Wright notes that the biggest commercial challenge facing the comics industry in the 1990s was to secure its traditional youth-focused role within a "glutted [popular cultural] market for adolescent obsessions" (284). Specialist television channels, pop music genres, computer games and other media had all successfully styled their products around an intimate connection with youth and adolescence. Yet Wright's observation of the struggle facing comic book publishers (partly allayed by successful exercises in synergy like the proliferation of superhero movies since the late 1990s) is merely a symptom of a wider phenomenon whereby notions equating youthfulness with hip appeal and acceptable taste have become embedded in the consuming mindset of the American bourgeoisie. This is a scenario in which apparent moments of youth-driven social upheaval such as the 1960s counterculture may be "more accurately understood as a stage in the development of the values of the American middle class, a colorful installment in the twentieth century drama of consumer subjectivity" (Frank 29). To understand the broad cultural narrative of American youth since the 1960s—a narrative that is vividly illustrated in superhero fantasies of dangerous and exhilaratingly powerful young people—is to grasp the dissociation of "youth" as a cultural value from the descriptive function of youth as a category of human biological development (Frith 380–32).

The veneration of youth as a desirable position within culture, identified by Thomas Frank in such loaded moments as Madison Avenue's creation of the "Pepsi Generation" in the 1960s (168–83), inevitably impacts upon studies of the reception of comics and their associated film adaptations, especially as the latter tend to manipulate their narratives and marketing around an ambiguous address that knowingly blurs age lines. Indeed, this wide but stratified appeal is a major catalytic reason for Hollywood studios' considerable recent investment in comic book properties; such knowledge helps studios to develop summer "tent-pole" releases like *Spider-Man*, *X-Men*, and *Fantastic Four* that will zone in on desirable audience demographics (those prone to repeat viewings and merchandise purchase). In the case of *Spider-Man*, the film's efficient cross-age targeting was highlighted by a mini-drama around classification that also earned the film free publicity. IMDB reported that concerns were raised among educationalists that the PG-13-rated film "may trigger anxiety and stress" in younger children, with the expert views cited implicitly connecting the movie's New York setting to the reception of images of September 11 (Anon). In the U.K., hesitation around the appropriate classification of the film centered on its depiction of physical violence and eventually led to the introduction of the brand new classification "12A," which permits youngsters below the age of twelve to view the film if accompanied by an adult. Such blurring of audience address across age lines, as witnessed in the release of *Spider-Man*, inevitably feeds into superheroic movie narratives themselves, resurfacing via signifiers and references that activate the nostalgic imaginations of different generations at different moments in the film's reception. For instance, *Spider-Man*, released in 2002, subtly downplays references to contemporaneity in its mise-en-scène. Settings like Peter's high school and Aunt May's home in Queens seem designed to resemble classic 1960s Steve Ditko artwork (Ditko being one of the visual stylists to embody the so-called "Silver Age" of superhero comics).[5] This stylistic choice serves to anchor the narrative in a register of sincerity that holds at bay more modern ironic tendencies, both in teen films and their viewers; yet, at the same time, it undeniably essays a crucial thematic function, situating the present of the narrative some time before the world-changing events of 9/11, even as the film's discourse of heroism places it squarely in a post-9/11 world. Furthermore, by depicting Spidey's initial battles with the Green Goblin (and restaging—in a less tragic version—the classic Gwen Stacy hostage scenario, seen in the comics in 1973), the film knowingly circumvents three decades of subsequent comic continuity to reflect a version of the character guaranteed to push the buttons of boomer audiences, effectively placing Spider-Man squarely in a "Silver Age" time capsule.

Turning the clock back in this way plucks Spider-Man out of contemporary social engagement and inevitably dilutes the film's ostensible representation of early twenty-first-century adolescence, but is undoubtedly a smart move in terms of cross-generational appeal (and more generally in supporting Raimi's rather quaintly classical design for the film, which cuts against certain preconceptions of contemporary spectacle cinema as obsessively courting youth audiences via the oft-noted utilization of an "MTV aesthetic"). Despite their various Oedipal wrangles, the principal teen characters in *Spider-Man* (Peter, Mary Jane, and Harry Osborn [James Franco]) conform to their "Silver Age" and newspaper strip precursors, and do not display traits of savagely defensive cynicism and highly coded, ironic inscrutability to adult eyes, much less engage in the kind of sexual and narcotic activities of recent teen "shock" films like *Kids* (Larry Clark, 1995) and *Thirteen* (Catherine Hardwicke, 2003). The qualities of "despair, ennui, and resistance" (Giroux 291) lacking in *Spider-Man*'s oddly sincere and stoic teens are precisely those qualities that *Ghost World* celebrates in its teen protagonists, Enid and Rebecca.

According to Thomas Hine, American culture "encourages individuals to be heroes of their own lives" (55). Implicit in this notion is the forging of one's own will and destiny, and the ultimate recognition of one's self as unique and powerful that is so often rehearsed in superhero narratives both in print and cinema.[6] *Spider-Man*, more than *Ghost World*—for obvious generic reasons—emphasizes the problem of violence in the contemporary world and posits as its solution the post-9/11 need for selfless heroism and community spirit (both Spidey installments include scenes dedicated to revealing the hero's sense of connection to ordinary New Yorkers). The narrative consequently crystalizes around the familiar problem of rising to a heroic destiny, conforming utterly to classic superhero stories. This problem is presented in terms of the dilemma of identity choice for Peter Parker, who begins his voiceover with the question, "Who am I?" The rest of the film narrates Peter's metamorphosis from this point of confusion until he answers his own question with his closing statement of unique identity ("I'm Spider-Man"). Generically, the film seems restricted to a presentation of teens that leans heavily towards the "traditional Hollywood narrative that chronicles teenage rebellion as part of a rite of passage towards a deeper understanding of what it means to join adult society" (Giroux 297). Hewing closely to the comic book source material (although dropping, as we have seen, any reference to Peter's parents), the movie privileges the idea of self-creation, of the young hero exploiting his newly acquired powers towards an end of forming a more powerful identity than the one dealt to him by everyday life (in an enjoyable montage sequence, we see Peter's inherent creativity and imagination infused and activated by his new powers as he literally designs the Spider-Man identity through working on ideas for a costume). Ex-Marvel editor Danny Fingeroth discusses how super-hero tales frequently incorporate the magical allure of making one's own destiny; the orphan status so often conferred as a precondition of super-heroic identity has a fantasy glamour all of its own, that of the identity as "tabula rasa" (69–71). Uncertainty about one's origins can be unsettling but leaves a loophole free so that the protagonist of the fiction may discover some distinguished secret of their birth later on (the revelation of Super-man's earthbound powers, for instance, or the fact that one is predestined to be the world's champion vampire slayer as in *Buffy* or *Blade*). Peter is already seen to be withdrawing from the faintly embarrassing presence of his aging guardians May (Rosemary Harris) and Ben (Cliff Robertson), as is shown in his disregard for Ben's advice during their final conversa-tion outside the library; Ben's death shortly after brings home to Peter that such fantasies of independence, while a natural part of growing up, hold the secret to the devastating truth of adult responsibility: that of one's es-sential moral aloneness.

Although their embedded nostalgia arguably qualifies their direct relation-ship to contemporary society, comic book adaptations like *Spider-Man* nevertheless can be seen to develop their discourses on youth in a way that takes advantage of comics' reputation for engaging with debates around childhood and adolescence in the wider social arena. According to Giroux, comic-derived narratives at their best can serve as a form of "public peda-gogy" for the airing of political questions to do with teen resistance and the entrapment of identity-forming processes within a late capitalist, re-lentlessly privatized model of social experience (293). This intervention of comic-related material in the public sphere of debate around youth iden-tities and the health of the American body politic explicitly situates both *Ghost World* and *Spider-Man* in relation to several youth-focused obses-sions informing cultural discourse since the millennium (Columbine, Sep-tember 11, pedophilia, the internet, and the rights of children in a global-ized world among them).

One strand shared by *Spider-Man* and *Ghost World* is the conceit of the irresponsible adult preying on the vulnerable teenager, although Peter Parker's battle with the Green Goblin/Norman Osborn (Willem Dafoe) is a rather more clear-cut case than the consensual but somehow sad sexual encounter between the middle-aged Seymour and Enid (rather than Seymour in particular, it is the adult world/symbolic order in general that plunges Enid into victim status). *Spider-Man* more obviously engages with another powerful theme that resonates with many other recent popular representations: that of the teen who possesses extraordinary power or talent, yet lacks the mature capacity to channel and control that power for the common good (and thus must either achieve agency by conforming to adult values, or remain a mysterious, abject threat). Such a representational trend highlights the child/teenager as a site of great anxiety within culture, a generalized fear gauged by Giroux in his citation of a Florida congressman's statement that contemporary youth "are the most dangerous criminals on the face of the earth" (McCollum qtd. in Giroux 284). Subtly varied treatments of this trope of the powerful, uncontrollable teenager can be found in a number of horror or fantasy narratives of the last two decades, including *The Lost Boys* (Joel Schumacher, 1987), *Akira* (Katsuhiro Otomo, 1988), *Edward Scissorhands* (Tim Burton, 1991), *Battle Royale* (Fukasaku Kinji, 2000), *Donnie Darko* (Richard Kelly, 2002) and, on television, *Smallville* and *Buffy the Vampire Slayer* (1997–2003). The same theme is explicitly articulated as a "social problem" in more conventional dramatic genres such as *Dangerous Minds* (John N. Smith, 1995), *Kids, Elephant,* (Gus Van Sant, 2003), and elsewhere rendered as comedy, both light (*Sabrina the Teenage Witch*, 1996–2003; *Malcolm in the Middle* 2000–) and black in form (*Heathers*, Michael Lehmann, 1988; *Election*, Alexander Payne, 1999). Defying easy generic classification but inhabiting an arthouse idiom similar to *Ghost World* is *The Virgin Suicides* (Sofia Coppola, 1999), a tragic, ironic tale of arrested adolescence, featuring teen icon and *Spider-Man* co-star, Kirsten Dunst. In Coppola's film, young female sexuality is a source of huge power and mystery, but one that is misdirected by parental interference into another layer of repression.

A symbolic repertoire of teen resistance, adventure, violence, and (frequently) rage that cannot be regulated or completely allied to Giroux's "traditional" Hollywood rite of passage narrative can appear as a threat to conservative norms. What is at stake in contestations of such violent fantasy representations as *Buffy*, *X-Men*, and others is their debatable value as models of empowerment; as Gerard Jones puts it, "[e]ducators and cultural commentators have been saying for decades that girls need more media role models of power and heroism, and those models have finally arrived. But, as usual, youth culture refuses to follow the patterns that adults wish it would" (152). In many of the above cited texts, the condition of adolescence (in both genders) is associated with uncommon power, hypersensitivity, insanity, sociopathic tendencies, violence, or death. Such an ambiguous (at best) understanding of children and teens in the public imagination has recently supported the imposition of a kind of "martial law" (Cassidy qtd. in Giroux 286) through numerous forms of surveillance on the young. At a time when American public schools resemble prisons and hysterical discourses about teen (female) gangs, incendiary computer games, hooded clothing, and Anti-Social Behaviour Orders (ASBOs) preoccupy British newspapers, the prevalence in popular film and TV of powerful, alternately heroic and threatening teens and older children can hardly fail to be noted. In the U.K., recent governmental policies, such as the introduction of the Anti-Social Behaviour Bill, respond to a series of popular anxieties around youth culture; an overview is provided by Casciani. British television has reflected recent anxious discourses on the behavior of children by commissioning several programs, all more or less in "reality" formats (with the attendant implications of surveillance that go with such formats), such as BBC's *Little Angels* (2003–) and *Who Rules the Roost?* (2004–), and Channel 4's *Supernanny* (2004–).

In terms of how this nebulous cultural anxiety has gelled into a representational pattern, a useful critical model has been articulated by John Stephens, who surveys a number of teen narratives from the late 1990s in terms of the journeys taken by their protagonists from a state of abjection to one of subjective agency. The overcoming of abjection and social marginalization is clearly the project achieved by a narrative like that of *Spider-Man*, which shows Peter Parker developing a sense of subjective agency that transcends "the lesser potentiality of childhood to [achieve] the greater potentiality of adulthood" (Stephens 124). As with related teen hero texts such as *Smallville*, this inscription of adolescence adumbrates the film's presentation of an archetypal narrative that idealistically and attractively frames youthful insurrection and confusion, while inevitably straightening these impulses out in due course. In this way, *Spider-Man* replays the appealing notion of permitted but limited rebellion written into popular culture's post-1960s adoption of the image, if not the substance, of a youth-led "revolution against conformity" (Frank 117–18). This allows the powerful teenager's function as a fearful fantasy figure to be kept in balance by its more overt role as a safe point of identification for diverse viewing inclinations and ages.

Unlike *Spider-Man*, the open-ended, multiply interpretable conclusion of *Ghost World* signals the intention of that film to resist either placing its protagonist Enid into a secure, narratively familiar "coming of age" trajectory, or to play into a cultural role of reassurance that problem teens will "turn out alright in the end." Indeed, although Rebecca does "assimilate" in the film (holding down a job, finding an apartment and buying into commodity culture), our sympathy seems inarguably directed towards Enid. The trauma of her (ideological) separation from Rebecca, and the confusing sexual turn of her friendship with Seymour, leave her with no other option than to simply disappear, an ending that politically may seem unsatisfying but is consistent with the film's patient and careful development of her character. At the end of the film, Enid has preserved her friendship with Rebecca but, on the grounds of censorship, been turned down for the arts college scholarship that promised her a different future. Seemingly unable to accept the new life of compromise that Rebecca has reluctantly embraced, the final scenes show Enid waiting at an apparently discontinued bus stop, before the bus mysteriously turns up and takes Enid away to an unknown destination.

The "traditionalism" in *Spider-Man*'s narrative is arguably thrown into relief by the "radically de-romanticized ambience of world-weariness" (Le Cain) that permeates *Ghost World*. Where *Spider-Man* focuses on the trials of identity choice, Zwigoff's film presents *cultural* choice, and the pressure to assimilate within the middle-class mainstream, as the emblematic obstacle in Enid's negotiation of the transition from youth to adult. Her transformation challenges her idea of herself as a unique arbiter of taste and opponent of vapid dominant culture. *Ghost World* purports to look askew at the impulse within American culture identified above by Thomas Hine; indeed, Enid builds her personality around her position as a critic of the kind of ersatz culture that inspires people to see themselves as "heroic" (witheringly manifested in her comments about the debilitated graduation ceremony speaker who delivers a banal homily on high school life: "I liked her so much better when she was an alcoholic and drug addict"). Enid's life is a constant struggle to prove her existence among the inhabitants of an utterly conventional, blandly middle class world; for instance, in her art class, her expressive and highly personal cartoons are initially overlooked by her patronizingly liberal teacher in favor of the facile social commentary of a classmate's work. In the incorporeal world of marginality and social invisibility that Rebecca and Enid inhabit, heroes are those whose oddness or seeming insanity trouble suburban, middle-class norms (such as Norman, the old man who waits doggedly for a discontinued bus service, or the eccentric wheelchair-bound quiz expert who is a regular at Rebecca's place of work). Of course, this position of invisibility derives substantially from the girls' age, their "in-between state" (just out of high school, not yet committed to college, work, or a stable romantic relationship) conferring a position of liminality (Hine 46–47).

Enid, more so than Rebecca, clearly *chooses* to haunt the margins; she is not interested in being "hero" of her own life—but the film nevertheless shows us that she is trapped all the same. That Enid has the wit and insight to see through the interpellatory structures of contemporary culture is repeatedly affirmed, but in steering our allegiance towards Enid, the film enforces a rather predictable hierarchy of value where her cynicism towards "the mainstream" replicates the film's own distaste for mass culture's shallow and mechanical cooptation of that which can be intrinsically (and mysteriously) valued about pulp material like comics. This view is developed in the ironic stance of the aforementioned "Catwoman" scene, which nevertheless became one of the most widely reproduced images of *Ghost World*, thus incorporating the affectation of a position outside "banal" everyday culture into the film's self-appraisal of its own distinctive qualities.

For all Enid's resistance to being positioned within a cultural landscape that she experiences as empty, facile, and, indeed, childlike, ultimately, and poignantly, she is powerless to transcend her own instinctual attachment to her past and the rarefied childhood from which she is taking leave. Significantly, this dilemma is expressed in the form of Enid's reaction to a product of mass culture that uncovers a treasured, and apparently authentic, memory. This is shown in a moving scene where Enid, preparing to move in with Rebecca and commence her anonymous new job at "Computer Station," listens to a record by the 1950s child pop act Patience and Prudence, obviously a much-loved childhood artifact for her. The refrain, made more haunting by the child's voice singing, is worth quoting in full:

A smile is something special
A ribbon something rare
So I'll be special and I'll be rare
With a smile and a ribbon in my hair

To be a girl they notice
Takes more than fancy dress
So I'll be special and I'll be rare
I'll be something beyond compare
I'll be noticed because I wear
A smile and a ribbon in my hair

The interpellatory promise of childhood for young females is adeptly revealed in the film's teasing out of the underlying ideological message of the song: to be noticed is to exist. The social order confers identity through a fantasy of remaining rare and special. Although, in keeping with the film's postmodern warping of cultural periods and Enid's eccentric tastes, Enid would be far too young to have experienced the success of the record during its actual time of release—suggesting that such valued totems of culture are passed on, perhaps by Enid's absent mother. It is notable that Enid locates and plays the record while preparing for her dreaded new job, arranged for her by Maxine (Teri Garr), an unwanted maternal interloper who represents yet another force of normalcy in relation to Enid. Enid is at once nostalgically, romantically devoted to the record's promise and acutely aware of the sheer emptiness of that promise; the song reiterates her consciousness that high school, which is now behind her, represented the very last moment where she could entertain a fantasy of her own uniqueness, through the cultural and verbal amour that she and Rebecca constructed around themselves. This realization proves to Enid that she cannot hold down a job at Computer Station and set up house with Rebecca in a "totally average" neighborhood without sacrificing some part of herself; oblivion, via a bus ride to nowhere, is preferable. Where Peter Parker takes up his Althusserian "hailing" by society without question, framed as it is by the familial and moral exigencies of the superhero, Enid recognizes that to be herself she must *refuse* to take up her allotted position; to embrace normality would be no more permanent and true to herself than her fleeting and unsuccessful experimentation with punk style earlier in the film.

That a defining scene such as this should unfold with Enid alone in her room is unsurprising; the liminal, threshold status of the bedroom as a place for experiment and the practicing of adult identities is recurrently depicted in recent films that feature teen characters negotiating the process of maturation, especially where the world in question is a middle class or suburban one.[7] In *American Beauty* (Sam Mendes, 1999), Thora Birch— *Ghost World*'s Enid—plays Jane Burnham, exploring escape routes from suburban conformity with her stereotypically drawn sensitive boyfriend Ricky (Wes Bentley). *The Ice Storm* (Ang Lee, 1997)—a text that explicitly cites superhero comics as a mirror for adolescent experience—stages scenes of sexual awakening and drug-taking in adolescent bedrooms (with a cast that includes actors such as Tobey Maguire, Christina Ricci, Elijah Wood, Katie Holmes, and David Krumholtz, all of whom have featured prominently in Hollywood teen films). That film shares *Ghost World*'s taste for representing America as a floating landscape of peculiar anonymity. In *Ghost World*, the only space that does not seem flat, "empty and grim" (Zwigoff qtd. in Said 22) is Enid's sacred bedroom. The colorful, richly cluttered mise-en-scène employed there—"[y]ou can almost smell the mouldering Doc Martens and cheap green hair dye" (Said 22)—is in stark contrast to other interior spaces where Enid, Rebecca, and their friend Josh (Brad Renfro) hang out: diners, convenience stores, and multiplexes, rendered in shallow focus with longer lenses to emphasize flatness and rob the image of texture. This visual regime emphasizes the perverse pull that the security of childhood and familiarity exerts on Enid; although her ultra-sardonic mode of humor and eccentric taste move her away from childhood and into mysterious adult spaces like the sex shop and Seymour's apartment, she pines for the simple pleasures and reassuring uniformity of youth ("God, just think, we'll never see Dennis again . . . it's actually totally depressing," she comments sadly about a marginal schoolmate at the graduation party).

Fig. 1. Teen bedrooms function in the texts as symbolic spaces for the cultivation of new selves for Peter Parker in *Spider-Man* . . .

Bedroom scenes in teen cinema are hugely important in setting up the notion of the barriers that postpubertal emotional and sexual development erect between teenagers and their families or guardians; bedrooms are places for cultivating new selves or retreating into comforting old ones. The key sequence depicting Peter Parker's transformation into Spider-Man occurs after Peter has returned to the sanctuary of his room, feeling ill and disorientated after receiving a spider bite on the class field trip. Mysteriously transpiring offscreen, as Peter succumbs to a bout of fever, his change is represented in terms of the magical substitution of a strong, healthy body for his previous unprepossessing physicality. Maguire's buff body is lingered over, and the sudden appearance of his new body in the mirror surprises and delights Peter, who has to this moment been distrusted by his conformist peers and defined by them solely in terms of intellect and his inclination to geekdom. Yet, the ambiguity of Peter's change—the fact that only he can ethically choose how to use his power, and that this emotional maturity comes separately from the physical alteration—is underscored by the fact that a parallel transformation (that of Norman Osborn into the lunatic Green Goblin) is presented to us in place of the details of Peter's mostly offscreen change. Although teasingly presented, Peter's transformation is vitally important in *Spider-Man*, and in some ways his true character only originates in this moment; Raimi's mise-en-scène supports this. Peter's bedroom has been dressed to appear just as cluttered as Enid's, yet the thin, generic quality of Parker as a science-inclined, geeky male teen is encoded through predictable signifiers: posters of Einstein and alien invasion, models of the space shuttle (references that again conjure cultural concerns that are evocative for older viewers). Such references lack the studied cultural specificity of Enid's Buzzcocks tapes and *H. R. Pufn-*

Fig. 2. . . . or the retreat into comforting old ones for Enid in *Ghost World*.

stuf paraphernalia, perhaps supporting a reading that Spider-Man is the dominant half of Peter's identity as far as the narrative is concerned.

Although they are places of great physical and emotional change and sometimes trauma,[8] both Enid and Peter seem to feel safe in their bedrooms, a use of space that halts a marked development in 1990s teen movie culture where the bedroom or parental home frequently becomes a site of horror, attack, and invasion. Scenes of violence, abduction, or sexual threat based around (overwhelmingly female) teens in domestic spaces are notable in *True Lies* (James Cameron, 1994), *Fear* (James Foley, 1996), *Scream* (Wes Craven, 1996), *Face/Off* (John Woo, 1997), and *Wild Things* (John McNaughton, 1998), among many others. Enid and Peter both move on eventually, but at a certain cost; Peter moves to Manhattan, where a suspicious Norman Osborn almost immediately violates his new apartment, and Enid leaves town. *Ghost World* shows us that, in the privacy of her own room, if nowhere else, Enid feels in control of the play of identities that characterizes this stage of life (clearly signaled through her grotesque artistic enhancement of a magazine photograph of a boorish alpha-male type). Yet, in Clowes's original comic, it is Rebecca and not Enid that articulates the fear of change that looms over these texts: "I don't want to go anywhere or do anything . . . I just want it to be like it was in high school" (Clowes 74).

As a structurally simple yet thematically rich form of expression, the comic book (and its associated movie adaptation) mines a repertoire of motifs linked to growth, evolution, identity, and the achievement of what Stephens terms "subjective agency." Interestingly, the discourses circling around comic books as a cultural commodity are similarly shot through with the language of change, identity, and development: fans are obsessed with "continuity"; the industry reviews distribution practices in line with changing demographics of age;[9] the comic format itself is considered by critics to have achieved "sophistication" and "complexity"—in other words, to have come of age—with the emergence of the ostensibly more serious and literary "graphic novel" in the 1980s (Wright 273). Although, this common line of argument risks reproducing earlier, conservative discourses used to attack the comic form and which contributed to the paradoxical position whereby comics (particularly horror titles) were labeled as intellectually juvenile, yet at the same time (according to opponents like Dr. Wertham), unfit for consumption by children, leaving them with an almost untouchable cultural status. This awkward position is enunciated by Warshow in his assessment of the notoriously graphic E.C. comics, when he notes, almost with embarrassment, that the comics' capacity to shock and appall is directly equivalent to their ability to provide aesthetic stimulation and thereby avoid the banality of other mass-circulated entertainments (67). The overarching metaphor of growth thus pervades comics both as an internal textual theme and as part of a wider interpretive and critical vocabulary and, naturally, emerges as an important issue in relation to the recent cycle of superhero and other comic adaptations for the cinema.

Like other teen subgenres, recent comic adaptations have addressed concerns with youth culture and behavior from a perspective sympathetic to the needs of adolescent viewers; however, a byproduct of this (and of generic exigencies) has been to represent teens as dangerous, or at least unable to control their own powers and potential, thus feeding into the current anxieties of older generations about the uncontrollability and ruthlessness of modern kids. Within this compromised and ambiguous climate of representation, and utilizing very different methods, *Spider-Man* and *Ghost World* present alternate, optimistic and pessimistic versions of the rite of passage that reflect "a particular crisis of the social" (Giroux 290) in contemporary culture; that is, the problem of forming a society where a child will be able to "find [their] way in the world without being subject to its most oppressive practices" (300). The traditional superhero narrative offers a character arc where the hero can reintegrate with society and fulfill their destiny, even if doubt, emotional turbulence and insecurity stay with them after they have taken up the hero mantle (which is very much the case in *Spider-Man 2*). However, interpellation into the adult world does not proceed as successfully with protagonists like Enid in *Ghost World*, whose ideological condition is to remain outside of the culture that identifies, hails, and celebrates heroes; she maintains a position of criticism and intransigence that eventually forces her to "freeze" her personal narrative at the crisis point of adolescence, rather than trade her nonconformist stance in return for the illusory promise of a full social identity.

However, readings of the two films under discussion must also acknowledge that the values—historical, cultural—associated with their divergent versions of growing up are ultimately qualified by the positions taken by each text towards their own likely reception and status. In *Spider-Man*'s case, the film's mass appeal is designed with several audiences in mind; those with a nostalgic familiarity with Peter Parker's ageless embodiment of troubled youth are directly addressed, anointing the movie with a romantic "Silver Age" grace that nevertheless pulls it back from a full engagement with contemporary social issues around young people. In the case of *Ghost World*, the problematic of "coming of age" is knowingly rendered as a cultural choice. Enid's "dropping out" of a stultifying world of normalcy, and her achievement of a literally impossible heroic journey to the "margins," underscores the film's idealized view of the teenager as the pure guardian of antagonism towards banal, phony middle-class culture; ironically, this is a stance that itself reproduces the dynamic by which the concept of an oppositional youth culture was appropriated and sold back as a "consuming attitude" to Americans of all ages.

IT'S A BIRD! IT'S A PLANE! NO, IT'S DVD!

SUPERMAN, SMALLVILLE, AND
THE PRODUCTION (OF) MELODRAMA

— RAYNA DENISON

Superman enjoys one of the largest intertextual franchises in the history of popular culture, and is also one of the most insistently multimedia of icons. He is one of the few icons to have appeared in prolonged radio, television, film, and print narratives and has been consistently reimagined by almost every generation from the 1930s onwards (Banks, Grossman, Alyn). Superman, in those various forms, has also proven a subject matter redolent with meaning and ripe for interpretation. This chapter takes as its focus just some of the constelled intertexts that currently circulate around the Man of Steel and uses them to interrogate the concept of genre in the comic book movie. The chapter uses a variety of production discourses, from advertising through to press releases and especially DVD, to rethink the shifting relationship that Superman's stories have to the genres of action and melodrama.

This approach differs somewhat from previous academic works on Superman. Umberto Eco in "the Myth of Superman" analyzed Superman's comic book narratives, finding him "by definition the character whom nothing can impede" who "finds himself in the worrisome narrative situation of being a hero without an adversary and therefore without the possibility of any development" (110). Skipping forward just two years and one media adaptation, however, this undeveloping character is viewed by Sarah

R. Kozloff quite differently. In "Superman as Saviour: Christian Allegory in the Superman Movies," Kozloff suggests that "these movies reflect a shift in public attitude" and that in fact these Superman texts "connect with the ideology of fundamental religious groups" (82). Jumping forward again to more recent work on the franchise, Miranda J. Banks reads Clark Kent in *Smallville* as "a new protagonist for the melodrama genre: beautiful, self-sacrificing, yet resilient" (Banks 18). Though Eco's points are well taken regarding Superman as a character, when considering Superman as a multimedia franchise, and critical interpretations of him, it would seem that development and variety have been central to his longevity.

The variety within this academic work is a testament to the changing roles the Superman icon has played through the decades, to his importance to the different popular culture currents into which his narratives have tapped. Moreover, the range of approaches taken to this superhero and his texts indicates how versatile the Superman concept has been, with new generations able to map economic, political, religious, mythic, and gender discourses onto the structures of Superman. This much can be read from the examples above. However, the mobile generic positioning of Superman has by and large escaped critical attention,[1] despite critical considerations of him as a modernist hero (Kipniss) and as a male melodrama protagonist (Banks). Superman is usually absent from critical discussions on action adventure and melodrama in film and television (Tasker, *Action and Adventure Cinema*; Tasker, *Spectacular Bodies*; King).[2] This chapter therefore seeks to unravel some of the complex generic codings of the franchise, in particular two of its most prominent recent incarnations. Taking action and melodrama as touchstones for this argument, this chapter will seek to uncover how genre has been created and recreated for *Superman: The Movie* (1978) (and to a lesser extent its 1980 sequel *Superman II*) and the recent media reinvention of Superman in the television series *Smallville* (2001–).

The choice of these sets of texts may seem somewhat arbitrary on the surface, separated as they are by over twenty years, different media, and the points in Superman's "life" on which they choose to focus. However, the commonalities greatly outweigh their differences. These range from the involvement of corporately "branded" companies (Warner Brothers Films and Warner Brothers Television) to production values (that of the blockbuster film and what might be termed blockbuster television) to modes of production (with the first two films made back to back in a not dissimilar fashion to episodic television productions) and through to their unknown leads, use of past stars and reliance on special effects.[3] It is not difficult, therefore, to find common ground from which to view these as connected texts, sharing common traits on deeper levels than subject matter. Especially salient to this discussion is the way each of these sets of texts has spawned its own intertextual network. Production information, played out in various print media, abounded around the release of the *Superman* films while *Smallville* has become the central hub in a web of texts that includes Internet sites, popular media coverage, and even its own comic book. The ways in which each of these intertextual webs functions in relation to developing understandings of Superman's genres will form much of the first half of this discussion.

To focus on the intertextuality of Superman no longer runs contrary to genre studies approaches to film. Reception studies have become closely linked with genre theory: Compare Barbara Klinger's influential approach to melodrama (*Melodrama and Meaning*) with more recent work on genre by Rick Altman (30). Altman's insistence on going back to industry discourse and examining the traces of the production event tallies closely with Klinger's historically specific contextual analyses of Douglas Sirk's films. Similar multidiscursive work on television genre has been also advanced by Jason Mittell. Building on this film and television work, this chapter will similarly interrogate the construction of genre by focusing not just on the messages in *Superman: The Movie*, nor by just looking at episodes of *Smallville* as self-contained texts. The production discourses will be thrown wide open here to include media coverage of both sets of texts, and it will incorporate crossover media like *Smallville*'s Internet–comic book–DVD intertext, "The Chloe Chronicles" (based on the show's teen investigative reporter, Chloe Sullivan), and the *Superman* films' repackaging and indeed generic reproduction on DVD in order to complicate notions of how and where genre can be read in relation to film and television. This is not to confuse the differing meanings of genre to film and television, but merely to posit that as these two sets of texts share a central "mythic" structure, they provide an instance in which to relationally explore the construction of generic meaning.

Casting a wide intertextual net allows for a rereading of the process of gentrification, not just at a textual, historical or industrial level, but also at a contextual, media-specific level. DVD plays a central role in this discussion. "Making of" documentaries and other DVD features, it will be argued, have important roles to play in terms of genre. For, unlike other "superintending" discourses (Klinger, *Melodrama and Meaning* xvi), such DVD extras appear in roughly the same temporal and spatial location as the "text" and act to add layers of nuance and meaning to it. In *The DVD Revolution*, Aaron Barlow claims two important things about the DVD Special Edition. First, he argues that it is a means of placing "movies in context, both that of the making and reaction after the fact" (83). Second, Barlow discusses how DVD "works well with our ways of remembering films, and is certainly becoming the physical repository, in a sense, of those memories" (79). In these ways DVD offers us not just the opportunity to reaccess film and television *post facto*, but also to access our memories of it and to have those memories reinscribed by the materials accompanying the text.

The argument here is therefore broken into two parts: the first will examine industry-inflected discourses around *Superman: The Movie* and *Smallville* on their initial releases, while the second will seek to show how those discussions were expanded and altered on the release of DVDs for the texts. Doing so should help to map shifts in dominant genres within the superhero genre between the 1970s and contemporary period. This chapter will also seek to expand Barlow's notions of the importance of DVD, seeing it not just as a means of remembering and contextualizing film and television, but as a forum in which new narratives can be inserted, and new meanings created.

Before launching into an assessment of contextual materials, it is important to rethink the way the terms "action" and "melodrama" are being mobilized hereafter. Unlike studies of melodrama that interpret it as the woman's film or soap opera (Gledhill; Jacobs; Kuhn; Landry), there are alternative theories that see an altogether more action-oriented history for the genre (Neale, "Melo Talk"; Altman 70–82). What these accounts suggest is that, historically, there was a sympathy shared by the action and melodrama genres. This sympathy seems to have ruptured around the rise of 1970s feminism and Reaganite politics in the 1980s. Action films of this period see the rise of hypermasculine bodies and heroes, with Arnold Swarzenegger and Sylvester Stallone the most frequently cited actors, and with female heroism, for example, *Wonder Woman* (1976–1979), appearing mostly on television in narratives where heroic female acts were orchestrated by male characters. These films and television programs tend to emphasize action-adventure, rather than melodrama, as the cause and effect of narrative events although academic work has pointed out the lingering traces of melodrama particularly within the film texts (Tasker, *Spectacular Bodies*). Subsequently, however, the rise of melodramatically motivated television action series could be seen to auger a new generic shift. In *Alias* (2001–2006), *Buffy the Vampire Slayer* (1997–2003), *Xena: Warrior Princess* (1995–2001), *The X-Files* (1993–2002), and now *Smallville*, the feminized version of melodrama ("marked by chance happenings, missed meetings, sudden conversions, last-minute rescues and revelations, *deus ex machina* endings" [Neale, "Melodrama and Tears" 6]) appears built into narrative structures as the cause of action segments. In these ways, melodrama and action, in television at least, have become intertwined once more.

The relationship between these melodramatic action films and television series is especially problematic when the texts are influenced by comic books, a medium with connotations that have led industry practitioners to distance themselves from it. When promoting *X-Men* in 2000, director Bryan Singer shied away from the category saying, "I'm making a sci-fi film which is based on this comic book. I was not making a comic book movie" (Salisbury 51). With the subsequent massive successes of numerous "comic book" movies including *X-Men* and *X2* (2000, 2003), *Spider-Man* and its sequel (2002, 2004), and the visibility of films such as *Blade 2* (2002), *The Punisher* (2004), and *Hulk* (2003), the comic book movie has regained some positive connotations. The renewed popularity of the comic book movie genre has been compounded in some respects by the large budget, slickly produced, comic book–derived television series developed in the wake of *X-Men*'s success. Amongst them *Smallville* is prime (a Batman derivation serial, *Birds of Prey* (2002–2003), and *Mutant X* (2001–2004) fared less well). Between the release of *Superman: The Movie* and the debut of *Smallville* then, the industry, audiences, and those who mediate between them have overseen shifts in the genre of the comic book movie. These appear to range from action (with occasional melodrama) to a more fully integrated form of melodramatic action. Moreover, the genre of the comic book movie has once more taken on the prestige markers it was associated with after the release of *Superman: The Movie*. However, the links between these genres have tended to be assumed, whereas in this chapter, production discourses will be questioned to see what it is that the comic book movie and television series mean to the industries that make them.

The origin text for *Smallville* is probably not the DC comic books starring Superman, but *Superman: The Movie*, which starred Marlon Brando, Gene Hackman, and Christopher Reeve. Reeve, along with co-stars Margot Kidder, Annette O'Toole (*Superman III*), and the voice of Terrence Stamp (replacing Brando as Superman's father Jor-el, after playing the villainous General Zod in the first two *Superman* films) have all made significant appearances within the first three seasons of *Smallville*. Moreover, the television series was carefully sold by playing with the clichés thrown up by the original films. Just as the texts speak to one another in a postmodern mélange of attractions to audiences, so too do the discourses surrounding these texts relate to one another. Beyond these knowing allusions, however, understanding the importance of genre to the superhero narrative requires an understanding of the sources of genre mediating the text. This study will embrace the differences between trade, promotional, and critical discourses in order to better view them as part of a dialogue between the relevant industry, its critics, and their potential audiences (Altman 72).

To begin with *Superman: The Movie*, it is possible to read three layers or expanding circuits of extra-textual genrification. First is an inter-industrial layer, involving the trade press and specialist journalism. Second is a layer of advertising that, though discussed here in relation to the trade press, saturated mainstream and specialist publications around *Superman: The Movie*'s release. Finally, there is a critical layer, where the film was assessed by journalists working in the mainstream presses. Within the first layer, press releases over the production period for *Superman: The Movie* come from numerous industry locations including Shepperton and Pinewood Studios in England (although always signed by Gordon Arnell and June Broom). Produced in the decade that saw the cultivation of the "B-movie Blockbuster" like *Jaws* (1975) and *Star Wars* (1977), these documents introduce two distinct (meta)generic issues: scale and special effects. One, dated 25 March 1977, indicated how important size was by compiling numerical indices for *Superman: The Movie*: locations (8), weeks of shooting (30), speaking roles (100+), and height of Christopher Reeve (6'4"). (Arnell and Broom, 1977a) The sheer spectacle of the production itself is grounded in these numbers, which in their fashion act as indicators of quality and the "epic" grandeur of the film to come. Similarly, a desire to sell *Superman: The Movie* on its special effects can be read from this and other examples. For instance, another release from later in 1977 proclaims that the production team "are now gearing up for a further five months of complex post production activity, concentrating on physical, optical, and flying effects" (Arnell and Broom, "'Superman' Touches Down"). The range of activities and their "complexity" again seem aimed at focusing discussion of the film onto its technical elements and its spectacle, away from issues of genre but perhaps toward measures of industrial legitimacy (that is, this movie is huge, and will be a blockbuster). However, as the following examples will show, spectacle is now a commonly cited trait of the comic book movie genre.

The *Superman: The Movie* advertising campaign placed similar emphasis on the aspects of the film that could be sold as spectacle. The campaign is perhaps nowhere better recorded that in the pages of *Variety*. From May 1977 through January 1979, *Superman: The Movie* was regularly featured in this trade publication. 11 May 1977, however, was a key advertising date for *Superman: The Movie*. Functioning as a teaser campaign, early production images were provided as full-page advertisements across eight pages of *Variety* (Superman Advertisements). The full-page images began with the film's "S" logo on a black background accompanied by the legend "Now Shooting," and the following page previewed one of the Krypton sets. Here then, the visual brand of *Superman: The Movie* is established, centering it on the comic book logo and futuristic, spectacular visuals. These advertisements were then followed by a series of star headshots drawing attention to the brand qualities of star names and images, with newcomer Christopher Reeve inserted only after images of Brando and Hackman. As these progress, stars share pages, with Glenn Ford (Jonathan Kent) and Ned Beatty (Otis) paired on the page following Reeve. On simple black backgrounds and sporting the film's logo in the bottom-right, these advertisements forge links between the text and perceived "quality" and Method-acting names, big stars and screen legends of the past. The teaser campaign, aimed at the film industry, therefore helped to forge links between the film's origins in comics, the process of adaptation (sets), and the cultural legitimacy of its performers, who included stars of screen and stage.

However, as well as comprehensive and prestigious advertising campaigns run in May 1977 and January 1979, two other concurrent industry narratives appear over the period.[4] The first is a series of what might be called cross-promotional advertisements. For example, Pinewood Studios put in a full-page article-interview with producer Ilya Salkind and Pierre Spengler discussing their experiences at the Studio. This cross-promotional interview seems aimed at promoting Pinewood (including its pub, which Spengler lovingly recalls, wishing "to sneak down there every so often and have a few pints with the rest of the crew"). Spengler is quoted as saying, "because of the very special nature of our picture, we also had to have the most advanced, up-to-date facilities available" (Salkind, "Super Studio 'Superman'"). As an advertisement of their facilities to the American industry, the emphasis on Pinewood's unique and cutting-edge technologies affords *Superman: The Movie* an air of quality and superiority to films made elsewhere.

In a more straightforward example, Dolby Laboratories, Inc. ran a full-page advertisement on 27 December 1978, just over a week after *Superman: The Movie*'s release. Bearing the film's logo it declared, "Superman is the 50th Motion Picture to be released with a Dolby encoded soundtrack" ("Dolby Stereo"). The relatively new technology is here cyclically sold through association with *Superman: The Movie*, while the film gains another positive experiential association (Sergi). These examples were presumably part of the Salkinds' negative pickup deal for *Superman: The Movie* in which they and not Warner Bros. became responsible for all production costs. To offset these, much like contemporary cross-promotion, here specialist companies within the American and British film industries likewise help to sell the film text alongside the benefits of their services. What they add to *Superman*'s generic discourse is a metageneric association with quality, spectacle, and epic grandeur.

Discussions of *Superman: The Movie*'s genre are perhaps most clearly stated in the review articles that accompanied its release. Susan Hellier

Anderson, writing for the *New York Times* in June 1977, did a behind-the-scenes article on the film and its production (Hellier Anderson 15). The article is peppered with generic terminology, particularly with allusive terms that come directly from Hellier Anderson as well as from the cast and producers. The terms "escapist entertainment" and "humor and fantasy, legend and sincerity" occur illustrating attempts to disperse different textual elements to the various audiences that might incline towards *Superman: The Movie*. However, "comic book" and "comic strip" are the most insistently used, appearing three times across the article. The phrases are used in relatively straightforward ways to link the film back to its origins and the article's visuals pair images from the film with the cover of "Action Comics" number 1 emphasizing the film's status as an adaptation from comic books. On one occasion Hellier Anderson refers to *Superman: The Movie* as "an updated version of the comic strip adventure," alluding to the film's origins but also differentiating it from the other major blockbuster film attractions of the period, including *Star Wars* (1977). Significantly here comic strip takes a supporting role to adventure, with *Superman: The Movie*'s newness and comic strip aspects providing contrast through which the film could be differentiated from other, similar, adventure films. Despite industry attempts to construct *Superman: The Movie* as an "A-Picture," then, a major Hollywood blockbuster, reviews still focused on the "mass-culture," comic book origins of the movie. However, as we will see, later media technologies wrote a new chapter in the generic classification of these movies.

A later "Superman" to take to screens provides an excellent comparative example of a media conglomerate cross-promoting its wares. Produced by Time Warner company Warner Bros. Television, based on a property owned by another of its companies, DC Comics, *Smallville* was launched with synergistic verve. Preceding its success Time Warner's *Entertainment Weekly* magazine discussed *Smallville* with detailed regularity. The coverage began in the form of a short preview article by Josh Wolk in September 2001 followed by an advertisement, taken out in October, only a few days prior to *Smallville*'s premiere on the Warner Bros. television netlet the WB (Banks 20; Wolk, "Fall TV Preview '01"; "Smallville Advertisement" 15). The article begins by introducing Clark Kent/Tom Welling and the "teening" of Superman for the new series. It then goes on to relate *Smallville*'s television and film lineage, how it contains stars from the previous *Superman* films ("Annette O'Toole, who coincidently played Lana Lang in *Superman III*") as well as from popular series like *The Dukes of Hazzard* (1979–1985) and emphasizing Welling's own beginnings in *Judging Amy* (1999–2005). These appeals work alongside ones that situate the new series as an action series *and* teen soap opera, quoting writer/creator Alfred Gough as saying, "It's puberty with super-powers" (Wolk, "Fall TV Preview '01" 66).

The advertising image provided some seven weeks later was the central one of *Smallville*'s first season, showing Clark Kent/Tom Welling strung up Christ-like in a cornfield with a red "S" painted on his naked torso. With the tagline, "Every story has a beginning," the image reworks previous notions of the Man of Steel. Age and the vulnerability of the naked body (tastefully smeared with "mud" in the image) are stressed suggesting difference from the previous men of steel. So too does the red *Smallville* logo, which shifts attention away from the protagonist. Interestingly the lighting for the image is dramatically different from the previous modernist interpretations of Superman, particularly as presented in the *Superman* films. For *Smallville*, Kent/Welling is photographed in heavy shadow, with a spotlight off to the left of the image picking up his muscled torso and the golden rope that binds him. This darkness provides a dramatically different visual than the previous poster images discussed for *Superman: The Movie* implying a textual shift towards a darker storyline. Difference from previous incarnations and key genre signifiers associated with melodrama (suffering, vulnerability, and small-town American life) thus became central markers for *Smallville*.

Subsequently in *Entertainment Weekly*, short articles recognized a building interest in *Smallville*. Lynette Rice for example drooled over Welling following the premiere and another article looked at the teen in the Superman franchise (Rice 66; "From Zeroes to Heroes" 102). In November 2001, following two articles in *Variety* that announced the serial's success, *Smallville* was conferred "hit" status with a cover image and longer article in *Entertainment Weekly* on 23 November 2001 (Adalian 21; Kissell 1). "Shows of Strength" is the first to deal with *Smallville*'s genre in depth (Jensen).[5] The article predominantly uses previously successful television shows as generic shorthand with which to discuss *Smallville*. *Smallville* in this article alone is lined up alongside *The X-Files, Dawson's Creek*

(1998–2003), *Twin Peaks* (1990–1991), and *Buffy the Vampire Slayer*. The intention seems to be to tap into two separate markets: one for teen narratives and the other for mystery, tinged by horror. These generic elements had begun to be brought together in *Buffy the Vampire Slayer*, and *Smallville*'s comparable genre-mixing formula was emphatically being signposted to potential crossover viewers in an attempt to cash in on the profitable markets that *Buffy* had tapped into. Interestingly though, co-developer and writer Miles Millar comments in the article, "Where *Buffy the Vampire Slayer* embraces camp, we can't and won't do that" (Jensen, "Shows of Strength" 28). Generic differences became central to the promotion of *Smallville*, with the wide range of comparison texts and Gough and Millar's distancing techniques illustrating how crowded the marketplace was, but also how hard the serial's producers were trying to appeal to audiences for multiple genres. Compared to the earlier discourse of *Superman: The Movie*, which emphasized its concordance with comic books, *Smallville* is clearly framed as "non-comic book," whether teen melodrama, horror, or mystery.

Conglomerate control of the kinds discussed above does not end at the cinema, or with broadcasting on television. New technologies are making an impact on the ability of conglomerates to exercise longer-lived control over their product. Like laserdisc before it the Digital Versatile Disc (DVD) is proving just that for conglomerates: versatile. Enabling complete repackaging of films, television, music videos, and even comic books, DVD as a format crisscrosses the media indiscriminately, reproducing them all in the domestic, televisual environment. Moreover, and particularly for film and television on DVD, inclusion of only the original text in question is becoming increasingly unusual. The industry now tends to juxtapose the original text with a variety of extras including advertising materials (trailers and TV spots), promotional texts (interviews, cast and crew biographies, "Making of" documentaries), and supplementary, cross-promotional, and trivia texts (for more on categories of extras see: Barlow 79–83). The American "Widescreen Special Edition" DVD of *Spider-Man 2* (2004), for example, contains a twelve-part documentary, a video-game documentary, and an "Ock-Umentary" about villain Doctor Octopus. It also has an "Art Gallery" featuring the work of comic book artist Alex Ross and a "Blooper Reel," a music video, weblinks, and two features delineating the hero's past and the women of the Spider-Man franchise. Putting these items together serves two main purposes: first, virtually every narrative, generic, and technical aspect of the film is explained by the filmmakers, and thereby sanctioned and mediated; and, second, these additional features help to sell the DVD to collectors (Klinger, "Contemporary Cinephile").

The increasing usage of Special Edition packaging suggests that audiences want these extra DVD materials, but so far little work has been done to investigate what uses audiences make of them.[6] Moreover, "Special Edition" is itself a category that can be misleading. For example, it is heavily associated with film rather than with music or television DVD releases. Furthermore, "Special Edition" can be used to differentiate little more than packaging. For instance, the U.K. release of Tim Burton's *Corpse Bride* (2005) has a "Special Edition," wherein the "specialness" is in the extra cardboard wrapper, booklet on production, and a series of eight art-postcards, while its disc is the same as the regular release. Taking this into account, the nature of these extras also needs to be better understood, as does their relationship with the texts they support. Barbara Klinger has discussed the role of such materials, and cautions us to remember that "Viewers do not get the unvarnished truth about the production; instead, they are presented with the 'promotable' facts, behind-the-scenes information that supports and enhances a sense of the 'movie magic' associated with the Hollywood production machine" (Klinger, "Contemporary Cinephile" 140).

Klinger's point about the mediation undertaken in the production of special features is a pertinent one. As the *Spider-Man 2* example shows, links to the music industry, Internet, and video game industry were all provided by the filmmakers in order to promote the franchise through its DVD. DVD in this way acts as a platform that filmmakers can use to launch or advertise the multimedia nature of contemporary film and television franchises. However, this does not explain the relationship of these extratextual materials to the original film or serial, nor how understanding of the original text can be changed by viewing them.

Once again, the importance of genre to the promotion of films and television, no matter what format they appear in, provides insights into the processes by which industries try to sell to, and understand, their audiences. In a further trend away from the division of media, the DVD format is now being used as a hub in which disparate media texts can be sewn together. One way in which this is being attempted is through the creation of additional storylines that comment on or feed into the core film or television text. A recent example of this can be found in *The Matrix* (1999, 2003, 2003) sequels and the animated features and video games created to supplement their narratives. Thus *The Animatrix* (2003) animated shorts, available on DVD, become required viewing for full understanding of the latter Matrix films.

Smallville's Season 2 and 3 DVD box sets follow a similar pattern with a series of episodic short video programs titled "The Chloe Chronicles."[7] "The Chloe Chronicles" were brought to life across a range of media initially: begun with short comic book narratives (less than half an issue) that led into web-posted video shorts that became, by Volume 2, a series of short episodic narratives shown weekly on the WB (Carpenter, Carpenter and Warshaw, 2001). The DVDs were the first instance in which these video clips and comic book narratives were packaged together as a unified whole.

"The Chloe Chronicles" are high school student-journalist (and friend to Clark Kent) Chloe Sullivan's (Allison Mack) "behind-the-scenes" investigations of *Smallville's* mysteries. It is this aspect of the original series that caused the comparisons to *Twin Peaks* and *The X-Files* discussed previously, as Smallville's inhabitants are changed by the presence of the meteor rocks that accompanied Clark Kent's arrival in their town. "The Chloe Chronicles" pick up from a Season 1 episode titled "Jitters" in which a LuthorCorp employee, Earl Jenkins, dies after contracting a meteor rock-related disease that causes him to shake uncontrollably. "The Chloe Chronicles" is formulated around a series of interviews recorded on a handheld camera, sometimes two, conducted by the Chloe Sullivan character as she interviews minor and new characters. Typically, where these branch off into sequences that would require special effects, the narrative shifts to the comic books where these can be produced more cheaply.

The conspiracy-inflected detective genre is the driving force behind this supplementary narrative, with Chloe Sullivan trying to discover those responsible for the experiments that killed Earl Jenkins. Crucially, this picks up on one of the least prominent generic elements within *Smallville*.

Gough has described the show as "Heart. Hero. Mystery. Family" (Jensen, "Shows of Strength" 28). Here it is the mystery part of the equation that is emphasized, whereas the plots of *Smallville* usually revolve around the romance, melodrama, and action genres represented in the other three terms. Ostensibly this is because the other three generic components relate directly to protagonist Clark Kent: his family, his relationships, his superpowers form the focus of the series. The mystery plots on the other hand are usually related to villains and to supporting character Chloe Sullivan's work for student newspaper *The Torch* (though these too are frequently related back to Clark Kent's secret heroic identity). In providing this secondary mystery narrative on the DVD, "The Chloe Chronicles" are able to reinforce the mystery plot lines and appeal to several audiences for *Smallville* simultaneously: those who became interested by initially browsing online or reading the comic books and those who view the series for its mystery elements. "The Chloe Chronicles" is therefore an example of just how intermedia such supplementary materials have become. They are able to draw attention to and supplement generic elements from the core text while cross-promoting other arms of the intertext circulating around that core.

If "The Chloe Chronicles" offers an example of supplementary narrative, then the repackaging of *Superman: The Movie* and *Superman II* into a Special Edition box set in 2001 illustrates how the DVD format can be used retrospectively to change conceptions of a film's genre. The extras for the box set feature trailers for both films, plus three "Making of" documentaries, a feature-length commentary, and screen tests, deleted scenes, and a "Vintage TV Spot," all for *Superman: The Movie*. It is the three "Making of" documentary features which undertake the translation of *Superman: The Movie* from prototypical action blockbuster to epic action melodrama.

Together the three documentaries, "Taking Flight: The Development of Superman," "Making Superman: Filming the Legend," and "The Magic Behind the Cape," last almost as long as *Superman: The Movie*. Charting the preexhibition life cycle of *Superman: The Movie*, from preproduction through to postproduction, these three films intersperse finished footage from both *Superman: The Movie* and *Superman II* with contemporary and new interviews and behind-the-scenes footage which together help to reinscribe the film with an additional and differently genred set of meanings.

"The Magic Behind the Cape" acts as an in-depth explanation of the *Superman* special effects, and it reinforces the emphasis on spectacle and is separated from the joint narratives of the other two documentaries. This commentary is closely linked to the emphasis on technology and newness seen in the original production discourses examined earlier. However, instead of focusing on Dolby or even the sets used, it is the *Superman* films' use of optical and other visual effects that are accentuated. It is, therefore, the history of visual effects technologies that are given screen time in "The Magic Behind the Cape," falling somewhere between Barlow's categories of "technical information" and "historical information."

The new genre is unmistakably laid out in Marc McClure's (who played Jimmy Olsen) opening narration for "Taking Flight," "The efforts of the filmmakers were of epic proportions," he says, and this is echoed in "Making Superman": "*Superman* overcame tremendous obstacles to become the success we know it as today." Superlative language in both cases ("epic," "tremendous") helps to build a narrative for the filming of *Superman: The Movie* that is filled with as much angst and difficulty as it is action packed. Director Richard Donner's attempt to make both the first and second *Superman* films back to back is provided in these "Making of" documentaries as the central and most melodramatic of the box set's narratives. As is common with commentaries and "Making of" documentaries, the director's, in this case Donner's, is the voice most frequently heard and also the one to whom the film is most often attributed (Parker and Parker). Donner is described by Creative Consultant Tom Mankiewicz in "Taking Flight" as "almost irresistible when he is pushing." Thereafter Donner is used to account for most creative decisions made on the *Superman* films, for instance the casting of Christopher Reeve ("he was Superman from day one") and the hiring of "big, tall, lanky genius" John Barry as Production Designer. However, in "Making Superman" the narrative alters from this one of Donner's authorship, to a narrative dealing with Donner's melodramatic heroism.

As the postproduction crew discusses the rush to get *Superman: The Movie* into cinemas for Christmas 1978, the discussion of the various difficulties segues into one of Donner's dismissal as director. Narrated in turn by McClure, Andrew Fogelson (credited as President of Warner Bros. marketing 1978–1980), Mankiewicz, Donner, Gene Hackman (who played Lex

Luthor), and Margot Kidder (Lois Lane), their explanations point to growing costs beyond the budget and poor management by the Salkinds as reasons for Donner's dismissal. Donner himself says, "It was a lonely period. It was a long period. It was tiring. It was exhausting, but I had taken on the project of making *Superman* and damn it nothing was going to stop me." Donner's dismissal thus signifies a different kind of narrative than that recognized by Klinger. Here, not all aspects of Hollywood filmmaking are glamorized and, although it is the Salkinds and not Warner Bros. who take the blame, a new auteur narrative is suggested. Donner's authorship of *Superman: The Movie* is built around "epic" difficulty, massive project management, and success in the face of almost unbearable pressure from production company villains. In essence, Donner's story, written over images from the film (especially ones from the production period that insert him into the frame with his stars), adds to the film a new melodramatic heroic narrative.

Donner's melodramatic heroism is carefully juxtaposed on the DVD—placed spatially close to the film texts and temporally blending archival and new footage so that its impact is naturalized. It adds a kind of heroic narrative to the 1978 and 1980 versions of Superman that are more like the hero of *Smallville*, the television version of Superman circulating most heavily by the time of the Special Edition DVD's release in 2001. The multiheroic narratives of Donner and *Superman* help to maximize appeals to audiences. They appeal to nostalgic audiences for the original films, to collectors for whom trivia is important, and to those audiences for whom melodramatic heroism is becoming a more natural construct than the action adventure heroism of Reeve in the *Superman* films.

Nor is the *Superman* film box set the only place in which such new "heroic" narratives have been produced. *Smallville's* third season box set contains a special feature titled "Producing *Smallville*: The Heroes Behind the Camera." Unlike Donner's tale of betrayal by the Salkinds, however, this "making of" featurette is entirely positive, detailing the working life of the crew with a special thank you during the end credits to the 250 people who help bring *Smallville* to life. Furthermore, the tone of the featurette is different, detailing the family atmosphere on set, with joking asides (particularly by Michael Rosenbaum who plays Lex Luthor in the series) interspersed with information about lighting, sets, and special effects among other behind-the-scenes roles. These help to maintain the soap opera feel to the production, likening "real" off-screen personae to the family orientation of many of *Smallville*'s story lines.

Two further important short documentaries appear on the Season 2 box set of *Smallville*, and it is these that most closely replicate the generic reconditioning undertaken for the *Superman* films. The first, "Faster Than a Speeding Bullet: The Visual Effects of *Smallville*" is set up as a text for technical information, but actually achieves a secondary goal more efficiently. The visual effects are used to showcase the serial's action genre status, as a series of "stunts" are explained for audiences, emphasizing their importance within the overall *Smallville* narrative. Newness and experimentation are emphasized in the documentary, as are the "heroic" efforts of the effects team, who as Millar explains are "always under the gun" when attempting to complete shots on time. The interesting effect of the "heroic" narrative is the way it emphasizes the relationship between film and televisual visual effects. Multiple references are made throughout the documentary to the way the effects for *Smallville* are, on the one hand, creating visual effects for the Superman franchise that have never been accurately produced in the past (especially X-Ray vision, which in *Smallville* is shown through CGI effects that replicate an X-Ray type of scan of Clark Kent's environment), while on the other producing effects that are of a comparable quality to those used in filmmaking.

The second featurette, "Christopher Reeve: The Man of Steel," is presented as a documentary about Reeve's appearance on *Smallville* as Dr. Virgil Swann, a character who tells Clark Kent about Krypton. Cross-promotion for a good cause, the featurette repeats the call for charitable donations to the Christopher Reeve Paralysis Fund, which first aired at the end of Reeve's episode ("Rosetta"). This call extends the narrative about Reeve "passing the torch" to Welling. (Greg Beeman, "Christopher Reeve: The Man of Steel") It is in this documentary that Gough states the differences between the two interpretations of Superman: "In the film, Superman is the character and Clark Kent is the disguise, and you know, in our show Clark Kent is the character and ultimately, down the road, Superman will be the disguise . . . it's a different take on the same material." Welling and Reeve also attempt to distinguish between the characters they play, with Reeve commenting that there are in fact two Clark Kents and that Welling's is more like the young version played by Jeff East in *Superman: The Movie* than it is like his own dualistic version of Kent/Superman. By separating out the different versions of the Superman story in this way the makers of *Smallville* provide an intertextual circuit in which the contemporary version of the story is informed and legitimated by Reeve's performances, while rekindling audience memories of the *Superman* films and fostering continued interest in them as source texts for *Smallville*. Separating the texts also enables a final definition to be created in the generic difference between *Superman: The Movie* and *Smallville*, between the action (Superman as character) and melodrama (Clark Kent as character).

Genre has always been an inconstant, nebulous concept that refuses absolute, permanent definition. This chapter has attempted to show how genre, even when linked to a single franchise or character like Superman, needs to be viewed as historically and contextually dependent. The shift between production narratives for *Superman: The Movie* that began by emphasizing comic book origins, spectacle, and cultural legitimacy through star performers, altered almost beyond recognition by the time the film came to DVD. Therein it was the melodrama of the making of *Superman* that most informed and augmented the film text. The advent of DVD technologies and how they influence our understanding of film and television texts implies the importance of considering genre as an intertextually dependent phenomenon. Although audiences are not forced to view such narratives as "The Chloe Chronicles" or the "Taking Flight" documentary, their presence is advertised in both the DVD packaging and repeatedly stressed in the DVD menus. As the market for DVDs increases, the special features they contain will also increase in importance as they reach growing audiences. Indeed, with moves towards more supplementary narratives rather than advertising or informational extras, DVD special features are being presented as audience draws alongside original texts. As special features continue to grow and change, they are becoming more and more useful as a means for understanding and extending textual enjoyment. As the investigation herein has shown, DVD extras do not simply add to their own texts, but, like the Christopher Reeve featurette, can be used to reinvigorate interest in entire franchises, and even charitable institutions.

DVD then encourages generic complexity and hybridity in ways that the popular and trade presses have neither scope nor interest in doing. Unlike *Entertainment Weekly*, where *Smallville* shared space with a multiplicity of other film, television, and music texts, the Internet and DVD provide dedicated spaces for production discourses, and additional revenue streams for producers. The WB's site for *Smallville* has links, for example, not just to "The Chloe Chronicles," but also to *The Torch*, Smallville High's fictional student paper, and to the *Smallville Ledger*, another fictional newspaper (http://www2.warnerbros.com/web/smallville/torch and http://www2.warnerbros.com/web/smallville/ledger). DVD is different from the Internet, however, because of its artifact status. As objects, DVDs have the sense of offering up a coherent, complete narrative, the object organizing its content and demanding recognition of the links between any separate contained texts. For this reason DVD might be better thought of as presenting not a text and extratextual materials, but as being itself a multitext, a multitext of layered, competing yet combined narratives, any of which potentially impacts on and changes the meanings of the others depending on which features audience members engage with.

This is not to suggest that DVD is "better" at disseminating generic or other information about films. The trade presses like *Variety* still dominate inter-industry discourses, and popular publications like *Entertainment Weekly* still serve a broader, more general community than those purchasing (often expensive) DVD box sets. Rather, DVD, as a format, with its ability to house disparate media texts, suggests, at a given historical moment, the relationships between not just the texts but the media themselves. It suggests also which genres are in ascendance at a particular moment. In the *Superman* box set, the repackaging of materials suggests a shift from a dominant action-adventure genre in the 1970s to a melodramatically inflected action genre in the present period. With *Smallville*, the special features provided give clear instances of the promotion of distinct component genres. Where "The Chloe Chronicles" showcases mystery, the Season 3 documentary "Producing Smallville: The Heroes Behind the Camera" provides another set of melodramatic struggles and "Faster than a Speeding Bullet: The Visual FX of Smallville" from Season 2 gives emphasis to action and spectacle. In each instance the special features are designed to accent, and in some cases actually create, generic codes to maximize audiences. DVD becomes an opportunity within a text's production life cycle in which the makers can put back or reemphasize missed or missing genre parts. The multitext DVD through these various means becomes a kind of supertext, a fitting format from which aspects of the Superman franchise can once again take flight.

AMERICAN SPLENDOR

TRANSLATING COMIC AUTOBIOGRAPHY
INTO DRAMA-DOCUMENTARY

— CRAIG HIGHT

American Splendor (2003) is a drama-documentary about the life
and art of seminal underground comic artist Harvey Pekar, the creator of
the long-standing autobiographical comic of the same name. All comic-
to-film adaptations have proved challenging, but apart from some notable
exceptions such as *Ghost World,* most have the advantage of characters
and scenarios which offer easy translation to mainstream action-adventure
cinema increasingly geared toward teenage audiences (fantastic superhero
characters, engaged in spectacular action against their enemies). In contrast, *American Splendor* (the comic) provided some unique challenges for
filmmakers Shari Springer Berman and Bob Pulcini. Pekar's idiosyncratic
and innovative comic has been published for over twenty-five years, it has
focused on mundane everyday details, employed a variety of styles and
featured a main character (Pekar) who has consistently articulated his antagonism toward the mainstream and the popular. The resulting film is
a hybrid of drama-documentary combining conventional aspects of this
form with elements of the graphic style of comic books. The film's innovative style opens up a space for an exploration of the nature of both autobiographical comic narratives, and drama-documentary codes and conventions.

This chapter discusses the translation of *American Splendor* into
mainstream film narrative, focusing upon the distinctive blend of representational strategies employed by the filmmakers, and the variety of levels

of commentary that it consequently borrows from both comic books and drama-documentary. The discussion below briefly positions Pekar's work within the wider genre of autobiographic comics, before tracing how the distinctive aspects of *American Splendor* the comic are remediated into audio-visual form.

Although comics are a medium as rich and complex as any other, the study of comic forms is a comparatively neglected field within media studies, with attempts to identify the defining characteristics of comic narratives and aesthetics still in their infancy.[1] A key reason for this academic neglect lies in the dominance of superhero narratives within the comic market, and the consequent assumption that comics are "just for kids." The medium, however, has consistently featured a variety of other genres, and in particular there is a long tradition of comic narratives within the overlapping genres of biography, autobiography, journalism, history, and other nonfiction related formats (Witek 13–57). Originating in underground comics, these more "adult" oriented narratives have increasingly sought both critical and popular recognition.

There is insufficient space here to fully explore the range of autobiographical comics which contextualizes Pekar's work. A key figure within this genre is Robert Crumb, whose work ranges from autobiographical to social satire comics (including collaborations with Pekar). The full spectrum of such comics incorporates work as diverse as Julie Doucet's *My New York Diary*, Joe Sacco's *Safe Area Gorazde: The War in Eastern Bosnia 1992–95*, and Marjane Satrapi's *Persepolis: The Story of a Childhood*. The breadth of aesthetic styles and thematics contained within just this highly selective cross-section of comic narratives demonstrates the broad territory which nonfiction comic creators range within.

Each of these works can be seen to draw, in varying degrees, from a number of specific visual discourses. Many nonfiction comic artists rely on the use of photographs as reference points for their drawings, to develop a sense of iconic authenticity in representing social and urban environments and natural landscapes. Within such settings, nonfiction comics will often move away from iconic representations of people, instead offering impressions or *interpretations* of characters. One resulting pattern is a distinctive visual dichotomy between character and setting, which especially characterizes autobiographical comics (such as Pekar's). The most extreme, and widely celebrated and debated, example of this pattern is Art Spiegelman's two-part *Maus* (*My Father Bleeds History* and *And Here My Troubles Began*). *Maus* dispenses with any semblance of iconic representation in the drawing of its characters, in favor of a cat-and-mouse metaphor to represent the power relations between representatives of the Nazi regime and European Jews.

Just as with documentary animation,[2] the graphic nature of comics opens up avenues for expression not available to prose writers, documentary filmmakers, or those working in the same genres in different media. Because most nonfiction comics are written and drawn by the same individual author/artist, these comics tend to have a highly individual style of expression. In fact, underlying many of these works is the explicit assumption that these artists' drawing styles are much more analogous to handwriting than might be the case for the writing style of prose writers. That is, that a comic author's style is derived directly from his/her personality and artistic sensibility rather than something that has been employed for deliberate effect. Again, a key originator in this regard within the autobiographical comics scene is Robert Crumb. Crumb's rhetorical justification of his work has tended to focus on claims that his art is an uncensored translation of his consciousness, which it is in some sense "unmediated," and therefore all the more valuable as artistic expression. Obviously, such a rhetorical stance has not prevented him from exploring a range of stylistic approaches.

Similarly, the content within autobiographical works is often marked by an apparent commitment to extremely intimate, almost confessional narratives. Although typically involving a focus on following a character through everyday events using first-person narration, the "authenticity" of the work is often judged on the apparent honesty of the writing or the emotional truth of a work. This means a focus on a brutal honesty in stories together with an often deliberately unflattering pattern of self-representation by comic artists. Harvey Pekar's work clearly operates within such broad tendencies within the genre of autobiographical comics.

American Splendor is an autobiography in progress, an account of Pekar's life and work told through a series of vignettes. The title is deliberately ironic, and an indicator of Pekar's sardonic and at times bitter

Fig. 1. "The Young Crumb Story," story by Harvey Pekar, art by Robert Crumb (Pekar, 2003). One of the many retellings of the beginnings of Pekar's comics career.

perspective on his life. The comic was originally self-published by Pekar, and he did not have a formal relationship with a publisher until the 1990s.[3] Pekar considers what he does autobiographical writing,[4] simply using graphic form to contribute to the wider body of this literature form (Pekar, "A Mensch for All Mediums"). He focuses particularly on the minutiae of life: "I concentrate, more than I think virtually any comic book artist has in the past, on the so-called mundane details of every day life—quotidian life. What happens to a person during a working day, marital relations, and stuff like that" (Pekar, "A Mensch for All Mediums").

The Pekar style is to capture the vernacular of language, to be faithful to the rhythms and idiosyncrasies of everyday conversation. *American Splendor* has an overwhelming reliance on episodic narrative, with his vignettes rarely having a punchline but usually focused instead on a turn of phrase or an everyday, often mundane, insight. As Witek notes, this provides for regular readers a "cumulative experience, unlike the self-contained gag strips in the newspapers" (Witek 137). Throughout these pieces, Pekar maintains both a consistent internal monologue (Witek 124), and an overall focus on the American lower and middle classes. His talent is in writing short storylines in ways that appear casual, and which resonate with his reader's own lives. (This is a style which offers obvious challenges for filmmakers tasked with transforming the comic into film narrative, as discussed below.)

Pekar has rarely enjoyed popular commercial success, but both himself and his admirers insist that this lack of popularity is in fact a clear marker of the authenticity of his work. He has been constructed as the antithesis of the superhero mainstream and championed as a bearer of the truth, someone who is committed to the integrity of his individual perspective, despite the personal and artistic sacrifices this entails. Here is Robert Crumb from his preface to *American Splendor Presents Bob and Harv's Comics*, speaking of Pekar's audience in Cleveland:

> And Harvey Pekar is their witness. He is one of them. He reports the truth of life in Cleveland as he sees it, hears it, *feels* it in his manic-depressive nervous system. There's nobody else to do it. Who would want to? There's no money in it. There no money in telling the truth. People want *escape*. They want *myths*. This slice-of-life stuff, with no spices added, no glamour, no heroes, it's only going to reach a small, select audience, no matter how eloquent or "poetic" it is done. [. . .] That's not to say there isn't *entertainment* here. Harvey is a great storyteller . . . he brings this mundane, work-a-day work to life, gives us its poignant *moments*, its humor, absurdity, irony . . . and mostly, it's absolute *truth*. There is no exaggeration in these stories. What you read is what *really* happened [emphasis in original]. (Crumb)

At times, Pekar's own description of his technique draws closely on the discourses of documentary: "I look at myself sometimes when I do these shorter pieces like a photographer walking down the street who runs into things; he sees things and he shoots them" (Harvey, *Art of the Comic Book* 235). The aesthetic style favored by Pekar's comics is consistent with this overall stance, as they eschew the complex, overlapping and visually dynamic layouts of superhero comics in favor of a conventional panel layout and commitment to eye-level perspective.

A key point to be made about Pekar is that he stands somewhat out-side of much of the autobiographical tradition in comics in that he does not draw himself but relies totally on collaboration with comic artists. *American Splendor* is written by Pekar, but actually illustrated by high-pro-file artists such as Crumb, Sacco, and Frank Stack. Ironically, in this Pekar in fact lies closer to the traditions of superhero comic writing, where teams of writer/artist/letterers are given opportunities to refashion a traditional superhero character.[5] Pekar chooses collaborators for particular stories; he attempts to match a particular story with an artist whose style he feels is appropriate for that material (Robinson).

Fig. 2. "A Marriage Album," story by Harvey Pekar and Joyce Brabner, art by Val Mayerik (Pekar, 2003). Arriving for the first time in Cleveland, Joyce tries to imagine which artist's representation of Harvey is the most accurate, a scene recreated for the film.

This reliance on collaboration with artists has resulted in a body of work which incorporates a variety of styles, and many different represen-tations of Pekar himself, as each artist folds his own interpretation of the writer into the overall body of work that constitutes the comic. A signifi-cant feature of *American Splendor* is consequently a high degree of reflex-ivity toward representations of individual identity (something recognized by the filmmakers of *American Splendor* the film, as outlined below). Un-like, for example, Crumb's autobiographical work, Pekar's narratives are not conceived initially in terms of images, but focus more on dialogue and the context of interactions between his characters. In this Pekar, quite self-consciously, follows more literary traditions of autobiography (Witek 130–32).

Consistent with other autobiographical comics, however, overall the portrayals of Pekar himself in both form and content are also quite negative and confessional. And, again, these aspects form part of the effort to appeal to reader's assumptions regarding the authenticity of the comic as a whole. When questioned on whether he was judging and portraying himself too harshly, Pekar has replied: "I don't want to play myself up as a hero, because it would make me unbelievable. I'd rather settle for people thinking that I'm a bum, but digging my stories, than liking me and not being able to believe in my stories" (Robinson, 2003).

Standing outside of the *American Splendor* comic, but consistent with Pekar's overall writing perspective, is *Our Cancer Year*, which provided the basis for the latter part of the narrative of the film itself. Co-written with wife Joyce Brabner and drawn by Stack, it chronicles Pekar's successful battle against cancer. This story was quite deliberately crafted and conceived by its authors as a singular graphic novel, with the authors selecting key events, and deliberately rearranging their chronological order to increase its emotional impact with readers. Throughout the book, Stack varies aspects of his style, using different drawing techniques for specific situations: sometimes crosshatching, sometimes in stark outline, with differing emphases on areas of black and white depending upon the mood of a chapter.

Overall, Pekar's work articulates some of the central tensions that are inherent to any effort to represent aspects of reality, and especially those which mark nonfiction forms within comics. Pekar is quite conscious of such tensions, and explicitly addresses them in his work, often directly asking readers to think about the nature of the representations he is offering. It is interesting to trace how this complexity of issues in regard to representation have been translated by the film adaptation of his work.

American Splendor the film was originally produced by HBO, but released to theatres after it won the Grand Jury Prize at the Sundance Film Festival. The film project originated from a collaborator's connection to independent film producer Ted Hope, who hired documentary filmmakers Shari Springer Berman and Robert Pulcini. Pekar and wife Joyce Brabner have co-writing credits, because parts of the film's narrative are based on *Our Cancer Year*. Pekar has claimed, including in the film itself, that he did not actually read the script before filming commenced and did not have real input into the creative production of the film, although he at least had access to the script in preproduction. In fact, Pekar has been consistent in voicing his cynicism toward the movie business itself, and the prospect of finding fame so late in his life that it offered him. He has insisted that he was involved simply as a means to increase the audience for his comics: "For me the movies were basically a one-shot opportunity to make some extra money" (Pekar, 2004).

As noted above, the film is a drama-documentary, a complex fact-fiction form[6] which combines the accessibility of mainstream film and television melodrama with an association with the factual discourse that underpins the documentary genre (Paget 35). A simple definition of drama-documentary is that it offers dramatized versions of actual events and is a form often chosen from a motivation to reach a wider audience than the documentary genre has traditionally attracted. Biographical films such as *American Splendor* tend to be centered on historical, political, or cultural figures already well known to the public. They are reintroduced to the audience with a suggestion that the film represents their "real story," containing an emotional truth less easily portrayed through the representational constraints of documentary.

Lipkin talks of drama-documentary as dealing with "quasi-indexical narrative" (2). Rather than an indexical representation of the real, the forms offers iconic representations couched within the narrative forms of melodrama. The rhetorical logic of an argument that is prioritized within documentary is present in the text but tends to be articulated more implicitly, at the level of thematics, the overall agenda of the text, and within the specific nature of its narrative constructions. Although largely reliant on iconic reconstruction, drama-documentary often directly integrates actual and re-created material, either in succession or together within a scene.[7] Crucially, however, melodramatic and documentary constructions are invariably used in ways that deny any tension or contradictions between these competing forms. Instead these serve to reinforce each other; any documentary materials used further authenticate the narrative, while the narrative works to add emotional weight to the rational discourses underlying a drama-documentary. The balance between these elements is crucial to the persuasive effect of a particular text. As Lipkin notes, the more complex sequences, those that particularly blur the boundaries between what is real and what is fictionalized, are often the most effective in this sense.

In terms of melodramatic narrative structure, drama- documentary typically employs techniques such as the telescoping of complex events and histories, creating a narrative arc out of an everyday story, and editing out aspects of a story that are repetitive, confusing, or simply extraneous to the main narrative thrust. And there are typically elements of a realistic dramatic style, such as key lighting, naturalistic sound, continuity editing, the use of actual locations for settings, (often unknown) actors that resemble the actual figures they portray, and a low-key or "realistic" style of acting. Other codes and conventions which may be used include some more typically associated with documentary, such as the use of captions to identify dates and locations, archival footage of events or issues, and voice-overs from actors or a real person featured in the text (Paget 61–89). Increasingly there is also the use of special effects within drama-documentary, but in ways that are consistent with their use within dramatic reconstruction sequences within documentary, with computer graphic imaging (CGI) used to reinforce a sense of the iconic authenticity of the text's version of events.

All of these forms of representation are used to increase the sense of a text's "proximity" (Lipkin 53–54) to actual social actors and historical events. In the case of *American Splendor*, remaining true to Pekar's original artistic vision also meant taking the collaborative nature of Pekar's work, and its consequent stylistic complexity, as a direct inspiration. The resulting film is a hybrid of different forms of representation. In Pulcini's words: "We thought we had the license to anything we wanted, because the comic books are so free form" (West and West 41). In the film, Pekar is represented in five different ways: as played by actor Paul Giamatti within the film's narrative sequences; as himself in interview footage shot for the film; as himself in archival footage from his appearances on American television; in comic form, within graphic and animation sequences derived from *American Splendor* the comic; and, briefly, played by actor Donal Logue in a stage play based on the comic. Similarly, Pekar's "voice," or his perspective, is represented in quite distinct ways through these representations. We hear him most often in scripted voice-over for the narrative sequences, although as noted above, he was not extensively involved in the writing of the film's script. He is also heard in direct-to-camera interview segments, within the archival footage, and through aspects of his writing lifted directly from the panels of his *American Splendor* comic.

With *American Splendor* the drama-documentary, the key issues become how these various representational strategies operate to support each other, and whether any tensions between them exist. To some extent, the distinct modes of representation within the film serve quite different purposes, although there is an obvious attempt to seamlessly integrate them into a coherent perspective on Pekar's work and life. This stylistic eclecticism is appropriate for the film's subject matter, and it allows the filmmakers to claim a commitment to authenticity in their approach. However, it is also true that it allowed them to produce a more entertaining and visually innovative film than is typically the case for the drama-documentary form (thus potentially increasing its appeal beyond the limited demographic of Pekar's original comic). This agenda clearly shaped the narrative structure of the film, which offers a considerably revised version of the extended and episodic narrative contained within *American Splendor* the comic.

The filmmakers were well aware of the challenges Pekar's work posed for adaptation to the screen. Co-director Pulcini observed, "Harvey's comic books are not really about traditional narrative structures. They're really just moments in his life, observations. The whole point of the *American Splendor* comics is that life doesn't really organize itself well, which is very daunting for a screenwriter. You want to stay true to the spirit of the books, but you also want to be able to fashion them into some kind of story" (West and West 41).

The film's revisions include the telescoping of some events, the changing of names to protect people's identities (Robinson), and the editing out of core aspects of Pekar's biography, including his intellectualism, his pride for Cleveland, and his long history of published jazz criticism.[8] Elsewhere the filmmakers have more explicitly stated the overall theme of the film: "an unlikely love story between a man and his medium, which in this case is a comic book, and how he got a life through comic books—he found love, or some version of love, a family, and a creative outlet" (West and West 41).

A sense of realism to the film is partly established through a selection of cinematographic styles. For the bulk of the film's narrative sequences, the filmmakers drew upon 1970s film traditions of realism, using muted earth tones for a "gritty, realistic look" (West and West 41). For later sequences, when Pekar is shown to beat cancer, the film's cinematography subtly brightens. As is consistently the case with drama-documentary, little-known actors Giamatti and Hope Davis were cast as Pekar and his wife Joyce Brabner. The middle part of the film follows the budding "romance" between these two, with the audience encouraged to warm to two dysfunctional characters who find each other. Co-director Berman has described their performances in ways familiar to the agenda of drama-documentary. "We didn't want Paul, or Hope, or any of the actors to do flat-out imitations of these people. We wanted them to capture something deeper, the essence of the character" (West and West 42).

Fig. 3. Hope Davis and Paul Giamatti play Brabner and Pekar in the film's narrative sequences.

Pekar's voice-over serves multiple purposes during these sequences. In part he simply repeats the perspective of his comic, at times voicing lines that he originally wrote for his comic (now part of the film's script). In this sense, his voice-over both reinforces the authenticity of Giamatti's interpretation of Pekar and also excuses any poetic license taken in the dramatic reconstructions of selected events in Pekar's life. However, Pekar also plays the role of commentator on the degree of mediation inherent to these sequences. In (scripted) voice-over for one early sequence of Giamatti at work as a clerk, he states: "Here's our man. Yeah, alright, here's me, the guy playing me, though he don't look nothing like me, but whatever . . . " This is a disclaimer that is consistent with the commentary on representation which is such a distinctive aspect of Pekar's comic, but is also an element of scripted reflexivity that is relatively rare for drama-documentary. This layered perspective continues throughout the film. For example, after a scene focused on a theatrical production of *American Splendor*, with Giamatti and Davis viewing actors Donal Logue and Molly Shannon playing Pekar and Brabner, we hear Pekar's voice-over: "If you think that reading comics about yourself is strange, try watching a play about it. God only knows how I'll feel when I see this movie."

Coexisting and often directly integrated with the film's narrative sequences are a variety of documentary sequences, with each strategy of documentary representation performing a specific function. For example, the final sequence of the film consists of handheld shots from Pekar's retirement party,[9] with Pekar celebrating with the real-life Joyce and their adopted daughter Danielle. Stylistically, this sequence stands in contrast to the rest of the film and serves to finally break the audience away from the narrative of Pekar's life and provide a sense of closure.

Throughout the film other key documentary elements are more seamlessly incorporated into the narrative. The key example here is the archival footage of Pekar's appearances on the American television program *The Letterman Show*. Davis and Giamatti are shown waiting nervously in the waiting room, and when he is called on-stage, Davis turns her attention to the television monitor in the room. She scrutinizes archival footage of Pekar's first appearance on the program, seemingly oblivious to the change in her husband's appearance (from Giamatti to Pekar). This is typical of the effort of drama-documentary to erase the boundary between the actors and their real life counterparts, and here the archival footage is used to reinforce our acceptance of the actor's portrayals.

The main documentary sequences within *American Splendor*, however, operate in a much more complex fashion within the film. They are filmed within a studio and provide spaces for the appearance of Pekar himself, where he can expound on aspects of his life experience and comment on the film itself. In contrast to the narrative sequences, and the film's final observational documentary scenes, these are more obviously constructed by the filmmakers themselves; "We wanted a very different style for the documentary parts of the film. We decided that would be the place where we'd have a very artificial look, where we'd create a comic book panel look, with very vibrant colors and just a few well-placed items in the frame amidst a lot of empty, white space. We thought that if we actually filmed Harvey in his own environment, the look would compete with the narrative, and we wanted to have a complete break" (Pulcini, quoted in West and West 42).

In the opening of the film, immediately after the credit sequences, we view the first of these studio scenes. The preceding scene has a voice-over from the real Pekar, as he introduces himself by reading from the script: "If you're the kind of person looking for some romance or escapism or some fantasy figure to save the day? Guess what? You got the wrong movie." On the line "guess what," there is a wipe to Pekar sitting on a stool, talking into a large studio microphone, in a bright white studio with some chairs and a sound recordist monitoring a tape recorder in the background. Pekar finishes his sentence, then comments that they have done enough takes, and begins a conversation with an off-screen female voice (co-director Berman). She asks him whether he likes the script, and he admits he has barely read it. During the exchange, we have inserts of closeups of Pekar's favorite drink (orange soda), and sound equipment.

Unlike Pekar's voice-over in the narrative sequences, here his *unscripted* words and on-screen presence are markers of authenticity. The short interview works as an explicit rupturing of the suspension of disbelief that is central to the narrative, and potentially opens an irreconcilable division between the competing forms of documentary and melodrama. Pekar's reading of the script is suddenly associated not with *his* perspective, but with the deliberate constructions of the filmmakers. Similarly, the sudden cut from Giamatti (and Davis) to the real Pekar (and Brabner) highlights how comparatively simplistic and two dimensional any actor's portrayal can be, when directly confronted with the complexity of the social actors they are based upon. It is a risky representational strategy and its success depends upon the audience accepting a creative tension between the competing meanings of these studio interviews.[10] The complexity of the film lies in the resulting space which is opened for the audience, a space which is then available for a critique of the narrative, and the nature of the representations which are offered by the film. The filmmakers invite this

Fig. 4. Joyce Brabner and Harvey Pekar in one of the film's documentary sequences.

critique, but still attempt to identify it with a commitment to representing the idiosyncratic perspective of Pekar.

Interestingly, these interview sequences are also the only space where Pekar's work in the comic medium is critiqued, ironically by his wife. After a montage of various representations of her by Pekar's collaborators, we cut to Brabner and Pekar being interviewed in the studio. She states that "Harvey tends to push the negative and the sour. He can be very depressed and therefore very depressing" and that he "won't put any happy things in there." Pekar, in response, admits that he does not put in all of the events which feature her, and that his perspective often tends to be all "doom and gloom." It is the only explicit suggestion in the film that his art might not be an absolutely accurate perspective on Pekar's experiences, but is in fact shaped by Pekar's negative personality as much as the selective portrayal of people and events that are central to any storyteller.[11]

The third key group of representational strategies employed in the film are elements of the graphic form of comics. Again, these are intended to increase the "proximity" (in Lipkin's terminology) of the film to Pekar's original work. In subsequent interviews, the filmmakers have also worked to reinforce the authenticity and validity of Pekar's original comic agenda, which also legitimates their own use of his comic panels as forms of "evidence." "We have a documentary film background, so we approached the comic books as if they were raw footage. You have to make connections between these moments, to find a way to piece them together, in the same way you do with documentary footage" (Pulcini, quoted in West and West 41). And, in fact, there are direct parallels to the ways in which the archival footage of Pekar on the *Letterman Show* operates in the film. When key collaborator Robert Crumb (played by James Urbaniak) draws Giamatti while both are sitting in his lounge, the resulting drawing is of the real Pekar, not of Giamatti. The drawing is authentic to that originally drawn by Crumb, and the fact that it looks nothing like Giamatti is ignored (just as Davis's viewing of the real Pekar on a television monitor causes no confusion for her character).

Similarly, the film's more openly graphic constructions are naturalized within the narrative sequences. Captions, a common convention in drama-documentary, here replicate the captions of comic panels rather than the sober style of documentary (they are in boxes on the top or bottom of the screen, in capitals, black on white, in typeface familiar from comics). There are also many sections of the film where we intercut easily between sequences showing the original *American Splendor* comic panels and the film's melodramatic constructions. The film's title sequence, for example, introduces both Pekar and examples of his art. From the caption "Our story begins," we cut to Giamatti, walking on the streets of Cleveland. He is framed by a comic strip border around the edge of the frame, then the camera tracks from one "comic panel" to the next, as if the viewer is reading a live-action comic book. The tracking mimics a reader following the layout of a comic book, and in each panel live action featuring the actor is alternated with actual panels from Pekar's *American Splendor*, with speech balloons that introduce the lead character. This deliberate blurring of the line between different forms of representation cues audiences to the expectation that such techniques will be used throughout the film.

Later in the film, there is a complex montage sequence which attempts to represent the scope of Pekar's *American Splendor* over the decades of its publication. Here dramatizations featuring Giamatti are intercut with the *American Splendor* panels that the scenes are directly based on, while this montage is accompanied by jazz music on the soundtrack. Each live action scene is played first, then freezes, and fades into the original comic panel. The panels selected represent highlights from the years of *American Splendor* comics, including many of the various key phrases and situations for which the comic has become known. Giamatti in live action, and the car-

Fig. 5. The opening credit sequence from *American Splendor*, the film, showing the use of live footage contained within the panels of a conventional comic layout.

toon Pekar, are seen reflecting on washing dishes, buying records, riding on the bus, gluing his coat together, drinking coffee in a café, and noting his disappointment at his reflection in a mirror.

In one sense, *American Splendor* here validates comics as simply another means of conveying information about Pekar. However, the inclusion of comics panels also highlights how difficult it is for audio-visual media to incorporate examples of Pekar's print media. To bridge the gap between the static print media of the comic and the moving images of film, the film uses a rudimentary form of animation (a comparatively innovative technique for drama-documentary[12]). The film takes individual panels from the comic and animates cutouts of sections of the panel (for example, only Pekar's hands and mouth moving while the rest of the panel stays static). These animations transform the original comic panels into a more accessible format for moving pictures.

Animation is used most extensively in the inevitable "epiphany" sequence; the scenes within a drama-documentary which portray a climactic point in the lead character life and/or work. Here we see Giamatti reach the moment when he realizes the artistic vision that will inspire his alternative approach to comics. Waiting to be served at a supermarket, we see and hear Giamatti's internal dialogue over the frustrations of waiting in queues. As we freeze on a closeup of Giamatti, a thought balloon appears next to his head: "Picking the right check-out line is an art . . . there's a lots of things you gotta consider" (the writing is in the same cartoon script used in the film's captions).

Fig. 6. One of the scenes featuring comic aesthetics: the frustrated internal monologue of Harvey (Giamatti), waiting in a queue at the supermarket.

As he is forced to wait behind an "old Jewish lady" engaged in a lengthy discussion with the store's manager we see a captioned thought balloon, then a cutout Pekar animation within a thought balloon, then a full-length cutout animation of Pekar in split-screen, then finally cutout animations of Pekar pop up each side of Giamatti's head. For each of these animations, Pekar's scripted voice-over serves as the soundtrack, as he rants against the injustice of waiting in supermarket queues. Inspired by the incident, Giamatti works all night, then meets future collaborator Crumb to articulate his (Pekar's) comic philosophy. He explains that while underground comics such as Crumb's are subversive and have opened things up politically there is still plenty more that could be done to attract an adult readership, that comics "could be more of an art form." Explaining that he has tried to write some material that is about real life, he states that this is no "idealized shit, no phony bullshit, it's the real thing. Ordinary life is pretty complex stuff." The last sentence is Pekar's slogan, appearing on his comics and his website.

As noted above, the more complex integration of documentary elements within conventional drama-documentary invariably serve to deepen a text's persuasive effect. In *American Splendor*, graphic elements and animation are added to the conventional mix of representational techniques, but here the effect is arguably that a more complicated relationship is established with the film's audience. These combinations do attempt to suggest a seamless flow between different modes of representation, but there is also the deliberate opening of a space for a commentary on both comic and drama-documentary forms. In one key scene, when Brabner (Davis) comes to Cleveland to first meet Pekar (Giamatti), animations are used to foreground the slippery nature of comic representation. Waiting at the train station, she surveys nearby people and imagines what Pekar actually looks like (having only seen his comics). We see full-size cutout animations of different cartoon versions of Pekar, in the variety of ways in which artists over the decades have drawn him (with varying degrees of attractiveness). She then meets Giamatti in the flesh, and the audience has the opportunity to recognize that he is simply another, more naturalistic, representation of Pekar himself.

There are also more explicitly reflexive scenes within the film. The key such scene occurs after Giamatti has a conversation about life and gourmet jelly beans with his workmate Toby Radloff (Judah Friedlander). As Giamatti ponders the beans, we cut to a side shot of director Pulcini behind the camera, directing Giamatti. After Pulcini yells "cut," the camera tracks from Giamatti over to a catering table, laden with food, where the real Pekar and Toby are conducting a similar conversation. Giamatti and Friedlander leave the table to sit on folding chairs at the rear of the studio. As the visuals cut to shots of Toby being photographed in the studio for publicity shots, we hear him interviewed in voice-over talking about loneliness and his relationship with Pekar. We then cut back to the conversation between Pekar and Toby, as they agree on strategies to combat loneliness.

There are multiple layers to this scene, arising from the sudden collapse of any boundary between the narrative and documentary sequences. The conversation between the real Pekar and Toby appears within the white studio of the documentary segments, but it is scripted. It allows the film to directly compare the performances particularly of the real and fake Tobys. It quite explicitly ruptures not only the fourth wall of the narrative sequences but of the documentary sequences as well, with co-director Pulcini appearing in frame and Giamatti and Friedlander straying into the "documentary" space where we have seen Pekar. These sequences explicitly foreground a key subtext from the previous sections of the film; that is, a commentary on the nature of any representation of reality (whether Pekar's comics, documentary or the drama-documentary form of the film). All are viewed as legitimate and perhaps equal forms of representing social experience.

In part this commentary also subverts the validity of the drama-documentary form itself, in that it so directly questions its own claims to an authoritative perspective on Pekar and his work. At another level, this strategy appears legitimate as a means of representing the overall perspective and agenda of Pekar and his comic books.

American Splendor, the comic, is a deliberate rejection of mainstream (superhero) comic narrative, just as *American Splendor* the film disrupts the audience's expectations of the realist mainstream (Hollywood) drama-documentary. Pekar has continued his own ruminations on the validity of strategies of representation in *Our Movie Year,* which collates his observations of the production, construction and reception of the film. The manner in which *American Splendor* the film incorporates elements of comic forms adds to this overall agenda; emphasizing the constructed nature of the film's narrative, expressing an irritation with the lack of representations of "real life" in popular media, questioning the motives of the filmmakers themselves, and so on. In turn, this constant emphasis on the nature of representation itself offers a commentary on the nature of comics as a medium. Paul Giamatti playing Pekar within the film is a mirror of Robert Crumb drawing Pekar in the comic; simply another means of representing the "reality" of Pekar's life, and just as implicated with issues of "authenticity" and "distortion" that are central to any such representation, within any medium. In other words, *American Splendor* the drama-documentary, precisely because it draws so self-consciously from both comic and film elements, allows for a foregrounding of a complex commentary on the distinctive nature of each of these forms of media. In the process the film demonstrates a respect for the comic book as an art form that other comic book adaptations (*Spider-Man, Batman, From Hell,* and the like) never even attempt.

EL SANTO

THE CASE OF A MEXICAN MULTIMEDIA HERO

— DAVID WILT

The relationship between comic strips (and later, comic books) and motion pictures began relatively early in the history of each medium. Cartoonist Winsor McKay created the "Little Nemo in Slumberland" newspaper comic strip in 1905, followed by a 1911 animated version (with J.Stuart Blackton), while Ham Fisher's "Mutt and Jeff" made their newspaper debut in 1907, and their first animated cartoon in 1913. These are just two examples: numerous Hollywood feature films, serials, and animated shorts of the silent and sound eras were based on comic strips and comic books.

Less frequent but far from unknown were cases in which actual people, usually movie stars or other celebrities, were honored by the creation of comics in their image. Charlie Chaplin was the star of live action movies, a newspaper comic strip, and an animated cartoon. U.S. readers could purchase comic books "starring" John Wayne, Frank Buck, Roy Rogers, Jerry Lewis, Bob Hope, and others. For the most part, these comic book "characters" were merely extensions of the star's public persona. For example, cowboy actor Roy Rogers appeared in Western adventure stories as if he were a "real" cowboy.

In Mexico, media crossovers were also not unknown. At least three fictional characters—El Monje Loco [The Mad Monk], Kalimán, and Carlos Lacroix—were featured in comic books, radio series, and motion pictures. As in the U.S., movie stars like Pedro Infante, María Félix, and comedian Gaspar Henaine "Capulina" appeared in comic book series utilizing their likenesses. And nearly two dozen live-action feature films were adapted from Mexican comic books between the late 1950s and the mid-1980s.

The case of Mexican wrestler El Santo is different. Rodolfo Guzmán Huerta, the man beneath the silver mask, was a professional athlete whose life and career were drastically altered by his forays into comic books and motion pictures. And, unlike Bob Hope or John Wayne, Guzmán Huerta *personally* participated in the production of the comic books bearing his name and image, at least for the first twenty-five years or so that the magazine was published.

Guzmán's wrestling career lasted nearly fifty years, and he continues to be instantly recognizable (and commercially viable) more than twenty years after his death. But this fame is not based solely on his exploits as a professional wrestler—the comic book and movie careers of El Santo elevated him from the status of a popular athlete (in a sport somewhat less marginal in Mexico than it is in the U.S.) to that of a national cult idol. Also significant is the manner in which comic books and films changed Santo's public persona: unlike most celebrity tie-ins designed to capitalize on an individual's existing fame, the Santo comics and movies materially enhanced and altered his public image from a tough-guy professional wrestler popular chiefly with aficionados of that sport, to a heroic multimedia superhero with a much broader fan base.

Although wrestling exhibitions (mostly featuring foreign grapplers) had been held in Mexico during the first three decades of the twentieth century, professional wrestling—known as *lucha libre*—really began in 1933 when Salvador Lutteroth González sponsored various matches in Mexico City and formed the Empresa Mexicana de Lucha Libre (EMLL). Originally, most of the participants were imported wrestlers, but Mexicans soon began to dominate the sport and the public responded positively. One convert was the teenaged Rodolfo Guzmán Huerta, a talented athlete whose favorite sport to that point had been American football. Since there was no opportunity for a professional football career in Mexico, Guzmán chose wrestling instead.

Rodolfo Guzmán Huerta was born in Tulancingo in the Mexican state of Hidalgo on 23 September 1917, one of seven children (three of Rodolfo's brothers would also become professional wrestlers). The Guzmán family moved to Mexico City in the 1920s. As a teenager, Rodolfo held various other jobs (painter, carpenter, mechanic) before and after beginning his wrestling career in 1934. In the ring he was first known as "Rudy" Guzmán, then switched to "El Hombre Rojo" [The Red Man], and later "El Murciélago II" [The Bat #2], capitalizing on the fame of another popular wrestler of the day, Jesús "Murciélago" Velázquez. Forced to drop this identity when the original "Bat" complained, Guzmán adopted yet another identity: El Santo, el Enmascarado de Plata [The Saint, the Silver-Masked One] (Cortés and Martínez 6, 8).

The name "El Santo" and the use of a silver mask were the fruits of a discussion between Guzmán and wrestling promoter Chucho Lomelí during which various potential names were proposed. In later years, Guzmán said he chose "El Santo" based on the popularity of the Leslie Charteris "Saint" novels and films; the idea of a silver mask was allegedly inspired by Alexandre Dumas's novel *The Man in the Iron Mask*.

Guzmán appeared in the ring as "El Santo" for the first time in July 1942, losing to El Lobo Negro (who—like Guzmán's erstwhile model "Murciélago" Velázquez—would later act in numerous movies, including many Santo films). From the first, Santo was a *rudo*, or tough-guy wrestler (as opposed to a *técnico*, or skilled wrestler). This denomination did not always signify a villainous ring character, but *rudos* are noted for their brutal fighting style and occasional dirty tricks.

Guzmán's new identity quickly became successful, both in the ring and with the fans. He won championships in the welterweight, middleweight, and light heavyweight classes in 1943, 1944, 1946, 1953, 1954, 1956, and 1966 ("Wrestling-Titles.com").[1] In 1944, El Santo formed a tag team with Gori Guerrero that was dubbed "La Pareja Atómica" [The Atomic Partners]. The *Santo* comic book which began publication a few years later was originally subtitled "Una Revista Atómica" [An Atomic Magazine], perhaps alluding to this well-known team's nickname.[2]

By 1950, El Santo was a star in the wrestling world, but relatively little known outside of the sport's aficionados. This would soon change. In May 1951, professional wrestling debuted on Mexico City's XEW-TV; by early the following year, the sport had become so popular with TV audiences that a special ring was erected in the television studios and a regular Saturday program of matches was initiated.[3]

Almost overnight, a sport previously accessible only to those who made the effort to attend matches in person, either in the Arena México in the capital or in one of countless smaller venues in the provinces, became freely available to anyone with access to a television set. While Mexican television was in its infancy and only a small percentage of the population owned sets, many more could view television in bars, stores, and other shared settings. Attendance at live wrestling matches was, like boxing, chiefly an adult male pastime prior to 1951, but televising the matches meant anyone who was curious about the sport—women, children, old, young, poor, rich—could see the event at no cost. This development probably encouraged at least some in the television audience to attend live events in person, and anecdotal evidence suggests that wrestling crowds became more heterogeneous in the 1960s and later. At the very least, television gave the sport a much higher profile than it had enjoyed previously.

The sudden surge in wrestling's popularity was not lost on other media. In 1952 alone, four motion pictures were made about professional wrestling. The comic book industry also responded.

Mexican comic books—known as *historietas*—evolved from newspaper comic strips like their counterparts in the U.S. While various newspaper supplements and magazines containing comic strips were issued in the early 1930s, the Mexican comic book is generally considered to have begun with the publication of *Adelaido el conquistador* [Adelaido the Conqueror]. *Adelaido* began in 1932, and lasted about one hundred weekly issues. However, the first long-running and successful comic magazine was *Paquín*, which started in 1934. Originally containing only reprints of U.S. newspaper comic strips (the title character was in fact the renamed "Henry" comic created by Carl Anderson), *Paquín* was soon joined by *Paquito* (1935), *Pepín*, and *Chamaco* (both 1936) (Aurrecoechea and Bartra I 46–49, 52). As the titles suggest, these comics were initially aimed at children, but were swiftly taken up by adults as well. More Mexican content was included, and eventually there was a fairly clear demarcation between reprints of U.S. material and books with most or all Mexican stories. *Pepín*, arguably

DAVID WILT

the most successful of the early anthology comic books, was originally a weekly comic, went to a thrice-weekly schedule in 1938, and was published *daily* after 1940. This title was so popular that the term *pepines* was often used generically in Mexico to refer to comic books (Rubenstein 18).

This frantic pace of publication—with mostly new material, not reprints—was possible because the comic books were composed of multiple stories by different artists. Each feature ran only a few pages, and was generally part of a continued story from day to day (or week to week). For example, *Pepín* number 1358 (10 Dec. 1942) contains nine separate comic stories (and a few single-page features) in its sixty-four interior pages, which measure 5.5 by 7.5 inches and usually have only two or three panels per page.

One of the artists who contributed to *Pepín* was José G. Cruz, who became something of a celebrity and received "above the title" credit on his series (Rubenstein 23). José Guadalupe Cruz was born in the state of Jalisco in 1917, the same year as Rodolfo Guzmán Huerta; in 1934, the year Guzmán first appeared in the wrestling ring, Cruz made his professional cartooning debut. Although some would later claim Cruz developed the *fotomontaje* technique to compensate for his artistic shortcomings, Cruz had been a successful artist for a number of years before turning to *fotomontaje*, and in later years would paint many evocative covers for the Santo comic book.

Cruz was an ambitious young man who branched out into other fields, including radio and motion pictures. In addition to using his own image as the hero of some of his comic books, he acted on the radio and appeared in dramatic roles in a dozen movies between 1947 and 1954. Twenty-two feature films during the same period were either adapted from his comic book stories and/or were based on screen stories specially written by Cruz.

In 1948, Cruz left *Pepín* and started his own publishing company, Ediciones José G. Cruz. Many of Cruz's stories for *Pepín* and for his own magazines were urban melodramas with crime elements, but he was also very successful with the long-running rural adventure strip "Adelita y las guerrillas" [Adelita and the Guerrillas] (published in *Pepín* and other venues and then as a separate title). However, his most successful publication was undoubtedly *Santo, el Enmascarado de Plata*.

DE PRONTO, LOS ENAMORADOS SE ENCONTRARON RODEA-
DOS POR LAS ALEGRES NINFAS DE LOS BOSQUES...LAS
HERMOSAS MUJERES CANTABAN A LA DICHA DE LOS AMAN-
TES ENVOLVIENDOLOS EN UNA BORRACHERA DE LOCURA
Y FANTASIA...

Fig. 1. Santo and his magical girlfriend Kyra, surrounded by photographs of "wood nymphs" (including Rita Hayworth, behind Santo) taken from various sources.

Curiously, for a magazine otherwise quite well known and documented, the date of the first *Santo* comic book is unclear. Armando Bartra cites August 1952, but October 1951 is given in other sources. (Bartra 47; Matamoros Durán 52) Originally a weekly, the comic book went to a thrice-weekly schedule (Mondays, Thursdays, and Saturdays) in September 1953. Horacio Robles, employed by Cruz on the magazine for many years, later said the publisher wanted to publish daily, but was dissuaded by his overworked staff. (Matamoros Durán, 55) Circulation figures vary widely. Bartra says a "conservative" estimate would be 300,000 copies per issue (47), while 550,000 copies (Matamoros Durán 56) and even "900,000 copies three times a week all over the Spanish-speaking world" (Rubenstein 138) have been cited. Even if the lowest number is used, 900,000 copies of the comic were sold weekly, and each magazine undoubtedly passed through multiple hands. Armando Bartra's research indicates new comic books were read by an average of five people and—as the used comic was sold, traded, rented, or read by patrons of barber shops and other places of business—the total reached a dozen readers. (Hinds and Tatum 6) Old issues of *Santo* comics were also bound into large compilation volumes of over 250 pages which increased readership even further.

Santo was distributed widely throughout Latin America. Issues published in Colombia during the 1970s and 1980s are labeled for sale in Colombia, Venezuela, the U.S.A., Puerto Rico, Ecuador, the Dominican Republic, Panama, Bolivia, Costa Rica, Honduras, El Salvador, and Guatemala. These reprints were published under license from José G. Cruz, with the exception of the final Colombian series that began in 1986 and which reprinted some of Santo's earliest adventures from the 1950s, although updated with a "new" image of Santo.

The original version of the *Santo* comic was like its predecessors, such as *Paquín* and *Pepín*, printed on newsprint (including the covers). Although the covers were in color, the interiors were printed in sepia tone (sepia or black-and-white interiors would be consistent throughout the magazine's run), as were most Mexican comic books until at least the 1960s. Later, glossy covers were added, alternating photographs of El Santo and artwork of him, usually drawings or paintings by José G. Cruz. The covers were usually not directly related to the story inside, instead depicting more abstract conflicts between Santo and the Loch Ness Monster, vampires, witches, werewolves, aliens, gangsters, spies, and so forth. Proof the *Santo* comic had an almost immediate impact is the speed with which movie company Filmex rushed a motion picture version into production. Shooting started in October 1952 on *El Enmascarado de Plata*, directed by René Cardona from a story by Cardona and José G. Cruz. Oddly enough, the star of the film was *not* Rodolfo Guzmán Huerta "El Santo," but another masked professional wrestler known as "El Médico Asesino" [The Killer Doctor, real name Cesáreo Manríquez González]. Guzmán wrote a letter to a contemporary sports magazine stating that "the truth was that the film [did not suit] my economic interests, and that is what I said . . . at the same time expressing my regrets for not doing it." To justify the use of the comic book's title for the movie, one of two masked *villains* was called "El Enmascarado de Plata," but for all other intents and purposes El Médico Asesino took the Santo role, and his white mask was close enough to Santo's silver mask to satisfy casual fans. El Médico Asesino adopted the comic book Santo's "origin story" (he became a crime fighter after his parents were killed by criminals), has a secret laboratory, is a popular wrestler, and never reveals his real identity. The film was released as a multichapter serial in U.S. Spanish-language theatres, but in Mexico it was shown as a rather long feature film.

Meanwhile, the *Santo* comic book continued its successful run. José G. Cruz wrote the stories (as he did for almost all of the magazines he published throughout his career), but the artwork was the product of a

Fig. 2. Santo and a friend travel back in time and meet Judas Iscariot at the scene of the Crucifixion. These panels demonstrate the "layered" look of early 1950s *fotomontaje*, combining multiple photographs and drawn elements.

team led by José Trinidad Romero and his brothers, along with Jesús Tovar, Arturo Dávila, "El Brujo" Velasco, and Horacio Robles (Matamoros Durán 54). After 1956, Trinidad Romero and his brothers went to work for another publisher and Robles took over *Santo*, adding his brothers Hugo and Oliverio to the team. They produced the book for Cruz until it ceased publication in 1980 (although some stories in the final years were revised reprints from the 1950s). The styles of the Trinidad Romero and Robles teams were rather different: the early issues are very dark and the *fotomontaje* is extremely

Fig. 3. The image of Santo is a photograph, while the rest of these panels are drawn art, a tendency of artist Horacio Robles, who replaced J. Trinidad Romero on the Santo magazine after 1956.

layered and intricate, while in later years the visuals are brighter and fewer elements are combined in each panel, resulting in a simpler look.

Rodolfo Guzmán Huerta also participated in the creation of each issue, posing for photographs that were used as part of the *fotomontaje* style, although Horacio Robles admits *he* sometimes filled in when El Santo was out of town on a wrestling tour. This made *Santo, el Enmascarado de Plata* "the only comic book where the protagonist really existed and [participated] in the creation of almost every issue" (Matamoros Durán 56). In the 1970s, José G. Cruz and El Santo had a falling out, with mutual lawsuits resulting, but "there was no winner and the only ones who received any money were, as always, the lawyers" (Matamoros Durán 57). The bitter dispute resulted in the replacement of Guzmán Huerta as the photographic model for El Santo—bodybuilder Héctor Pliego, the new hero, was given a mask with an "S" on the forehead. Later reprints of 1950s *Santo* stories were touched up so that El Santo wore the "new" mask, and in some cases photos of Pliego's body were pasted over the old images of Guzmán Huerta— although the rest of the panels were original—to complete the revision. The *Santo* comic ran advertisements promoting the "new, rejuvenated, and modernized Santo!"

By the end of the 1970s, circulation of the now weekly comic had dropped to 100,000 per month (Herner 124). *Huracán Ramírez,* also featuring a wrestler-superhero,[4] was selling twice that, but the most popular comic of this era was *Kalimán,* another superhero title, which sold two million copies of each weekly issue (Herner 122). In 1980 José G. Cruz— who had become extremely wealthy thanks to his publishing activities— abruptly canceled the title (in the middle of a continued story) and moved to Los Angeles, where he died later in the decade.

Santo's comic book legacy did not completely end with the cessation of the José G. Cruz magazine. In 1985, a new comic book starring El Hijo del Santo (Santo's son, himself a professional wrestler and occasional movie star) began publication, although it was a traditional (drawn artwork) comic rather than in *fotomontaje* style. This was not immediately successful, nor was a later series. El Santo was featured in at least one issue (number 425) of the comic *Sensacional de Luchas,* and in 2001 an English-language Santo comic was planned for U.S. release, but canceled after negotations between El Hijo del Santo (who owns the rights to his father's character) and the publishers broke down. However, a new comic—*Santo, la Leyenda de Plata* [Santo, the Silver Legend]—began publication in February 2005 by Carol Ediciones in Mexico. This comic book (with drawn art) features the fictional adventures of El Hijo del Santo (although in the magazine as well as the ring he is now generally referred to just "El Santo").

A discussion of the formal attributes of the *Santo* comic is in order. If a "comic book" is a magazine composed of *drawn* comic strips, then *Santo* does not qualify, since the artwork was created via a technique known as *fotomontaje.* This style should not be confused with the *fotonovela* ("photo-novel"), a format consisting of comic strip-style stories composed solely of photographs (usually posed specifically for the story, although stills from TV shows or movies are sometimes used for magazine "tie-ins"). Only rarely were modifications (other than dialogue balloons and the occasional "sound effect") made to these photos. For example, *Fotomisterio* 182 (3 Jan. 1976) consists of fifty pages with at least four panels per page, and only *one* panel is not a simple photograph (and that one is merely a pasteup of two photos). Comic "strips" consisting of posed photographs date back to the 1920s in Mexico, but the magazine-length *fotonovelas* were most popular in the 1960s and 1970s, to some degree replacing the more elaborate *fotomontaje* process. According to Mexican comic historians Juan Manuel Aurre-coechea and Armando Bartra,

> *Fotomontaje* is something else. It substitutes photos for drawings, maintaining the language of the comic, which signifies overlaying balloons . . . drawing "force lines," drawing [sound effects] and, if necessary, cutting and pasting different photos, retouching them and, frequently, adding the missing elements with the pen. The Mexican *fotohistorieta* of the 1940s isn't the work of photographers that ventured into the narrative genre, it is an amplification of the language of the comic, developed by professional cartoonists who found in photographic collage a fruitful extension of the pen and pencil. And it is also, and above all, an effort to introduce the maximum verisimilitude possible in the comic books, appropriating the proverbial faithfulness to reality of the photographer. (Aurrecoechea and Bartra II 194)

Fotomontaje emerged in Mexican comic books around 1943, and seems to have been developed almost simultaneously by Ramón Valdiosera and José G. Cruz. Aurrecoechea writes that even if Cruz didn't invent the technique, "there is no argument that he is its most prolific and creative practitioner" (Aurrecoechea II 195, 197).

The *fotomontaje* process was arguably more labor intensive than traditional, drawn comic books, requiring not only the original conception of each comic book panel, but a painstaking elaboration of this image by means of photographic and artistic collage (as compared to a comic book artist simply drawing the images). The choice of *fotomontage* over artwork therefore required a decision on the part of the publisher, a philosophical or artistic decision rather than a purely financial one (at least in terms of production costs). The *realism* of *fotomontaje* was its selling point: although the images were manipulated, sometimes extensively, they were still intrinsically more "real" than a cartoon drawing.

Some publishers, like José G. Cruz, committed themselves to *fotomontaje* for most or all of their titles, while others printed both traditional comic books and titles in *fotomontaje*, depending upon the genre. *Fotomontaje* was not necessarily limited to use in comic books with urban, contemporary settings. José G. Cruz and others published magazines with "cowboy" and other rural and period themes, and even humor series were done in the *fotomontaje* format. It appears, however, that the most popular and enduring series utilizing *fotomontaje* were contemporary dramatic genres, including crime stories, adventure books like *El Santo*, and urban romantic melodramas such as the anthology series *Ayúdeme Doctora Corazón*. Humor comic books (*Los Supersabios* and *La familia Burrón*, for example), and titles with "exotic" settings (*Kalimán, Chanoc, Alma Grande*) were more often done in the traditional (drawn) cartoon format.

When used for contemporary urban melodramas, *fotomontaje* seems relatively innocuous, although the use of photographed rather than drawn faces adds an air of verisimilitude to the stories. Various Cruz comics in this format were adapted to motion pictures, and at least one of his "models," Roberto Romaña, actually made the transition from comic book "actor" to movie actor. But *El Enmascarado de Plata* was a radical departure from realistic melodrama: Cruz and José Trinidad Romero used the *fotomontaje* process to create a fantasy world (Bartra 48–49). Through the addition and manipulation of photographs and drawings—whether new or recycled from other publications—the "real" (photographed) Santo faced vampires, werewolves, and aliens, traveled to Hell, the jungle, tropical islands, flew through the air, and generally behaved like "fictional" superheroes in other comics.

PERO AL FIN TU-
VO LA SUERTE
DE ATINAR UNO
DE LOS GOLPES
EN EL CUELLO
DE UNO DE AQUE
LLOS FORMIDA-
BLES ENGENDROS
Y LA CABEZA
VOLÓ POR LOS
AIRES LANZANDO
BORBOTONES DE
SANGRE...

12615

Fig. 4. Santo beheads a giant, a combination of various photographic and drawn elements by Horacio Robles.

What effect did the *fotomontaje* process have on the impact of the *Santo* comic books? The use of photographs of a "real person" (since El Santo never revealed his face or true identity, he was not perceived as an "actor" playing a role) led to an almost subliminal perception of "reality" on the part of readers. Horacio Robles says El Santo once complained to him about the flying ability of the comic book Santo, saying audiences expected him to do the same at personal appearances (Matamoros Durán 56). It is unlikely that a comic book featuring drawn artwork would have made such an impression on its readers. An additional touch of verisimilitude occurred when—at least in the early years—the comics sometimes contained topical references suggesting that the stories were happening almost in real time: Bartra cites a recreation of the famous Santo-Black Shadow wrestling match, and another story set at the Atayde circus, which had just been playing the Mexico City area (Bartra 54).[5]

Consequently, although Santo's printed adventures soon veered into the realm of the fantastic, they were still rooted in a photographic pseudo-reality. This may have even made Santo's transition to motion pictures smoother. For example, readers of *Superman* comics may or may not have been pleased with the way the titular superhero was portrayed on the screen: perhaps they disliked the actor chosen, or the overall "look" of the

movie. However, *Santo* comic aficionados were seeing the same person in the same costume, whether they were reading the magazines or watching the films.

"He began as an almost normal wrestler, who fought on Sundays, defended good-hearted people, and had his [own] apartment. But later, José G. Cruz began to enjoy himself with his character and had him travel the world, through strange places and dimensions, meeting fabulous and terrifying personages such as the Devil himself or the Virgin of Guadalupe" (Bartra 56).

Rodolfo Guzmán Huerta in the professional wrestling ring was a *rudo*, noted for his furious style and often bloody matches. But, as comic book historian and anthropologist Armando Bartra notes, "if Santo, the one in the ring, was a *rudo* . . . the Santo of the comic books is an avenging archangel, a warrior of the Lord and the greatest enemy of Satan" (53). In creating the comic *Santo, el Enmascarado de Plata*, José G. Cruz borrowed little more than the physical likeness of Santo and his identity as a wrestler (although the latter trait would later be dispensed with almost entirely, with Santo becoming a full-time superhero). In fact, the Santo "origin" story in the comic books was reminiscent of other comic characters like Batman: Santo's parents were killed by criminals, and he became a crimefighter to bring the murderers to justice, then decided to help other people with their problems. None of this was related in any way to the wrestling persona of El Santo (although at least his name was appropriate for a heroic figure).

The *Santo* comics over the years featured a wide variety of villains, from run-of-the-mill gangsters and sinister Communist agents to demons, vampires, aliens, and other fantastic creatures. The latter type of stories seemed to predominate—as they did in Santo's movies—elevating the hero to something beyond a "simple" enforcer of the law. Santo did not just capture bank robbers, he saved people from horrible supernatural fiends, serving as a representative of Good versus Evil incarnate. José G. Cruz's tales, particularly in the first decade of publication, helped cement El Santo's larger than life image: "the writer took plots from films, novels, short stories, legends, truculent stories [told by one's] nanny, police station gossip, historical events, newspaper articles. Also Greek-Latin mythology . . . some epic poems, and above all the sacred Scriptures" (Bartra 28).

The *Santo* comic book helped broaden the wrestler's fan base. *Historietas* had become more specialized, beginning in the early 1950s, although there was a split between "adult" and "children's" titles as early as the 1930s. But the multistory and multicharacter publications like *Pepín* began to disappear as more focused titles emerged: "*Historietas* began to aim themselves at increasingly well-defined segments of their audience, rather than offering something for everyone . . . consumers could choose among rural romances and urban humor comics, among comics starring superheroes, real-life matinee idols, or wrestlers" (Rubenstein 33).

While the *Santo* magazine was read by adults, it also targeted a younger audience. The youth readership of the comics was specifically addressed a

Fig. 6. This combination of photographs with drawn embellishment is typical of the *fotomontaje* technique of J. Trinidad Romero. From *Santo* no. 54 (30 April 1953).

number of times. For example, the cover of a December 1955 issue shows Santa Claus *and* El Santo bringing toys to a sleeping child on Christmas Eve. A 1958 issue features Santo and a child on the cover—he is saying "All children should be attentive and studious in school and obey their parents!" An issue from 1954 depicts Santo handing a little girl a doll, with the caption "Not only is Santo the greatest idol of the public, but he is also the best friend that children have ever had." Of course, to prove the magazine was not aimed solely at young readers, these covers alternated with those showing Santo being strangled by a mummy, punching gangsters, confronting aliens, wrestling vampires and robots, witnessing an atomic explosion, and enjoying the company of various scantily clad women. Nor were the contents aimed at young children, with gory murders, monsters, streetwalkers, children in peril, and similar situations frequently appearing in the stories.

Just as television had expanded the audience for professional wrestling, the *Santo* comic captured a new segment of the public for Rodolfo Guzmán Huerta's character. However, the connection only went so far: the two worlds of El Santo—professional wrestling and comic books—were only peripherally connected. In the early years of the comic book, some mention was made of Santo's "real" profession, and a few stories even revolved around wrestling, but as time went by the comic book stories largely

DAVID WILT

ignored Santo's career as an athlete, and presented him as a full-time super-hero. Similarly, Santo (still a *rudo*) in the ring generally faced conventional opponents rather than robots, mummies, werewolves, or vampires. The heroic character, supernatural villains, and exotic settings of the comic book stories were not at all replicated in the professional wrestling aspect of Santo's public life. Motion pictures completed the process of mythmaking and thus elevated El Santo to the status of a national idol.

The success of professional wrestling on television inspired a brief wave of wrestling-related films in 1952. The four major movies made that year varied in theme. *La bestia magnífica* [The Magnificent Beast] was a sports melodrama about two best friends who become wrestling rivals. The stars were real-life wrestler Wolf Ruvinskis and athletic actor Crox Alvarado, supported by glamorous actress Miroslava and various professional wrestlers. *El luchador fenómeno* [The Phenomenal Wrestler] was a fantasy-comedy starring Adalberto Martínez "Resortes." This movie was a sequel to *El beisbolista fenómeno* [The Phenomenal Baseball Player] and illustrates how wrestling had suddenly leaped to national prominence in Mexico: in the first film, Resortes became a famous pitcher thanks to the supernatural aid of a ghost; in *El luchador fenómeno*, he originally wants to extend his prowess to soccer, but a deceased wrestler supplants a ghostly soccer player and Resortes enters the ring instead. *El Enmascarado de Plata*, discussed earlier, was a crime film with a masked superhero in the lead, an imitation of Hollywood serials and American superhero comics. The fourth and final picture in the 1952 quarter was *Huracán Ramírez*, a wrestling melodrama-comedy about the son (David Silva) of an aging pro wrestler who wrestles as the title character wearing a mask so his father will not know.

However, this brief wave of wrestling-related movies did not last. Over the next few years there were some references to wrestling in Mexican cinema, but relatively few movies specifically about the sport. Masked heroes were also present, but not in a wrestling setting. The most popular of these characters was La Sombra Vengadora [The Avenging Shadow]—played by wrestler Fernando Osés, who had a long career as a stuntman, actor, screenwriter, producer, and director—who appeared in a quartet of 1954 movies and occasional films thereafter. La Sombra eventually made the leap from screen to ring but was not very successful (as with Huracán Ramírez, a fictional character would later be impersonated in the ring by various journeymen professional wrestlers, losing the unity of identity—and the concomitant link to reality—which marked Santo's career in various media).

In late 1958 El Santo agreed to appear on the screen. His first two movies—low-budget efforts shot in Cuba shortly before Fidel Castro's rise to power—are unusual experiments. In the first picture, *Cerebro del mal* [Evil Brain], Santo is not referred to by name at all, is not identified as a professional wrestler, and spends a large portion of the film brainwashed into helping the villain. A second masked hero, "El Incógnito" (played by Fernando Osés) handles most of the heroic action. In the second Santo film, *Santo vs. hombres infernales* [Santo vs. Infernal Men], he plays an agent of the police but once again shares the hero's role, this time with actor Joaquín Cordero. At the end of the movie he departs to fight evil elsewhere. Although Santo had no particular personality (and virtually no dialogue) in either of these films, the character is closer to the comic book version than his ring persona, and ads for the films (released in Mexico several years after they were shot) clearly ballyhooed him as a superhero in crime movies, not a wrestler in sports dramas.

Despite their rather poor quality overall, the first Santo movies proved popular and Rodolfo Guzmán Huerta signed a contract to make films in Mexico. The first Mexican-made Santo picture, *Santo contra los zombies* [Santo vs. the Zombies] went into production in March 1961 (in fact, some months before the Cuban-lensed pictures had even been shown in Mexico City). He made three more films that year, including one (*Santo contra el rey del crimen*) which features a Santo "origin story" (similar to Lee Falk's "The Phantom"—the Santo identity is passed from father to son, generation after generation). After a brief period in which he was utilized chiefly as a *deux ex machina*—with the "plot" being handled by professional actors—Santo was soon entrusted with the full burden of stardom in his movies, including glimpses of a "personal life," such as (varied) girlfriends, a secret crime-fighting headquarters, and flashy sports cars (usually Santo's real-life personal vehicles).

Unlike the comic book series, Santo's identity as a professional wrestler was reinforced in virtually all of Santo's movies, which usually included several full-length wrestling matches. Some bouts were integrated into the plots, others inserted strictly to allow Santo to demonstrate the reason for his fame (much as musical numbers would be included in films starring popular singers). However, the influence of the comics on the movies was strong. Just about any genre or setting was fair game: there are straight crime films, sports crime films, science fiction movies, horror movies, jungle movies, a Western, rural adventure films, spy movies, even an outright comedy. Santo's opponents included witches, vampires, werewolves, various iterations of the Frankenstein monster, mummies, Martians, a giant outer space blob, Nazis, neo-Nazis, Communists, and headhunters.

A few representative titles illustrate the tenor of Santo's movie adventures: *Santo contra las mujeres vampiro* [Santo vs. the Vampire Women, 1962], *Profanadores de tumbas* [Grave Robbers, 1965], *Santo el Enmascarado de Plata contra la invasión de los marcianos* [Santo the Silver-Masked Man vs. the Martian Invasion, 1966], *Santo y Blue Demon contra los monstruos* [Santo and Blue Demon vs. the Monsters, 1968], *Santo y Blue Demon contra Drácula y el Hombre Lobo* [Santo and Blue Demon vs. Dracula and the Wolf Man, 1972], *Misterio en las Bermudas* [Mystery of the Bermuda Triangle, 1976]. Compare these to some of Santo's comic book opponents: Rasputin, the Cyclops, the Minotaur, Dr. Death, the Headless Horseman, the Invisible Man, the Wolf Man, Merlin the Magician, the Killer Dove with the Poisoned Beak, the Zombies, and the Giant Octopus. Thus, the Santo movies contain aspects of *both* his wrestling and his comic book personas (Bartra 52).[6]

Curiously, it appears El Santo, even when he was working amicably with José G. Cruz, did not make a significant effort to cross-promote the various aspects of his career. The Cruz comics did not feature adaptations of Santo movies, and as noted above, his professional wrestling career was rarely mentioned in the comic stories after the early years. Nor did Santo's films include scenes in which his comic books were shown or mentioned. Some of this can be attributed to legal restrictions: Santo did not own the comic book nor did he produce his own films (until the early 1970s), so the rights to each medium's representation were in the hands of others. It is also possible he felt no need to help Cruz sell more copies of the comic book (it is not known if his fee was tied to sales).

While Santo did not promote the comic book in his motion pictures the *Santo* comic showed up in some non-Santo movies, including *El Águila Descalza* [The Barefoot Eagle, 1969], a superhero parody (based on a short-lived comic book itself), and *Las cariñosas* (1978). These attest to the ubiquitous nature of the publication, and depict its adult (albeit working-class) readership. In *El gran perro muerto* [The Big Dead Dog, 1978], two dim-witted provincial policemen have an argument about who is the greater superhero, Superman or El Santo. This latter example illustrates part of Santo's appeal: he was a home-grown, Mexican superhero, not an import from *gringolandia*. Although popular in other countries, Santo never reached the status of national idol that he did in Mexico, where he was revered as a *Mexican* sports idol, movie star, and popular culture icon.

Between 1958 and 1982, El Santo appeared in fifty feature films, shot in Mexico, the United States (Florida and Texas), Haiti, Ecuador, Spain, Colombia, Puerto Rico, the Dominican Republic, and Cuba. These movies were made by various companies, with many different directors, writers, and performers. Sometimes Santo had a crime lab, sometimes not; sometimes he had a girlfriend, sometimes not (and in any case, never the same one twice); sometimes he had a sidekick (his real-life manager Carlos Suárez filled this role in various pictures), sometimes not. In many movies Santo is a "freelance" superhero, fighting evil wherever he finds it, but in other movies he works for the police, Interpol, even the FBI. The only consistent facet of the movies was Santo himself.[7]

After El Santo became a movie star, other masked wrestlers caught the eye of Mexican movie producers. Blue Demon, a bitter rival of Santo in the ring, ironically found himself cast as Santo's partner in nearly a dozen films and also starred in his own series. There were also at least three Blue Demon comic book series—a *fotomontaje* version in the 1950s, a *fotonovela* style comic in the late 1960s, and a drawn-art comic in the 1990s. Also cast as movie superheroes were wrestlers Mil Máscaras, Tinieblas, Octagón, Atlantis, Máscara Sagrada, Vampiro Casanova, and other lesser lights, in addition to "created-for-film" masked heroes like Huracán Ramírez and Superzán. But none achieved or even approached the same level of popularity or lasting fame as El Santo.

Although Santo was a popular figure in the wrestling world during the late 1940s, it took the popularity of televised matches to provide the impetus

DAVID WILT

for the *Santo* comic book's publication. Similarly, even though the comic had been in existence for a decade, it was not until Santo became a movie star that he changed his ring style to complement his fictional persona. On 5 July 1962, Santo made his first ring appearance as a *técnico*, discarding his previous *rudo* identity: "it was no longer necessary to be the bad and violent one of the story. Santo had achieved fame among children; thanks to the hallucinogenic comic books of José G. Cruz and his first films, he was completely renovated. From then on the Silver One never doubted his heroic identity [as] one chosen by God to do good on Earth" (Rivera Calderón 43).

Santo's movie career was the final piece of the puzzle that elevated him to the status of a major celebrity. Beginning in the 1960s, Santo was more than just a wrestler, he became a popular idol who toured Mexico, Spain, Latin America, and the United States—not only in wrestling matches, but appearing on stage, in celebrity bullfights, at political rallies, and other events. His name and image were ubiquitous: people all over Latin America could visit their local sports arena and watch El Santo wrestle live; they could see the matches on TV; they could go to the theatre and view Santo in the movies; they could read Santo comic books every week, buy Santo toys—including "action figures" and mask-and-cape sets—and, if they were lucky, they might even meet El Santo at a public appearance and get his autograph.

In 1982 the sixty-five-year-old Santo retired from wrestling. Or more accurately, he was forced to retire: after suffering a heart attack in the ring in 1981 and having a pacemaker implanted, Santo lost his license to wrestle professionally and made a farewell tour, participating in his final match in 1982. But Santo was not ready for retirement, and continued to make personal appearances in various venues. In January 1984, he appeared on a TV talk show with several other wrestlers and surprised everyone by partially removing his mask, exposing most of his face. Less than two weeks later, while appearing in a comedy skit at the Blanquita theatre in Mexico City, El Santo suffered a heart attack and died. Thousands attended his funeral; Rodolfo Guzmán Huerta was buried wearing the silver mask he had made famous, and the marker on his tomb also features his masked image.

There is no simple explanation for El Santo's enduring fame. His status as a wrestling celebrity was the reason for the creation of the comic book that bore his name and image. The comic book's popularity—added to his sports renown—resulted in an offer to make movies. His movie roles completed the long starmaking process, which stretched from the 1940s (wrestling) to the 1950s (comic book) and the 1960s (motion pictures). This was by no means a coordinated campaign to create a multimedia star (Guzmán Huerta was the only person involved in all of the areas and he seems to have been more reactive than proactive in terms of new endeavors). However it happened, each aspect of Santo's career was an essential building block for his persona, and the result was that for two decades— the 1960s and 1970s—El Santo was a top professional wrestler *and* a major movie star *and* featured in a comic book selling hundreds of thousands of copies a month.

Twenty years after his death, El Santo is still an icon of Mexican popular culture. Although the comic book that originally helped propel him to widespread celebrity is long gone (and eagerly sought by collectors), his films are still readily available on tape and DVD (including subtitled versions recently released for the first time in the U.S.). In 2004, the Cartoon Network in Mexico aired a new animated series about the Silver-Masked Man, and in 2005 a new comic book series using his image began publication. While Rodolfo Guzmán Huerta is no longer alive, it appears El Santo is truly immortal.

DAVID WILT

FROM BLOCKBUSTER TO FLOP?

THE APPARENT FAILURE (OR POSSIBLE TRANSCENDENCE) OF RALF KÖNIG'S QUEER COMICS AESTHETIC IN *MAYBE . . . MAYBE NOT* AND *KILLER CONDOM*

— PAUL M. MALONE

Ralf König, Germany's best-known comics artist, has been able to parlay his satirical and often frank tales of the German gay scene into such a degree of mainstream appeal that their adaptation into film became virtually inevitable, though not unproblematic. The first film, *Der bewegte Mann* (U.S. title: *Maybe . . . Maybe Not*, 1994), was a huge hit but deeply unsatisfying for König personally, while subsequent film projects, whether disappointing or fulfilling for the artist, have fallen far short of the first film's commercial and relative critical success. This failure is all the more surprising given König's own popularity and his willingness to address a wider—that is, a heterosexual—audience. König's negotiation of his own openly gay identity, and that of his work, with a mainstream sensibility raises tensions that have prompted Elmar Klages to suggest that his solution to this problem might be described as a "coming in" (58).

König's comics—and their translation into films—illustrate aspects of the ideology of gay issues in Germany and its representation in different media. This chapter explores two of his comics and their respective film versions: the more mainstream *Der bewegte Mann* and the more graphic and niche-oriented *Kondom des Grauens*. After discussing the ideological similarities and differences between the two comics and their cinematic versions, this chapter will conclude with a consideration of König's other film and television projects, as well as his own position in the context of gay issues in German film and comics.

Ralf König was born in 1960 in the small Westphalian town of Soest. Although he had always enjoyed drawing, after leaving school he trained as a carpenter, a trade his parents thought practical (Voigt 35). In 1979, however, he came out as a homosexual; his participation in Homolulu, a weeklong festival in Frankfurt (23–29 July 1979) celebrating the German *Schwulenemanzipationsbewegung* or gay liberation movement, inspired him to give up the tradesman's life for good (Voigt 35–36; Klages 59). He moved to Dortmund and began publishing short comic strips in local gay newspapers and magazines such as *magnus* and *Siegessäule*, as well as contributing to "straight" humor and satire magazines. He also began studying graphic arts at the State Art Academy in Düsseldorf. In the following five years he produced four volumes of short cartoons, compiled under the title *Schwulcomix* 1–4 ("Gay Comix").[1] During this period he not only honed his craft as a cartoonist, but also developed what can be called, with some reservations, a queer aesthetic.

The term "queer" can itself be applied only awkwardly to German homosexual culture. For one thing, whereas English "queer" has taken on connotations of active resistance not only to a heterosexual mainstream culture but also often to essentializing views of both sex and gender in general, the word occurs only as a rare and academic loan word in German, lacking the emotional resonance that it has for native English speakers (Kuzniar 6–7). The German cognate *quer*, meaning "sideways, odd," lacks any sexual connotation, as does its close synonym *schräg* ("diagonal, offbeat"). The German word *schwul*, on the other hand, originated as a pejorative term for homosexuals but has been appropriated by the gay community in a manner analogous to "queer"; however, it lacks the English term's overtones of general oddness or difference. Depending on context, *schwul* can thus be translated roughly equally as "queer," "gay," or "fag(got)" (Wright, "From Outsider" 105; Kuzniar 6–7). Not everyone or everything that is *schwul*, then, is necessarily "queer."

At the same time, it is true that German homosexuals have had to rally against a basically conservative mainstream culture and the strictures of Paragraph 175 of the German Criminal Code (which from 1871 on forbade both "lewd acts" between men and until 1969, bestiality). Nonetheless, they have also experienced relative social tolerance, particularly during the days of the Weimar Republic (1919–1932) and again in the last few decades. In the intervening period, the Nazis infamously both broadened and strictly enforced Paragraph 175 from 1935 on, interning homosexuals in concentration camps. It is less widely known that this interpretation of the law was not repealed, but rather confirmed, by postwar West German courts. Thus, well into the 1970s gays in Germany, though no longer herded into camps, were liable to social persecution, public prosecution, and private blackmail (Wright, "From Outsider" 102), leading to thousands of convictions and countless suicides.

In the loosening social climate from the late 1960s on, however, the law was mitigated by setting twenty-one as an age of consent for homosexual activity in 1969 (further lowered to eighteen in 1973). These first steps were an important factor in the upswing in the German gay liberation movement that culminated in the 1979 Homolulu festival (Wright, "From Outsider" 102). However, in contrast to its American counterpart the German movement lacked a "Bill of Rights to which to appeal," the black civil rights movement as a model (Kuzniar 260), and a set of "specific, achievable goals" (Wright, "From Outsider" 98). Faced with increasing liberalization, after its post-1969 heyday the *Schwulenemanzipationsbewegung* largely dissipated into a sense of assimilation and apolitical consumerism (98). Paragraph 175 was finally abolished altogether in 1994, and the sense of oppression that continues to fuel aggressively queer cultural strategies in the Anglo-American sphere has thus ceased to exist in Germany (115). As a result, by the turn of the twenty-first century German gay filmmaker Rosa von Praunheim (*né* Holger Mischwitzky) could declare, "Especially in Germany, gay people seem passive and unpolitical ever since they got a piece of the cake. They are no better than heterosexuals" (Kuzniar 260).

Ralf König's comics aesthetic is nonetheless queer insofar as it fulfils Edd Sewell's demand: "Queer characters must be allowed to live in a queer world doing queer things with the dominant culture playing a marginalized role" (271). From early on, König's characters have been a stark contrast to the gay supporting characters Sewell describes in North American mainstream comic strips. These figures "are well integrated into heterosexual society in that they look and act 'straight' before coming out as queer, and they look and act in a manner appropriate to the dominant heterosexual culture after coming out. . . . They come out and fade back in rather quickly with no lasting consequences" (253).

For the sociohistorical reasons outlined above, the "emancipatory narrative of 'coming out'" has never played as important a role in German gay society as in the American scene (Kuzniar 18–19). König's characters are thus always already "out," whether conservative dressers, transvestites, or leathermen; König is also queer in his refusal to privilege any particular model of (male) homosexuality. This does not mean that gays and their milieu are idealized: König is as merciless in satirizing their pretensions, petty jealousies, and rivalries as he is sympathetic in depicting their longings for real love, good sex, or both. In either case, the straight world is marginalized, though hardly antagonized: if represented at all, heterosexuals are often depicted as foolish and pitiably inhibited, but seldom as a threat. In one of König's cartoons, for instance, a gay customer addresses a waitress: "First, we're gay [schwul], and second, we'll have two helpings of assorted ice cream." The man's partner rolls his eyes at this self-outing, but the blasé waitress only replies, "The first doesn't interest me, and the second with or without whipped cream?" (Knigge 309).

Even more marginalizing, and arguably less queer, is König's ambivalent depiction of women, regardless of their sexual orientation. König's 1987 adaptation of Aristophanes' Lysistrata, for example, portrays the eponymous character almost as the villain: her plan to deny the men of Athens sexual favors until peace is declared with Sparta is motivated in part by her own lesbianism and her desire to consort with her Spartan friends. She is undone, however, when the transvestite Hepatitos (König's invention and the real hero) convinces the Athenian warriors to engage in "compulsory homosexuality." By the end, the men have learned to do without women in both kitchen and bedroom, and peace with Sparta ensues only because the battles have become orgies. Lysistrata is shunned, and Zeus himself threatens to descend and rape her, after which "you sure won't be lesbian any more!" (König, Lysistrata 125). Is this a satirical critique of patriarchy, or uncritical reinforcement? König has hardly defused criticisms of his attitude to women with his famous rejoinder, "Women can no longer simply be wished off the streets of a big city" (Bartholomae, Mal mir mal 43). Accusations of outright misogyny, however, underestimate both the occasional sympathy he shows for women and the jaundiced eye that he often casts on both gay and straight men in his work. It might nonetheless be justified to argue that König perceives and depicts an essential—and essentializing—difference between men and women far greater than the distance between gay and straight men.

As his confidence as an artist increased, König was pleased by the relative success of the *Schwulcomix* volumes, but frustrated by the invisibility of his gay-themed work on the larger cultural scene: published by the homosexual Verlag Rosa Winkel (literally, "Pink Corner Press"), the *Schwulcomix* series was generally relegated to gay bookstores, of which there were then only four in all of West Germany ("Ralf König"). It is not only due to the relatively peripheral position of homosexuals in society, however, that König's first major publications were published in gay magazines or collected in paperback form by gay publishers, rather than appearing as either mainstream or alternative "comics." Germany had never developed an active comics culture comparable to those in other western European countries, in part because "the crucial events that marked the comic in its development—the adventure comic, the comic book, etc., occurred precisely during [the Nazi era]," and pictorial storytelling in Germany therefore remained "stuck in the nineteenth century" (Gasser et al. 24). The postwar influx of American comics had only convinced German parents and authorities that the victors possessed a far more impoverished culture than the vanquished (Springman 414): comics were regarded as *Schmutz und Schund* ("smut and trash"), accused of fomenting illiteracy and encouraging brutality and pathological behavior. As Germany regained much of its political autonomy, these criticisms had culminated in the well-known law against "disseminating publications that endanger youth" (*Gesetz über die Verbreitung jugendgefährdender Schriften*) of 1953 (Gasser et al. 25). This law would eventually be applied against König, when his 1992 book *Dicke Dödel I: Bullenklöten!* ("Thick Willies I: Bull's Balls!") was seized and prosecuted in Bavaria. The presiding court did not uphold the case, finding König's work to be " 'art' in the sense of Article 5 of the German Basic Law" (Bartholomae, "Herr König" 7–9).

During the 1950s, only essentially conservative artists such as the popular adventure artist Hansrudi Wäscher and the Disney-inspired entrepreneur Rolf Kauka had escaped censure, though without creating a united and viable German comics culture (Dolle-Weinkauff 117–25, 154–57). In the 1960s, however, the rise of a youth-oriented popular counterculture in reaction to the conservatism of the previous decade had raised the profile of comics. The German comics industry nonetheless still relied overwhelmingly on licensing translated versions of foreign comics such as René Goscinny and Albert Uderzo's *Astérix* and the work of the American underground artist Robert Crumb (Gasser et al. 24, 27). It was such foreign comics, including *Astérix*, Crumb, Phillipe Druillet, and Charles Schulz's *Peanuts*, that would inspire Ralf König and other artists of his generation later in the early 1980s (Klages 79–81). Besides König, chief among these were Walter Moers (1957–), who was equally capable of writing charming children's cartoons such as *Käpt'n Blaubärs Seemansgarn* (*Cap'n Bluebear's Seaman's Yarn*, 1988–), or of appealing to adults with his imaginatively obscene comics series *Der kleine Arschloch* (*The Little Arsehole*, 1990–); and Brösel (Rötger Feldmann, 1950–), creator of a bucktoothed, beer-swilling slacker motorcyclist named *Werner*, whose anarchic adventures became a cult hit, so far filling eleven volumes (1981–). Although the styles of all three artists show similarities, it was the sexually transgressive König who was ultimately to become the most popular.

When he finished his art degree in 1986, encouraged by the fact that straight readers were beginning to take notice of his work and by the increasing acceptance of homosexuality by the left-wing and alternative scenes in Germany, König quite deliberately set his sights on a wider audience. At the prompting of one of Germany's most respected mainstream publishers, Rowohlt Verlag, he produced his first book-length comic, introducing a straight man into a gay milieu. The book's title, *Der bewegte Mann* (1987), is something of a challenge to translate: here the phrase is a satirical use of *bewegt*, which can mean "moved" in either the physical or emotional sense, to describe a man who is taking part in the "men's movement" (*Männerbewegung*) by participating in consciousness-raising support groups and so on. Thus the German title could be rendered as "The New Man" or "The Enlightened Man."

The man in question is Axel Feldheim, whom we first see making a halfhearted suicide attempt after being left by his girlfriend Doro. Doro's shock and remorse become anger and disgust when she goes to the Düsseldorf hospital only to discover that he has been discharged; the sleeping tablets he took were too weak and too few even to bother pumping his stomach. The first few pages also introduce Norbert Brommer, a gay nebbish who is constantly being taken advantage of by his lovers and mocked by his effeminate best friend Walter (who prefers to be addressed by the woman's name Waltraud). Waltraud takes part in a straight men's group in order to explain gay issues to them, but he is also attracted to fellow member Axel, whom he later invites to a party. Axel accepts in order to take his mind off Doro, but after getting drunk at the party ends up at Norbert's flat, where he confesses to a brief homosexual experience in the army and Norbert develops a crush on him.

Axel and Norbert end up as part-time roommates, since Axel wants to avoid his own flat with its memories of Doro. During a visit to Axel's place to watch *Casablanca* on television, however, Norbert begins performing fellatio on Axel; suddenly they are interrupted by Doro, who still has a key. Axel shoves Norbert into a wardrobe, where the suspicious Doro, expecting to find a woman, finds him instead. Norbert dresses and escapes hastily while a shaken Doro reveals that she is pregnant with Axel's child. Axel then breaks off his friendship with Norbert and marries Doro— though the wedding is spoiled somewhat by the uninvited arrival of a teary Norbert and his friends in drag.

Rowohlt had set König certain conditions for *Der bewegte Mann*: no explicit sex or erect penises, for example (Klages 67). König had willingly complied, and the book appeared under Rowohlt's humor-oriented paperback "rororo tomate" imprint; in the same year, Rowohlt also published König's *Lysistrata*. With Rowohlt's backing, *Der bewegte Mann* became an even greater success than König could have dared hope. As a result, only a year later the sequel, *Pretty Baby: Der bewegte Mann 2* (1988), appeared from the same publisher. *Pretty Baby* takes up the story only a few months later, when Norbert has taken up a new relationship with a macho butcher who prefers football and slasher films to sex. Meanwhile, Doro is nearing the end of her pregnancy; Axel finds her condition increasingly unerotic, and his gaze has begun to wander. His constant excuses for not having sex cause Doro to worry that Axel may after all be gay. When Axel runs into old flame Elke, visiting from America, he makes a date with her for the coming weekend, when Doro will be out of town. Doro, of course, cancels her trip, forcing Axel to run to Norbert and inveigle him into lending Axel his flat for the evening; back home, Doro finds a hastily scribbled telephone number and suspiciously dials it. When Norbert answers, her worst fears seem to be confirmed. Axel invents a school reunion in Cologne and goes off to meet Elke, while Norbert, Waltraud, and the butcher go to the movies to see Visconti's *Death in Venice*.

From this point, everything goes spectacularly and predictably wrong. Elke has brought a gift from America: "Bull Power," a powerful drug intended for breeding bulls. However, its effect on Axel is anything but aphrodisiac: he is reduced to naked, grunting, crouching catatonia. Meanwhile, Norbert and friends fall into an altercation at the cinema with a gang of hooligans; they are forced to return early to Norbert's flat to clean up the bloodied Waltraud, where they find the insensible Axel, and Elke discovers that Bull Power does indeed have the intended effect on the butcher. Enter Doro, enraged, who is so upset to discover her husband crouching naked and surrounded by homosexuals that her contractions begin. Norbert is forced to drive her to the hospital, while Waltraud brings a recovered Axel only later. Axel arrives to discover he has missed the birth—a traumatized Norbert took his place—and Doro threatens divorce. The arrival of the titular "pretty baby" in a nurse's arms, however, reconciles the two, and Norbert and Waltraud steal away, relieved to have nothing more to do with the overwrought world of heterosexuality.

The tremendous success of the Rowohlt books solidified König's status as the "best-known German comics artist" (Knigge 309)—notably, not only as Germany's best-known gay comics artist. Much of this broad appeal can be attributed to König's visual style: like his early influences—the Americans Robert Crumb and Vaughn Bodé (*Cheech Wizard*), and the French artists Albert Uderzo (*Astérix*) and Claire Bretécher (*Les Frustrés*)—and much like his German contemporaries Moers and Brösel, König draws his characters in the so-called "bigfoot style." The equivalent German term, which invariably pops up whenever König's work is discussed, is *Knollennasen* (literally, "tuber-nosed" characters; the alleged Freudian relationship that both feet and noses have in common will not be belabored here). König's cartoony figures can graphically indulge in both gay and straight sexual antics without much discomfort for a straight or prudish reader—

though König's work for mass-market publishers such as Rowohlt is constrained to be less frank than his books published by gay and alternative presses. Thus the comics form serves as a distancing device, which has permitted König to enjoy a broad readership throughout Europe, based on the wit of his art and writing and his satirical targeting of homosexuals and heterosexuals alike. In the years immediately following, König would be awarded several important prizes for his work: in 1990, at the International Comic Salon at Grenoble, he was named "Best German-Language Cartoonist," while two years later in 1992, a jury at the Erlangen Salon voted him the Max und Moritz Prize as best German-language comics artist. That same year, he was honored outside Germany: the Barcelona International Comic Salon named him "Best International Cartoonist." It was this sudden prominence, in fact, that made it virtually impossible for him to publish *Bullenklöten!*, his return to a mainly gay audience, without both disappointing some of his wider readership and attracting the attention of the Bavarian authorities (Klages 58).

Given König's new success and celebrity, it is hardly surprising that the newly revived popular German cinema soon turned its attention to his work. Like its comics culture, Germany's far more glorious cinema-producing career had been tragically interrupted by the Nazi era; then it had been crippled by postwar conservatism and Hollywood competition (Hake 104–12). Only since 1982, when government subsidies had been transferred from art films to more commercial projects, had a popular and more varied domestic film industry begun to develop in earnest (168–71). König was not the only cartoonist to be seen as offering prospective film material for this revitalized industry: Brösel's *Werner* was turned into a hit animated film in 1990 (sequels would follow in 1996, 1999, and 2003). König, however, had little interest in seeing his characters spring to life in animated form, arguing that "a failed animated film would hurt me more than a live one" ("Ralf König"). Director Sönke Wortmann had wanted to film the *Der bewegte Mann/Pretty Baby* books soon after their publication, but until he had established a reputation with the success of *Allein unter Frauen* (*Alone Among Women*, 1991) and *Kleine Haie* (*Little Sharks*, 1992) he was unable to attract either a producer or government subsidies for such a subject. As a rising star, however, Wortmann was able to draw the attention of Bernd Eichinger, one of Germany's most successful and most international producers, who had produced Jean-Jacques Annaud's 1986 *The Name of the Rose*, for example—as well as the 1990 *Werner* film.

With Eichinger's support, Wortmann's resulting live-action comedy *Der bewegte Mann* (*Maybe . . . Maybe Not*, 1994) was, in the context of the small German film industry, a blockbuster. Featuring two of Germany's most recognizable young stars, Til Schweiger and Katja Riemann, as Axel and Doro, and hard-working character actor Joachim Król in the role of Norbert, the finished film not only won several national awards—the prestigious Golden Screen, as well as three German Film Awards, for the picture, Wortmann's direction and Król's performance—but also went on to become one of the highest grossing German films of all time, with six and a half million tickets sold in Germany alone and fifteen million worldwide ("König mit Geldsorgen").

The film is remarkably faithful to its source, with much of Wortmann's screenplay following König's dialogue in the two books *verbatim*. At the same time, however, it is "typical of these new situational comedies" labeled "New German Comedy"—a trend to which Wortmann would come to be seen as a major contributor, and which relied on newly established young stars such as Schweiger and Riemann to provide "glamour as well as commercialization" (Coury 356, 363). Sabine Hake, indeed, goes so far as to label Schweiger and Riemann the German equivalents of Tom Cruise and Meg Ryan (185). Moreover, if König had already deliberately broadened his appeal by including straight major characters in his stories, Wortmann went further. He made the heterosexual couple the centre of the film, thus underscoring the New German Comedy's "reliance on traditional elements of the classic cinema: causality, linear narrative, closure, and the most necessary element of all, a happy end" (Coury 356). Both books end with Axel reconfirmed in his heterosexuality, first as a new husband and then as a new father, and Norbert isolated, lonely and forced to recognize the futility of his love for Axel. Wortmann, however, ends his film with Axel and Doro still unreconciled; Norbert, however, as the voice of reason, is certain that Doro will calm down and take Axel back. At this, Axel invites Norbert for breakfast, and they go off together: "In the end [Norbert] is compensated with Axel as a buddy" (Halle 21), while in the book he is consoled only by the thought that heterosexuals' compulsion to reproduce reduces them to mindless slaves (König, *Pretty Baby* 117). Thus Sabine Hake's claim that in Wortmann's film, "the re-education of the arrogant macho [typical of an entire strain of the New German Comedy] comes about through his gay friend," (183) clearly does not apply to König's books.

In fact, while Randall Halle has identified the plot of *Der bewegte Mann*, like several other examples of New German Comedy, as a "temporary-gay narrative," in which a straight leading man loses a relationship and undergoes a sexual identity crisis before being successfully reintegrated into heterosexual relations (12), Wortmann's film in fact conforms to this pattern much less than does König's original story. In contrast to Axel's attempted suicide in the book, for instance, the film introduces Axel cheating on Doro by having sex with a woman customer at the nightclub where Axel and Doro both work as waitstaff. Catching him in the act—we later learn that this is not his first offence—Doro throws him out (in the film, again unlike the comic, they are already living together). Thus, from the very beginning we are reassured that Axel is really heterosexual. So too, Axel's confession to a brief homosexual experience in the army, followed by his drunken attempt to push Norbert's face into his crotch (König, *Der bewegte Mann* 51-52), and his later musings on the possibility of his being capable of a gay relationship (91–92) are completely missing from the film. Even the compromising situation in which Doro almost catches Norbert and Axel (in Axel's bachelor place in the book, but in the flat that he formerly shared with Doro in the film) is not taken as far in Wortmann's version as in the original, where Axel obviously allows Norbert to perform fellatio on him, even while imagining a woman who clearly is not Doro (101). Likewise, for these reasons neither the book nor the film can really be classified as a "coming-out" story, or even as a parody of one, as Les Wright attempts to do ("From Outsider" 115-16, "Genre Cycle" 332-35). In both cases the gay characters are already "out" in typical König fashion, and the heterosexuals are ultimately confirmed in their ways.

While Wortmann's "heterosexualization" of König's story is likely to have played some part in the film's great success, the appealing cast and strong performances also helped turn the film into a major event. In particular, Til Schweiger and Joachim Król are well cast as Axel and Norbert; Schweiger succeeds in making Axel's irresponsible behavior the result of boyish emotional immaturity rather than malice, while Król underplays

Norbert's angst and infatuation to create a completely credible character. Rufus Beck also manages both to embody König's caricature of Waltraud as a flaming stereotype and to provide sympathetic emotional depth. Only Katja Riemann, generally the poster girl of the New German Comedy and "perfect embodiment [of the] new female ideal" (Hake 183), has little to play beyond Doro's anger and homophobia; her last-minute reconciliation with Norbert during the drive to the hospital is too little and too late to carry much weight. Of course, Schweiger's chiseled good looks and Riemann's gaminesque beauty—and even Król's nondescript features—are miles removed from König's minimalist *Knollennasen*; only Beck's hawk-like profile comes close to the comic's original.

The film was also promoted via a Hollywood-style "collateral marketing" campaign (Lischke-McNab 403), in which tie-in products served both to advertise and commemorate the film. Though minimal by American (or current German) standards (Töteberg 91), the media blitz accompanying the film's release included as a matter of course a single-volume reissue of König's original comics, now advertised as "the book of the film," and the soundtrack album, which featured rerecordings of German popular songs of the 1920s, '30s and '40s. These songs helped the movie ride a current wave of nostalgia for the old hits (Lischke-McNab 403, 409); the use of the songs as witty commentary on events in the film, however, also has some precedent in König's ironic use of self-composed verse in both the prologue and epilogue to *Pretty Baby* (5, 117).

The film's success, thanks to its high technical quality, broad appeal, and collateral merchandising, further confirmed Ralf König's celebrity status and reputation as an artist—again, no longer merely as a gay artist. As a result, Christian Gasser, writing about a nascent German comics avant-garde in 1999, could definitively count König's work among "mainstream comics" that had served as inspirations for films, along with *Batman*, *Spawn*, and *Astérix* (Gasser 18).

In 1995, however, when Wortmann's *Der bewegte Mann* was exported to America under the title *Maybe . . . Maybe Not*, the reaction indicated that given the cultural differences between the two countries, the film was not going to be accepted as "mainstream" or repeat its German success. Stephen Holden, in the *New York Times*, wrote: "Who knows why Sonke [*sic*] Wortmann's mildly entertaining sex farce . . . has become one of the highest grossing German films in history. . . . The gay characters are downright creepy. . . . How funny is 'Maybe . . . Maybe Not'? It delivers some laughs, but they are really titters stored in a junior high school locker of the mind."

Maybe . . . Maybe Not, whose English title seems to cast a doubt on Axel's heterosexuality that the film never fully explores, was further disadvantaged by the lack of any collateral merchandising. König's name and work were virtually unknown, and there was certainly no American nostalgia for the 1930s German music used on the soundtrack; hence there were no ancillary publications or soundtrack albums. Thus, too, the American poster featured a photograph of Til Schweiger as Axel posed sitting on a gigantic ladies' shoe, rather than the iconic König cartoon which has been a feature of every poster for a König film in Germany. Moreover, the release of the film in a subtitled version—by far the preference of the relatively few American cinema-goers who are already interested in foreign films as art films—was unlikely to attract the mass audience interested in light comedy and overcome the traditional postwar prejudice against German films in particular (Segrave 174–79, 169–70). Finally while the film had been viewable by anyone twelve years old or over in Germany, in the U.S. *Maybe . . . Maybe Not* received an R rating, restricting it to viewers over seventeen unless accompanied by an adult. Ultimately, the film did respectably well, but failed to approach the American success of *Das Boot* (*The Boat*, 1981) or even of Wim Wenders's comparatively esoteric *Der Himmel über Berlin* (*Wings of Desire*, 1987), both of which ranked in the fifty highest grossing foreign films in U.S. release up to 2000 (Segrave 214–15).

Der bewegte Mann's disappointing performance in North America did not detract from its phenomenal success on the German market. Ralf König found his initial pleasure in the film adaptation's domestic success quickly soured, however, upon realizing how much his cartoon grotesques had been adulterated for straight consumption: "It wasn't my story any more. The plot and the dialogue were mine, yes, but the comic is narrated from the viewpoint of the gay protagonist and the hetero is more the object of desire. In the film it was turned exactly the other way round. There the gays were only the comic attractions. It isn't a bad film and I owe it a lot, of course, but I had the feeling that I really had nothing to do with the product and it wasn't so hot sitting in chat shows and talking my way out of it" (Wieland; see also Voigt 29–31).

However much he owed the film in terms of publicity, ultimately he came to feel that "the film sticks to my name as if with Velcro, and it gets on my nerves" ("Ralf König"). Almost immediately afterward, nonetheless, he found himself involved in another film project of a very different character.

Shortly after completing the three above-mentioned books for Rowohlt, König had also produced a second, more graphic two-book series, better suited to a niche publisher. Vogel Verlag, usually a publisher of gay and S/M porn, thus published *Kondom des Grauens* ("Condom of Horror," 1988) in a small run of only five hundred copies: given the macabre subject matter, König writes, "I didn't figure there would be more than five hundred readers" (König, "Tappajakondomi" 7). Relegated to gay bookstores, the volume nonetheless sold steadily, and at König's first comics convention in Erlangen the tiny Edition Kunst der Comics ("Comic Art Press") expressed interest in republishing it for a wider audience. This would provide König with his first exposure to a primarily comics-oriented readership; Kunst der Comics brought out both the original *Kondom des Grauens* (republished 1989) and its sequel *Bis auf die Knochen* ("Down to the Bones," 1990). Both volumes are subtitled "*Ein Knollennasen-Horrorfilm*." In these editions, the books were so successful as to be among König's most translated and exported works (König, "Tappajakondomi" 8). They also became the stepping stone to his long relationship with Germany's most venerable comics publisher, Carlsen Verlag, who began by reprinting selections from his older *Schwulcomix*, beginning with *Prall aus dem Leben* ("Drawn from Life," 1989). Thus, since 1989 König has truly served three different markets, "Gay scene, mainstream, and comics ghetto" (Klages 57–58), publishing largely but not exclusively through one publisher for each: respectively MännerschwarmSkript, Rowohlt, and Carlsen. The cinema audience, of course, has come to constitute a fourth market, if only intermittently.

The *Kondom des Grauens* stories mark König's only full-length excursions so far into the realm of horror fantasy, a genre in which he has little interest for its own sake (Buhre). Here, however, his satirical imagination targets the conventions of Hollywood, particularly those of the *film noir* detective story and the 1950s-style science-fiction/horror film, gleefully inverting their usually conservative and normalizing heterosexual dynamic. The filmic parody extends to furnishing the comics with English-language opening and (in the case of *Bis auf die Knochen*) closing credits (for example, "Special kondom-effects [*sic*] by William Wabbel"). The books' protagonist is tough-as-nails New York police inspector Luigi Mackeroni, a Sicilian by birth, who is seldom seen without his trademark trench coat, dark glasses, cigarette, and permanent five o'clock shadow. Mackeroni is almost the typical macho loner cop: unbelievably hardboiled, ridiculously well endowed, and constantly aggravating his superiors by not sticking to the rules—though in this case, atypically, his rebellion extends to his being openly and unashamedly gay.

The plot of *Kondom des Grauens* begins at the disreputable Hotel Quickie, where the clientele usually rents by the hour. Lately, several customers have been bizarrely and inexplicably emasculated, and Mackeroni is put on the case. During a tryst with a local leather boy in whom he has developed an interest, Mackeroni almost falls victim himself: it seems that one of the prophylactics provided by the management is in reality alive— a voracious, toothed monster that, once employed, severs the user's penis. Mackeroni only loses a testicle to the creature, but of course his superiors refuse to believe his story. He continues to stake out the hotel, and fails to prevent it from striking again. Finally, he discovers that the condom has tracked him to his apartment, since the size of his phallus makes him irresistible to it. Grappling with the thing, Mackeroni falls out of the window and finds himself dangling from his fingertips on the twenty-fourth storey. The condom bites one of his fingers off, spits it out, moves to the next . . .

In the nick of time, Mackeroni's leather boy arrives, drags the detective back in to safety, and declares his love. Mackeroni hits on an idea to trap the monster: using his penis as a decoy, he lures the condom into pouncing. At the last second, he substitutes a hose hooked up to the gas tap behind the stove; he inflates the creature and ties it off like a balloon, then lets it float off from the balcony and pulls his gun to blast it out of the sky: "Go to hell, condom!" (53).

The sequel, *Bis auf die Knochen*, takes place three years later. Almost twice as long as the first book, the second concerns a grotesque series of

murders in which homosexuals are found reduced to picked-clean skeletons. Mackeroni is naturally assigned to the case, and given a straight partner, family man Brian Plumley. The subplots here include a gay porn star,
Billy Bullcock, who becomes the object of Mackeroni's affection but also
seems to be implicated in the murders, and Mackeroni's rather callous practical jokes on his partner Plumley, who is sent undercover as a leatherman
with a yellow hankie in his back pocket, thus setting him up to be subjected to golden showers. In the end, the monster turns out to be another
artificial creature, this time a flesh-eating monster named Raoul, whose
phallus-like appendage is actually an elastic mouth that devours gays whole
to digest them with acid and spit out their bones. Mackeroni discovers that
both Raoul and the toothed condom are the creations of Dr. Riffelson, a
radical feminist religious fanatic who is using drugs to control the brilliant
Russian geneticist Professor Smirnoff. Unfortunately, by this point Mackeroni is himself a prisoner, and is about to become a test subject for the new
and improved killer condom when Plumley interrupts. The condom, once
released, emasculates both Smirnoff and Riffelson (who is in fact a schizo-
phrenic transvestite to boot) before biting off Raoul's appendage and thus
being dissolved by acid itself. Raoul, in its death throes, sprays acid every-
where, finally destroying Riffelson's face before she can shoot Mackeroni
and Plumley, who has just come out to his partner. In the happy ending,
though Smirnoff and Riffelson have both survived, Mackeroni expresses
his hope that another sequel is not in the offing; Plumley takes up the gay
scene with a new crewcut (a typically unproblematic König coming-out);
and Mackeroni finally takes Billy home with him.

As even a synopsis demonstrates, in contrast to the basically realistic
milieu of *Der bewegte Mann*, the *Kondom des Grauens* stories are so queerly
over the top that König's deliberately overwrought dialogue in defense of
the joys of anal sex and fairly graphic depictions of fellatio do not stand
out much from the bizarre and conceptually disturbing, if still cartoon-
ish, body-horror violence. Despite the extreme and parodic tone, however, these books' emotional core is easily as serious as that of *Der bewegte
Mann*. Beneath his aggressive exterior, Mackeroni is no less lovelorn than
Norbert Brommer, and instead of Norbert's essentially supportive gay milieu, Mackeroni chooses to work among straight colleagues from whom
he constantly has to demand tolerance and acceptance. His job also makes

him unusual among König's gay characters, incidentally, most of whom get by with no sign of gainful employment (Klages 74). Moreover, Mackeroni's move from finding a lover who loves him for himself, rather than because of his huge phallus, at the end of the first book to finding a man with whom the emotional connection is more important than the sex in the second volume's conclusion—"When we got to my place we smoked a little pot . . . and in bed we listened to music by Verdi . . . at some point he dozed off" (*Bis auf die Knochen* 105)—is ultimately both a dramatic and a romantic development. Hovering over all of this is the killer condom (or the flesh-eating monster) itself, which was originally less a direct reference to the threat of AIDS than a metaphor for the young König's reaction to the pleasure-inhibiting strictures of safe sex (König, "Tappajakondomi" 6–7). However, in the finished work the monster effectively symbolizes the anxiety caused by AIDS and the correspondingly intensified homophobia (König would first deal explicitly with AIDS only in a later book, *Superparadies*, in 1999).

Notwithstanding his disappointment with his previous film experience, König accepted an offer to adapt these two books to the screen as *Kondom des Grauens* (*Killer Condom*, 1996). This time, however, König made a point of co-writing the screenplay—he had already adapted the books into a successful touring puppet play in 1992 (Knigge 310; König, "Tappajakondomi" 8–9). The finished screenplay, based on the puppet show and co-written with director Martin Walz and Mario Kramp, effectively compresses the action of the two books by simply jettisoning the entire second monster, that is, Raoul and its skeletonized victims. Instead, the number of deadly condoms is multiplied, and the denouement of the second book is tacked on to the first, while certain elements of the second plot are integrated into the resulting structure. Mackeroni gets a straight partner already during the investigation into the Hotel Quickie attacks, for instance, and his love interest is a young rent boy named Billy, combining the unnamed leather boy of the first book with the porn star Billy Bullcock.

Notably, in the film, Mackeroni's heterosexual partner—now given the more macho name Sam Hanks, rather than Brian Plumley—does not experience a coming out; instead, he learns to be more tolerant of homosexuality, in part because at the story's end Mackeroni saves his life, rather than the other way around. However, a new character, created for the puppet play but carried over into the film, is Babette, a transsexual lip-sync artist at the hotel, who was formerly Mackeroni's partner Bob. A one-night stand with Mackeroni caused Bob to change his gender identity, but he/she still has an inconvenient crush on the Sicilian and is unable to let go. Babette too will learn to be independent in the course of the plot. Although Mackeroni's role in Bob/Babette's life-changing decision is much more active than his part in Plumley's coming out, the displacement of the "conversion" of an apparently straight partner into the past serves to minimize any potential anxiety such an event might produce in a heterosexual audience. Interestingly, while in the original text Mackeroni's leather boy helps him kill the condom that finds its way to his flat, in the film it is not the analogous character Billy, but rather Babette, who both inadvertently brings the condom from the hotel in her handbag and is convinced to help trap and destroy the creature.

An additional new character is a Croatian woman—a conflation of the relatively novel presence of eastern Europeans in Germany and the image of America as melting pot—whose nose is attacked by a condom in Central Park. Because she later sees Dr. Riffleson's Chinese henchman, who is also linked to Professor Smirnoff, at the hospital, she is able to lead Hanks to Riffleson's secret laboratory. Billy is brought along, too, since it turns out that he understands Croatian. Thus they are all captured, so that Mackeroni can rescue all of them—as well as Babette and the hotel manager, Robinson, both of whose capture goes unexplained.

Even with some of the sexual aspects of the books toned down, it would have been extremely unlikely to find financial support for a film version of *Kondom des Grauens* had it not been for the phenomenal domestic success of both *Der bewegte Mann* and the animated *Werner* films. Given that Ralf König's name now appeared to be box-office gold in itself, even Martin Walz, a relatively inexperienced director, was able to gain the support of producer Ralph S. Dietrich and his Ascot Elite Entertainment Group. Ascot Elite had been founded by Dietrich's father, the Swiss producer Erwin C. Dietrich, whose career had been even longer than that of Bernd Eichinger, but much less distinguished. Variously described as "the European Roger Corman" (Blatter) or the "Trash-Pope" (Buttgereit 22), in the 1960s and '70s the elder Dietrich had produced numerous exploitation films with titles such as *Porno Baby* (1969) or *Tempting Roommates* (1976), turning later to internationally cast actioners (*Code Name: Wild Geese*, 1984). Son Ralph had served an apprenticeship of sorts under Joel Silver in Hollywood before returning to take over Ascot Elite, though his father still played an active role in the company. Such a background was arguably not inappropriate for producing a film that would be advertised as history's first "condomedy" (*Kondomödie*), but it also did not necessarily promise either a large budget or much sympathy for the subject matter.

The film was nonetheless fortunate to attract a strong German cast, including Udo Samel, who bears a passing resemblance to Bob Hoskins, and who takes the proceedings extremely seriously as Mackeroni. Compared to his model in the books, Samel spends far too much time with his dark glasses off, but he also establishes Mackeroni's absurdly hard-boiled persona by smoking almost incessantly, including in the shower; in one scene, he manages to keep a cigarette in one side of his mouth while downing a drink with the other. Peter Lohmeyer plays Sam Hanks as uptight and homophobic, but committed enough to his job to aid Mackeroni despite his misgivings; and Iris Berben, a well-known television actress, makes the most of her chance to play a villain, taking Dr. Riffleson to the heights of maniacal scenery-chewing in the film's climax. Babette is played by Leonard Lansink, an actor usually cast in tough guy and cop roles, but who had also appeared briefly in *Der bewegte Mann*. In both films, humor is derived from the contrast between Lansink's stocky frame and a drag costume: in the earlier film, he appears dressed briefly as Jeannie from *I Dream of Jeannie*, while in *Kondom des Grauens* he dons a series of glitzy showgirl outfits.

As tribute to König's popularity, a number of even bigger stars and other celebrities appear in walk-on roles in the film, including such well-known actors as Otto Sander and his daughter Meret Becker, fellow film director Dani Levi, and members of the rock band Einstürzende Neubauten. There were celebrities off camera as well: special effects were supervised by Jörg Buttgereit, whose low-budget and often satirical body-horror films (*Nekromantik*, 1987; *Schramm*, 1993) had earned him a cult following and exercised the German censors on several occasions; while a consulting role in designing Dr. Riffleson's laboratory was played by the famous Swiss artist and eccentric H. R. Giger, whose relatively peripheral participation in *Kondom des Grauens* and connection with Ridley Scott's *Alien* (1979) were played up in the film's publicity.

In keeping with König's use of actual photographs of New York City as the background of many of the pictures in the comics, director Walz and a few of the cast and crew flew to New York late in the filming for a week of exterior shooting. Much of the film's bizarre effect relies on the contrast between the authentic locations, often strikingly photographed, and the German dialogue. However, the price of this authenticity is the fact that the interiors, constructed on a soundstage in Berlin, look all the more like badly painted flats. Moreover—according to the director's commentary on the American DVD release—the fatigue of the overseas trip took its toll on filming the already hectic climactic scenes in the final week of the production schedule.

Once the actual filming had concluded, problems continued, with the producers evincing some squeamishness over some of the remaining overtly homosexual content and a certain amount of the film's gory violence. Although there is no attempt to show frontal male nudity, at one point the shadow of Mackeroni's massive erection is cast upon the hotel room wall; a later shot was cut, however, in which it is clear, though not explicitly shown, that Billy is being penetrated anally. The Dietrichs had apparently decided late in the game to pitch the film, like *Der bewegte Mann*, at an audience twelve and up; Walz was forced to reedit early scenes that had already been edited and even scored, resulting in awkward and sudden cuts. The film's second half, however, also becomes increasingly ragged in the editing, until the denouement threatens to become totally incoherent. The final version was judged suitable for viewers sixteen and over, though the question of who its intended audience might be remained open. Walz claimed to have been promised a restored "director's cut" for the DVD release of the film (Blatter); but if his claim is true, the film's failure no doubt put paid to any chance of his being allowed another reedit.

For despite a similar collateral merchandising campaign—as with *Der bewegte Mann*, the original comics were issued in an omnibus format (labeled a "Doublefeature") and a soundtrack album was released, as well as two further books about the film, one published by Alpha Comics and the other by old standby Rowohlt—*Kondom des Grauens* flopped dismally, drawing less than half a million viewers in Germany. König disowned it in even stronger terms than he had *Der bewegte Mann*: "The second film, *Kondom des Grauens*, was a complete disaster. After the success of *Der bewegte Mann* they wanted to use my name to make a quick buck, and it turned into amateur night. During the filming in Berlin I stupidly blabbed into any microphone in sight that the film would be great and off beat— because I couldn't imagine that anyone could make such a pitiful mess of this story. I refused to show up at the première and to this day I still haven't seen it in a cinema" ("Ralf König").

König's bitterness notwithstanding, *Kondom des Grauens* arguably captured his provocative cartoon sensibility more accurately than *Der bewegte Mann* had. Thus it may be a backhanded compliment when Sabine Hake writes: "Whereas a few comedies offered a critique to the upwardly mobile yuppie culture [of the 1990s] through their defiant affirmation of petty-bourgeois lifestyles, the vast majority expressed their opposition and resentment through extreme crudeness. . . . Film adaptations of popular cartoons proved particularly effective in satisfying the younger audience's demand for shock value and vulgarity, whether in the juvenile humour of *Werner Beinhart* (1990), based on the books by Brösel, or in the gay humour of *Kondom des Grauens* (1996, *Killer Condom*), inspired by the work of Ralf König" (Hake 184–85). It should be noted, however, that in contrast to her equation here between "popular cartoons" and "vulgarity," or for that matter, between "vulgarity" and "gay humor," Hake makes no mention of König as the originator of *Der bewegte Mann* in her generally positive description of that film (183).

Surprisingly, *Kondom des Grauens* was in some regards better received critically upon export to the U.S. than its predecessor had been. In part this is because it was distributed by Troma, a small independent company with a twenty-five-year history of "determined resistance to the aesthetics of the mainstream Hollywood film industry" (Kidnie 102), based on "campy humor, high-threshold sex and violence, and political themes" (Taylor 14): Troma's most famous product is the series of *Toxic Avenger* films, chronicling the adventures of a low-rent mutant superhero (1985–). Retitled *Killer Condom*, with the tag line "The Rubber that Rubs You Out," a subtitled print of the film was given a limited theatrical run without an MPAA rating. *New York Times* reviewer Lawrence van Gelder found the film far from perfect, but possessing "a level of deadpan humor considerably above [Troma's] usual adolescent subnorm," and referred to König's comics, apparently from firsthand knowledge, as "far out and sometimes dead on." An English translation of the *Kondom des Grauens* comic, also titled *Killer Condom*, had in fact been published in 1991 by comics publisher Catalan Communications, but was already out of print. Meanwhile, the German soundtrack album, although it included standards by Etta James and Brenda Lee, could not have been repackaged for American merchandising because of copyright issues affecting several of the tracks. Thus there was no possibility of collateral marketing; given the film's already limited release, it sank without a trace until its release on DVD two years later.

König has so far participated directly in only one other film project, *Wie die Karnickel* ("Like Bunnies," 2002), for which he wrote the original screenplay (only later adapting his screenplay into a comic book, published first by Achterbahn in 2002 and then in an expanded and revised edition by Rowohlt in 2003). König also exercised casting control, with the result that the actors are far from the stereotypical movie-star good looks of Til Schweiger and Katja Riemann. Although this film was also no great success, König has declared himself more than satisfied with the result, which proved to him that his ideas could be translated to the screen on his own terms (Wieland, "Ralf König"). Meanwhile, the mixed reviews emphasized *Wie die Karnickel's* similarity in both form and content to *Der bewegte Mann*, to which the later film is almost explicitly a reply. The major difference is that in *Wie die Karnickel*, the heterosexual character is meant to be the protagonist from the beginning. Nonetheless, König maintains, "this film is gayer than *Der bewegte Mann*, because it shows the gay perspective on heteros. For the gays in my comics heteros are sometimes like unreachable gods, and for a change here's one who can't get anything right at all" (Lippitz). Moreover, the moral of the story is ultimately queer insofar as the straight protagonist finally finds self-fulfillment by learning to act upon his sexual desires like his gay neighbor (and in fact, more successfully).

A further project, with which König had almost no connection, was a Spanish/Catalan film adaptation of his 1987 comic *Lysistrata*, directed and written by Francesc Bellmunt (*Lisistrata*, 2002). Despite the language barrier, König felt that Bellmunt's film was the most faithful translation yet of his comics work into film, and went to great effort to have the film dubbed for a German release, which finally took place in December 2004 to lackluster reviews. Notably, Bellmunt's film alters the main character's appearance: while in König's original story Lysistrata is a stereotypical stocky dyke with an anachronistic blond crew cut, the Spanish film casts the long-haired, slender, dark and attractive Maribel Verdú, turning her into the equally stereotypical "hot lesbian" of male heterosexual fantasy. König's reaction is pragmatic: " . . . if the gays in the film are once again TOO sissy, the straight men unfortunately all too often somewhat too unappetizing, and in contrast the women mainly turned out too young, thin and beautiful . . . well, sigh . . . that's how it is when heteros do the casting" ("Ralf König"). In a gesture that can be read as either approval or resignation, König's design for the German version's poster represents the film's Lysistrata—with allowances for the trademark König nose—rather than his original.

König thus seems to have found himself in a position where the broader audience required by cinema sometimes constrains him from replicating the work that brought him fame as a creator of comics. He accepts these constraints with apparent willingness: "[Writing a screenplay] I don't need anyone at all to tell me, 'That just won't work.' In the dialogue I get away with a good deal. That's probably true, but there I know what I'm doing, and I know what will or won't work. I don't have to worry about that in a comic. In a comic I can get away with an awful lot more, because they're little *Knollennasen* people, and you can even show a gay man with sperm stuck to his nose. You can't do that easily in a film" ("Wie die Karnickel").

König's acceptance of this situation may seem particularly ironic given the strength and vitality of a specifically gay and lesbian German cinema—an avenue in which, like animated film, König seems to have little or no active interest, and to which films such as *Der bewegte Mann* are indeed held up as the stereotype-ridden and regressive counterexample (again, with no mention of König himself; Kuzniar 3–4). Nonetheless, there is still common ground between König and queer figures such as Rosa von Praunheim, whose early film work Les Wright describes as the "catalyst for the post-1969 *Schwulenemanzipationsbewegung* in the then West Germany" ("Genre" 311), as König's comments on the younger generation of German gays make clear: "It must be a completely different kind of gay existence [*Schwulsein*] that the kids are living today, at least in a metropolis like Cologne. In our day we still handed out gay political pamphlets against [conservative politician] Franz Josef Strauss when he wanted to become chancellor [in 1979–80]. Just try telling that to one of these techno-bunnies jumping around in a kilt at the Lulu. I think that anyone who had to fight a bit to be gay is bit more conscious of sociopolitical things. Just dancing, techno, ecstasy is too little. But they have another kind of fun nowadays— God, I'm talking like an old man!" (Voigt 19).

As a result, it should be noted, König's forbearance is not limitless: in April 2003 a new situation comedy series arrived on Germany's satellite television network Sat1. Entitled *Bewegte Männer* ("Enlightened Men"), this show's promotional materials emphasized its basis in Wortmann's successful film. As with many television series based on feature films, the premise of *Bewegte Männer* relies on undoing the closure of the film and freezing the situation at an earlier point in the plot. In the series, Doro never became pregnant; instead, she succeeded in dumping Axel, and though he still has hopes of reconciliation, she has moved on. However, since in this version she owns the café where Axel works, they still see each other constantly. Axel has moved in with Norbert on a permanent basis; Norbert's unrequited love for Axel is complicated by the fact that outside a small circle of friends, he has never come out, especially to his mother Margarethe. Also sharing the flat with Axel and Norbert are Waltraud and his boyfriend Frank (based on a character from *Pretty Baby* not used in the film). In this more family-friendly configuration, all of the featured homosexuals are thus either monogamous or safely closeted, with Norbert's attempts to keep his sexual orientation a secret from his overbearing mother providing much of the supposed hilarity. Notably, although the program's opening credits have a comic strip motif, Ralf König's name appears nowhere in any of the promotional material, and he claims to have been neither consulted nor compensated by the producers (who include Bernd Eichinger, through Constantin Film, and Oliver Berben, son of Iris Berben). The artist himself, in general no fan of television to begin with (Buhre), has labeled the show "a piece of shit" ("König mit Geldsorgen") and "miserable, lying, homo- and humor-phobic crap" ("Ralf König"). Nonetheless, the series was popular enough to earn a second season in 2004.

Despite such disappointments in his dealings with the entertainment industry, which have in part contributed to his recent claims of money problems ("König mit Geldsorgen"), König has no qualms about writing further screenplays ("Wie die Karnickel"). His primary focus nonetheless remains the creation of comics. Rowohlt recently published a König comic titled *Dschinn Dschinn*, inspired by the *Thousand and One Nights*, and future plans even include a science fiction story: "I'm daring to tackle other themes, because just laughing at funny queens isn't enough for me" (Klink 20). To this extent, the cinema has played a role in transforming not only his work but the artist himself: in spite of his proudly queer sensibility, thanks to his exposure via film he has reached the point where he can be quite certain that he is no longer addressing only either a comics readership or a gay audience. As Elmar Klages has observed, since 1989 Ralf König "writes for everyone . . . or not at all" (58).

OLD MALAY HEROES NEVER DIE

THE STORY OF HANG TUAH IN FILMS AND COMICS

— JAN VAN DER PUTTEN AND TIMOTHY P. BARNARD

Takkan Melayu hilang di dunia ("Malays will never vanish from this world") is a phrase that often appears in speeches throughout the Malay Peninsula and Sumatra to indicate the resilience of Malay culture. It is widely believed to have been pronounced by the hero of the *Romance of Hang Tuah* (*Hikayat Hang Tuah*)—a classical tale of a fifteenth-century hero who is the epitome of loyalty and service to his sultan, the ruler of the Malay state of Melaka—but it actually cannot be found in any existing form of the text, as one scholar has frankly admitted (Milner, *Invention of Politics* 102, 112). The phrase probably originated in a popular theatre version of the story that was staged during the 1920–30s,[1] which marks the beginning of an era when the tale was revived and popularized through different media such as theater, film, comics, and songs. The height of this revival occurred in the 1950s when an influential film and numerous comic books were released with the goal of boosting nationalistic feelings among Malays who were on the brink of independence, which was finally obtained from the British in 1957. The tale went through a second revival in the 1980s when it was used ironically to hold up a mirror to Malay culture and governance as a commentary of how the image of a Malay hero had emerged and shifted in the previous decades.[2]

The basic story of Hang Tuah focuses around loyalty to family, friends, and ruler, and is contained in numerous accounts that are collected in a number of overlapping tales found in a score of manuscripts over the past four hundred years. The tales usually begin when a young Hang Tuah travels with his four closest friends—Jebat, Kasturi, Lekir, and Lekiu—to attain mystical knowledge and powers from spiritual teachers. During this period they manage to defeat pirates from neighboring islands and, upon their return to the port of Melaka, engage in another brawl with thugs who plan to murder the *bendahara*, a chief dignitary in the Malay court. Hang Tuah and his friends save the bendahara and are taken into service by the Malay sultan. They distinguish themselves and soon grow into important servants at the court, especially the main protagonist of the story who, after securing a Javanese bride for the sultan, is appointed *Laksamana* ("Admiral") in charge of the defense of Melaka. This speedy promotion, however, evokes envy among the older servants and, as is common in Malay stories, results in slander being used to defame the main protagonist, which serves as one of the most important driving forces behind the plot. The dramatic climax revolves around a duel between Tuah and Jebat, the protagonist's closest friend, who has defied the ruler's orders and taken over the palace. Death was the only possible punishment for this act of treason, and it is Hang Tuah who must fight, and ultimately kill, his best friend Jebat.

The tale of Hang Tuah is one of the most popular legends in the Malay world, leading to it being reinterpreted in a variety of media throughout the twentieth century. Popularized versions of the tale even continue to appear in the twenty-first century. Among these new versions is a 2004 film, *Putri Gunung Ledang* ("Princess from Mt. Ledang"), which once again shifts the understanding of Hang Tuah in the perception of the Malay audience. Instead of focusing on nationalistic sentiments, the film portrays the complex hero as a romantic, martial arts aficionado with few political undertones. It is an attempt, in the words of the lead actress, to "rewrite history."[3] In another recent form—the comic strip *Eh, Tuah!*—the heroic status of Hang Tuah, together with his comrade Hang Jebat, has vanished as they are portrayed as modern youngsters clad in traditional clothes who make comments on certain specifics from the Hang Tuah tradition or current events in Singapore. In the illustration we find the above mentioned phrase being ironically used when Hang Tuah sinks into an anthill. But it is only temporary, as Jebat's comments run: "He is in luck. Ravenous ants will not make Tuah vanish!"

Fig. 1. *Eh, Tuah!* by Soffyan A. Halim
(*Berita Minggu*, 24 October 2004).

In this chapter we will trace the development of Hang Tuah's image in comics and film, as well as the original source material, and how these different genres dealt with a contested hero in the 1950s, a period in which colonialism, loyalty, and individualism were fluid values as Malaya was moving toward independence. During this period, Hang Tuah's loyalty to the sultan—a symbol of traditional subservience—became controversial, making his role in comics and film ambivalent, which subsequently led to another transformation of this image in the early years of the twenty-first century. In short, representations of Huang Tuah in comics and films helped shape a modern Malay identity and our focus in this chapter is the way in which those forms helped reshape the legend into a usable history.

During the period from 1945 to 1957 no less than 145 new Malay-language magazine titles were published in Singapore and the Malay Peninsula (Hamedi Mohd. Adnan). These popular magazines were important for the regional development of comic strips and comic books, which have received very little attention in academic studies of the Malay world.[4] The magazine *Kenchana* published the first Malay comic strip in biweekly/(bi)monthly installments beginning with its first issue in January 1947. The same issue also incorporated an article about the development of an indigenous form of comic art against the background of the Western comic strips such as Flash Gordon, Mickey Mouse, Tarzan, and Prince Valiant. The author of the article defines the different comic types as caricature (*gambar sindiran*), cartoon-film (such as Snow White), serialized drawings (such as *Tunggadewa* by Achnas; see figure 2) and several other techniques. He predicts a glorious future for comics as a means of education:

In the future comic art (*seni kelawak*) is going to develop rapidly, because it is not only important for amusement but it can also be used for education and clear explanations about science (such as now in America there is *Science Comics*, which reflect a dynamic and interesting way to understand modern sciences, such as atomic energy).[5] For history, which often is boring for children, or to inculcate children with goodness, comics may be the best and clearest instrument. Comic stories from America or from the West in general are of course not in accordance with our Eastern soul and feelings. Furthermore, the local conditions, the characters and their traditions and behavior will often offend our Eastern feelings, which will affect and harm our souls. We must appreciate the fact that *Kenchana* from its first issue has endeavored to publish a serialized comic about the Golden Age of our country, which has been written by a young artistic Indonesian, because with it the Malay nation will also be able to taste the beautiful flowers of the art of comics, especially comics that are connected to the history of the Malay homeland. (. . .) With *Tunggadewa* by Achnas we begin the history of Malay comic art and continue Indonesian comic art. We hope that the respected readers of *Kenchana* will welcome it with enthusiasm and happiness. Long live the Malay nation! Independence! Indonesia! (Nazif 13, 21)

From this quotation it becomes clear that for its author comic art was directly connected with the education of children and also adults, believing that it would surely strengthen Malay pride, a necessary precursor for the coming independence of the Malay nation. The article must be read in the context of the relationship between the people of the Malay Peninsula with their "brothers" across the Melaka Straits in the former Dutch East Indies who were participating in a struggle for independence against the Dutch in the late 1940s. The Indonesian artist Naz Achnas, who introduced comic art to Malaya, was a refugee who fled his homeland during the Indonesian Revolution (1945–49).[6] Naz also offered free drawing lessons to the readers of *Kenchana* who won a competition, as an editorial in the first issue stated (Naz 6).

The key figure in the development of popular writing during the period between World War Two and independence in Malaya was Harun Aminurrashid, who was involved in at least fourteen other magazines besides *Kenchana*, and also wrote the forewords for several of the comic books that began appearing from 1952 onwards.[7] In one of these forewords he deplores the paucity of Malay comics published since 1947, claiming that less than ten stories had appeared, whereas developed countries published them by the thousands, reviving stories such as Tarzan and Superman for years on end. According to Harun, Malay children could be taught loyalty, kindness, and a desire for self-improvement through the publication of comics.[8] In a foreword to another publication he offered backhanded compliments about its quality: "The two comics published here, if one counts that they are beginners' efforts, are a compliment to their writers-drawers, who have seriously worked to reach their goals. The flaws found in the drawings and the story line I am convinced will be improved by the publisher *Nilam*, so that in the near future *Nilam*'s publication will reach a level that may satisfy the readers" (Harun Aminurrashid in *15 tahun dahulu* 1952 15, quoted in Gallop).

Apparently Harun's criticism did not fall on deaf ears since several publishers began to venture into the publication of comic books in the early 1950s, resulting in an increase in both the quality of the drawings and the printing. The most productive publishers during the 1950s were Geliga Press in Singapore, The Malay Press in Kuala Pilah (on the Malay Peninsula), and Keluarga-Zawyah Publishing House in Singapore-Johor Baru. This last mentioned publisher deserves special attention since its comics reflected the vicissitudes of the enthusiastic and flamboyant entrepreneur Sabirin Hj. Mohd. Annie.

In May 1952 Sabirin Hj. Mohd. Annie began publication of a serial under the title *Majalah Comic Melayu* (Malay Comics Magazine). Each issue comprised a single comic story in Latin script, most of which were drawn and written by Razak Ahmad from Penang. This series of comics replaced the film magazine *Dunia Film* (World of Film), another of Sabirin's publications which folded in its fourth year of publication in July 1952.[9] Twelve issues of the comic series were advertised and at least eleven were published, most of them legendary historical tales, such as *Meminang Putri Gunung Ledang* ("Proposing to the Princess of Mount Ledang") and

JAN VAN DER PUTTEN AND TIMOTHY P. BARNARD

Karena Roboh Kota Melaka ("Because Melaka fell"). All of these issues were introduced with an editorial by the publisher in which he vigorously defended his publications. Sabirin tried to mobilize his readers to look for subscribers: "anyone who managed to round up 10 subscribers to subscribe to a minimum of 6 issues each would receive 6 issues free; subscribers to more than 6 issues were promised a numbered badge inscribed 'Warga Mujalah Comic Melayu' [Member of the Malay Comic Magazine] which would entitle the owner to discounts from Zawyah Publishing House" (Gallop). Another scheme to boost sales was a raffle on New Year's Eve of 1953 in which the winner would receive a bicycle; however, if contenders would continue to send in five ten-cent stamps every month, they could even win a prize of ten dollars each month (Razak).

Sabirin's attempts to secure money from his subscribers as well as his distributors in the Malay Peninsula and several cities in Indonesia, and at the same time sell other products, continued. Among his schemes were promotions for "Zetpiech perfumed oil for smelly armpits" (Zetpiech Obat Katiak Hamis), capsules for venereal diseases, ointment for skin ailments, and his infallible cure for almost anything: Zetpiech Iron Tonic (see figure 2). In short, Sabirin's Zawyah Publishing Home printed his comics and magazines at his Annie's Printing Works and distributed them through a network of medicine-book-shoe-shops together with his pills and ointments. He may have started as early as 1939 with Annie's Medical Hall as his first imprint,[10] continued during the 1940s with nationalistic, entertaining, and literary magazines, and moved on to comics in the early 1950s. The *Majalah Comic Melayu* in Latin script seems to be continued in a new series that surprisingly was published in the "old" Perso-Arabic script. Sabirin probably foresaw that Latin script would become more popular as independence, and the modernity it entailed, drew near, and therefore had the comic series published in that "fancy" script.[11] But he also had his commercial interests to consider, and therefore Sabirin announced in an advertisement in the last known issue of *Majalah Comic Melayu* that the following issue would employ the Perso-Arabic script to meet the general demand from subscribers. It would however take more than two years to start the new series entitled *Penerbitan Keluarga* (Family Publication) which comprised the same type of legendary stories featuring one of the most artistically refined versions of the Hang Tuah story that appeared in Malay comic form. It was through this and other popular media that the old tales of Tuah were further disseminated and reinterpretations made possible.

The first Malay comic version of the Hang Tuah story did not appear in the Peninsula but in Indonesia. In 1951 the Dutch-established government publishing house Balai Pustaka published the story for children, as was explicitly stated on the front cover.[12] The comic, drawn and written by Nasjah Djamin, a painter and writer hailing from North Sumatra but living in Jakarta at the time, faithfully and in great detail follows *Hikayat Hang Tuah*, from the childhood scuffle with pirates until the confrontation with Jebat, a man he considered to be his brother, over the latter's treasonous behavior towards the sultan. The remaining pages describe diplomatic missions to India and China, and the subjugation of the Malay polity of Trengganu is dealt with in four frames. The story ends with the message that after that last episode Melaka only increased its power, for obvious reasons leaving out the fall of the empire to the Portuguese and the alienation of the hero and his ruler. Balai Pustaka by this time was in the hands of newly established Indonesian government which tried to boost nationalistic feelings by teaching children about their heroic predecessors, focusing on their triumphs.

With the 1951 comic publication of the tales of Hang Tuah, Balai Pustaka dug in its heels against foreign comics that had began to flood the market in the early 1950s. These comics were translated American stories or the odd Indonesian version of a Chinese legendary adventure, which were severely criticized by educators who wanted to erase Western influences. These critics were silenced when by 1954 comic designers such as Kosasih and Johnlo developed an indigenous type of comics that explored the Sundanese-Javanese tradition of stories based on the Indian epics Ramayana and Mahabharata (Bonneff 19–31). This early Balai Pustaka publication of a story based on the Malay tradition may have been a one-off edition that served as a model for the commercial publishers in Bandung and Jakarta, where the indigenous comic industry converged. Nationalistic discourse, however, was to be directed towards the Javanese roots of the Indonesian nation, rather than traditions in old Malay tales. Thus, further comic tales of Hang Tuah can only be found in British held territories in Singapore and the Malay Peninsula.

JAN VAN DER PUTTEN AND TIMOTHY P. BARNARD

By the early 1950s Malay legendary tales were becoming the prerogative of Malay nationalists who were reinterpreting them in an attempt to write and draw—or create—a nation in the Peninsula. The story of Hang Tuah was the one that was most frequently exploited for nationalistic and commercial purposes. There were at least nine different comic versions of the story which were published in the Peninsula during the 1950s. One of the first appeared as issue 11 of *Majalah Comic Melayu* entitled *Perjuangan Hang Tuah dan Jebat* ("The fight between Hang Tuah and Jebat," 1953), drawn and written by Razak Ahmad. In sixteen pages the story from Hang Tuah's banishment from the court until Jebat's death is depicted in large frames which are rather coarsely drawn but also aptly reflect the dynamics of the confrontation between the two Malay warriors. However, the story is rather hard to follow if one is not familiar with it because the writer leaves out certain essential information that links some of the scenes depicted in different frames. In accordance with the commercial intentions of its publisher, every page except the first shows an advertisement at the bottom (see figure 2); the back cover—both inside and outside—is adorned with page-long notifications and advertisements for the publisher's medicines.

The other comic versions all employ the Perso-Arabic script and either revolve around Hang Tuah's adventures on the island of Java, where he defeated the Javanese warrior Taming Sari and received a magically empowered *kris* (dagger) (*Hang Tuah di taman larangan* ["Hang Tuah in the forbidden garden"], 1955(?) and *Taming Sari*, 1957), and of course the fight between the two friends (*Jebat Derhaka* ["Jebat's Treason"], 1956 and *Keris Hang Tuah*, 1957). Saidin Yahya drew a series of five comics in which he depicted the story of Hang Tuah in two volumes (Saidin), and apparently reserved three volumes for a newly developed story about the brave warrior Hang Derahman who was acknowledged as Hang Tuah's son (*Putra Hang Tuah* 1–3, 1952–53) but it is not clear if he published the latter three volumes (Zainab).[13] Interestingly, the publisher of both series was the Malay Teacher's Association in Kedah, a Malay state near the Thai border. The chairman of this organization expressed his hope that the publication would be beneficial to Malay writing as well as of use to children who were studying history, writing, reading, drawing and other topics in school. He called upon readers to help expand the writings on the Malay nation, which he believed was lagging far behind other nations. Still his organization had

Fig. 2. Hang Jebat has taken over the palace. Note advertisement at the bottom of the page (*Perjuangan Hang Tuah dan Jebat*, p. 6).

difficulties in securing funds for future publications of comics and therefore, in a supplement to the chairman's introduction, the caretaker of the organization inculcated the subscribers to enclose a money order or stamps with their orders for copies (Saidin). And although the publication was co-sponsored by several companies that promoted their services and goods by way of advertisements, eager readers apparently had to wait for about one year to be able to read the second part of this series (Saidin).

Apart from a shortage of funding, the comic industry in the Peninsula was also short of artists who could draw and write a decent comic, although there were a few very accomplished artists active in the field. This is clear from the difference between the spectacular drawing on the front cover of *Keris Hang Tuah* by Muhammad Ibrahim and the rather simplistic drawings inside by Husin Ahmad, who added his name and address in the last frame, probably to attract fan mail from girls. This was surely the intention of the very young Embong Ahmad who added his photograph to the comic *Laksamana Bintan* ("Admiral of Bintan") in 1954. In the introduction to *Hang Tuah di Air Masin* ("Hang Tuah at Sea") we find another example of this phenomenon of young artists seeking recognition. The young artist K. Bali, who was at school in Southern Thailand, asked for "constructive criticism," and if youngsters wanted to make their acquaintance, and could send newspapers and books, they were welcome to send him a letter. This appeal to readers was apparently successful, as in one of his other comics (*Raden Mas* [a proper name]) he emphasized that his fans should enclose stamps with their reactions. His efforts at self-promotion included embellishing his next comic with a large photograph of himself on the back cover and a smaller one inside. It also contained reactions by some of his readers, drawings of flower patterns for women and a poem for close friends. K. Bali published three comic books in total, *Pembela Tanahair* ("Defender of the Homeland"), *Hang Tuah di Air Masin,* and *Raden Mas I,* the sequel to the latter serialized in *Hiburan* (Bali *Dari Tendong ke Borneo* 96–97). K. Bali based his work on youth literature the comic publisher sent to him with the request to make them into comic books (Bali, *Hang Tuah di air masin,* introduction).

The role of inexperienced young artists in the comic industry of Malaya in the 1950s was similar to developments in the United States at the same time. It was a new medium that appealed to youth. Unlike the United States, however, the stories were not original, with superheroes representing anxieties of the times. Instead Malay comic artists tapped into ancient tales and their heroes, a natural fodder for both the comic and film industries. The reinterpretation of these tales would reflect nationalist ideals and modernity (in the Malay Peninsula a word that is almost the equivalent of individuality and anti-"feudalism"). To understand the role that these traditional heroes, and particularly Hang Tuah, played in the comics and film, and vice versa, in a time of intense political debate, we first need to look at the origins of the tale and presentation in other forms of popular media during colonial rule.

The genesis of the story of Hang Tuah, and any reality behind it, is still a mystery. The main text is known as *Hikayat Hang Tuah*, which exists in about twenty manuscripts, of which the oldest extant one is from the mid-eighteenth century. The tales refer to the fifteenth-century Malay state of Melaka, which at that time was a prosperous and powerful polity in insular Southeast Asia, and relate various adventures of Hang Tuah, a formidable dignitary at the Melaka court who saves his master time and again from precarious situations or conflicts with powerful adversaries.

These tales may be read and interpreted in many ways, whether as an allegoric history of the relationship between the Malay polities Johor and Jambi in the second half of the seventeenth century, the period during which they may have been written down, or as a symbolic story, using Tuah's youth, adventures, actions, and illness to refer to the Melaka's development, decline, and fall (Braginsky). The *hikayat*—a Malay term for romance or story—can also be interpreted as a Malay vade-mecum for the public with advice on how to behave and act in a proper manner (Maier). The moral lessons that are given in the tales about the loyalty subjects should observe towards their ruler are linked to the prosperity of the state, and form another aspect of the tale that has been interpreted in many ways.

Although the tale is divided into many episodes, the central theme is encapsulated in the conflict between Hang Tuah and Jebat. Both characters are equal in many respects and Jebat may be even seen as the alter ego of Tuah. Jebat is as courageous, handsome, well mannered, and well behaved as Tuah until the moment he is appointed as Tuah's replacement. Hang Tuah is the ultimate example of a servant who has an almost sickening loyalty to his sultan, while the penalty of disloyalty is clearly shown in the consequences of Hang Jebat's rebellion. Jebat kills all of the female servants and royal concubines at the palace when he is challenged by Hang Tuah, and after he is mortally wounded by Tuah's *kris*, Jebat recovers to kill thousands of people around the palace before his own demise. The theme of loyalty is in accordance with the environment in which much "classical"

Malay literature was written, namely the Malay courts where scribes and authors worked together on the production of books which had a certain sacral meaning for the courts where they were produced. Such themes are found throughout premodern Malay writing, although some Malay texts depict the ruler as a tyrant who alienates many of his subjects through his unjust rule, thus emphasizing that the ruler also had obligations towards his subjects. These lessons are almost totally lacking in the *Hikayat Hang Tuah*, except for the tale of Jebat's rebellion. In that tale Jebat temporarily becomes ruler of the palace and polity, acting as tyrannical leader who does nothing but drink, fornicate, and kill the people who are subjected to his whims and wishes.

The *Hikayat Hang Tuah* was very much embedded in the literary traditions of premodern Malay courts. Along with *Sulalatus Salatin* or *Sejarah Melayu* ("Malay Annals")—another text that focuses on precolonial Melaka and contains some truncated versions of Hang Tuah's tales—accounts of Hang Tuah can be classified as typical *kerajaan* (royal) texts (Milner, *Kerajaan*) in that they consolidate and strengthen the position of the ruling elite, and the manuscripts were highly respected receptacles if not sacred objects at the courts where they were produced. These texts were only supposed to be read in public on certain occasions and only before a limited audience. Outside court circles they were probably only known to a few Western scholars who studied Malay literature and collected manuscripts, although the populace also knew them in some form through oral traditions. For colonial scholars both *Hikayat Hang Tuah* and *Sulalatus Salatin* had a certain appeal for they were historical tales without too many fantastical or mythic legends, which were common and often the focus of severe criticism by colonial scholars of Malay literary tradition. The two texts that described the tales of Hang Tuah were also in accordance with colonial policies that promoted loyalty to the ruler among Malays as a praiseworthy characteristic since it could be transferred to the new holders of power in the region, the British. The tales balanced nicely alongside texts that were highly critical of the Malay elite, the most famous written by the British supported author Abdullah Munsyi, which were all published by the British to provide reading materials for their vernacular colonial educational system (Proudfoot 16).

Moreover, both the *Sulalatus Salatin* and *Hikayat Hang Tuah* are written in clear and simple Malay not riddled with Arabic loan words, and therefore in line with nineteenth-century Western ideals of a "pure," original language which was important for Western understandings of a Malay "nation." The lucidity of the language in these texts was considered important for the development of a standard form of Malay which was to be used in the colonial education system that European officials in British Malaya and the Dutch East Indies established in the latter part of the nineteenth century. Since the colonial authorities needed texts to develop a certain pride among Malays for their history and language, which in colonial conceptions were characterized by the domination of the aristocracy and marred by foreign words, both of these texts were seen as exemplary. These officials, such as R. J. Wilkinson, ensured that the *Hikayat Hang Tuah* and *Sulalatus Salatin* were in the first batch of texts published. It was through this publication that the story of Hang Tuah gained a certain familiarity among a larger Malay public. Eventually *Hikayat Hang Tuah* went through four editions in the ubiquitous Malay Literature Series, which was published as part of the colonial educational service in the early twentieth century.

The story of Hang Tuah was further popularized in the early twentieth century through *bangsawan*, a form of popular Malay opera that developed under the influence of Indian theatre groups touring Southeast Asia in the last decades of the nineteenth century. These theatre groups staged a host of different stories hailing from Indian and Western traditions in one of the Indian languages. The performances were accompanied by music and dance and were interspersed with comical and musical interludes, which often did not have any connection with the story but received enthusiastic reactions from the audience (Cohen 315–17). From the 1890s onwards this type of commercial theatre was "imitated" in the Malay world and developed into a form of Malay drama that flourished in the two decades prior to World War Two. *Bangsawan* theatre depended upon ticket sales and therefore was subject to the popular tastes of the viewing audience (Rahmah Bujang 46–48; Tan 165–67).

Some of the tales of Hang Tuah were incorporated into the repertoire of *bangsawan* theatre, quickly becoming a staple of the performances (Abdul 17). In a list of stories staged by *bangsawan* troupes between 1914

JAN VAN DER PUTTEN AND TIMOTHY P. BARNARD

and 1956, there are at least three plays that are directly taken from *Hikayat Hang Tuah*: "Hang Tuah," "*Keris Taming Sari*," and "*Cinta di negara Hang Tuah*" ("Love in the land of Hang Tuah"; Rahmah Bujang appendix D). The latter title is interesting because *Hikayat Hang Tuah* is almost void of episodes in which love is the main theme; only the episode in which Hang Tuah abducts Princess Teja may be classified as such and it may have been the subject matter of this play.

The socioeconomic and political environment in which the *bangsawan* theatre developed gradually changed beginning in the 1930s. The Depression made it hard for theatre groups to stage large productions and the audience found it increasingly difficult to pay the price of the tickets. In addition, nationalistic groups calling for independence from British colonialism were growing in popularity. Such nationalistic feelings were considered incongruent with plays that contained the message that loyalty of subjects to their masters was something to be celebrated—after all Hang Tuah killed his best friend for insulting the ruler. During World War Two the first drama staged took the Hang Tuah story as its subject material and tried to convey a "serious" message to the audience, but in this case to focus on how the era of Hang Tuah differed from contemporary times. Japanese restrictions prevented any new or more explicit interpretation of the story; thus, the play *Hang Tuah Pahlawan Melayu* ("Hang Tuah the Malay hero") only reminded Malays of glorious days that had passed (Abdul 24–26). The version presented during the War was important, however. It was the beginning of a reinterpretation of the basic story. In the following decades the tales of Hang Tuah would give vent to nationalistic feelings, which invariably undermined their position as the sublime champion of those in power. At the core of these reinterpretations would be the new media of film and comics that transformed the subject material.

Malay film began during the 1930s as theatre owners searched for a product that would appeal to local audiences. The *bangsawan* tradition was quite influential in the nascent film industry, as well as the comic strip production that followed in its wake, for it provided the stars as well as the stories for many of the films that were made in the decade after the war. It also provided the industry with an audience that was familiar with and appreciative of the players, stories, and conventions. These early films were shot on a small stage, with little movement from the actors and the camera, and no use of close ups. The rarity of seeing Malay language dramas through the modern medium of film, however, drew large crowds despite the limited technical quality of the product (Jamil Sulong 1993: 9). World War Two brought this early era of Malay language film to a close. Although only a handful of films had been produced, and were of limited influence, they laid the ground for a vibrant Malay film industry in the 1950s and early 1960s that was based in Singapore.

The Malay film industry that flourished in Singapore following World War Two was centered on two companies: Malay Film Productions (MFP) and Cathay Keris. MFP was the local branch of Shaw Brothers, a Chinese theatre and film production organization that was influential throughout Southeast Asia. They were to dominate the Malay film industry until the late 1950s, when Run Run Shaw—the maverick responsible for much the organization's success—returned to Hong Kong and a series of labor strikes that followed crippled production capabilities. Following these developments, Cathay Keris surpassed MFP in terms of productivity and creativity. Like MFP, Cathay Keris was a major Chinese-owned theatre chain and film producer, although its founders were based in Singapore (Barnard). At their respective peaks, both studios produced films about Hang Tuah, with each reflecting the political and social issues of the time, as well the reasons for the studios' popularity.

The main reason for MFP's success in the 1950s was an actor and singer named P. Ramlee. Although he was not a conventionally attractive man, being skinny with acne scars on his face, Ramlee was charismatic and had a musical ability that helped him earn a contract to lead the studio orchestra in the late 1940s. Since practically every Malay film of the period featured songs, he often appeared before the cameras either leading the orchestra or singing a musical number in many of the early postwar films. Ramlee soon moved away from the orchestra pit and took increasingly larger speaking roles in films and by 1950 he was a leading man. For the next twenty years he dominated all aspects of the Malay film industry as an actor, writer, and director. He eventually appeared in forty-three films, directing sixteen of them. In addition, Ramlee often wrote the scripts, while also composing and performing the music that would appear in the film. The turning point in his career was the film *Hang Tuah*, a drama that

JAN VAN DER PUTTEN AND TIMOTHY P. BARNARD

was not only influenced by Malay storytelling traditions but also the new medium of comic art. The production reflected the coming together of a number of modernizing influences of the 1950s in Malaya.

Expatriate Indian directors dominated the early film world in which P. Ramlee participated since Shaw Brothers felt they could bring an expertise to the industry, as well as be easily controlled since they could be deported if they caused trouble. While these Indian directors brought a certain amount of technical knowledge to early Malay film, there were cultural boundaries that limited their acceptance among the Malay actors and assistants on the sets. One of the most common complaints in the memoirs and oral histories of participants was the inability of Indian directors to communicate in Malay and the control the Indian directors had over the stories told on screen. Scripts and advice to actors usually had to undergo a laborious process of translation from various Indian languages into English and then into Malay, and back again (Hamzah 82–83; Jamil 24, 47, 50–51). The result was direct translation of popular Indian film plots along with the songs that were a combination of Indian cinema and *bangsawan* traditions, performed in Malay.

As MFP productions grew in popularity in the 1950s, Shaw Brothers' executives searched for a story that would appeal to a Malay audience in the midst of a growing nationalistic movement and be appropriate for their first color film.[14] They decided on filming the story of Hang Tuah, as it had become a popular tale among the populace following the numerous comic versions. The executives then turned to Phani Majumdar, a newly imported Indian director, to helm the film. Shaw Brothers originally hired Majumdar, an activist in the Bengal film industry, in 1955 to reorganize the studio. He accomplished this task by promoting Malays who had been working behind the scenes as assistant directors, cameramen, and editors to increasingly important positions, while also supporting new story lines and ideas. Majumdar wanted to introduce some of the activism he advocated in India into the Malay film industry by encouraging innovation, and this provided opportunities for many young activists who had worked in the publishing industry. Backed by the increasing popularity and status of P. Ramlee, Mujamdar directed one of the most important films ever made in Singapore, and, by returning to the tale of the Melakan warrior, tapped into the growing popularity of the story as reflected in earlier comic versions.

Majumdar wrote the screenplay for *Hang Tuah* with the assistance of Jamil Sulong, a nationalistic artist, and Mubin Sheppard, a British civil servant and historian who eventually stayed in Malaya following its independence in 1957. In addition, the director asked for input from Mahmud Ahmad, Abdullah Hussain, and Haji Buyong Adil, all of whom were leading writers or cultural activists at the time. The input of these activists resulted in the incorporation of traditional sayings (*gurindam*) and poetry (*pantun*) as an integral part of the plot and dialogue. Shaw Brothers' high hopes for the film pushed Majumdar to complete the film so that it could qualify for competition in the Asian Film Festival circuit in 1955. The filming process, which involved flying the film to London for processing, however, took too long. Shaw Brothers finally released the film in January 1956, featuring it in their marquee cinemas in Singapore and Kuala Lumpur, something they rarely did with Malay films.[15] *Hang Tuah* went on to win prizes at film festivals in Hong Kong and was shown in Indonesia, Thailand, and the Middle East, as well as at the Berlin Film Festival, all firsts in the Malay film industry (Ahmad 80–81; Jamil 86).

Despite such success, the film received harsh criticism from the Malay activist community, becoming a focus of complaints that artists had at the time toward both MFP and Cathay Keris, as well as British rule in the region. Reflecting much of this criticism is an article by Mahmud Ahmad in the Malay magazine, *Majalah Bintang* (Star Magazine) that came out the month after the film was released. In the piece Mahmud distances himself from much of the production, claiming that he had little input into the film since he only attended one or two meetings as well as a ceremony celebrating the first day of filming. For his efforts, Mahmud received a few meals, three shanty drinking sessions, and a pair of complimentary tickets to a Shaw Brothers cinema. He then claims that Mubin Sheppard had an inordinate amount of input into the film. Although Sheppard had published a popular children's book on Hang Tuah in 1949, such a role was unwelcome during a period in which Malay artists were trying to get their own versions of such iconic tales before the public. In addition, Mahmud claims that the only formal meeting he attended was conducted in English, another point of irritation as it was seen as a tool of colonial oppression. Finally, he criticizes the costumes that the characters wore claiming that they were not authentic. This last point may seem fairly petty, but it was a

JAN VAN DER PUTTEN AND TIMOTHY P. BARNARD

point of contention since an earlier promotional article for the film made great efforts to address this issue, claiming it was necessary for the colors to appear vibrant on screen.[16]

While the costumes and the participation of Sheppard and Majumdar were the focus of much criticism, activists also questioned the limited number of tales and the inclusion of two songs in the film. While the "singing Hang Tuah" led to charges that the film was "too Indian" (Harding and Ahmad 72), the contempt of many of the activists was directed at a simplification of a complicated and subtle text since the film only contained an account of four of the most famous tales. It begins with the tale of young Tuah and his friends fighting pirates and then receiving instructions in the martial arts at the mysterious Mt. Ledang. The film then turns to three of the most common tales: the trip to Majapahit and the gift of the dagger "Taming Sari," the seduction of Teja and Tuah's exile due to slander, and finally the rebellion of the treasonous Jebat. The film ends with Hang Tuah's murder of Jebat. The last shot focuses on P. Ramlee as Hang Tuah, who states "Who was right, me or Jebat?," leaving the audience to question whether Hang Tuah's loyalty to the ruler was justified. The questioning of Tuah's actions in the last lines of the film, as well as Ramlee's status in the community, did temper some of the criticism, however. This twist to the tale, which previously had been used as the template for blind loyalty, represented a push in a new direction, opening the story up to an examination of Jebat's motivations and perhaps a justification for rebelling against colonial and traditional authority, to which the popular comics of the day had also drawn attention. This was clearly seen when the two main actors, P. Ramlee and Ahmad Mahmud, promoted the film through traveling theatre presentations during the mid-1950s. During reenactments of the Tuah-Jebat clash, Jebat always received the greatest amount of applause (Josselin de Jong 146).

The reassessment of Hang Jebat's actions was made in a context of increased social and cultural activism that was related to growing nationalistic feelings. One of the most influential organizations at that time was a group of Malay artists and writers, known as the ASAS 50 (an acronym for *Angkatan Sasterawan 50*—Generation of the Writers of the 1950s), who promoted the ideal of "art for society." While best known for their poems and short stories, many ASAS 50 members also worked in the film industry.

Many of these artists, such as Jamil Sulong and S. Roomai Noor, originally came from the publishing industry, where Harun Aminurrashid had acted as a mentor. Harun's initially employed these future actors and directors to write for his entertainment magazines, and the nationalism and use of popular culture that he promoted became influential in their future positions in the film industry. One of their common complaints at the time among these activists was that the films did not reflect the concerns of the Malay community, for which the Indian directors were harshly criticized. However, Majumdar provided greater opportunities for Malay input into the filmmaking process, with *Hang Tuah* being the first step. The criticisms of these Malay activists and the development of ASAS-50, however, were rooted in the earlier developments in the magazine industry, in which comic strips were a vibrant medium for new ideas.

The interactive influence of comics and film became apparent in comics that were published after the release of the film. Released the same year as the film, Muhammad Ibrahim's *Jebat Derhaka* contains drawings that are quite detailed with many frames on one page, which does tend to cause problems for reader. While the author decided to insert many quotations taken directly from the original *hikayat,* the film was the inspiration for the drawings, since they are quite accurate caricatures of P. Ramlee as Tuah and Ahmad Mahmud as Jebat. Much of this is ironic since P. Ramlee had not been the first choice to play Hang Tuah. During the planning stages for the film, one of the main Malay advisors, Haji Buyong Adil, insisted that Hang Tuah must be tall and muscular with light-colored skin, and thus rejected P. Ramlee for the role. After a few disastrous screen tests with unknowns, studio executives forced the director to accept the Malay film icon—the biggest and most charismatic star of the era—for the part. Distraught at the choice, Haji Buyong Adil insisted that the actor did not fit the part. However, when pressed to prove that Hang Tuah is even described as such in the original texts and twentieth-century interpretations, he eventually conceded that the character in each medium fit the expectations of the audience, and came to accept P. Ramlee as Hang Tuah, as well as Ahmad Mahmud as Hang Jebat (Abdullah, *Sebuah Perjalanan* 600–601). Thus, what had previously been a blank slate with regard to the appearance of Hang Tuah had now become standard. P. Ramlee was Hang Tuah. In the comic illustrations in *Jebat Derhaka,* however, there is a flaw: For the

Fig. 3. P. Ramlee and Ahmad Mahmud as
the models for an illustrated Hang Tuah and
Hang Jebat (*Jebat Derhaka* 1956, p. 31).

film the actor shaved off his trademark mustache, which does appear in
the drawings.

The publisher of *Jebat Derhaka* was none other than Sabirin Hj. Mohd.
Annie, and it appeared in his new series *Penerbitan Keluarga*. In the introduction he expressed a conviction that, although the story was already
well known, the publication would be warmly welcomed for the entertainment it provided and for its repetition and commemoration of the virtues
of its hero in the past. Hopefully this comic would help the reader learn
progressive lessons (*Jebat Derhaka*, 1956). This introduction not only refers
to the commercial help the readers would provide to the publisher; it also
clearly alludes to the progress the nation would experience through pend-
ing independence from the British. The introduction was dated 30 June
1956, thirteen months before Malayan independence materialized, and five
months after the release of a film version of the Hang Tuah story that ended
with an ambivalent twist that questioned loyalty to a traditional ruler. The
proliferation of these comics—which would subsequently influence, and

be influenced by, a film—may be interpreted as an expression of hope that the efforts of the comic industry, and connected artists, would lead to developing pride in the nation by a retelling and perhaps reinterpretation of legendary tales for children and grown-ups.

The story of Hang Tuah has seen many artistic reinterpretations. Abdul Rahman Napiah (1994) and Solehah Ishak (2002) have dealt extensively with the dramatized representations of the Hang Tuah tale, which revolve exclusively around the Tuah-Jebat duel. The 1958 radio play *Tragedi Hang Jebat* (later retitled *Hang Jebat Menderhaka* [Hang Jebat commits treason] and produced as a stage play) by Ali Aziz, is considered a turning point for the shift towards Jebat as hero in the struggle against the old forces obstructing the full development of an independent Malay nation. This shift was further refined in Usman Awang's *Matinya Seorang Pahlawan* ("Death of a Warrior," 1961), which was frequently staged to boost patriotic feelings in the new-born nation. About two decades later the tale inspired three playwrights in compiling absurdist plays which featured Jebat as champion of the underprivileged in Malaysian society (Solehah 7–8). Another very interesting reinterpretation of the tale may be found in a short story by Fatimah Busu (1984), in which the hero Jebat rises from his grave, which has become a garbage dump, and eternally travels around the country while bleeding from his mortal wound. Every Thursday night Jebat is visited by hundreds of thousands of small skulls who sing for him and eagerly listen as he tells them the legendary tale of Hang Tuah. The skulls claim that he is better off than them because he still wears his earthly body, but Jebat counters with the tales of the people he encounters who are tortured in hell. At dawn the following day he continues his journey. This version, the first by a female author, blends Islamic symbolism and legends, such as the "Tale of King Skull" (*Hikayat Raja Jumjumah*), the Camus-inspired Sisyphus tale, and homoerotic allusions with the Malay legend (Khoo).

The *Romance of Hang Tuah* holds a pivotal position in the development of the Malayan film industry in the 1950s. It also played an important role in a thriving popular literature industry, in which comics were a new development. Although some comic books were modeled after Western prototypes, the comic industry in the Peninsula quickly developed an indigenous style during this period, and much of this can be related to the

JAN VAN DER PUTTEN AND TIMOTHY P. BARNARD

impeding possibility of independence. Throughout the Malay Peninsula and Singapore, the idea of a modern nation, focused on progress, became a mantra in the publishing and film industry. Thus, the stories depicted in films and comics promoted ideals of sacrifice and modernity (Barnard and Barnard), while only later shifting to more commercial stories. This led to a questioning of traditional tales that was only hinted at in the comics and the ending of *Hang Tuah*, the 1956 film.

While the MFP film and numerous comics had reintroduced the story of Hang Tuah and Hang Jebat to the general public in the 1950s, this trend continued with the 1961 production of another film that focused on the story, this time titled *Hang Jebat*, which was made by Cathay Keris. In contrast to earlier versions of the tale, however, this one focused on the usual villain of the piece, Hang Jebat, making him a modern hero who did not participate in "feudal" worship of loyalty, but made individualistic decisions in favor of his friends and family. Under the direction of Malay auteur Hussein Haniff, the film clearly places the tale in a modern context. By focusing on the traditional antagonist, who was treasonous to the ruler in the name of justice and friendship, Cathay Keris presented a revolutionary—modern—interpretation of the Malay historical legend (Jamil 229; Lim 65, 130–31).

The discussed reinterpretations of the tale were only possible because of the popularity and familiarity the producers and the audience had with the story of Hang Tuah. This popularization began in the 1920s through theatre performances, which led to a rewriting of the story in youth literature during the 1940s and 1950s. Each of these reinterpretations then influenced highly popular forms of comics and film beginning in the 1950s. In this period after World War Two legendary tales were used to inculcate Malays with a feeling of pride for their history so they would feel united as one nation to overcome the problems decolonization would bring. But a tale that contains the choice one has to make between loyalty to one's superiors or towards one's friends and next of kin as one of its major themes, is of course prone to be used and reused as inspiration for future interpretations. These heroes are sure to be resurrected from the grave and will haunt Malay artistic expression for generations to come.

ENKI BILAL'S INTERMEDIAL FANTASIES

FROM COMIC BOOK *NIKOPOL TRILOGY* TO FILM *IMMORTALS (AD VITAM)*

—SOPHIE GEOFFROY-MENOUX

A Franco Yugoslavian artist traumatized by the civil war in Bosnia, Enki Bilal was born in Belgrade in 1951, and immigrated to Paris (France) at the age of ten. His glamorous comic books exude a haunting sense of desperate and tragic love in the midst of political and economic disasters (dictatorship, globalization, eugenics), and ecological cataclysms (climate changes). Urban guerillas in devastated cities reminiscent of the Sarajevo that haunts his childhood memories, and underground movements led by unwilling and all-too-human, often schizoid antiheroes are featured among his idiosyncrasies.

This chapter offers a semiotic approach to Enki Bilal's science-fiction film *Immortals (ad vitam)*, released in France in March 2004 and starring Charlotte Rampling, ex-Miss France Linda Hardy, and Thomas Kretschmann. The film was adapted by Bilal from his own well-known comic books: *The Nikopol Trilogy* (*Carnival of Mortals* [1980], *Woman Trap* [1986] and *Cold Equator* [1992]). Bilal's fantastic *Nikopol Trilogy* is a surrealistic, dreamlike dystopia based on what he sees as the harrowing realities of our postmodern world: a cynical approach to money and power, coupled with a morbid fear of aging and of death, to which the film title—*Immortals (ad vitam)*—refers. *Immortals (ad vitam)* engages and critiques the role of images in society—and the potential for such images to be used as a form of social control. As such, Bilal's postmodernist work offers interesting possibilities for the media of comics and film as social critique.

Taking up the timeless theme of the quest for eternal life and ever-lasting beauty, youth, and love, Bilal depicts a decadent albeit futuristic world where the immediate impact of visual images generates and guaran-tees political domination. From plastic surgery to the adulteration of visual images, the power of corrupt dictator Ferdinand Choublanc (Senator Kyle Allgood in the film) is based on manipulations of all kinds aimed at eras-ing, then replacing people's memories (knowledge, language, the ability to express themselves and to communicate) with the hypnotic-like state of oblivion induced by spectacular shows and performances broadcast on ubiq-uitous video screens, and overwhelmingly and lethally beautified "masks": fake images and government-sponsored fashion and makeup pasted onto void, alienated, and coldhearted robotlike individuals without a past.

The equilibrium and the order based on this strategy—artificial memo-ries and personal amnesia considered as weapons—is disrupted by the ap-parently absurd interruption of a flying pyramid inhabited by the Egyp-tian gods Anubis, Bastet, Thot, and others in the sky of New York. When one central character's frozen leg suddenly falls down from outer space into the streets, the surrealistic story turns into a politico-fantastic thriller.

A technical tour de force, the film results from Bilal's deconstruction/transposition of his own comic books, which themselves are very filmic in style. It offers an interpretative synthesis and selection of the basic ele-ments of the comic book trilogy, arranged to fit the cinematic format and satisfy the expectations of the targeted audience: young viewers expecting a cult movie. Thus, not only does the reconstruction entail a transposition into a different, emphatically hybrid medium (film, video, cartoon, virtual images, animation film), but it also brings about a shift in the work's genre, and therefore a shift in its intended reception.

The comic book trilogy focuses on the improbable love story of a mu-tant journalist (Jill Bioskop), the Egyptian god Horus, and Alcide Nikopol (whose leg is referred to above), a human dissenter frozen by the all-powerful Eugenics Society "Globus," then accidentally thawed and flung into a terri-fying world decades ahead of the chosen time, and whose refuge is Baude-laire's decadent poetry. The *Trilogy* spans the years 2023 to 2034, and moves from ultramodern cityscapes (New York, Paris, Berlin, London) in devel-oped countries ruled by tyrants to African desert landscapes (especially in

Egypt), peopled by civilized animals and threatened by tribal conflicts and militias fueled by western countries.

The first volume, *La Foire aux Immortels* (*Carnival of Mortals*, 1980), is set in March 2023 Paris, where an Egyptian flying pyramid has just run out of fuel. Taking advantage of that failure, Horus rebels against his fellow creatures' universal rule, and to make them surrender to his will, blackmails dictator Ferdinand Choublanc, granting immortality in exchange for Horus's control of the city's fuel supply. The capsule in which dissident Nikopol has been frozen is hit by a missile and plummets down. Nikopol's frozen leg is cut off in the process. The volume focuses on the bargain between the two dissenters, Nikopol and Horus. In exchange for survival, a new leg (made out of a metallic subway rail), and divine strength, Horus inhabits Nikopol's human body, while Nikopol, possessed by Horus, but haunted by Baudelaire's *Flowers of Evil*, becomes a hero and a leader. He nevertheless collapses when Horus is chased from Paris by the gods, and ends up in a lunatic asylum.

Volume II, *La Femme piège* (*Woman Trap*, 1986) begins in Paris, on 22 February 2025, then moves to London, and focuses on the white-skinned, blue-cropped-haired mutant journalist Jill Bioskop, her reports, her "blue" feelings (and, literally, blue tears), her loves, fatal both to herself and to her lovers, and her amnesia. She and Nikopol are brought together by Horus's telepathic influence. The latter, punished by the gods after his rebellion, looks for a female partner to reach immortality through procreation. He uses Nikopol's body to impregnate Jill. The book ends with Nikopol and Jill, in love, flying over Egypt in a vessel piloted by Horus.

In volume III, *Froid équateur* (*Cold Equator*, 1992), all the characters, plots, and subplots converge. Nikopol, his son and twin Niko, Horus— alternately inside and outside Nikopol—and Jill Bioskop, but also the gods (Anubis, Bastet among others) in their flying pyramid, Choublanc and other dictators converge, somewhere in Africa on the Equator line, the territory of the mafialike organization KKDZO. The unifying devices are the filming of *Amor/Amore* (Jill and Nikopol's love story), Nikopol's fight against dictatorship, and Niko's love story with yet another character, Yelena. The book ends with an amnesiac Jill finishing the film, unaware that the catatonic Nikopol (oblivious through madness) whose hand she absentmindedly shakes, used to be her lover, and the medium through which Horus made her pregnant.

A comparison of the comic books and the screenplay reveals that the film is no mere adaptation and rather a totally new visual artifact. Two hundred talented young designers, some of whom had worked with Spielberg, Lucas, Wim Wenders, Jeunet (*City of Lost Children*), and Sting, spent over four years working with Bilal to make the film. They used well-known video clip maker Duran's 3D animation software to keep and develop the "Bilal touch." A condensation of the three comic books on which it is recognizably based, the film differs from them by highlighting certain features. For example, the bewildering travels through space, switches from city to city, and travels from cityscapes to African natural desert scenery, have been replaced by the breathtaking horizontal trajectories of cars flying across the sky of the one location where the action is concentrated: New York City, especially Central Park, in the winter of 2095. This shift in the spatiotemporal locus turns the film into a science fiction film. Urban filth and vertical concrete submerge everything, movements are cramped or guided (with the noteworthy exception of Horus's free flight), and the stifling atmosphere generates a claustrophobic sense of impending doom.

This feeling is enhanced by the film's focus on the main characters (unlike the comic books' numerous minor characters), whose functions and actions are more explicitly motivated, whereas in the comic they had remained implicit. The film thus hinges on the triangular love story (Nikopol-Horus-Jill), but the perspective has changed, warding off the simplifying effects of such dramatic tightening up. Counterbalancing Nikopol and Horus's male "heroism," Jill here becomes the film's poignant "center of consciousness." The film focuses on her alienness, her feelings of displacement, of not belonging,[1] and her painful transformation into a human woman. This is a physical and psychic transformation,[2] the symptoms of which are visually represented (the shedding of her blue hair symbolically represents her fall into oblivion) and eagerly watched over by scientist Dr. Emma Turner (Charlotte Rampling), the filmic counterpart to the comic books' Yelena Prokosh-Tootobi (Niko's lover). The film opposes "the original world of primary symptoms, drives and instincts" which "incorporates both futurism and archaism"³ and in which male characters are tied to the heroines, who try to find and show them the way out (Deleuze 194–95), because they have to, even if, in the process, they must "forget everything before starting from scratch."⁴ From *ur-topos* to *u-topos*.

Physically attracted to Jill's strange beauty and childlike purity, and scientifically fascinated by her extraterrestrial vitality, Emma Turner is the film's sole human being, and, like Nikopol, a rebel against Globus Eugenics Society. Her experiments aim at preserving the original, unadulterated human species, and fighting against the ongoing genetic manipulations and the ideology of her time—some people are disposable, others must be protected. This concern is the dominant theme of the film, which opens with the traumatic sequence of a raid, in which Jill is caught, by Eugenics militias to capture sane human "guinea pigs" whose organs will be removed for VIP's needs.

Absent from the comic books, the characters of Inspector Froebe and his crew turn the film into a political thriller reminiscent of American action films and survival stories, and Nikopol into a political savior-of-the-world Bruce-Willis-type hero. The absence of his son-twin, Niko, makes him all the more unique: the film chooses not to duplicate the treatment of the theme of dual personalities beyond the couples Horus/Nikopol and Jill-before/Jill-after. This move sets off the individuality of Emma Turner's character and emphasizes the medical theme as well as her scientific rebellion.

The rhetoric of Bilal's images in both mediums is based on a pessimistic vision of reality and characterized by his aestheticist though dysphoric representation of urban, postmodern life. The iconic and linguistic codes he uses to represent reality are an apt translation of his pessimistic imagination. His graphic pages are saturated by "emotionalist images" (Deleuze's "*images émotion*"), since the scale of his panels ranges from medium close shots to close shots, closeups, and extreme closeups. The saturation of the frames sets off faces in an emotionally efficient way.⁵ Readers are all the more easily overwhelmed by the feeling of empathy such closeups force on them, as other devices contribute to Bilal's violently, cruelly beautiful representation of brute force and crime.

The all-but-speechless characters seem to have been frozen as in snapshots, with their vacant stares and robotlike movements, their silence and

SOPHIE GEOFFROY-MENOUX

inability to communicate in any direct way—when he is not speaking Horus's words, Nikopol quotes from Baudelaire instead of expressing himself. The feeling aroused by the rigidity and fixity of the faces of these hieratic characters creates a mixture of fascination and awe. These robotlike masks, statues, idols, golems, or freaks are the brutal though beautiful consequence of the political tyranny of aesthetics: government controlled and sponsored fashions impose the use of certain colors, hairstyles, and dress codes, which artificially compensate for the lifeless anonymity of these nonexpressive androgynous creatures. And fashions, such as people's faces, change whenever revolutions or coups occur.[6]

The violent, dysphoric atmosphere generated by such graphic options is exacerbated by the psycho-physiologic effects of Bilal's chromatic idiosyncrasies. The whole range of grayish and greenish tints and crude lights he predominantly uses in his comic books, translated into the black and white effect or grey monochromes of the film, result in an expressionist's universe as much as a futuristic world. Indeed, the dominant impression is that of a subterranean, or subaquatic, aquariumlike backcloth upon which rare red or orange touches—crimson patches of blood—stand out. These colors arouse tactile sensations such as those associated to the nonorganic life of metallic, sleek, cold, shiny, hard, opaque, tasteless objects (connoting ideal, noble absolute, nonhuman perfection), as opposed to the soft, warm, resilient, mat, comforting grain of left-over, residual humanity (seen as trivial, grotesque, carnivalesque, excremental, and obscene), as Nikopol's selection among Baudelaire's *Flowers of Evil* shows.[7] Bilal's semiotic system of colors and forms is structured as a network of binary oppositions: mutants vs. siblings (interbreeding), supernatural rapes vs. natural procreation, and so on.

Bilal's dystopic representation of the world appears, at times, twice removed from reality by the explicit or implicit references to literature. For instance Nikopol quotes from Baudelaire's *Flowers of Evil*. His missing leg is reminiscent of Théophile Gautier's "Pied de la momie" ("The Mummy's Foot"). The general atmosphere and ideology of the work are redolent of H. P. Lovecraft's Chthulhu mythos, style, and prejudices. Furthermore the name of the telepathic cat Gogol Algol is a knowing wink at the Russian author Gogol and at Julien Green's *Château d'Algol*.

Other iconic linguistic codes are superimposed on Bilal's visual and intertextual codes. Pictorial modes, especially Dali and Magritte, and, more generally speaking, Surrealism are imitated. References to cartoons, like Roland Topor's *La Planète Sauvage*,[8] and applied arts like fashion design, through references to Jean-Paul Gaultier or Philippe Découfflé, are also present. Bilal also pastes newspaper articles onto his panels and a fake issue of *Libération* is inserted in the comic book. The reality effect of some of its referential elements ("Thursday 14th October 1993"; Serge July's editorial note) is counterbalanced by the derealizing effect of other clearly science fiction elements such as titles like "The Day When the Future Sent a Telecopy," or "Today, 3 February 2025 Meets 14 October 1993".[9] The drawn pseudo-photographs that illustrate it are ambiguous; traces, and therefore revelations and proofs, of what-really-took-place, they nevertheless exhibit impossible scenes. They ultimately work as indice-like epiphanies. To these cases of intertextuality that reference a literary canon and give the comic books a glamorous dimension, the film adds a cult effect of numerous references to cinema. For example, the long black coats worn by the characters remind the viewer of *The Matrix*, while their makeup and violence is reminiscent of Stanley Kubrik's *A Clockwork Orange*. Nikopol's hibernation capsule waltzing through space naturally brings to mind the same director's *2001: A Space Odyssey*. The brutal hockey matches contain a hint of *Rollerball*, while the thriller dimension evokes *Blade Runner*. Luc Besson's *The Fifth Element* is suggested by the action taking place a hundred meters above ground, amid the skyscrapers, where cars and trolleys zoom about, as well as by the performance, the plastic perfection, and the Jean-Paul Gaultier outfit of actress Linda Hardy (Mila Jovovich's blue-haired double). Nikopol himself, who has become, during his hibernation, the leader of an underground movement, "Spirit of Nikopol," is endowed with a role redolent of American action films. Intertextuality thus contributes to the shift from comic book to cult movie. Moreover, the rhetoric of Bilal's fiction and the structuring of his comic book discourse rely on constant shifts from book form to photography and the cinema, and vice versa. In the same way as the comic books are written and drawn like film shots/ sequences or composed like photographs, the film resorts to the techniques of drawing.

Indeed, the comic books sometimes look like fine photomontages and read like a film's storyboard. The cinema is at the core of volume III, which

SOPHIE GEOFFROY-MENOUX

opens in the studios of Dembi Dolo, where director Giancarlo Donadoni is showing Niko the rushes of the film *Amor/Amore* featuring his father, Nikopol, and mother, Jill. The story is from then on a retrospective narrative, aiming at explaining the disappearance of the heroic pair, at trying to understand why the film was never finished, and at presenting the film's completion. In other words, the book is offered as an equivalent to the lost film, and designed like the film it is meant to replace. Thus, the filming of *Amor/Amore* may be absent from the film itself, which may lose the *mise en abîme* effect present in the comic books, it nevertheless capitalizes on self-referentiality. For Bilal's fans, the film they view is the one shot in the comic book.

The initial sequence of the book shows Niko watching the image-by-image reel: the comic panels read like the film's actual storyboard. The fictional film is thus represented as a series of almost identical snapshots cut from the intended film, with the intradiegetic spectators' comments superimposed in squares pasted above the images: the director's technical comments counterpoised by Niko's emotional ones. An emotional climax is reached with the final sequence shot ("It's the last scene I was able to shoot with him"), which freezes on closeups of Jill and Nikopol's kiss. The hallucinatory fixity of the filmed images is compensated by the movement created by the succession of images barely different from one another. The first closeup of the pair, kissing, with their eyes shut, is followed by a close shot of the same kiss, with their eyes open. The kiss is then interpolated by the director's information, after a zooming out of the kiss, now seen as part of a medium long shot of the green, desert movie house including the two viewers, the director and Niko, facing the prolonged, enlarged kiss on the giant screen, with their backs to us. The next image zooms in on the director's blue hair (blue, as an homage to lost Jill), and a final, lateral pan shows the two men in profile, silhouetted against the screen, reduced by the dilated closeups of the romantic pair. The filmlike changes in the framing, or in the scale of the camera shots, alter the spectator's point of view and understanding of the scene: what is out of frame is necessarily fantasized or imagined.

Other aspects of filmmaking can be pinpointed in Bilal's inherently cinematographic drawn work. His rhetoric includes references to casting (Niko meets the actors impersonating lost Jill and Nikopol), to camera moves, to editing, and even to dialogue and the direction of actors. For instance, the typography of Bilal's speech balloons and thought bubbles turns these supplements of the drawn image into precinematographic stage directions. Typed in white ink on a black page, inside a speech balloon (even though Bilal's balloons are square!), the dialogue between Jill and Jeff is both high brow and literary, given as a piece of reported speech very much in the manner of Céline's brutal prose: " 'when, how and where are we going?' I ask, slightly drunk . . . 'Tomorrow morning, by aero-taxi, to Berlin,' he answers").[10] The film skillfully adapts the comic book generic, traditional association of text and image. An example of Bilal's transposition of speech balloons into a compelling sound track is the actors' voices: disquietingly, embarrassingly telltale, they echo the comic book character's impersonal, flat tones suggested by the typography and style. For instance, Charlotte Rampling/Dr. Turner's cold tone and foreign accent somehow belie her benevolent proposals. The sound effects that accompany Horus's penetration of Nikopol's body remind one of a rape, especially as they are similar to those accompanying Horus-Nikopol's repeated rapes of Jill. The sound track enhances the extreme violence of these scenes, as well as the double-sided personality of the "hero" and his victimized "beloved" Jill.

The visual representation of dialogues is of particular interest because of Bilal's "editing" technique. For example, Jill's telephone conversations (Vol. I, 50), or Niko and Yelena's encounter and subsequent face to face in a train full of African animals (Vol. I, 14), or their rendezvous at the Savoy Hotel (Vol. II, 81) are given rhythm by filmic editing techniques (shot/reverse shot; over-the-shoulder cutting pattern) that structure the sequences around camera moves compensating for the lack of expression of the faces themselves, in the purest classical Hollywood style. The camera moves account for the paradoxically gripping aspect of these uniformly square, immobile faces whose set, rigid expressions turn into opaque, stubborn, impenetrable, and somewhat caricatural, enigmas. Contrary to the male characters, most often facing and looking at the onlookers, Jill is shown looking at something else, into another frame or beyond, her eyes averted. On page 72 (Vol. II), she gazes at a crowd of people who look askance at her: thus is her role subtly defined as the central focal point of other people's (including the readers') voyeuristic gaze: a melancholy, victimized "*femme piège*"; a Woman Trap indeed.

Bilal's preference for "emotionalist images" and closeups is all the more compelling as it is set against remarkable pictures of landscapes and cityscapes composed like panoramic shots. The panoramic view of London seen from above Tower Bridge with yellow aero-taxis and a blood-red Thames (Vol. II, 87) is particularly striking and paradigmatic of Bilal's postmodern perception of the urban fabric as a juxtaposition of disjointed places or heterogeneous spatiotemporal microcosms, where waste lands, shanty towns, dockyards and warehouses, closed down and disused factories coexist with ultramodern, sleek concrete and glass designer buildings and high tech advertisings. It is a kind of urban wilderness, in which the few existing landmarks are confusingly similar. Piles of girders and scrap heaps are the common denominator of all sites, demolition or (re)-construction sites alike, that arouse the same emotions of anguished impatience.

Bilal's play on depth of focus, perspective, and decentering[11] can best be appreciated in Volume II, 95. The bottom lefthand side interior daylight shot is interestingly decentered. Framed by a slightly out of line window, a view of the hall of the Savoy hotel shows us, in the foreground, a woman in a bathing suit diving into an out of frame swimming pool; in the middle distance, a group of spectators are looking away from her at the disquieting background outside the window: a lonely soldier standing guard in the cold streets of Berlin. The image is built on the surrealistic juxtaposition, within the same square, of three heterogeneous and apparently unrelated scenes or spheres (all the characters look away from the others). The reader fights against the sense of the absurd evinced by the overall scenography, especially the foreground scene (a diver without a pool), by looking for the hidden meaning outside the window.

On page 149, Bilal likewise skillfully combines the effects of framing/ decentering and camera angle. The first frame encloses a low angle shot of Anubis being carried by Thot and accompanied by other birds flying away from the Egyptian pyramid, which can be seen floating in the snow laden sky (as the swarm of rockets in the background shows). In the next frame, another low angle shot shows the naked legs of a man apparently flying between skyscrapers: the white shanks and feet of Anubis, seen, magnified, from ground level. The framing here excludes the god's escort, to concentrate on the sole part (the flying leg) viewed by the human beings in the streets. Then Bilal zooms in on a close shot of Anubis's face (right pro-file), looking down and revealing his intentions to descend among people (*"dépose-moi en bas"*). In the final low angle shot, the people in the street, wide-eyed and frightened, are gaping at Anubis's body from his foot and his leg up. The low-angle shots enhance the humans' surprise and sense of overwhelming, supernatural forces and imminent doom.

The meaningful choice of framing can also be underlined in the two conflicting images of the death of Ferdinand Choublanc. The first one is a gruesome grey, green, and crimson view of Nikopol staring at the ob-scenely enormous body of the dictator he has just found dead, smeared in blood, blankly staring at him, and gripping a gun in his hand. The gore effect is suppressed in the next frame, even though the very same scene is represented: the reframed black-and-white photograph, from which Chou-blanc's gun and embarrassing colors have been erased, published in the newspaper and completed by the headline: "Nikopol shoots Choublanc."[12] What is at stake here is the indictment of the political manipulation of im-ages and the government's control of the press. Nikopol's challenge con-sists in revealing the political nature of media agendas.

The perspectivist relativism inherent in Bilal's choice of nonlinear editing—his use of duplicating devices and confrontation of diverging views of the same thing or of a scene shown from several, differing angles unified by cuts-away—is one of Bilal's idiosyncrasies. Another example is the hockey match in which Nikopol (inhabited by Horus) unwillingly takes part. The reader sees it alternately from the players' viewpoint, from the perspective of the officials' tribune (Vol. I, 33), and from that of the Egyptian gods (37), each viewpoint evincing a different significance.

Unlike Bilal's film, the comic books capitalize on the expressive ed-iting effects of the montage of the pages.[13] Page 137 exploits to the full the contrast between the top rectangular frame (a close shot of the five KKDZO top officials impressive and massive), the middle frame (their five dictionary-like biographies), and the bottom rectangular frame (the same five officials, seen from behind, gazing at the pyramid floating in a snow laden African sky, looming above troops of penguins). A sense of surre-alistic improbability is generated by the artful juxtaposition, or rather ed-iting, of these three images. The improbable encounter of alien cultures is likewise conveyed through expressive editing in numerous cases. Page

120 associates the futurist image of scientific progress and symbols of ancient cultures and archaic beliefs brought together in the rocket driven by Horus. Disjointed universes are set in parallel when Bastet, Anubis, Toth are shown playing Monopoly (Vol. I, 5) or when the African deserts are contrasted to urban settings such as New York, London, Berlin, and Paris.

Conversely, page 77 in volume II is carefully composed of frames within frames. Within the squared space of the pub in Camden Town framed by the page, the square frame of a TV set broadcasting, in bluish tints, the evening news bulletin, induces a documentary kind of reading, together with a holograph effect, a *mise en abîme*. The registrational extracts from *The KKDZO Daily News* pasted onto page 163 similarly link up a familiar journalistic layout with fantastic contents. The pseudoscientific medical headline—"Ivo Kohl: acute cementitis!"—contrasts with the surreal black-and-white photograph of Kohl's head transformed into cement and severed from his body.

Some images actually work as meta-images. Niko, page 157, wonderingly examines his face in the mirror; the camera moves closer and closer to his reflection, so that the vertical crack in the mirror now looks like a scar across his face: an appropriate symbol of his split identity and the outcome of his anguished soliloquy ("Is this a murderer's face?"). The climax of this revealing anamorphous occurs when a gecko suddenly runs over the reflection. The potentially deflating effect is warded off by his assistant's question ("You do not shave so as to save up your energy for the match, is that it? . . . You are Loopkin, aren't you?")[14] and his bewildered reaction. This epiphany of Loopkin, Nikopol's boxing alter ego, is completed and commented on by the final supplementary image of the gecko running across his face and partially covering his forehead and right eye. The symbolic significance of such an image is supplemented by the wordplay, in French, on *lézard* (gecko, lizard) and *(se) lézarder* (to be cracked, to crack up). Thus, the apparently disconnected item (the gecko) is an apt example of Bilal's surrealistically meaningful cuts-away.[15]

These techniques (cut-away and meta-image) ultimately resemble collage techniques, and are endowed with the same role: pasting in an item meant to replace and hide what has been cut off and taken away. These instances of a painter's use of "the wet sponge and the varnish bottle" are remarkably relevant to Bilal's obsessional leitmotivs: dismemberment/rememberment/remembrance.

But in this violently beautiful world, where the beautiful is used as the most efficient ideological tool to make people blindly surrender to any authority, not only is aesthetic perfection obtained through the obliteration and the masking of human traits, but aesthetic coercion also entails the sacrifice of the human body, and is symbolically represented by the visual prevalence of fragmentary or fragmented bodies. Images of torn-up bodies, of limbs torn apart, of dismembered bodies are the apt symptoms and representations of the motive of split identities. These "*images-pulsions*" ("impulse images")[16] coincide with the predatory type of relations prevailing in Bilal's albums. "What the subject instinctually desires is inevitably the partial object or the fetish."[17] Taking place within the hero's mind, this results in a psychomachia the outcome of which is alienation, amnesia, and madness.

The significance of all those fragments is twofold. First, they are a sign and a symptom of mutilation and mutilating processes (caused by the war, torture, or ultra-violent sports); but they also signify the healing process through the image of grafting—transplanted organs, Nikopol's congealed body, his cut-off then welded leg, plastic surgery—the sole problem being the links and joins. In this sense, the comic book form is particularly adept—image by image snapshots brought together in the page layout—while the film, because the images are linked by editing, is an inadequate medium and translation of the healing process. The linking up of fragments is a key issue in this postmodern work saturated by both homosemiotic and heterosemiotic intertextual references.

As a result, it is difficult to define the generic and ontological status of Bilal's film. Is it a poetic, surrealistic, fantasmatic, and oniric mixture of fable and SF, as Bilal claims in his interview of 24 March 2004? A science-fiction movie? A fantastic film? Viewer-response criticism can barely help us here, as it seems difficult to define its effects: the blurring, the epiphany, or the apocalypse of the real? Indeed, just as the comic books use filmic devices and techniques, this truly intermedial film[18] incorporates derealizing effects. The shift from the real to the unreal is permanent, as is the tension between derealizing and documentary devices and reception.

Indeed, reality effects are counterbalanced by the hyperreality effects generated by the insertion, onto a neutral, uniform background, of filmed images, virtual images or characters, video games, or cartoon characters: "we are not in the real," Bilal declared. As Charlotte Rampling explained, the three flesh and blood actors playing Jill, Dr. Turner, and Nikopol (the only nonhybrid creatures featured in the film) had to act "in a void," without any scenery or film set, visual landmarks, or props.[19] Even if "the actors were not allowed to wander off the script, and everything was written down" (Bilal), they moved amid imaginary beings tapped from their own minds, in a setting amounting to the filmic equivalent of *u-topos* or what Deleuze called "*espace quelconque*" (amorphous space):[20] a green back-cloth, a no-man's land into which the actors had to conjure up partners, and into which the other elements were inlaid afterwards. In some cases, the actors' images were artificial as well: they had to wear green overalls and electrodes registering their skeletons' movements, which were then modeled and digitalized, and transposed onto drawn characters like those of animated cartoons.

Bilal's backgrounds, but also the way he resorts to coloring, definitely result in an unreality effect. The last scene can be taken as a case in point, when the characters tread on an ostensibly hand-painted, then animated surface that seems unstable under their feet, until we realize it is flooded with filmed water. The total absence of the sun and the compelling wash-drawn grisaille that pervades everything set off the only patches of color: those provided by the comic book characters (they seem, like Jill, to have been penciled or delineated in charcoal), cartoon characters (cruel, blood-thirsty Dayaks), virtual characters (Dr. Froebe, John), or hybrid, interme-dial creatures. The Egyptian gods, notably Horus, with their human bodies and animal heads, look like crosses between comic book, drawn charac-ters and photographs of human beings, the result of superimposed im-ages. The same technique applies to the flying pyramid: a digitally modi-fied photograph superimposed onto the hand-painted New York sky.

The movements—which, according to Deleuze, after Bergson, define cinema, contrary to the superlative fixity of comic book creatures—of these intermedial creatures and images cause a strange, uncanny, and even a surrealistic effect. Either arrested and jerky—imitating video games—

or supersonic—for instance the vehicles speeding around the city in all dimensions—they symbolize and reveal their ultimate inhumanity, their superlative alienness.

Yet, there is a remarkable structural and formal, aesthetic correspondence between these technical options—aiming at surrealistic, unrealistic, hyperrealistic effects—and Bilal's vision of hidden, secret, painful realities. The recurrent motives of grafting, pasting, joining can be understood in relation to a morbid relation, foreclosure, repression or denial, to the traumas of History. The absurd pyramid, because it is displaced, has the same function as the apple which replaces the man's face in the Magritte surrealistic picture "Son of Man." It is the concrete manifestation of the filtering function of the collective memories (screen-memories, indeed) artificially composed and conveyed by history manuals: fake, imported, appropriated memories from the archaic past of other cultures instead of the traumas of modern, but repressed history (in Bilal's case, Sarajevo's civil war). The ancient Egyptian pyramid serves to occlude, mask, and fill in the blanks of the hollowed out memories of Bosnia. It is the sign and the symbol of "collective memory," which "like all memorials, is probably a machine meant to make people oblivious, by blocking their subjective ability to remember, and organized so as to eliminate the individuals' sense of identity, to the sole benefit of their collective sense of belonging to a national community."[21]

The illusion of immortality to which the image of the pyramid is linked enables the characters to prolong their protective denial of time-induced metamorphoses and of mutations caused by History: memories, suffering, and madness are associated, and opposed to the protective effects of oblivion, amnesia, and beauty; hence, Jill's pills, hence Nikopol's Baudelaire. The eternal return of the past, its endless, degrading, maddening repetition: such is Bilal's definition of immortality. The father and his son are the same age and look like twins; their very names (Nikopol/Niko) are a denial of progress and difference. Dual personalities and the inability to move forward (fixation) entail a sense of dissemination, fragmentation (Niko, Nikopol, Loopkin, Horus), and dissolution of identity: symptoms of schizophrenia (Nikopol-Horus; the two Jills), signs of a life dominated by the death instincts (Thanatos), and in which the life instincts (Eros) are perverted (Jill's rapes). Immortality is but another name for the "en-

SOPHIE GEOFFROY-MENOUX

chaining, degrading repetition of the past" (Kierkegaard), and is quite different from resurrection as the "gift of the new, of the possible,"[22] associated with Jill's "child."

This romantic love story targeted at young spectators also functions as an apocalypse of the real, precisely because of its symbolic surrealistic aspect.[23] Yet one can contend that the science fiction induced fictionalizing reading (relying on unreality effects) constantly undermines the documentary type of reading (relying on registrational reality effects). The realizing process—favored by the film adaptation of the comic books—is deconstructed by the derealizing process—the vanishing of the real—generated by the paradoxical hyperreality effects of intermediality and mediated representations (heterosemiotic and homosemiotic intertextuality). Overwhelmed by aesthesis and poiesis, the viewer's catharsis is undermined by the borderline state induced by the identity troubles of the heroes, a state he/she mimetically and vicariously experiences. Such hesitation undoubtedly reflects Bilal's own evolution: haunted by the recurrent war memories of his childhood in Yugoslavia, he shows that growing up is a process of transformation whereby humans are changed into mutants by their blessed forgetfulness. In spite of inescapable flashes demonstrating the absurd but threatening, towering presence of the Past, oblivion is the key to evolution and happiness.

Viewing or reading Bilal's intermedial, truly fantastic artifacts is a decidedly deceptive and misleading borderline experience. His idiosyncratic aestheticist drawing of the realities he sees, imagines, remembers (or cannot forget), wavering between archaic, futuristic, decadent representations, their intermedial aspect and the transmediality we have dealt with (from comic book to film, and vice versa) account for the mixed affects and effects generated by such a blurred ontological object, surreal, hyperreal, and virtual, as well as real, and fraught with a political and a moral message.

NOTES

1. My translation of a French quote by Alain Resnais (Thomas 247): "Toujours est-il que jusqu'ici je n'ai jamais vu de film tiré d'une bande dessinée qui me paraisse ajouter quelque chose à l'œuvre d'origine, ça a toujours été des soustractions."

2. For instance in the recent *1001 Movies You Must See Before You Die* (Schneider, 2003) there is only one live action adaptation of a comic, namely Tim Burton's *Batman*. Also in other lists comics adaptations seldom appear: *Les films-clés du cinéma* (Beylie, 1987) or *Beste films aller tijden* (Hofman, 1993).

3. It is not unusual to read reviews such as "Another Movie Based on Comic Book Disappoints" (Baxendell, 2005). The Spanish scriptwriter and critic José Miguel Pallarés (2003) devotes a complete book to adaptations of comics, but explicitly excludes the superhero genre because in his view those films get already too much promotion. On the contrary adaptations of "graphic novels" such as *Ghost World, American Splendor, Immortel,* or *Sin City* seem to please more the film critics. Only exceptional superhero adaptations such as *Spider-Man* or *X-Men* get a quite positive press (Boogaerts 83–88, 157–62).

4. For instance at *ALAS (a blog),* fans of *Watchmen* say that they would not like to see *Watchmen* adapted to film.

5. Of course, not all comic adaptations were as financially successful; Altman's *Popeye* (1980) or Ang Lee's *Hulk* (2003) were viewed as box office disappointments.

6. Benoît Peeters (1996) states: "Si les rencontres entre cinema et bande dessinée n'ont pas donné naissance à beaucoup de chefs-d'œuvre, elles ont par contre conduit à un grand nombre de films curieux."

7. Art Spiegelman (1998): "I don't want to see *Maus* as a movie. I've had lots of offers. I fired my first agent because he wanted to make a movie, and I kept telling him I didn't want it. (. . .) I'm not interested in it because (A) that aforementioned line about large groups of people [Spiegelman's father told his son not to trust large groups] and (B) the fact that it took so long for me to find the proper way to get it told in panel form, thirteen years—it would have been eleven and a half if I hadn't tried to stop smoking for a year and a half. But thirteen years to learn about animation and adapt it again. And it required a lot of the abstraction that came with the comics medium."

8. After my query at the comix-scholars list in May 2005 various persons responded that they experience such a primacy effect. Among others Chris Hayton wrote (19 May 2005): "To a greater or lesser extent, depending on fidelity to the original story, I become irritated or disappointed by the departure from, for example, the *Tales to Astonish/Incredible*

Hulk stories that the latest *Hulk* movie was based on, even the *Spider-Man* movies, because I read the stories month by month in the 1960s and so I want to see a movie that is faithful to the plot and the characters as a I experienced them in their original form."

9. Excluded in this analysis are the following categories: a) films loosely inspired by comics such as Spielberg's *Raiders of the Lost Ark* (1981) or Resnais's *L'Année Dernière à Marienbad* (1961), b) films by comics artists but not based on comics like *Delicatessen* (Jeunet & Caro, 1996), c) films where comic artists collaborated only on storyboard, costume, and prop design, d) films entirely made up of panels of a comic such as Oshima's *Ninja Bugeicho* (1967). Moreover there is also a category of films that use some elements of comics (like superheroes) but avoid the narrative clichés, as in Shyamalan's *Unbreakable* (2000).

10. Of course, original artwork of a comic can be shown in an exhibition, but these penciled and inked pages differ from the printed version: mostly there are no colors, no texts, and the format of the original plates are generally bigger than the printed books.

11. Walter Benjamin (223) explains: "By making many reproductions it substitutes a plurality of copies for a unique existence. And in permitting the producton to meet the beholder or listener in his own particular situation, it reactivates the object reproduced. These two processes lead to a tremendous shattering of tradition which is the obverse of the contemporary crisis and renewal of mankind. Both processes are intimately connected with the contemporary mass movements. Their most powerful agent is the film. Its social significance, particularly in its most positive form, is inconceivable without its destructive, cathartic aspect, that is the liquidation of the traditional value of the cultural heritage."

12. Of course one can view a video or a DVD also alone at home, but films are made in the first place for theatres.

13. My translation of a French interview with Alan Moore (Mouchart 30): "Je m'efforce de ne pas avoir d'opinion. Ces long métrages ne ressemblent pas beaucoup à mes livres. Si ce sont de bons films, le mérite en revient aux réalisateurs. Ça n'a rien à voir avec moi. De même si ces films sont médiocres. Ça m'intéresse de les voir, mais comme je n'ai pas envie de travailler pour Hollywood et que le cinéma n'est pas l'un de mes médiums préférés, je ne me sens pas très impliqué dans ces projets."

14. Only by using a video or a DVD player can the viewer control the pace of the projection.

15. Only exceptionally does a comic artist like Bilal for *Le Sommeil du monstre* (1998) draws each panel separately on a support and in a later phase tries to combine those separate panels. The newest digital techniques (like Photoshop) make this approach more easy.

16. Only recently multiple-frame imagery is becoming somewhat more accepted thanks to popular American television series such as *24* (since 2001).

17. Special printing methods combined with special viewing spectacles can give the viewer the impression of a really three-dimensional space. But the prints will always be flat—except for a single experiment of a comic printed in relief.

18. The fact that a single frame of a film is also a printed and static image does not matter because the viewer looks only at the projection: nobody can see twenty-four still frames per second separately. Our eyes and minds will be fooled into seeing movement (Bordwell & Thompson 2).

19. Christiansen (115) contends that there are a number of films in which there is no movement (such as Oshima's *Ninja Bugeicho*, 1967), but he believes that the viewer of such a film can presume that there will be movement in the image, while this is never a possibility in still images.

20. Though since the coming of the digital age images can easily be created without lenses, generally the creators disguise them as photographical images. Digital images in

cinema are predominantly created in an optical denotation system. The idea is that the digital must not be recognized as such; it must look real as much as possible.

21. Creative film directors use also some of these picture elements, but they are harder to manipulate and control on a film set than a drawer can with a pencil on paper. Given some drawing talent, leaving out elements—stressing the major lines—is easier on paper: what you do not draw does not exist. While a drawer has to add details, a director has to leave out details.

22. My translation of a French article by Peeters (1996): "Réussir un film convaincant à partir des Aventures de Tintin semble décidément un pari presque impossible. L'ambiguité est probablement constitutive, car l'œuvre d'Hergé se tient sur une corde raide entre réalisme et caricature. Le trait du dessinateur—la fameuse «ligne claire»—est l'élément qui unifie l'œuvre et garantit sa cohérence, sitôt qu'il disparaît, c'est la confusion et la perte de crédibilité qui s'installent. Au bout du compte, l'intérêt premier des films adaptés de *Tintin* est de prouver par l'absurde à quel point les qualités de l'œuvre d'Hergé sont liées à la bande dessinée et à son langage."

23. My translation of an Italian text by Costa (25): "Molto spesso si è rimproverato al cinema di finzione ispirato ai personaggi dei fumetti l'incapacità di restituire l'incanto, la magia, in una parola lo stile di quell'universo figurativo. In realtà, molti dei problemi posti dalla relazione tra il cinema e il fumetto sono analoghi a quelli che si pongono tra cinema e pittura: la staticità della pittura e quella del fumetto, rispetto al movimento del cinema, reagiscono in maniere diversa, in quanto la grafica dei comics ha inventato e codificato forme di dinamismo dalle quali dipende gran parte del suo fascino figurativo. Il cinema può cercare di restituirlo solo attraverso complesse operazioni di selezione e stilizzazioone dei suoi propri mezzi espressi."

24. Though the combination of digital animated actors with real actors in one frame is sometimes problematic in *Immortel*.

25. In some films (as Oshima's *Ninja Bugeicho*) naturalistic spoken dialogue and sound effects are added to the still images from a comic (in our example panels from the Sanpei Shirato's manga of the same name). But Oshima's fast cutting of stylized still images, naturalistic spoken dialogue, and richly musical sound effects produce a strange and often very striking disjunction (Burch 738–39).

Michael Cohen, "Dick Tracy: In Pursuit of a Comic Book Aesthetic"

1. In the original comic strip this character is called "Junior." At the end of the film the Kid must choose a proper name for himself, and decides on "Dick Tracy Jnr."

2. Measurements have been taken from a cross section of strips reprinted in Gould, *Dick Tracy: The Thirties*.

3. John Belton explains that when a soundtrack was added to film, the old standard ratio of 1.33:1 was lost. In 1932 the Academy of Motion Picture Arts and Sciences established the Academy ratio, only it was now 1.37:1. He notes that although it is a slightly different ratio, it is still referred to as 1.33:1 (43–45).

Kerry Gough, "Translation Creativity and Alien Econ(c)omics: From Hollywood Blockbuster to Dark Horse Comic Book"

1. Many thanks go to the editors for suggestions on an earlier draft of this chapter, Lee Dawson for his continual availability, and Randy Stradley for all the information provided surrounding the development of the Aliens comic books. Lee Dawson is publicist for Dark

Horse Comics, and Randy Stradley is Senior Editor of the Original Alien Comic Books at Dark Horse.

Derek Johnson, "Will the Real Wolverine Please Stand Up? Marvel's Mutation from Monthlies to Movies"

1. See "Welcome to Comic-Con International: San Diego!" Emphasis has been added to the original text.

2. See McAllister and Raviv.

3. For more detailed statistics, see "Weak Finish to a Strong Comics Year" at *ICv2 News.* http://www.icv2.com/ articles/home/2080.html.

4. See "Top July Comics Flat" at *ICv2 News* to view the rest of the best-sellers during summer 2003. http://www.icv2.com/articles/news/3317.html.

5. See "ICv2's Top 300 Comics and Top 50 GN's Index" for this statistic and other monthly sales figures. www.icv2.com/articles/home/1850.html. The quoted figure here does not represent a severe monthly downturn in sales from previous issues. While sales improved for *Ultimate X-Men* over the next two years, the number of issues sold only increased by around 10,000 copies (see "Top July Comics Flat" www.icv2.com/articles/ new/3317.html).

6. These statistics have been compiled from *Entertainment Weekly* (16 May 2003, 18 July 2003, and 8 Aug. 2003) and the internet site Box Office Mojo, www.boxofficemojo.com.

7. In comparisons to the Ultimate Universe, this original "classic" universe is generally referred to as the "Marvel Universe" or the "616" universe. But for purposes of clarity here, I will continue to refer to it in this generic way as the "classic" universe.

8. One of the primary ways in which this is done in the films is through character identification. The lack of character depth and screen presence for Cyclops makes him hard to identify with as he and Wolverine vie for her affections in the first film. As the central protagonist, on the other hand, Wolverine's deeper characterization makes him more sympathetic as a potential suitor for Jean.

9. By 2004, the relationship between Cyclops and Jean Grey had ended as the result of the former's extramarital affair with Emma Frost. This was, of course, another "adult" issue, but it also left the door open to a couple more steamy encounters between Wolverine and Jean, particularly at the end of Grant Morrison's run on *New X-Men.*

10. For example, the psychic powers of Emma Frost were supplemented by her ability to assume a "diamond form" whereas Henry McCoy, AKA the Beast, became more catlike and even less-human appearing than before. See *New X-Men* #114–16.

11. See Moreels, 28. Feb. 2004. While Whedon (creator of *Buffy the Vampire Slayer, Angel,* and *Firefly*) began his tenure on *Astonishing X-Men* in May 2004, the exact start date for Singer to take on his role as "producer" of *Ultimate X-Men* was to be determined, and at the time of this writing, seems unlikely to ever happen.

Neil Rae and Jonathan Gray, "When Gen-X Met the X-Men: Retextualizing Comic Book Film Reception"

1. All interviewee names are pseudonyms.

Mel Gibson, "'Wham! Bam! The X-Men Are Here': The British Broadsheet Press and the X-Men Films and Comic"

1. In Britain the form of the newspaper, until very recently when some broadsheet papers began to release tabloid editions, has been seen as a physical indicator of certain as-

pects of the approach and concerns of the paper. Generally, the term "broadsheet" has been seen as indicating "quality," a term attached here to notions of complex debate, whilst the term "tabloid" has been seen as indicating "popular" and more simplistic. This shorthand, whilst it does not take into account the political perspectives of the newspapers, also suggests class allegiances, with the broadsheets, the focus of this chapter, often being seen as representing a middle-class and educated set of perspectives.

2. Most articles exhibited this slippage. In contrast, few articles consciously explored the relationship between comics and film. Those articles that did often focused on the problems of translation between the two media, as is the case with, for instance, Mark Salisbury in the *Guardian*, 4 August 2000.

3. One of the more enthusiastic articles in the *Telegraph*, that by John Hiscock (4 August 2000), focused on why Stewart and McKellen were happy to do the film. The Royal Shakespeare Company connection served as a "high cultural" justification for the articles "serious" interest in this example of "mass culture," an alternative to apologizing.

4. The term fan marked, as it is, by assumptions about age and maturity. Clive King, for instance, (29 July 2000) referred to "geekdom" when discussing fans (24).

5. This Act and the campaign which led to it are discussed in depth in Martin Barker's *A Haunt of Fears*.

6. One could argue that the *X-Men* comics and film encourage such reflection in adult readers, given the parallels between the experience of becoming a teenager and becoming a "mutant," this being one interpretation of the sense of difference throughout the text.

7. Although there were occasions when even this was not enough to redeem the film. For instance, Macaulay states that, "The confrontations between Magneto and Xavier have the Shakespearean aspirations of the more ambitious *Star Trek* episodes" (24). Science fiction television, too, must know its place, again focusing the reader on notions of hierarchies of culture.

8. Aspiration is also a factor, given the perpetual concern about the health of the British film industry.

9. In this tradition, as is suggested by the way in which the term "anarchy" functions as a synonym for popular culture in *Culture and Anarchy*, such culture represents disorder and decline.

10. Arnold was profoundly influential on Leavis, who saw the twentieth century as marked by increasing cultural decline.

11. Simultaneously, Leavis both created a space for the study of popular culture, and in seeing popular culture solely as decline created problems for its study.

12. Particularly ironic given that whilst this may be part of the image conveyed to the reader, they are, of course, simultaneously engaged with and part of popular culture.

13. Hence Hoggart has been described as left-Leavisite.

Aldo J. Regalado, "*Unbreakable* and the Limits of Transgression"

1. Although most fan histories acknowledge the character appearing in "The Reign of the Super-Man" as a curious precursor to the more famous comic book character, none have explored in detail the thematic connections that link the two.

Martin Flanagan, "Teen Trajectories in *Spider-Man* and *Ghost World*"

1. The main superhero publishers sharply differentiate their products in terms of age. DC and Marvel both offer "Mature" classifications (DC's "Vertigo" line, Marvel's "Max" and "Knights" imprints) while Marvel has recently launched an introductory "Marvel Age"

line, suitable for any age but deliberately slanted towards preteen children. Twelve-and-overs are catered to by Marvel's "Ultimate" family of titles, with the forthcoming *Fantastic Four* movie from Fox rumoured to derive from the teen-centric take on the characters in *Ultimate Fantastic Four*.

2. Exemplary works in the first category include Frank Miller's *Batman Year One* (1988) and *Daredevil: Man Without Fear* (1993) and Mark Millar's *Red Son* (2004); notable in the latter are the works of Alan Moore, including but not limited to *Watchmen* (1986) and *Supreme* (with Rob Liefeld, 1996–97). Michael Stracynzki's recent updating of minor Marvel superhero team "Squadron Supreme" in the form of *Supreme Power* (2003–) cheekily appropriates the Superman origin myth.

3. Spider-Man created by Stan Lee and Steve Ditko; the Hulk created by Lee and Jack Kirby; Daredevil created by Lee and Bill Everett.

4. For an historical account of Dr. Frederic Wertham's assault on the comic book industry in the mid 1950s, see Wright (154–79). An interesting contemporaneous commentary on Wertham's crusade can be found in Warshow (53–74).

5. The "Silver Age" is frequently identified as beginning with Marvel's *Fantastic Four* #1 (November 1961) and running throughout the rest of the 1960s. See Simon.

6. This notion supplies, for example, the dramatic arc of M. Night Shyamalan's film *Unbreakable* (2000), a pseudo-"realistic"/psychological take on the process of discovering one's own super-powers.

7. The teen bedroom is a "threshold" in the sense conceptualized by Mikhail Bakhtin; that is, as a symbolic space where crisis or "radical change" unfolds, where "one is renewed or perishes" (169).

8. Enid is seen crying in her bedroom several times, and Peter is comforted by Aunt May in his room after Uncle Ben's funeral.

9. For example, the shift from newsstand distribution to "direct sales" to fans through dedicated stores (Wright 254–62).

Rayna Denison, "It's a Bird! It's a Plane! No, It's DVD!: *Superman, Smallville*, and the Production (of) Melodrama"

1. A notable exception to the lack of scholarly discussion of genre discussions of Superman is Ian Gordon's work on *Lois & Clark (The New Adventures of Superman)* (1993–1997), which details the romantic and nostalgic aspects of the serial's success (Gordon, "Superman on the Set").

2. Although the first in the 1970–1980s cycle of Superman films does appear in some recent work on genre itself, as will be discussed later. See, for example, Neale 250 and Altman 117.

3. This is not intended to insist upon a totalizing or universalizing approach to these two distinct media. However, in an age where more films are viewed on television than in cinema and where television has improved its production values so as to compete with film, it is an important moment in which to begin rethinking the relationship they share.

4. The first campaign ran 11 May 1977 and consisted of an eight-page spread beginning with the famous "S" logo and the legend "NOW SHOOTING." Subsequent pages gave examples of the sets and full-page star headshots with character names. The second, advert series includes a thank you message to the British film industry and a full-page poster with the "You'll Believe a Man Can Fly" tagline and production information.

5. The one reference to genre in the "Fall Preview '01" article reads, "Think a cross between *The X-Files* and *Justice League 90210*. As this re-covers the more detailed comparative analysis of the longer issue, its impact for the show can be thought of as similar.

6. The first major conference on DVD took place in April 2005, and if this is any indication, it would seem that academic work on DVD is a quickly expanding field ("What Is a DVD?" University of Warwick, U.K., 23 April 2005).

7. "The Chloe Chronicles" came in two volumes, split across the Season 2 and 3 box sets. Both contain reproductions of frames from the *Smallville* comic book short stories and documentary footage.

Craig Hight, "*American Splendor:* Translating Comic Autobiography into Drama-Documentary"

1. See, for example, Eisner, *Comics and Sequential Art*; McCloud, *Understanding Comics*; Eisner, *Graphic Storytelling*; Harvey, *Art of the Comic Book*; Sabin, *Comics, Comix and Graphic Novels*; Carrier. McCloud offers the most useful definition of comics as "juxtaposed pictorial and other images in deliberate sequence, intended to convey information and/or produce an aesthetic response in the viewer" (McCloud, *Understanding Comics* 9).

2. Animation sequences are quite common within documentary and have a long history. There is also a small subgenre of fully animated documentaries, hybrid forms which typically employ the codes and conventions of the genre with elements such documentary soundtracks, or other forms of evidence.

3. See http://www.harveypekar.com/about.html for a brief biography of Pekar.

4. Pekar has also done isolated examples of biographical work, such as *Unsung Hero— The Story of Robert Mc Neill*, but otherwise concentrates completely on autobiography.

5. Batman, for example, has endured immeasurable makeovers, and in the process the character has been deconstructed at several levels. He now exists in a variety of published forms, some of which are completely contradictory, but which collectively provide for a rich variety of thematics and highly reflexive articulations of comic traditions.

6. See Corner, Paget, Rosenthal, Lipkin, 2002.

7. Lipkin distinguishes here between the typical drama-documentary strategies of modeling, sequencing, and interaction (Lipkin 13).

8. Although this is implied through the mostly jazz music which appears on the soundtrack.

9 This is presumably real (that is, unstaged observational) footage, but by this stage the relationship between the fictional and the actual is ambiguous.

10. There have been contrasting reactions to such techniques from most commentators of the film. Some acknowledged this as an innovative technique which reflects Pekar's perspective. Others complained that these frequent interruptions to the narrative sequences added nothing to viewers' understanding of Pekar's life, and undermined their engagement with Giamatti's performance (see, for example, Hampton). Some critics were also irritated by the device of using comic aesthetics on the cinematic screen. See http://www.mrqe.com/ for a variety of links to newspaper and online reviews for the film.

11. At a different level, however, the inclusion of the conversation happily works to validate the filmmakers' revisions of Pekar's original comic narrative.

12. Although, as noted above, there is a long tradition of animation within the documentary genre.

David Wilt, "El Santo: The Case of a Mexican Multimedia Hero"

1. This information can also be found in print in Royal Duncan and Gary Will, *Wrestling Title Histories*. Revised 4th edition. Waterloo, Ontario: Archeus Communications, 2000.

2. Coincidentally, Gori Guerrero was also the protagonist of a 1950s comic book. Other wrestlers "starring" in comic books in the first "wave" of wrestling's popularity (after its television debut in 1951) include Blue Demon, Black Shadow, Cavernario Galindo, and the Médico Asesino (Bartra 48).

3. The traditional day for wrestling matches in Mexico City arenas was Sunday, so the Saturday TV matches in a way promoted the next day's "live" event. Televised wrestling was banned in 1956 by Ernesto P. Uruchurtu, the "Iron Regent" (an official roughly equivalent to a mayor) of Mexico City, who cited the sport's bad influence on youth (the prohibition was later removed). Uruchurtu is also remembered for forbidding a proposed Beatles concert in the capital in 1965.

4. "Huracán Ramírez" was a character created for a 1952 movie, which spawned numerous sequels. The owners of the character later allowed various professional wrestlers to use the name in the ring. The *Huracán Ramírez* comic was also done in *fotomontaje* style.

5. Some of these events occurred only a few weeks before the comic book was printed. Two decades later, the *Huracán Ramírez* comic book made a foray into contemporary events, with a story set at the famous September 1971 Avándaro rock festival (*Huracán Ramírez* 152 [2 Nov. 1971]).

6. While Santo's ring career and the sales of the comics were undoubtedly helped by his movie stardom, there was not much cross-promotion—the movies didn't specifically promote the comic and the comic books did not feature adaptations of Santo movies. There were *some* film references in the comics, however—José G. Cruz painted various covers in the 1970s showing Santo with well-known horror movie images, including aliens wearing *Destination Moon*-style spacesuits, Hammer Films monsters, the giant frog "key art" from *Frogs*, Princess Leia from *Star Wars*, etc.

7. The comic books, on the other hand, did feature some recurring characters in addition to Santo. In the 1950s, for example, "white witch" Kyra appeared in several stories as Santo's supernatural love interest. Other characters—sidekick "Mala Facha," an adolescent boy named "Bobby"—were used in more than one story cycle. In some 1970s comics, Santo had an aide named "Ik." Allegedly an alien being, Ik was portrayed by a young boy with a pencil-thin moustache, wearing a pirate costume.

Paul M. Malone, "From Blockbuster to Flop? The Apparent Failure (or Possible Transcendence) of Ralf König's Queer Comics Aesthetic in *Maybe . . . Maybe Not* and *Killer Condom*"

1. All translations from the German are my own; Ralf König's website includes an English version in an excellent colloquial translation, but the quotations here are also my own translations of the German pages.

Jan van der Putten and Timothy P. Barnard, "Old Malay Heroes Never Die: The Story of Hang Tuah in Films and Comics"

1. The first reference that could be found for the phrase is in Budi Negoro's "Hang Tuah Pahlawan Bangsa" in the magazine *Kenchana*, Oct. 1948. The author ends his article by stating that "Hang Tuah was not only a Malay hero, but also a valuable son (of the nation) in our present struggle, for with him the important motto 'Malays will not vanish from this world' was preserved. Freedom!" (*Hang Tuah bukan saja pahlawan Melayu tetapi pula saorang putera yang sangat berharga dalam perjuangan kita hari ini, kerana padanya tersimpan semboyan yang utama "Tidak Melayu hilang didunia." MERDEKA.*).

2. In the last quarter of the twentieth century three newly written plays were staged in

Malaysia, all of which featured absurdist theatre in which Tuah's friend and adversary Jebat becomes the hero for characters in the seamy margins of society (Abdul).

3. The actress's name is Tiara Jacquelina. The quote comes from an interview done at the Palm Springs International Film Festival. http://www.filmthreat.com/Interviews.asp?Id=904. Accessed on 1 June 2005.

4. Mulyadi Mahamood's recent study (2004) only discusses cartoons and a few serialized comic strips that were published in newspapers. The only studies that concentrate on comic books from the 1950s are by Zainab Awang Ngah (1984) and Annabel Gallop (1995). For a comprehensive study of Malay language comic books from Indonesia, see Bonneff (1998).

5. *Seni kelawak* is a neologism derived from *lawak* ("comic, funny"). It does not seem to have lasted long, as we fail to find it in any dictionary.

6. This is suggested by Harun Aminurrashid, the chief editor of both *Kenchana* and *Hiboran*, another popular magazine that was published at the time. Looking back in the tenth anniversary issue of *Hiboran* in 1956, he recalls that he met Achnas during a discussion about setting up the new magazine *Kenchana*. He engaged the young Indonesian who was in the same predicament as Harun had found himself after World War Two. Achnas did the technique and layout of *Kenchana* until it folded in 1950. He also drew political cartoons about developments in Indonesia, which were published in *Hiboran*. In 1956 Achnas began a career as a director of Malay and Indonesian films (Harun 15).

7. It is probable that *Tunggadewa* was the first published comic book after it had been serialized in *Kenchana*. An advertisement in *Kenchana* announced that the comic in full color was published in a compilation together with Indonesian strips and illustrated short stories. It was published by the Malayan Indonesian Book and Magazine Store (MIBS) based on Arab Street in Singapore. The publication is so far unknown from the collections in the British Library or the University Malaya Library. Gallop conditionally designates *Pesaka dato' moyang* as the strongest contender for the title of "earliest Malay comic book."

8. Foreword by Harun Aminurrashid in *Pesaka dato' moyang*, 21 April 1952, quoted in Gallop.

9. See Gallop's discussion about this publisher, where she notes that the first issue of the comic magazine is printed with the old masthead of *Dunia Film*. See Hamedi Mohd Adnan for details about the magazine.

10. The British Library in London holds the title *Tiga bulan di dalam penjara* by Shamsuddin Salleh, which mentions Annie's Medical Hall, Johor Baharu as its imprint (BL 14654.d.82). Conspicuously, several novels by this author were published by Annies Printing Works (see Chambert-Loir 277–79).

11. One of his earlier publications, *Suara Timor* (October–December 1942), also had been published in Latin script, which was called an important script (*huruf yang terkemuka*) for that time (Hamedi).

12. This version was recently republished in a translated Dutch facsimile edition (*Hang Tuah*, 2003); for details about the author/artist, see Soemargono (209–47).

13. We have been unable to check the story of his *Putra Hang Tuah*, information from Zainab Awang Ngah (10).

14. *Hang Tuah*, however, was not the first Malay film made in color. This honor goes to the Cathay Keris produced *Buluh Perindu* (Bamboo of Yearning—1953) (Barnard 126–27).

15. The film cost $300,000, at a time when most productions were made for less than $30,000. At that time, the Malaysian dollar (or ringgit) was two shillings, four pence (a British pound is worth twenty shillings). *Majalah Bintang*, 19 (2 Jan. 1956): 8.

16. Abdullah Hussain claims they were only paid a cup of coffee for their efforts, although he implies that Haji Buyong Adil may have pocketed all of their advisory fees

(Abdullah Hussain, 2005: 599–603). Mahmud Ahmad's account of his role is titled "Behind the Scenes at Hang Tuah: Was Mahmud Ahmad an Advisor?" ("Di belakang layer di Filem 'Hang Tuah.' Mahmud Ahmad sebagai penasihat," *Majalah Bintang*, 20 (16 Feb. 1956): 8. The earlier article is found in *Majalah Bintang*, 19 (2 Jan. 1956): 8–9.

Sophie Geoffroy-Menoux, "Enki Bilal's Intermedial Fantasies: From Comic Book *Nikopol Trilogy* to Film *Immortals (ad vitam)*"

1. "You are a displaced person" ("Tu es une déplacée"); even her organs are "displaced," "not in the right place" ("pas à leur place").
2. "There is a sort of blank in my memory" ("Il y a comme un trou dans ma mémoire"). My translation.
3. "Le monde originaire des symptômes et pulsions" qui "embrasse le futurisme et l'archaisme" (Deleuze 194–95).
4. "Tout oublier pour tout recommencer."
5. "The closeup tears the image up from its spatiotemporal context and generates crude affects." My translation. "Le gros plan a le pouvoir d'arracher l'image aux coordonnées spatio-temporelles pour faire surgir l'affect pur . . . " (Deleuze 137). Deleuze defines closeups as "emotionalist images" or "images affection"; see his chapter 6, entitled "L'image-affection: visage et gros plan" (Deleuze 125).
6. "New trends: green lips and red hair, beard, moustaches and any other body or facial adornment. A pale complexion is a must" (Vol. 1, p. 61). This cosmeto-political revolution triggers off a visual turning point in the comic book: women, who used to be second-class citizens, are more present, in a pseudo-medieval and carnivalesque atmosphere.
7. See B. Berenson's well-known theory of "tactile values." *The Florentine Painters of the Renaissance*. New York: G. P. Putnam's Sons, 1896.
8. *The Wild Planet*. My translation.
9. My translation. "Le Jour où le Futur Téléscripta," "Aujourd'hui, le 3 février 2025 rencontre le 14 octobre 1993."
10. My translation. " 'Quand, comment et pour aller où?' je demande un peu bourrée . . . 'Demain matin, en aéro-taxi, destination Berlin,' me répond-il . . . " (Volume II, p. 81).
11. Analyzing the examples of frames that cut the object filmed, or faces cut by the screen, Pascal Bonitzer defines decentering (*Décadrage*) as "abnormal view points" which "must not be mistaken for oblique perspectives or paradoxical angles, and are suggestive of the image's other dimensions." ("Ces points de vue anormaux qui ne se confondent pas avec une perspective oblique ou un angle paradoxal et renvoient à une autre dimension de l'image," Pascal Bonitzer, "Décadrages" in *Cahiers du cinéma*, N° 284, janvier 1978, quoted in Deleuze 27–28).
12. "L'assassinat de Choublanc par Nikopol" (Vol. III, p. 138–39).
13. See 1920 Russian filmmakers' definition of montage: the association of two shots produces a significance that is present in neither shots taken separately.
14. My translation. "C'est pour garder l'influx que vous ne vous rasez pas? . . . Vous êtes bien Loopkin?"
15. See Deleuze about the "*montage d'attractions*": it consists in "inserting special images—theatre or cinema representations, or sculptural or plastic images, which apparently interrupt the course of the action." My translation of: "insertion d'images spéciales, soit représentations théâtrales ou scénographiques, soit représentations sculpturales ou plastiques, qui semblent interrompre le cours de l'action" (247).
16. My translation.

17. "L'objet de la pulsion," according to Deleuze, "c'est toujours l'objet partiel ou le fétiche" (Deleuze 180).

18. Serge Raffy, for want of a better word (nonexistent in French), called it a "*film mutant*" (a mutant film) in *Le Nouvel Observateur*, 28 March 2004.

19. Charlotte Rampling, Interview, *France Inter*, 24 March 2004.

20. This "amorphous space" (Deleuze 168) is the perfect locus for "virtual conjunctions" ("*conjonction virtuelle*," Deleuze 155) to occur, and the place where death instincts and elementary drives are acted out. See his "Mondes originaires et pulsions élémentaires" (Deleuze 173). It is "a pure background, without a form, without an end, made of unformed matter" ("on le reconnaît à son caractère informe, c'est un fond pur, ou plutôt un sans-fond, fait de matières non formées," Deleuze 174).

21. "Cette mémoire collective, comme toute machine de mémoire, serait une machine à fabriquer de l'oubli, dans la mesure où elle s'opposerait à la mémoire subjective et où il s'agirait d'éradiquer la subjectivité au profit d'un discours collectif" (Alain Brun quoted in Joly 163).

22. "Une répétition du passé enchaînante, dégradante" (Kierkegaard quoted in Deleuze 184–85). For Kierkegaard, the eternal repetition of the past is opposed to "l'éternel retour comme résurrection, comme don du nouveau, du possible" (Deleuze 185).

23. "It is a very romantic film." Rampling, Interview, *France Inter*, 24 March 2004.

REFERENCES

Aaker, David A. Building Strong Brands. New York: Free Press, 1996.

Abbott, Lawrence L. "Comic Art: Characteristics and Potentialities of a Narrative Medium." Journal of Popular Culture 19.4 (Spring 1986): 155–76.

Abdul Rahman Napiah. Tuah-Jebat dalam Drama Melayu. Satu kajian Intertekstualiti. Kuala Lumpur: Dewan Bahasa dan Pustaka, 1994.

Abdullah Hussain. Sebuah Perjalanan. Kuala Lumpur: Dewan Bahasa dan Pustaka, 2005.

Abdullah Hussain, and Nik Safiah Karim, eds. Memoranda Angkatan Sastrawan '50. 2nd ed. Petaling Jaya: Fajar Bakti, 1987.

Adalian, Josef. "'Smallville' Gets Super Order." Daily Variety. 25 Oct. 2001. 21.

Affron, Charles, and Mirella Jona Affron. Sets in Motion: Art Direction and Film Narrative. New Jersey: Rutgers University Press, 1995.

Ahmad Sarji. P. Ramlee: Erti yang Sakti. Petaling Jaya: Pelanduk, 1999.

Alias. Prod. J. J. Abrams and Ken Oilin. Perf. Jennifer Garner. ABC. 2001– .

"Alien vs. Predator Production Notes." Planet AVP. 2004. 12 Jan. 2005. www.planetavp.com.

"Alien Vs Predator Snatches $38.3 Million." MovieWeb. 16 Aug. 2004. 17 March 2005. http://www.movieweb.com/news/71/4871.php.

"All Things Considered." NPR. Washington, D.C. 19 July 2002. Transcript accessed via Proquest. 9 Oct. 2003. http://www.library.wisc.edu.

"All-Time Domestic Blockbusters." Box Office Guru. 12 Mar. 2006. http://www.boxofficeguru.com/blockbusters.htm.

Althusser, Louis. "Ideology and Ideological State Apparatuses." Literary Theory: An Anthology. Eds. Julie Rivkin and Michael Ryan. Oxford: Blackwell, 2001. 294–304.

Altman, Rick. Film/Genre. London: BFI Publishing, 1999.

Alyn, Kirk. A Job for Superman. Hollywood, Calif.: K. Alyn, 1971.

American Splendor. Dir. Shari Springer Berman and Bob Pulcini. Perf. Paul Giamatti, Hope Davis, James Urbaniak, Harvey Pekar, and Judah Friedlander. HBO Films/Fine Line Features, 2003.

Anderson, Paul W. S. "Final Fight: Q & A Paul W. S. Anderson." Total DVD 71 (2005): 18–23.

Andrew. "Best Superhero Film Ever?" Online posting. 22 April 2003. Peterdavid.net. http://www.Peterdavid.net/.

Arnell, Gordon, and June Broom. "'Superman' Takes Off March 28." Press Release. 25 Mar. 1977.

Arnell, Gordon, and June Broom. "'Superman' Touches Down after 30 Weeks of Flight." Press Release. 28 Oct. 1977.

Arnheim, Rudolf. Art and Visual Perception: A Psychology of the Creative Eye. Berkeley: University of California Press, 1971.

Arnold, Matthew. *Culture and Anarchy*. London: Cambridge University Press, 1960.

Atkinson, Mike. "Delirious Inventions." *Sight and Sound* 5.7 (July 1995): 12–16.

Aurrecoechea, Juan Manuel, and Armando Bartra. *Puros cuentos II: Historia de la historieta en México 1934–1950*. Mexico: Grijalbo, 1993.

Bacon-Smith, Camille, with Tyrone Yarborough. "Batman: The Ethnography." *The Many Lives of the Batman: Critical Approaches to a Superhero and His Media*. Eds. Roberta E. Pearson and William Uricchio. London: BFI, 1991. 90–116.

Bakhtin, Mikhail. *Problems of Dostoevsky's Poetics*. Ed. and Trans. Caryl Emerson. Minneapolis and London: University of Minnesota Press, 1997.

——. *Rabelais and His World*. Bloomington: Indiana University Press, 1984

——. *Speech Genres and Other Late Essays*. Trans. Vern W. McGee. Austin: University of Texas Press, 1986.

——. *The Dialogic Imagination: Four Essays*. Ed. Michael Holquist. Trans. Caryl Emerson and Michael Holquist. Austin: University of Texas Press, 1981.

Bali, K. *Dari Tendong ke Borneo. Memoir karyawan DBP Cawangan Sabah*. Kuala Lumpur: Dewan Bahasa dan Pustaka, 2002.

——. *Hang Tuah di Air Masin*. Kuala Pilah: Sentosa Store Press, 1954.

Baney, Jack. "American Blender: A Reporter Sifts Through the Many Realities of Hanging Out with Harvey Pekar the Movie Star." *The Comics Journal* 255 (Oct. 2003). 17 Oct. 2004. http://www.tcj.com/255/n_pekar.html.

Banks, Miranda J. "A Boy for All Planets: Roswell, Smallville and the Teen Male Melodrama." *Teen TV: Genre, Consumption and Identity*. Eds. Glyn Davis and Kay Dickinson. London: BFI Publishing, 2004. 17–28.

Barber, Nicholas. "Is It the Follow-up, the Prequel, or the Prologue to the Sequel?" *Independent* 4 May 2003. 13 Feb. 2006. http://enjoyment.independent.co. uk/film/reviews/article103422.ece.

Barker, Martin. *A Haunt of Fears: The Strange History of the British Horror Comics Campaign*. London: Pluto Press, 1984.

——. *Comics: Ideology, Power and the Critics*. Manchester: Manchester University Press, 1989.

——. "News Reviews, Clues, Interviews and Other Ancillary Materials—A Critique and Research Proposal." *Scope: An Online Journal of Film Studies* (Feb. 2004). 12 Jan. 2005. www.nottingham.ac.uk/film/scope archive/articles/ news-reviews.htm

Barker, Martin, and Kate Brooks. *Knowing Audiences: Judge Dredd, Its Friends, Fans and Foes*. Luton: University of Luton Press, 1998.

Barlow, Aaron. *The DVD Revolution: Movies, Culture, & Technology*. Westport, Connecticut: Praeger, 2005.

Barnard, Timothy P. "Vampires, Heroes and Jesters: A History of Cathay Keris." *The Cathay Story*. Ed. Wong Ain-ling. Hong Kong: Hong Kong Film Archive, 2002. 124–41

Barnard, Timothy P., and Rohayati Paseng Barnard. "The Ambivalence of P. Ramlee: *Penarek Beca* and *Bujang Lapok* in Perspective." *Asian Cinema* 13.2 (2002): 9–23.

Barol, Bill. "Batmania." *Newsweek* 26 June 1989: 70.

Barta, Armando. "Las viñetas del apocalipsis." *Luna Córnea* 27 (Sept./Nov. 2003): 46–63.

Bartholomae, Joachim. "Herr König, Sie sind doch nicht selber schwul, Sie zeichnen so was doch nur, weil es sich gut verkauft?" *Mal mir mal nen Schwulen: Das Buch zu Ralf König*. Ed. Joachim Bartholomae. Hamburg: MännerschwarmSkript, 1996. 4–10.

——, ed. *Mal mir mal nen Schwulen: Das Buch zu Ralf König*. Hamburg: MännerschwarmSkript, 1996.

Batman. Dir. Tim Burton. Perf. Michael Keaton, Jack Nicholson, and Kim Basinger. Warner Brothers, 1989.

Baxendell, Blake. "Another Movie Based on Comic Book Disappoints." *The Rocket* 25 Feb. 2005. 25 Jan. 2006. http://www.theonlinerocket.com/media/paper 601/news/2005/02/25/ Entertainment/Another.Movie.Based.On.Comic.Book.Disappoints-877682.shtml.

Bazin, André. *What Is Cinema?* Vol. 1. Trans. Hugh Gray. Berkeley: University of California Press, 1967.

Benjamin, Walter. "The Work of Art in the Age of Mechanical Reproduction." *Illuminations.* London: Fontana, 1973. 219–54.

Bell, Matthew. "Oppressed Minorities Lurk Beneath the Razzle-dazzle." *Guardian* 6 May 2003. 13 Feb. 2006. http://www.guardian.co.uk/editor/story/0,,94989 4,00.html.

Belton, John. *Widescreen Cinema.* Cambridge, Mass.: Harvard University Press, 1992.

Bennett, Tony. "Holy Shifting Signifiers: Foreword." *The Many Lives of the Batman: Critical Approaches to a Superhero and His Media.* Eds. Roberta E. Pearson and William Uricchio. London: BFI, 1991. vii–ix.

Bennett, Tony, and Janet Woollacott. *Bond and Beyond: The Political Career of a Popular Hero.* London: MacMillan, 1987.

Berkowitz, Harry. "Marvel's Movie Mania." *Newsday* 29 Apr. 2005: A57.

Berman, Shari Springer, and Robert Pulcini. "Splendid Misery: An Interview with Robert Pulcini and Shari Springer Berman." By Dennis West and Joan M. West, with Anne Gilbert. *Cineaste* 28.4 (Fall 2003): 40–43.

Bernière, Vincent. "Enki Bilal. Le bleu dans les yeux." *Bang* 6 (printemps 2005): 10–25.

Beylie, Claude. *Les films-clés du cinema.* Paris: Larousse, 2002.

Bierbaum, Tom. "As Typical Comics Reader Skews Older, More Adult Themes Raise Questions and Eyebrows." *Variety* 8 July 1987: 24+.

Bilal, Enki. *La Trilogie Nikopol.* Genève: Les Humanoïdes Associés, 2002.

Biochel, Bill. "Batman: Commodity as Myth." *The Many Lives of the Batman: Critical Approaches to a Superhero and His Media.* Eds. Roberta E. Pearson and William Uricchio. London: Routledge, 1991. 4–32.

Birds of Prey. Dir. David Carson and Shawn Levy. Perf. Asley Scott, Dina Meyer, and Rachel Skarsten. Warner Brothers. 2002–2003.

Blade 2. Dir. Guillermo Del Toro. Perf. Wesley Snipes, Kris Kristofferson, Norman Reedus, and Leonor Varela. New Line Cinema, 2002.

Bond, Matthew. "Fun Was Never Such Work." *Telegraph* 18 Aug. 2000: 8.

Bonifer, Mike. *Dick Tracy: The Making of the Movie.* New York: Bantam Books, 1990.

Bonneff, Marcel. *Komik Indonesia.* Jakarta: Kepustakaan Populer Gramedia, 1998.

Boogaerts, An. "De comic book helden op het grote scherm. Vergelijking van comic books met hun adaptatie in speelfilms. Case-study: Spider-Man en X-Men." MA Thesis. K.U. Leuven, 2005.

Bordwell, David, and Kristin Thompson. *Film Art: An Introduction.* New York: McGraw Hill, 2001.

Bowles, Scott. "Marvel's 'New Avengers' Draws on Familiar Faces." *USA Today* 21 Oct. 2004. 25 Jan. 2006. http://www.usatoday.com/life/2004-10-21-coming-attractions_x.htm.

——. "Summer Movie Preview." *USA Today* 25 Apr. 2003: A1.

"Box Office." *Entertainment Weekly* 16 May 2003: 55.

"Box Office." *Entertainment Weekly* 18 July 2003: 59.

"Box Office." *Entertainment Weekly* 8 Aug. 2003: 55.

"Box Office Figures." *Box Office Guru.* 12 Apr. 2005. 12 Apr. 2005. www.boxofficeguru.com.

"Box Office Figures." *Box Office Mojo.* 12 Apr. 2005. 12 Apr. 2005. www.boxofficemojo.com.

"Box Office Figures." *The Internet Movie Database.* 12 Apr. 2005. 12 Apr. 2005. www.imdb.com.

"Box Office Figures." *Variety* 2005. 12 Apr. 2005. www.variety.com.

Boyd, Robert. "Unbreakable." Online posting. 28 Nov. 2000. Comic.con Panels. 16 Feb. 2006. http://www.comicon.com/cgi-bin/ultimatebb.cgi?ubb=get _topic;f=42;t=001314.

Bradshaw, Peter. "A Most X-cellent Adventure." *Guardian* 18 Aug. 2000: 4.

———. "X-Men 2." *Guardian* 25 Apr. 2003. 13 Feb. 2006. http://film.guardian.co.uk/News_Story/Critic_Review/Guardian_review/0,,942734,00.html.

Braginsky, V. I. "Hikayat Hang Tuah: Malay Epic and Muslim Mirror." *Bijdragen tot de Taal-, Land- en Volkenkunde* 146.4 (1990): 399–412.

Brodesser, Claude. "Marvel Faces Rivalry from Catwoman & Co." *Variety* 14 July 2003: 7.

Brooker, Will. *Batman Unmasked: Analyzing a Cultural Icon*. London: Continuum, 2000.

———. *Using the Force: Creativity, Community, and Star Wars Fans*. New York: Continuum, 2002.

Brooks, Brad. "Re: [comixschl] Shyamalan." E-mail to Comics Scholars' Discussion List. 4 Mar. 2005.

Brooks, Karen. "Nothing Sells like Teen Spirit: The Commodification of Youth Culture." *Youth Culture: Texts, Images, and Identities*. Eds. Kerry Mallan and Sharyn Pearce. Westport and London: Praeger, 2003. 1–16.

Brooks, Tim, and Earle Marsh. *The Complete Directory to Prime Time Network and Cable TV Shows, 1946–Present*. New York: Ballantine Books, 2003.

Brooks, Xan, "The X Factor." *Guardian Unlimited* 18 Aug. 2000. 15 Feb. 2006. http://film.guardian.co.uk/News_Story/Critic_Review/Guardian_review/0,,355574,00.html.

Brown, Jeffrey A. "Comic Book Fandom and Cultural Capital." *Journal of Popular Culture* 30.4 (Spring 1997): 13–31.

Brownstein, Charles. "Revamped Marvel Looks to Sell Books." *Publishers Weekly* 24 Sept. 2001: 25.

Buffy the Vampire Slayer. Prod. Joss Whedon. Perf. Sarah Michelle Geller. Fox. 1997–2003.

Burch, Noël. "Nagisa Oshima and Japanese Cinema in the '60s." *Cinema: A Critical Dictionary*. Ed. Richard Roud. London: Secker & Warburg, 1980. 735–41.

———. *To the Distant Observer: Form and Meaning in the Japanese Cinema*. London: Scolar Press, 1979.

Butler, Robert. " 'Sixth Sense' Maker's Follow-up Thrills and Confuses." *Kansas City Star* 21 Nov. 2000. *EBSCO*. www.ebsco.com.

Buttgereit, Jörg. "Es muß organisch wirken." In *Kondom des Grauens: Das Buch zum Film*. Ralf König and Martin Walz. Reinbek bei Hamburg: Rowohlt, 1996. 22–23.

Carpenter, Clint (w), Tom Derenick (a), Tom Grummett (p), and Adam DeKraker, Kevin Conrad (i). "Chronicle." *Smallville* #7 (May 2004), NY: DC Comics: 7–31.

Carpenter, Clint, Mark Warshaw (w), Renato Guedes (a), Tom Derenick (p), and Adam DeKraker (i). "Exploit." *Smallville* #8 (July 2004), NY: DC Comics: 6–28.

Carrier, David. *The Aesthetics of Comics*. University Park: Pennsylvania State University, 2000.

Casciani, Dominic. "Are We Criminalising Teenagers?" *BBC News* 12 Nov. 2004. 25 Jan. 2006. http://news.bbc.co.uk/1/hi/uk/3188726.stm.

Chambert-Loir, Henri. "Golongan nasionalis Indonesia di mata novelis Shamsuddin Salleh." *Hubungan Budaya Dalam Sejarah Dunia Melayu*. Eds. Daniel Perret and Puteri Rashidah Megat Ramli. Kuala Lumpur: EFEO, DBP, 2001. 245–79.

Chin, Bertha, and Jonathan Gray. " 'One Ring to Rule Them All': Pre-Viewers and Pre-Texts of the *Lord of the Rings* Films." *Intensities: The Journal of Cult Media* 2 (Autumn/Winter 2001). 3 Feb. 2006. http://www.cult-media.com/issue2/Achingray.htm.

Christiansen, Hans-Christian. "Comics and Film: A Narrative Perspective." *Comics & Culture: Analytical and Theoretical Approaches to Comics*. Eds. Anne Magnussen and Hans-Christian Christiansen. Copenhagen: Museum Tusculanum Press, 2000. 107–21.

Clegg, Sam. "Message 9: Screw All of You That Didn't Like This Film! I Loved AVP!!!!" On-line posting. 2 Sep. 2004. Alt.cult-movies.alien Forum. 30 Nov. 2004. http://groups. google.com/group/alt.cult-movies.alien.

Clover, Carol J. *Men, Women and Chainsaws*. London: BFI, 1992.

Clowes, Daniel. *Ghost World*. London: Jonathan Cape, 2000.

Cohen, Matthew Isaac. "On the Origin of the Komedie Stamboel. Popular Culture, Colonial Society, and the Parsi Theatre Movement." *Bijdragen tot de Taal-, Land- en Volkenkunde* 157.2 (2001): 313–57.

Combs, Richard. Rev. of *Dick Tracy*, dir. Warren Beatty. *Monthly Film Bulletin* Aug. 1990: 215–17.

"Comic Book Adaptation Figures." *Box Office Mojo*. 12 April 2005. 12 April 2005. www. boxofficemojo.com/genres/chart/?id=comicbookadaptation.htm.

"Comics Economics." *Comics International* 180 (Jan. 2005).

"Company Overview: The Story of Dark Horse." *Dark Horse Comics*. 2004. 7 Feb. 2005. www.darkhorse.com/company/overview.php.

Complete Superman Collection DVD, Warner Bros., 2001.

Corner, John. *The Art of Record*. Manchester: Manchester University Press, 1996.

Cortés, Ana María, and María Eugenia Martínez. "Superhéroe de carne y hueso." *Somos* 1941 (October 1999): 6–13.

Costa, Antonio. *Il cinema el le arti visive*. Torino: Giulio Einaudi, 2002.

Coury, David N. "From Aesthetics to Commercialism: Narration and the New German Comedy." *Seminar* 33.4 (1997): 356–73.

Croal, N'Gai. "Marvelous Makeover." *Newsweek* 17 Feb. 2003: 50.

Crumb, Robert. "A Mercifully Short Preface." *American Splendor Presents Bob and Harv's Comics*. By Harvey Pekar (w) and R. Crumb (a). New York: Four Walls Eight Windows, 1996.

Dan. "Unbreakable." Online posting. 27 November 2000. Comic.con Panels. 16 Feb 2006. http://www.comicon.com/cgi-bin/ultimatebb.cgi?ubb=get_topic; f=42;t=001314.

Daniels, Les. *DC Comics: Sixty Years of the World's Favorite Comic Book Heroes*. Boston: Bulfinch Press, 1995.

Dark Horse Comics. 2005. 18 April 2005. www.darkhorse.com.

"Dark Horse Comics Licenses." *Dark Horse Comics*. 2005. 7 Feb. 2005. www.darkhorse.com/company/licenses.php.

"Dark Horse Services." *Dark Horse Comics*. 2004. 5 August 2004. http://services.darkhorse.com/.

Dawson's Creek. Prod. Kevin Williamson, Perf. James Van Der Beek, Katie Holmes, Michelle Williams, and Joshua Jackson. Warner Brothers. 1998–2003.

Dawson, Lee, 2005. "Re: Aliens Comic Book Chapter." E-mail to Kerry Gough. 4 March 2005.

Decklinger, Mike. "The Downfall of Comics." *CAPA-Alpha* 1 (1964).

De la Cruz, John. Bug Hunt Letters. Letter column appearing in *Aliens #2*. July 1989. Milwaukee: Dark Horse Comics.

Deleuze, Gilles. *Cinéma1: L'image-mouvement*. Paris: Minuit, 1983.

Der bewegte Mann. Dir. Sönke Wortmann. Perf. Til Schweiger, Katja Reimann, and Joachim Krol. Orion Classics, 1994.

"'Dick Tracy' Is Arresting Interest of Comics Fans." *St. Petersburg Times* 23 August, 1989: 5.

"Dolby Stereo." *Variety* 27 Dec. 1978: 31.

Dolle-Weinkauff, Bernd. *Comics: Geschichte einer populären Literaturform in Deutschland seit 1945*. Weinheim/Basel: Beltz, 1990.

Doucet, Julie. *My New York Diary*. Montreal: Drawn & Quarterly, 1999.

Duncan, Royal, and Gary Will. *Wrestling Title Histories*. 4th ed. Waterloo, Ontario: Archeus Communications, 2000.

Dyer, Geoff. "American Dreams." *New Statesman* 17.789 (Jan. 2004): 42–44.

Eco, Umberto. "The Myth of Superman." *The Role of the Reader: Explorations in the Semiotics of Texts*. London: Hutchinson, 1979. 107–24.

Eisner, Will. *Comics and Sequential Art*. Tamarac, Fla.: Poorhouse Press, 1985.

———. *Graphic Storytelling*. Tamarac, Fla.: Poorhouse Press, 1996.

Ellen, Barbara. "X Marks the Spotty Script." *Times* 1 May 2003: A12–13.

Ellis, John. *Visible Fictions: Cinema Television Video*. New York: Routledge, 1993.

"El Santo." *Wrestling-Titles*. 2006. 2 Feb. 2006. www.wrestling-titles.com/ wrestlers/santo/.

Eshun, Ekow. "Wham! Bam! The X-Men Are Here." *Independent on Sunday* 6 Aug. 2000: C1.

Fabrikant, Geraldine. "The Media Business: Advertising; In Land of Big Bucks, Even Bigger Bucks." *New York Times* 18 Oct. 1990: D23.

"February 2005 Market Share: 2004 Year in Review." *Diamond Comic Distributors*. Mar. 2005. 29 Mar. 2005. www.diamondcomics.com/ market_share.html.

Fell, John L. *Film and the Narrative Tradition*. Norman, Okla.: University of Oklahoma Press, 1974.

Fierman, Daniel. "Bat Outta Hell." *Entertainment Weekly* 29 Apr./6 May 2005: 30–35.

Fingeroth, Danny. *Superman on the Couch*. New York: Continuum, 2004.

Fish, Stanley. *Is There a Text in This Class? The Authority of Interpretive Communities*. Cambridge, MA: Harvard University Press, 1980.

Flores, Marc. "Comics on a New Adventure." *USA Today* 21 Feb. 2003: D16.

Frémion, Yves. "Dessinateurs à la caméra." In *CinémAction HS: cinéma et bande dessinée*. Paris: Corlet—Télérama, 1990. 163–67.

French, Philip. "Can You Really Have a Superhero Called Xavier?" *Observer* 20 Aug.2000. 13 Feb. 2006. http://observer.guardian.co.uk/review/story/0,,3 56258,00.html.

———. "X2." *Observer* 4 May 2003. 13 Feb. 2006. http://film.guardian.co.uk/News_ Story/ Critic_Review/Observer_review/0,,949028,00.html.

From Hell. Dir. Albert Hughes and Allen Hughes. Perf. Johnny Depp, Heather Graham, Ian Holm, and Robbie Coltrane. 20th Century Fox, 2001.

"From Zeroes to Heroes." *Entertainment Weekly* 26 Oct. 2001: 102.

Gallop, Annabel Teh. "Malay Comic Books from the 1950s and 1960s." Unpublished paper presented at the World Congress on Malay Language. Dewan Bahasa dan Pustaka, Kuala Lumpur. 21–25 Aug. 1995.

Gambaccini, Paul. "I Was a Teenage Gambaccini! Or Blecch!" *CAPA-Alpha* 1 (1964).

———. "Listen Here!" *CAPA-Alpha* 6 (1964).

Gartner, Lloyd P. *The History of the Jews of Cleveland*. Cleveland: Western Reserve Historical Society, 1978.

Gasser, Christian, ed. *Mutanten: Die deutschsprachige Comic-Avantgarde der 90er Jahre*. Ostfildern-Ruit: Hatje Cantz, 1999.

———. "Mutantenkosmos: Von Mickey Mouse zu Explomaus." *Mutanten: Die deutschsprachige Comic-Avantgarde der 90er Jahre*. Ed. Christan Gasser. Ostfildern-Ruit: Hatje Cantz, 1999. 5–18.

Gasser, Christian, et al. "Das große Entenhauser Max-und-Moritz-Symposium: Warum gibt es keine deutschsprachige Comic-Kultur?" *Mutanten: Die deutschsprachige Comic-Avantgarde der 90er Jahre*. Ed. Christan Gasser. Ostfildern-Ruit: Hatje Cantz, 1999. 24–28.

Geipel, John. *The Cartoon: A Short History of Graphic Comedy and Satire*. London: David and Charles, 1972.

Geraghty, Christine, and David Lusted. *The Television Studies Book*. London: Arnold, 1998.

Ghost World. Dir. Terry Zwigoff. Perf. Thora Birch, Scarlett Johansson, and Steve Buscemi. MGM Distribution Company and United Artists Films Europe, 2000.

Gifford, Dennis. *Discovering Comics*. Tring, Herts.: Shire Publications, 1971.

Giger, H. R. *Giger's Alien: Film Design 20th Century Fox*. London: Big O Publishing, 1979.

Giroux, Henry A. "Teen Girls' Resistance and the Disappearing Social in *Ghost World*." *The Review of Education, Pedagogy and Cultural Studies* 24 (2002): 283–304.

Glassman, Irving. "Conversations." *Alter Ego* 1.3 (1961).

Gledhill, Christine, ed. *Home Is Where the Heart Is: Studies in Melodrama and the Woman's Film*. London: BFI Publishing, 1987.

Gombrich, Ernst H. *Art and Illusion: A Study in the Psychology of Pictorial Representation*. Oxford: Phaidon Press, 1987.

Gondek, Jeff. "Best Superhero Film Ever?" Online posting. 23 Apr. 2003. Peterdavid.net. http://www.Peterdavid.net/.

Gordon, Ian. *Comic Strips and Consumer Culture, 1890–1945*. Washington: Smithsonian Institution Press, 1998.

———. "Superman on the Set: The Market, Nostalgia and Television Audiences." *Quality Popular Television*. Eds. Mark Jancovich and James Lyons. London: BFI, 2003. 148–62.

Gould, Chester. *Dick Tracy: The Thirties. Tommy Guns and Hard Times*. Ed. Herb Galewitz. New Jersey: The Wellfleet Press, 1990.

Grainge, Paul. "Branding Hollywood: Studio Logos and the Aesthetics of Memory and Hype." *Screen* 45.4 (Winter 2004): 344–62.

Gray, Jonathan. "New Audiences, New Textualities: Anti-Fans and Non-Fans." *International Journal of Cultural Studies* 6.1 (2003): 65–82.

Groensteen, Thierry. "Acteurs de papier." In *CinémAction HS: cinéma et bande dessinée*. Paris: Corlet—Télérama, 1990. 254–63.

———. "Du 7ᵉ au 9ᵉ art: l'inventaire des singularités." In *CinémAction HS: cinéma et bande dessinée*. Paris: Corlet—Télérama, 1990. 16–28.

Grossman, Gary. *Superman: Serial to Cereal*. New York: Popular Library, 1976.

Gustines, George Gene. "Even Superheroes Can Use Some Buffing of the Brand." *New York Times* 9 May 2005: 8.

Hake, Sabine. *German National Cinema*. London: Routledge, 2002.

Halle, Randall. "'Happy Ends' to Crises of Heterosexual Desire: Toward a Social Psychology of Recent German Comedies." *Camera Obscura* 15:2 (2000): 1–39.

Hamedi Mohd. Adnan. *Direktori Majalah-Majalah Melayu sebelum merdeka*. Kuala Lumpur: Penerbit Universiti Malaya, 2002.

Hampton, Howard. "Instant Authenticity." *Film Comment* 39.4 (July/Aug. 2003): 25–27.

Hamzah Hussin. *Memoir Hamzah Hussin: Dari Cathay Keris ke Merdeka Studio*. Bangi: University Kebangsaan Malaysia, 1997.

Hang Tuah. Getekend door Nasjah. Vertaald uit het Indonesisch door Fred Dijs, verbeterd door Ibu Guru Kwee-Tan, met een essay van Rudy Kousbroek. Amsterdam: Bulaaq & In Beeld, Tekst en Uitleg, 2003.

Hanson, Eric. "State of the Art: The Comic-book Industry Is Flexing Its Muscles after Heroic Successes on the Big Screen." *Star Tribune* 4 June 2003: 1E.

Haraway, Donna. "A Cyborg Manifesto: Science Technology and Socialist Feminism in the Late Twentieth Century." *Simians, Cyborgs and Women: The Reinvention of Nature*. New York: Routledge, 1991. 149–81.

Harding, James, and Ahmad Sarji. *P. Ramlee: The Bright Star*. Petaling Jaya: Pelanduk, 2002.

Harvey, Robert C. "The Aesthetics of the Comic Strip." *Journal of Popular Culture* 12.4 (Spring 1979): 640–52.

———. *The Art of the Comic Book: An Aesthetic History.* Jackson: University Press of Mississippi, 1996.

Harun Aminurrashid. "Saya dengan Hiburan. 'Awak Siapa?'" *Hiburan 10 tahun: keluaran khas untuk peringatan genap umur majalah Hiburan sepuluh tahun (Januari 1946 hingga Januari 1956).* Singapore: Abdullah 'Ali, 1956.

Hatfield, Charles. *Alternative Comics: An Emerging Literature.* Jackson, MS: University Press of Mississippi, 2005.

Hellier Anderson, Susan. "It's a Bird! It's a Plane! It's a Movie!" *New York Times* 26 Jun. 1977: 15.

Henderson, Carl. "Inside the Comic Book Industry." *Rec.arts.comics.misc.* 2005. 18 Apr. 2005. http://users.rcn.com/kateshort/faqs/miscfaq3.htm.

Hermes, Joke. *Reading Women's Magazines: An Analysis of Everyday Media Use.* Oxford: Polity, 1995.

Herner, Irene. *Mitos y monitos: Historietas y fotonovelas en México.* Mexico: UNAM-Editorial Nueva Imagen, 1979.

Hesmondhalgh, David. *The Cultural Industries.* London: Sage Publications, 2002.

Hick, Darren. "Based on a True Story." *The Comics Journal* (2002). 17 Oct. 2004. http://www.tcj.com/3_online/e_hick_090899.html.

Higson, Andrew, and Ginette Vincendeau. "Melodrama: An Introduction." *Screen* 27.6 (Nov./Dec. 1986): 2–5.

Hikayat Hang Tuah. *Hikayat Hang Tuah (menurut naskhakh Dewan Bahasa dan Pustaka) Di-selenggarakan dengan di-beri Pengenalan dan Chatatan oleh Kassim Ahmad, M.A. (Malaya).* Kuala Lumpur: Dewan Bahasa dan Pustaka, 1964.

Hills, Matt. *Fan Cultures.* London: Routledge, 2002.

Hine, Thomas. *The Rise and Fall of the American Teenager.* New York: Avon Books, 1999.

Hinds, Harold E., Jr., and Charles M. Tatum. *Not Just for Children: The Mexican Comic Book in the Late 1960s and 1970s.* Westport, CT: Greenwood Press, 1992.

Hiscock, John. "Cartoon Mutants—RSC Trained." *Telegraph* 4 Aug. 2000: A8.

Hochberg, Julian, and Virginia Brooks. "Movies in the Mind's Eye." *Post-Theory. Reconstructing Film Studies.* Eds. David Bordwell and Noël Carroll. Madison, Wisconsin: University of Wisconsin Press, 1996. 368–87.

Hofman, Robert. *Beste films aller tijden.* L. Korteland, 1993.

Hoggart, Richard. *The Uses of Literacy.* Harmondsworth: Penguin, 1957.

Holden, Stephen. "She Wants Him Back, Without the Roommate." Rev. of *Maybe . . . Maybe Not,* dir. Sonke Wortmann. *New York Times* 28 June 1996. 6 Nov. 2004. http://www.nytimes.com.

Holson, Laura M. "Can Little-Known Heroes Be Hollywood Hits?" *New York Times* 26 July 2004: C2.

Hughes, Kathleen A. "Batman Fans Fear the Joke's on Them in Hollywood Epic." *Wall Street Journal* 29 Nov. 1988: 1.

Hulk. Dir. Ang Lee. Perf. Eric Bana, Jennifer Connelly, Sam Elliot, Josh Lucas, and Nick Nolte. DVD. Universal Pictures, 2003.

Hunt, Nathan. "The Importance of Trivia: Ownership, Exclusion and Authority in Science Fiction Fandom." *Defining Cult Movies: The Cultural Politics of Oppositional Taste.* Eds. Mark Jancovich, Antonio Lazaro Reboll, Julian Stringer, and Andy Willis. Manchester: Manchester University Press, 2003. 185–201.

"ICv2's Top 300 Comics and Top 50 GN's Index." *ICv2 News.* 2003. 26 Oct. 2003. www.icv2.com/articles/home/1850.html.

Inge, M. Thomas. *Comics as Culture.* Jackson: University of Mississippi Press, 1990.

Itzkoff, Dave. "The Vendetta behind 'V for Vendetta.'" *New York Times* 12 Mar. 2006: B1, 13.

Jacobs, Lea. "The Woman's Picture and the Poetics of Melodrama." *Camera Obscura* 31 (1993). 120–47.

Jamil Sulong. *Kaca Permata: Memoir Seorang Pengarah.* Kuala Lumpur: Dewan Bahasa dan Pustaka, 1993.

Jenkins, Henry. "Will the Web Save Comics? Critics Rave. Markets Shrink. It's the Internet to the Rescue." *Technology Review* 1 May 2002. 13 Mar. 2006. http://www.technologyreview. com/BioTech/wtr_12839,304,p1.html.

———. *Textual Poachers: Television Fans and Participatory Culture.* London: Routledge, 1992.

Jensen, Jeff. "Comic Heroes Return to Root as Marvel Is Cast as Hip Brand." *Advertising Age* 8 Jan. 1998: 69.

———. "Shows of Strength." *Entertainment Weekly* 23 Nov. 2001: 26–28.

Joly, Martine. *Introduction à l'analyse de l'image.* Paris: Nathan, 2005.

———. *L'image et son interpretation.* Paris: Nathan, 2002.

Jones, Gerard. *Killing Monsters: Why Children Need Fantasy, Super Heroes, and Make-Believe Violence.* New York: Basic Books, 2002.

Jones, Gerard, and Will Jacobs. *The Comic Book Heroes.* California: Prima Publishing, 1997.

Josselin de Jong, P. E. de. "The Rise and Decline of a National Hero." *Journal of the Malayan Branch of the Royal Asiatic Society* 38.2 (1965):140–55.

Khoo Gaik Cheng. "Nationalism and Homoeroticism: A Feminist Reading of the Hang Tuah and Hang Jebat Debate." *Risking Malaysia: Culture, Politics and Identity.* Eds. Maznah Mohamad and Wong Soak Koon. Bangi: Penerbit Universiti Kebangsaan Malaysia, 2001. 45–72.

Kidnie, Margaret Jane. " 'The Way the World Is Now': Love in the Troma Zone." *Shakespeare, Film, Fin de Siècle.* Eds. Mark Thornton Burnett and Ramona Way. Houndmills, Basingstoke and London: Macmillan, 2000. 102–21.

King, Clive. "When in Tights." *Times* 29 July 2000: M24.

King, Geoff. *Spectacular Narratives: Hollywood in the Age of the Blockbuster.* London: I. B. Tauris, 2000.

Kipniss, Marc. "The Death (and Rebirth) of Superman." *Discourse* 16.3 (Spring 1994): 144–67.

Kissell, Rick. " 'Smallville' Bow Super for the WB." *Daily Variety.* 18 Oct. 2001. 1.

Klages, Elmar. "Aber der Arsch: von dem Arsch, wißt ihr . . . Diese prallen, runden Hinterbacken, mit so einem leichten Flaum überzogen . . . " *Mal mir mal nen Schwulen: Das Buch zu Ralf König.* Ed. Joachim Bartholomae. Hamburg: MännerschwarmSkript, 1996. 56–87.

Klinger, Barbara. "The Contemporary Cinephile: Film Collecting in the Post-Video Era." *Hollywood Spectatorship: Changing Perceptions of Cinema Audiences.* Eds. Melvyn Stokes and Richard Maltby. London: BFI Publishing, 2001. 132–47.

———. *Melodrama and Meaning: History, Culture, and the Films of Douglas Sirk.* Bloomington: Indiana University Press, 1994.

Klink, Roman. "Ein Gespräch mit Ralf König." *Ralf Königs Lysistrata.* 13 Nov. 2004. http:// nzettl.han-solo.net/kw_presse/material/kfv/ralfknigslysistrata/ Lysistrata_Presseheft.pdf..

Knigge, Andreas. *Comics: Vom Massenblatt ins multimediale Abenteuer.* Reinbek bei Hamburg: Rowohlt, 1996.

Kondom des Grauens. Dir. Martin Walz. Perf. Udo Samel, Peter Lohmeyer, Iris Berben, Marc Richter, and Leonard Lansink. Troma Team, 1996.

"König mit Geldsorgen." *Yahoo! Nachrichten.* 8 Nov. 2004. http://de.news.yahoo .com/ 041108/12/4aadm.html.

König, Ralf. "Wie die Karnickel: Drehbuchautor Ralf König im Interview." *wdr.de Kultur.* 10 Nov. 2004. http://www.wdr.de/themen/kultur/film/ralph_koenig /index .jhtml.

———— (w,a). *Bis auf die Knochen*. Thurn: Edition Kunst der Comics, 1990.

———— (w,a). *Der bewegte Mann*. Reinbek bei Hamburg: Rowohlt, 1987.

————. Home Page. 2004. 18 June 2004. http://www.ralf-koenig.de.

———— (w,a). *Kondom des Grauens*. Sonneberg: Edition Kunst der Comics, 1988.

———— (w,a). *Lysistrata*. Reinbek bei Hamburg: Rowohlt, 1987.

————. "'ne dicke Nase müssen sie haben: Interview mit Ralf König." By Matthias Wieland. *SUBWAY Magazin* July 2002. 10 Nov. 2004. http://www. subway-net.de/magazin/2002/07ralfkoenig.shtml.

————. "Pornos und Gitterbetten: Interview mit Ralf König." By Ulf Lippitz. *ULTIMO.* 10 Nov. 2004. http://www.ultimo.devcon.net/kr-film/i-ralf.htm.

———— (w,a). *Pretty Baby: Der bewegte Mann 2*. Reinbek bei Hamburg: Rowohlt, 1988.

————. "Ralf König: Ich habe sehr viel Spaß am Zwischenmenschlichen." By Jakob Buhre. *Planet Interview.* 18 June 2004. http://www.planet-interview.de /interviews/pi.php?interview=koenig-ralf.

————. "Tappajakondomi—Jäykistävää Kauhua." In *Kondom des Grauens: Das Buch zum Film*. Ralf König and Martin Walz. Reinbek bei Hamburg: Rowohlt, 1996. Reinbek bei Hamburg: Rowohlt, 1996. 6–13.

———— (w,a). *Wie die Karnickel*. Reinbek bei Hamburg: Rowohlt, 2003.

König, Ralf, and Martin Walz. *Kondom des Grauens: Das Buch zum Film*. Reinbek bei Hamburg: Rowohlt, 1996.

Kozloff, Sarah R. "Superman as Saviour: Christian Allegory in the Superman Movies." *Journal of Popular Film and Television* 9.2 (1981): 78–82.

Krantz, Matt. "Marvel's Profit Sense Is Tingling as Superhero Films Prevail." *USA Today* 7 May 2003: B1.

Kuhfeld, Al. "Kid Stuff." *CAPA-Alpha* 4 (1964).

Kuhn, Annette. "'That Day *Did* Last Me All My Life': Cinema Memory and Enduring Fandom." *Identifying Hollywood's Audiences: Cultural Identity and the Movies*. Eds. Melvyn Stokes and Richard Maltby. London: BFI, 1999. 135–46.

————. *Women's Pictures: Feminism and Cinema*. London: Routledge, 1982.

Kunzle, David. *The History of the Comic Strip, Vol. 1: The Early Comic Strip*. Berkeley: University of California Press, 1973.

————. *The History of the Comic Strip, Vol. 2: The Nineteenth Century*. Berkeley: University of California Press, 1989.

Kuzniar, Alice. *Queer German Cinema*. Stanford: Stanford University Press, 2000.

Kyle, Richard. "Wonderland." *CAPA-Alpha* 1 (1964).

Lacassin, Francis. "The Comic Strip and Film Language." *Film Quarterly* 26.1 (Fall 1972): 11–23.

Landesman, Cosmo. "Scratch Beneath the Surface" *Sunday Times* 20 Aug. 2000: C6.

————. "On the Nail." *Sunday Times* 4 May 2003: C8–9.

Landry, Marcia, ed. *Imitations of Life: A Reader on Film and Television Melodrama*. Detroit: Wayne State University Press, 1991.

Lat. *Lat 30 Years Later*. Petaling Jaya: Kampung Boy, 1994.

Lauro, Patricia Winters. "With a Stable of Heroes, Marvel Casts a Wide Net." *New York Times* 8 May 2003: 3–4.

Leary, Timothy. Foreword. *Giger's Alien: Film Design 20th Century Fox*. By H. R. Giger. London: Big O Publishing, 1979.

Leavis, Frank Raymond, and Densys Thompson. *Culture and Environment*. Westport, CT: Greenwood Press, 1977.

Le Cain, Maximilian. "The Shadow of Time Passing: *Ghost World*." *Senses of Cinema* 21 (July/Aug. 2002). 28 Oct. 2004. http://www.sensesofcinema. com/contents/02/21/ghost_world.html.

Lee, Stan. "Interview with Stan Lee (Part 3 of 5)." By Kenneth Plume. *IGN FilmForce.* 28 June 2000. 25 Jan. 2006. http://filmforce.ign.com/articles /035/035883p1.html.

———. "'Nuff Said—An Interview with Stan Lee." By Kenneth Plume. *IGN FilmForce.* 30 Apr. 2002. 25 Jan. 2006. http://filmforce.ign.com/ articles/358/358217 p1.html.

Lefèvre, Pascal. "Willy Vandersteens Suske en Wiske in de krant (1945–1971). Een theoretisch kader voor een vormelijke analyse van strips." Diss. K.U. Leuven, 2003.

Leith, Sam. "Black and White and Noir All Over." *Daily Telegraph* 14 May 2005: ART4.

Levinson, Paul. *The Soft Edge: A Natural History and Future of the Information Revolution.* New York: Routledge, 1997.

Lim Kay Tong. *Cathay: 55 Years of Cinema.* Singapore: Landmark, 1991.

Lindlof, Thomas. "Media Audiences as Interpretive Communities." *Communication Yearbook* 11 (1998): 81–107.

Lipkin, Steven N. *Real Emotional Logic: Film and Television Docudrama as Persuasive Practice.* Carbondale: Southern Illinois University Press, 2002.

Lischke-McNab, Ute. "Gender, Sex, and Sexuality: The Use of Music as a Collateral Marketing Device in *Maybe . . . Maybe Not." Queering the Canon: Defying Sights in German Literature and Culture.* Eds. Christoph Lorey and John L. Plews. Columbia, SC: Camden House, 1998. 403–19.

Lisistrata. Dir. Francesc Bellmunt. Perf. Maribel Verdú, Juan Luis Galiardo, and Javier Gurruchaga. Laurenfilm S.A, 2002.

Lott, Jeremy. "Smash! Pow! Bam!: Why Superheroes Go Bankrupt." *Reason* Oct. 2002: 68.

Lovell, Jarret. "Nostalgia, Comic Books, and the 'War Against Crime!' An Inquiry into the Resurgence of Popular Justice." *Journal of Popular Culture: Comparative Studies in the World's Civilizations* 36.2 (Fall 2002): 335–51.

Lusted, David. "The Popular Culture Debate and Light Entertainment on Television." *The Television Studies Book.* Eds. Christine Geraghty and David Lusted. London: Arnold, 1998. 175–90.

MacDonald, Heidi. "Comics Go to the Movies." *Publishers Weekly* 16 June 2003: 30.

Macaulay, Sean. "A New Breed of Monster Hit." *Times* 17 July 2000: 24.

Maeder, Jay. *Dick Tracy: The Official Biography.* New York: Plume, 1990.

Magid, Ron. "Comic Book World Springs to Life for *Dick Tracy." American Cinematographer* Dec. 1990: 80–87.

Maier, H. M. J. "Tales of Hang Tuah: In Search of Wisdom and Good Behavior." *Bijdragen tot de Taal-, Land- en Volkenkunde* 155.3 (1999): 342–61.

Marr, Merissa, and Kate Kelly. "Budget Busters: With Special Effects the Star, Hollywood Faces New Reality." *Wall Street Journal* May 12 2006: A1.

Mars-Jones, Adam. "If It Ain't Broke, Don't Fix It." *Times* 28 Dec. 2000. *OCLC First Search.* http://www.oclc.org/firstsearch/.

Matamoros Durán, Mauricio. "El Santo en las historietas." *Somos* 1941 (October 1999): 52–58.

Mathews, Kevin. Bug Hunt Letters. Letter column appearing in *Aliens #4.* March 1989. Milwaukee: Dark Horse Comics.

May, Elaine Tyler. *Homeward Bound: American Families in the Cold War Era.* New York: Basic Books, 1999.

McAllister, Matthew P. "Ownership Concentration in the U.S. Comic Book Industry." *Comics and Ideology.* Eds. Matthew P. McAllister, Edward H. Sewell Jr., and Ian Gordon. New York: Peter Lang, 2001. 15–38.

McAllister, Matthew P., Edward H. Sewell Jr., and Ian Gordon, eds. *Comics and Ideology.* NY: Peter Lang Publishers, 2001.

McCloud, Scott. *Reinventing Comics: How Imagination and Technology Are Revolutionizing an Art Form.* New York: Perennial, 2000.

————. *Understanding Comics: The Invisible Art.* New York: Paradox Press, 1993.

McIntee, David. *Beautiful Monsters: The Unofficial and Unauthorised Guide to the Alien and Predator Films.* Tolworth: Telos, 2005.

McKenzie, Alan. *How to Draw and Sell Comic Strips for Newspapers and Comic Books.* London: Macdonald Orbis, 1987.

McLuhan, Marshall. *Understanding Media: The Extensions of Man.* Cambridge, Massachusetts: MIT Press, 1997.

Meehan, Eileen R. " 'Holy Commodity Fetish, Batman!': The Political Economy of a Commercial Intertext." *The Many Lives of Batman: Critical Approaches to a Superhero and His Media.* Eds. Roberta E. Pearson and William Urrichio. London: Routledge, 1991. 47–65.

Meyrowitz, Joshua. *No Sense of Place: The Impact of Electronic Media on Social Behavior.* New York: Oxford University Press, 1985.

Milner, Anthony. *The Invention of Politics in Colonial Malaya: Contesting Nationalism and the Expansion of the Public Sphere.* Cambridge: Cambridge University Press, 1995.

————. *Kerajaan: Malay Political Culture on the Eve of Colonial Rule.* Tucson: University of Arizona Press for the Association of Asian Studies, 1982.

Mittell, Jason. *Genre and Television: From Cop Shows to Cartoons in American Culture.* New York: Routledge, 2004.

Moreels, Eric J. "Arad's Mega Marvel Movie, TV Update." Online posting. 13 Nov. 2003. Comixfan Forums. 6 Dec. 2003. http://www.comixfan.com/xfan /forums.

————. "Jemas to Exit as Marvel Comics President." Online posting. 9 Sept. 2003. Comixfan Forums. 6 Dec. 2003. http://www.comixfan.com /xfan /forums.

————. "Marvel to Bid on Artisan." Online posting. 2 July 2003. Comixfan Forums. 6 Dec. 2003. http://www.comixfan.com/xfan/forums.

————. "Quesada Responds to More X-Issues." Online posting. 21 Oct. 2003. Comixfan Forums. 6 Dec. 2003. http://www.comixfan.com/xfan/ forums.

————. "Quesada Talks Another X-Men Spring Cleaning." Online posting. 9 Sept. 2003. Comixfan Forums. 6 Dec. 2003. http://www.comixfan.com/xfan /forums.

————. "Wolverine Set to Change Face." Online posting. 2 June 2003. Comixfan Forums. 6 Dec. 2003. http://www.comixfan.com/xfan/forums.

————. "12 Month Tenures for Whedon, Singer on *X-Men*." Online posting. 28 Feb. 2004. Comixfan Forums. 10 March 2004. http://www.comixfan.com/xfan /forums.

"Morning Edition." NPR. Washington, D.C. 29 Nov. 2000. Transcript accessed via Proquest. 9 Oct. 2003. http://www.library.wisc.edu.

Mouchart, Benoît. "Alan Moore. Un gentleman extraordinaire." *Bang* 5 (hiver 2004): 10–31.

Mulyadi Mahamood. *The History of Malay Editorial Cartoons (1930s–1993).* Kuala Lumpur: Utusan Publications, 2004.

Mutant X. Prod. Avi Arad. Perf. John Shea, Victoria Pratt, Victor Webster, Forbes March, Laura Lee Smith (2001–2003), and Karen Cliche (2003–2004). Fireworks Entertainment/ Tribune Entertainment. 2001–2004.

Murphy, A. D. "Forman to Salkinds: 'Your Profit Mine': Charge Funding Was Siphoned." *Variety* 13 Dec. 1978: 3.

Nadel, Dan. "The Unknown Comic." *Print* 57.4 (July/Aug. 2003): 86–93.

Naz Achnas. "Editorial." *Kenchana* 1 (Jan. 1947): 6.

Nazif Bin Achmadin. "Comic dan Cartoon: Dalam Zaman Ini." *Kenchana* 1 (Jan. 1947): 13, 21.

Neale, Steve. *Genre and Hollywood.* London: Routledge, 2000.

————. "Melo Talk: On the Meaning and Uses of the Term Melodrama." *Velvet Light Trap* 32 (1993): 66–89.

————. "Melodrama and Tears." *Screen* 27.6 (Nov./Dec. 1986): 6–22.

Norcliffe, Glen, and Olivero Rendace. "New Geographies of Comic Book Production in

North America: The New Artisan, Distancing, and the Periodic Social Economy." *Economic Geography* 7.3 (July 2003): 241–63.

O'Sullivan, Charlotte. "X Misses the Spot." *Independent* 2 May 2003. 13 Feb. 2006. http://enjoyment.independent.co.uk/film/reviews/article102871.ece.

Paget, Derek. *No Other Way to Tell It: Dramadoc/Docudrama on Television.* Manchester: Manchester University Press, 1998.

Pallarés, José Miguel. *Viñetas de celuloide. El comic en el cine.* Madrid: Metrópolis Milenio, 2003.

Parker, Deborah, and Mark Parker. "Directors and DVD Commentary: The Specifics of Intention." *Journal of Aesthetics and Art Criticism* 62.1 (Winter 2004): 13–22.

Parsons, Patrick. "Batman and His Audience: The Dialectic of Culture." *The Many Lives of Batman: Critical Approaches to a Superhero and His Media.* Eds. Roberta E. Pearson and William Urrichio. London: Routledge, 1991. 66–89.

Pearson, Roberta E., and William Uricchio. "I'm Not Fooled by That Cheap Disguise!" *The Many Lives of Batman: Critical Approaches to a Superhero and His Media.* Eds. Roberta E. Pearson and William Urrichio. London: Routledge, 1991. 182–213.

Peeters, Benoît. *Cinéma et BD / Film en strip.* Brussels: Musée du Cinéma/Filmmuseum, 1996.

Peirce, Charles Sanders. *Ecrits sur le signe.* Paris: Seuil, 1978.

Pekar, Harvey. "A Mensch for All Mediums: TIME Comix Talks to 'American Splendor' Creator, Harvey Pekar." By Andrew D. Arnold. *Time* 8 Aug. 2003. 17 Oct. 2004. http://www.time.com/time/columnist/arnold/article /0,9565,474360,00.html.

———. "Harvey Pekar: My Film Future." *Cleveland Free Times* 11 Jan. 2004. 17 Oct. 2004. http://www.freetimes.com/modules.php?op= modload&name= News&file=article&sid=928.

———. "What Me Worry? Yes: *American Splendor* Is One of the Most Celebrated Movies of the Year, and Everybody Loves My Comics Again. But . . . I dunno." *Austin Chronicle* 5 Sept. 2003. 17 Oct. 2004. http://www.austinchronicle.com/issues/dispatch/2003-09-05/screens_feature.html.

Pekar, Harvey (w), and David Collier (a). *American Splendor: Unsung Hero—The Story of Robert Mc Neill.* Milwaukee: Dark Horse Comics, 2003.

Pekar, Harvey (w), Dean Haspiel, Josh Neufeld, Joe Sacco, et al (a). *Best of American Splendor.* New York: Ballantine Books, 2005.

Pekar, Harvey, and Gary Dumm. "American Splendor on the Web." *Modern Tales.* 2004. 17 Oct. 2004. http://www.moderntales.com/longplayfeature.%20php?name= americansplendor&view=toc.

Pekar, Harvey, Joyce Brabner, and Danielle Batone. *From Off the Streets of Cleveland Comes Harvey Pekar.* 2004. 17 Oct. 2004. http://www.harvey pekar.com/.

Pekar, Harvey, Joyce Brabner (w), and Frank Stack (a). *Our Cancer Year.* New York: Four Walls Eight Windows, 1994.

Pekar, Harvey (w), Robert Crumb, Gary Dumm, Mark Zingarelli, et al (a). *Our Movie Year.* New York: Ballantine Books, 2004.

Pekar, Harvey (w), Robert Crumb, Gregory Budgett, Gerry Shamray, et al (a). *American Splendor: The Life and Times of Harvey Pekar.* New York: Ballantine Books, 2003.

Pekar, Harvey (w), and Robert Crumb (a). *American Splendor Presents Bob and Harv's Comics.* New York: Four Walls Eight Windows, 1996.

Pellitteri, Marco. "Re: [comixschl] Shyamalan." E-mail to Comics Scholars' Discussion List. 4 Mar. 2005.

Perry, George, and Alan Aldridge. *The Penguin Book of Comics: A Slight History.* Middlesex: Penguin Books, 1971.

Peters, Jan-Marie. *Pictorial Signs and the Language of Film.* Amsterdam: Rodopi, 1981.

Petrou, David Michael. *The Making of Superman: The Movie*. London: W. H. Allen and Company, 1978.

Plowright, Frank, ed. *The Slings & Arrows Comic Guide*. London: Aurum Press, 1997.

Potton, Eric. "X-Men." *Times* 19 Aug. 2000: M24.

"Prepare for Battle: Alien vs. Predator Gets Ready to Make a DVD Killing." *DVD Monthly* Feb. 2005: 32–35.

"Press Release, Dark Horse Goes to the Movies (and Vice Versa)." *Dark Horse Comics.* 14 Dec 2004. www.darkhorse.com/news/horsepower.

Proudfoot, Ian. *Early Malay Printed Books: A Provisional Account of Materials Printed in the Singapore-Malaysia Area up to 1920, Noting Holdings in Major Public Collections.* [N.p.:] Academy of Malay Studies and the Library University of Malaya, 1993.

Pumphrey, George H. *What Children Think of Their Comics*. London: Epworth Press, 1964.

The Punisher. Dir. Jonathan Hensleigh. Perf. Thomas Jane and John Travolta. Lions Gate Film, 2004.

Pustz, Matthew J. *Comic Book Culture: Fanboys and True Believers*. Jackson: University Press of Mississippi, 1999.

Quinn, Anthony. "Mutants with an Unconvincing Message." *Independent* 18 Aug. 2000: 10.

Radford, Bill. " 'Unbreakable' a Must-See for Comic-Book Fans." *Colorado Springs Gazette* 7 Dec. 2000. *EBSCO*. www.ebsco.com.

Raffy, Serge. "Un film-mutant surgi d'entre deux mondes." *Le Nouvel Observateur* 28 mars 2004.

Rahmah Bujang. *Sejarah Perkembangan Drama Bangsawan di Tanah Melayu dan Singapura.* Kuala Lumpur: Dewan bahasa dan Pustaka, 1975.

Ramin, Sue Berger. "Screenings: Worth a Thousand Words." *Publishers Weekly* 27 Oct. 2003: 16.

Ramirez, Fernando. "Unbreakable." Online posting. 29 Nov. 2000. Comic.con Panels. 16 Feb 2006. http://www.comicon.com/cgi-bin/ultimatebb.cgi? ubb =get_topic;f=42;t=001314.

Raviv, Dan. *Comic Wars*. New York: Broadway Books, 2002.

Rawson, Philip. *Drawing*. Philadelphia: University of Pennsylvania Press, 1987.

———. *Seeing through Drawing*. London: British Broadcasting Corporation, 1979.

Razak Ahmad. *Perjuangan Hang Tuah dan Jebat*. Majalah Comic Melayu, Johore Bahru: Sabirin Bin Mohd. Annie (Zawyah Publ. Home), 1953.

Rea, Steven. "Shyamalan Is in Fine Scary Form in 'Signs.' " *Philadelphia Inquirer*. 21 Nov. 2000. *EBSCO*. www.ebsco.com.

Regalado, Aldo. "Bending Steel with Bare Hands: Modernity and the American Superhero in the Twentieth Century." Diss. Uni of Miami, 2006.

Reitberger, Reinhold, and Wolfgang Fuchs. *Comics: Anatomy of a Mass Medium*. London: Studio Vista, 1972.

Rice, Lynette. "On the Air." *Entertainment Weekly* 19 Oct. 2001: 66.

Richardson, Mike. "Interview: Licensing the Franchise: Alien vs. Predator—The Comic Book." *Alien vs. Predator Two Disc Extreme Edition*. DVD. 20th Century Fox, 2005.

Richardson, Mike, Randy Stradley, and Paul Gulacy. "Mike Richardson and Randy Stradley and Paul Gulacy—News: Interviews." *Dark Horse Comics*. 2004. 14 Dec 2004. www.darkhorse.com/news/interviews.

Rivera Calderón, Fernando. "Un rudo bajado el cielo." *Somos* 1941 (October 1999): 38–45.

Robbins, Trina. "Re: [comixschl] Shyamalan." E-mail to Comics Scholars' Discussion List. 4 March 2005.

Robey, Tim. "X-Men Excel at Excess." *Telegraph* 2 May 2003. 13 Feb. 2006. http://www.telegraph.co.uk/arts/main.jhtml?xml=/arts/2003/05/02/bfxmeno2.xml.

Robinson, Tasha. "Harvey Pekar." *The Onion A. V. Club.* 10 Sept. 2003. 17 October 2004. http://www.theonionavclub.com/feature/index.php ?issue=3935&f=1.

Ron, M. "Message 8: Screw All of You That Didn't Like This Film! I Loved AVP!!!!" Online posting. 31 Aug. 2004. Alt.cult-movies.alien Forum. 30 Nov. 2004. http://groups.google. com/group/alt.cult-movies.alien.

Rosenthal, Alan, ed. *Why Docudrama? Fact-Fiction on Film and TV*. Carbondale: Southern Illinois University Press, 1999.

Rozanski, Chuck. "How Ronald O. Perelman Caused Harm to the Comics Industry." *Mile High Comics*. 2004. 14 Dec. 2004. www.milehigh comics.com.

Rubenstein, Anne. *Bad Language, Naked Ladies, & Other Threats to the Nation: A Political History of Comic Books in Mexico*. Durham, NC: Duke University Press, 1998.

Russo, Tom. "Clash of Titans." *Entertainment Weekly* 24 June/1 July 2005: 26.

Sabin, Roger. *Comics, Comix and Graphic Novels: A History of Comic Art*. London: Phaidon Press, 1996.

———. "The Crisis in Modern American and British Comics, and the Possibilities of the Internet as a Solution." *Comics & Culture: Analytical and Theoretical Approaches to Comics*. Eds. Anne Magnussen and Hans-Christian Christiansen. Copenhagen: Museum Tusculanum Press, 2000. 43–58.

Sacco, Joe. *Safe Area Gorazde: The War in Eastern Bosnia 1992–95*. Seattle: Fantagraphics Books, 2001.

Said, S. F. "The Misfits of Zwigoff." *Sight and Sound* 10:8 (Aug. 2000): 20–22.

Saidin Yahya. *Hang Tuah 1–2*. [Kota Star:] Jabatan Pelajaran dan Persuratan PGMK, Cawangan Kota Star, 1953–1954.

Salisbury, Mark. "At Last, Earthlings, You Have Seen the Light." *Guardian* 4 Aug. 2000: 6.

"Salkind Denies Rumor 'Superman' Coin Was Tainted." *Variety* 22 Nov. 1978: 9.

"Salkind, From Swiss Clinic, Denies Forman Charges; Reply Readying." *Variety* 19 Dec. 1978.

Salkind, Ilya, and Pierre Spengler. "Super Studio 'Superman': Ilya Salkind and Pierre Spengler Discuss Their Multi-Million Dollar Epic at Pinewood." *Variety* 13 Dec. 1978: 27.

San Diego Comic-Con International. 2003. 26 Oct. 2003. http://www.comic-con. org/Pages/CCIWhatsNew.html.

Satrapi, Marianne. *Persepolis: The Story of a Childhood*. New York: Pantheon Books, 2003.

Schneider, Steven Jay. *1001 Movies You Must See Before You Die*. Hauppauge, N.Y.: Barron's, 2003.

Segrave, Kerry. *Foreign Films in America: A History*. Jefferson, NC: McFarland, 2004.

Sergi, Gianluca. *The Dolby Era: Film Sound in Contemporary Hollywood*. Manchester: Manchester University Press, 2004.

Sewell, Edward H. "Queer Characters in Comic Strips." *Comics and Ideology*. Ed. Matthew P. McAllister, Edward H. Sewell, Jr., and Ian Gordon. New York: Peter Lang, 2001. 251–74.

Sheppard, M. C. *The Adventures of Hang Tuah*. Singapore: Donald Moore, 1955.

Shyamalan, M. Night. "In the Director's Chair with M. Night Shyamalan (part 1)." By Joel Siegel. *MovieWeb*. 23 July 2004. 24 Jan. 2006. http://www.movie web.com/news/15/4615.php.

———. "In the Director's Chair with M. Night Shyamalan (part 2)." By Joel Siegel. *MovieWeb*. 23 July 2004. 24 Jan. 2006. http://www.movieweb.com/news /16/4616.php.

———. "The Man with a Vision: An Interview with M. Night Shayamalan." By Wilson Morales. *Blackfilm*. 23 Aug. 2002. 24 Jan. 2006. http://blackfilm.com/200 20823/features/mnightshyamalan.shtml.

———. "The Night in Question." By Tom Roston. *Premiere*. 24. Jan. 2006. http://www.premiere.com/article.asp?section_id6&article_id=1735.

Siegel, Jerry. "Special Interview: Jerry Siegel." *The 1975 San Diego Comic Con* Dyna Pubs, 1975.

Siegel, Jerry, and Joe Shuster. *DC Archives: Superman the Action Comics*. Vol. 1. New York: DC Comics, 1998.

———. "The Reign of the Super-Man." *Science Fiction Magazine* 3 (1933). 24 Jan. 2006. http://superman.ws/seventy/reign/.

Siegel, Jerry, Joe Shuster, and Joanne Siegel. "Of Superman and Kids with Dreams. A Rare Interview with the Creators of Superman: Jerry Siegel and Joe Shuster." By Tom Andrae, Geoffry Blum, and Gary Coddington. *NEMO: The Classic Comics Library* 2 (Aug. 1983): 6–19. 24 Jan. 2006. http://superman.ws/seventy/interview/.

"Smallville Advertisement." *Entertainment Weekly* 12 Oct. 2001: 15.

Smallville. Prod. Alfred Gough and Miles Millar. Perf. Tom Welling, Michael Rosenbaum, and Kristin Kreuk. Warner Brothers. 2001– .

Smallville Season 1 DVD, Warner Bros., 2003.

Smallville Season 2 DVD, Warner Bros., 2004.

Smallville Season 3 DVD, Warner Bros., 2004.

Smith, Greg M. "Shaping *The Maxx*: Adapting the Comic Book Frame to Television." *Animation Journal* 8:1 (Fall 1999): 32–53.

Soemargono, Farida. *"Sastrawan Malioboro" 1945–1960. Dunia Jawa dalam Kesusastraan Indonesia.* Mataram: Lengge, 2004.

Solehah Ishak. "Death of a Warrior or Long Live Feudalism." *Malay Literature* 15.2 (2002): 1–11.

Somigli, Luca. "The Superhero with a Thousand Faces: Visual Narratives on Film and Paper." *Play It Again, Sam: Retakes on Remakes.* Eds. Andrew Horton and Stuart Y. McDougal. Berkeley: University of California Press, 1998. 279–94.

Spider-Man. Dir. Sam Raimi. Perf. Tobey Maguire, Willem Dafoe, Kirsten Dunst, and James Franco. Sony Pictures, 2002.

Spider-Man 2. Dir. Sam Raimi. Perf. Tobey Maguire, Kirsten Dunst, and James Franco. Sony Pictures, 2004.

Spiegelman, Art. Comix 101 talk. Herbst Theatre, San Francisco. 13 October 1998. Unpublished transcription by Peter Stattler.

——— (w,a). *Maus I: A Survivor's Tale—My Father Bleeds History.* New York: Pantheon Books, 1986.

——— (w,a). *Maus II: A Survivor's Tale—And Here My Troubles Began.* New York: Pantheon Books, 1991.

Spigel, Lynn, and Henry Jenkins. "Same Bat Channel, Different Bat Times: Mass Culture and Popular Memory." *The Many Lives of the Batman: Critical Approaches to a Superhero and His Media.* Eds. Roberta E. Pearson and William Uricchio. New York: Routledge, 1991. 117–48.

Springman, Luke. "Poisoned Hearts, Diseased Minds, and American Pimps: The Language of Censorship in the *Schund und Schmutz* Debates." *The German Quarterly* 68.4 (Fall 1995): 408–29.

Stack, Tim. "Claw power." *Entertainment Weekly* June 9 2006: 17–18.

Stephens, John. "I'll Never Be the Same after That Summer: From Abjection to Subjective Agency in Teen Films." *Youth Culture: Texts, Images and Identities.* Eds. Kerry Mallan and Sharyn Pearce. Westport and London: Praeger, 2003. 123–38.

Stradley, Randy. Bug Hunt Editorial Response. Letter column appearing in *Aliens #4.* March 1989. Milwaukee: Dark Horse Comics.

———. "A Conversation with Randy Stradley. SBC Interviews." By Mike Jozic. *Silver Bullet Comicbooks.* 2004. 15 Dec. 2004 www.silverbullet comicbooks.com/features.

———. "Interview: Licensing the Franchise: Alien vs. Predator—The Comic Book." *Alien vs. Predator Two Disc Extreme Edition.* DVD. 20th Century Fox, 2005.

———. "Re: Comic Book Chapter." E-mail to Kerry Gough. 10 Dec. 2004.

———. "Re: Ripley Questions." E-mail to Kerry Gough. 3 Mar. 2005.

Strauss, Bob. "Where It All 'Begins': Director, Writers Access a Deeper, Darker Place in Re-imaging Batman's Origins." *Daily News (Los Angeles)* 12 June 2005: U6.

Superman Advertisements. *Variety* 11 May 1977: 9–16.

"'Superman' Is PG." *Variety* 22 Nov. 1978: 9.

"'Superman': It's Adult." *Variety* 19 Dec. 1978.

Superman: The Movie. Dir. Richard Donner. Perf. Christopher Reeve, Gene Hackman, Margot Kidder, and Marlon Brando. Warner Brothers, 1978.

Superman II. Dir. Richard Lester. Perf. Christopher Reeve, Gene Hackman, and Margot Kidder. Warner Brothers, 1980.

Surridge, Matthew. "Comics and Codes: Biography as Genre: A Reply to 'Based on a True Story.'" *Comics Journal* (2002). 17 Oct. 2004. http://www.tcj.com/3_ online/b_surridge_092299.html.

Sutherland, John. "How Superheroes Took Over the Cinema." *Guardian* 31 May 2002. 11 June 2004. http://film.guardian.co.uk/features/feature pages /0,,724656,00.html.

Tan Sooi Beng. *Bangsawan: A Social and Stylistic History of Popular Malay Opera.* Singapore: Oxford University Press, 1993.

Tasker, Yvonne. *Spectacular Bodies: Gender, Genre and the Action Cinema.* London: Routledge, 1993.

———, ed. *Action and Adventure Cinema.* London: Routledge, 2004.

Taylor, Elayne. "Crash! Splat! Kershplooie! Writing a Troma Film." *Creative Screenwriting* 7.3 (2000): 14–15.

Terkel, Studs. *Hard Times.* New York: Avon Books, 1970.

Thomas, François. "Entretien avec Alain Resnais: de la littérature de catacombes à la destruction de la planète." In *CinémAction HS: cinéma et bande dessinée.* Paris: Corlet—Télérama, 1990. 236–51.

Thompson, David. "Mutant Heroes to the Power of X." *Independent* 14 July 2000: 12.

———. "The Spider Stratagem." *Sight and Sound* 12.4 (Apr. 2002): 24–26.

Tondro, Jason. "Re: [comixschl] Shyamalan." E-mail to Comics Scholars' Discussion List. 4 Mar. 2005.

"Top July Comics Flat." *ICv2 News.* 12 Aug. 2003. 26 Oct. 2003. http://www. icv2.com/articles/news/3317.html.

Töteberg, Michael. "Als die Nasen laufen lernten." *Mal mir mal nen Schwulen: Das Buch zu Ralf König.* Ed. Joachim Bartholomae. Hamburg: MännerschwarmSkript, 1996. 88–100.

Tulloch, John, and Henry Jenkins. *Science Fiction Audiences: Watching Doctor Who and Star Trek.* New York: Routledge, 1995.

Twin Peaks. Prod. David Lynch and Mark Frost. Perf. Kyle MacLachlan and Michael Ontkean. ABC. 1990–1991.

"2004 Comics, Graphic Novel, and Magazine Publisher Actual Reorders Dollar Market Share: 2004 Year in Review." *Diamond Comic Distributors.* March 2005. 29 March 2005. www.diamondcomics.com/market_share.html.

"2004 Year in Review." *Diamond Comic Distributors.* Feb 2005. 18 Feb. 2005. www.diamondcomics.com/market_share.html.

Unbreakable. Dir. M. Night Shyamalan. Perf. Bruce Willis and Samuel L. Jackson. Touchstone Pictures, Blinding Edge Pictures, and Limited Editions Production, 2000.

Van Gelder, Lawrence. "Safe Sex It Is Not." Rev. of *Killer Condom,* dir. Martin Walz. *New York Times* 31 July 1998. 6 Nov. 2004. http://www.nytimes.com.

Verheiden, Mark (w), and Mark A. Nelson (a). *Aliens* #4 (March 1989), Milwaukee: Dark Horse Comics.

Vincent, Laurence. *Legendary Brands: Unleashing the Power of Storytelling to Create a Winning Market Strategy.* Chicago: Dearborn Trade Publishing, 2002.

Voigt, Thomas. "Manchmal bin ich selbst meine beste Comicfigur." [Interview with Ralf König]. *Mal mir mal nen Schwulen: Das Buch zu Ralf König.* Ed. Joachim Bartholomae. Hamburg: MännerschwarmSkript, 1996. 16–41.

Walz, Martin. "'Kondom des Grauens': Interview mit Regisseur Martin Walz." By Martin Blatter. *Cinenet.* 12 May 2000. http://old.kino.ch/previews/k/ KondomDes Grauens/Walz/.

Warner, Chris. "Interview: Licensing the Franchise: Alien vs. Predator—The Comic Book." *Alien vs. Predator Two Disc Extreme Edition.* DVD. 20th Century Fox, 2005.

Warshow, Robert *The Immediate Experience.* Cambridge, Massachusetts: Harvard University Press, 2002.

Wasko, Janet. *How Hollywood Works.* London: Sage Publications, 2003.

———. *Understanding Disney: The Manufacture of Fantasy.* Malden: Polity Press, 2001.

Waugh, Coulton. *The Comics.* New York: Macmillan, 1947.

"WB Owns Salkinds' 'Superman' Overseas." *Variety* 19 Dec. 1978.

"Weak Finish to a Strong Comics Year." *ICv2 News.* 26 Dec. 2002. 26 Oct. 2003. http://www. icv2.com/articles/home/2080.html.

Weingroff, Rick. "Whiz-Bang 7." *CAPA-Alpha* 13 (1964).

Weintraub, Brian. "Cinema: The New Life of Bryan." *Observer* 16 July 2000: 8.

Wertham, Frederic. *The World of Fanzines: A Special Form of Communication.* Carbondale: Southern Illinois University Press, 1973.

Wie die Karnickel. Dir. Sven Unterwaldt Jr. Perf. Anna Böttcher, Elke Czischek, and Michael di Mugno. Constantin Film/Achterbahn, 2002.

Wilkinson, R. J. *Papers on Malay Subjects—Malay Literature Part I. Romance; History; Poetry.* Kuala Lumpur: Federated Malay States Government Press, 1924.

Williams, Jeff. "Comics: A Tool of Subversion?" *Journal of Criminal Justice and Popular Culture* 2.6 (1994). 14 Dec. 2004. www.albany.edu/sjc/jcjpc.

Williams, Linda. "When the Woman Looks." *Horror: The Film Reader.* Ed. Mark Jancovich. London: Routledge, 2002. 61–66.

Willats, John. *Art and Representation: New Principles in the Analysis of Pictures.* Princeton, New Jersey: Princeton University Press, 1997.

Wilt, David. *The Mexican Filmography, 1916–2001.* Jefferson, NC: McFarland & Company, 2004.

Winstedt, Richard O. *A History of Classical Malay Literature.* Kuala Lumpur, New York: Oxford Univeristy Press, 1969.

Witek, Joseph. *Comic Books as History: The Narrative Art of Jack Jackson, Art Spiegelman, and Harvey Pekar.* Jackson: University Press of Mississippi, 1989.

Wolk, Douglas. "Big Films Mean Big Comics Sale." *Publishers Weekly* 17 June 2002: 28.

———. "Marvel Gets Its House in Order." *Publishers Weekly* 18 Mar. 2002: 32.

Wolk, Douglas, and Calvin Reid. "Comics Create Big Buzz at BEA." *Publishers Weekly* 16 June 2003: 27.

Wolk, Josh. "Fall TV Preview '01: Smallville." *Entertainment Weekly* 7 Sept. 2001: 66.

Wrestling-Titles.com. 15 Mar. 2006. www.wrestling-titles.com/wrestlers/santo/.

Wright, Bradford W. *Comic Book Nation: The Transformation of Youth Culture in America.* Baltimore and London: Johns Hopkins, 2001.

Wright, Les. "From Outsider to Insider: Queer Politics in German Film, 1970–94." *European Journal of Cultural Studies* 1.1 (1998): 97–121.

———. "The Genre Cycle of German Gay Coming-Out Films, 1970–1994." *Queering the Canon: Defying Sights in German Literature and Culture.* Eds. Christoph Lorey and John L. Plews. Columbia, SC: Camden House, 1998. 311–39.

Wyatt, Justin. *High Concept: Movies and Marketing in Hollywood.* Austin: University of Texas Press, 1994.

The X-Files. Prod. Chris Carter. Perf. David Duchovny and Gillian Anderson. Fox. 1993–2002.

X-Men. Dir. Bryan Singer. Perf. Hugh Jackman, Patrick Stewart, Ian McKellen, Famke Janssen, James Marsden, Halle Berry, Anna Paquin, Tyler Mane, Ray Park, and Rebecca Romijin. 20th Century Fox, 2000.

Xena: Warrior Princess. Prod. John Schulian and Robert G. Tapert. Perf. Lucy Lawless. Syndicated. 1995–2001.

X2. Dir. Bryan Singer. Perf. Hugh Jackman, Patrick Stewart, Ian McKellen, Famke Janssen, James Marsden, Halle Berry, Anna Paquin, Rebecca Romijin, Brian Cox, Alan Cumming, Aaron Stanford, Shawn Ashmore, and Kelly Hu. 20th Century Fox, 2003.

Zainab Awang Ngah. "Malay Comic Books Published in the 1950s." *Kekal AbadiJil.* 3.3 (Sept. 1984): 4–11.

CONTRIBUTORS

TIMOTHY P. BARNARD is an associate professor in the Department of History at the National University of Singapore. He has published works on the history and culture of the Melaka Straits region, with a particular focus on issues of identity and the environment. Among his publications are *Mulitiple Centres of Authority: Environment and Society in Eastern Sumatra, 1674–1827* (Leiden: KITLV, 2003) and *Contesting Malayness: Malay Identity across Boundaries* (Singapore: Singapore University Press, 2004). He was until recently the editor of the *Journal of Southeast Asian Studies*. He is currently working on a history of Malay film from 1945 to 1965.

MICHAEL COHEN'S chapter on Dick Tracy is based on his completed masters thesis in cinema studies from La Trobe University in Australia. His MA analyzes superhero films that reveal formal and stylistic choices which attempt to capture a comic book aesthetic. He is also the editor and senior writer of film reviews for the *Experience: Events* section of The Scene.com.au, an online lifestyle site.

RAYNA DENISON is a lecturer in media and film studies at the University of Sussex. She has recently completed a PhD titled "Cultural Traffic in Japanese Anime: The Meanings of Promotion, Reception and Exhibition Circuits in Princess Mononoke" and has published on the international flows in anime culture. She is also researching film sound, children's media, the blockbuster, and investigative narratives in television and film. To this end she is currently co-editing a collection titled *Mysterious Bodies: Investigating the Corporeal in Television Drama* with Mark Jancovich.

MARTIN FLANAGAN is course leader and senior lecturer in film and media studies at the University of Bolton. His thesis was concerned with the cinematic relevance of the theories of Mikhail Bakhtin, and he has recently published an article applying Bakhtinian ideas to action film aesthetics in the collection *Action and Adventure Cinema* (Routledge, 2004). He has also published work on Ang Lee's *Hulk* in the *New Review of Film and Television Studies*, and explored authorial issues in articles on Robert Rodriguez and Terrence Malick.

SOPHIE GEOFFROY-MENOUX is professor at the University of La Réunion (France). Her teaching and research areas are intertextuality and intermediality, especially in fantastic literature. She has published critical editions (*Hawthorne, by Henry James*, Paris: José Corti, 2000), unpublished correspondence ("Henry James and Family: Eleven Unpublished Letters," *Sources*, Spring 2003), and numerous books and articles on Henry James, Nathaniel Hawthorne, Vernon Lee (*La voix maudite*, Terre de Brume, 2001), and Angela Carter. She has contributed thirty-five entries in the forthcoming *Dictionnaire des Littératures de l'Imaginaire* (L'Atalante, 2007).

MEL GIBSON is a senior lecturer in childhood studies at the University of Northumbria. She has published on a range of issues around comics and audiences. She also works with libraries and schools in developing comic collections.

IAN GORDON is an associate professor in history and convener of American studies at the National University of Singapore. He is the author of *Comic Strips and Consumer Culture* (Smithsonian Institution Press, 1998); "Superman on the Set: The Market, Nostalgia and Television Audiences," in *Quality Popular Television* (BFI, 2003); and a co-editor of *Comics and Ideology*.

KERRY GOUGH is a lecturer in media theory at the University of Central England, Birmingham. She is currently completing her PhD "*Ever Been Mistaken for a Man?: Ripley as a Shifting Cultural Signifier*" with the University of Nottingham. Her thesis examines the historical reception of the *Alien* film saga and the function that Lt. Ellen Ripley fulfils within the reception materials, as a historically specific located nexus for societal discourse and debate surrounding the body, social behaviors, and gendered norms.

JONATHAN GRAY is assistant professor of communication and media studies at Fordham University. He has published on various issues of textuality and audiences in *Critical Studies in Media Communication*, *International Journal of Cultural Studies*, *Intensities: Journal of Cult Media*, *American Behavioral Scientist*, and books on *Blade Runner* and *Lord of the Rings*. His recent book is entitled *Watching with the Simpsons: Television, Parody, and Intertextuality* (Routledge, 2006).

CRAIG HIGHT is a senior lecturer with the Screen and Media Studies Department at the University of Waikato. With Dr. Jane Roscoe, he has co-written *Faking It: Mock-Documentary and the Subversion of Factuality* (Manchester University Press), the first major work on mock-documentary as a documentary hybrid form. His recent research focuses on digital technologies, including their relationship to documentary practice, and aspects of the production, construction, and reception of documentary hybrids.

MARK JANCOVICH is a professor of film and television studies at the University of East Anglia in the U.K. His books include *The Cultural Politics of the New Criticism* (Cambridge University Press, 1993); *Rational Fears: American Horror in the 1950s* (Manchester University Press, 1996); and *Quality Popular Television* (edited with James Lyons) (BFI, 2003).

DEREK JOHNSON is a PhD candidate in media and cultural studies at the University of Wisconsin—Madison. His research focuses on the production, marketing, and reception of serialized transmedia franchises in film, television, comic books, video games, and other commodity forms.

PASCAL LEFÈVRE first studied social sciences and American studies at the University of Leuven (K.U. Leuven). While working as a producer at the Belgian national broadcasting corporation (BRTN), he started publishing and organizing conferences on comic strips. From 1996 till 1999 he was attached part time as a scientific advisor to the Belgian Centre of Comic Strip Art in Brussels. Since 1997 he has been lecturing on comics at two Flemish art schools (in Brussels and Antwerp). Selected publications are *Pour une lecture moderne de la* *bande dessinée* (with Jan Baetens) and *The Comic Strip in the Nineteenth Century* (co-edited with Charles Dierick). In October 2003 he completed his PhD on the formal analysis of comics at the University of Leuven.

PAUL M. MALONE is an associate professor of German in the Department of Germanic and Slavic Studies at the University of Waterloo, Canada. He is the author of *Franz Kafka's The Trial: Four Stage Adaptations* (Frankfurt: Peter Lang, 2003), and has also published on German drama, film, theatre/performance theory, and virtual reality computer technology.

MATTHEW P. MCALLISTER is an associate professor in film, video, and media studies at Penn State University. He is the author of *The Commercialization of American Culture: New Advertising, Control, and Democracy* (Sage, 1996); "Selling Survivor: The Use of TV News to Promote Commercial Entertainment," in A. N. Valdivia (ed.), *The Blackwell Companion to Media Studies* (Blackwell, 2003); and a co-editor of *Comics and Ideology*.

NEIL RAE is a doctoral candidate in media and communication studies at Goldsmiths College, University of London. His dissertation examines the global publication, circulation, and consumption of manga.

ALDO J. REGALADO is a doctoral candidate in history at the University of Miami in Florida. His doctoral dissertation, "Bending Steel with Bare Hands: Modernity and the American Superhero in the Twentieth Century," is a cultural history that examines the origins and construction of superheroes in American popular culture as they have been shaped by the tensions inherent in the modernizing forces of an emergent capitalism and its relationship to shifting American notions of race, class, gender, and nationalism. His essay, "*Unbreakable* and the Limits of Transgression," appears in *Comics as Philosophy* (University of Mississippi Press, 2005). Mr. Regalado is currently teaches history at the University of Miami and at Palmer Trinity School.

JAN VAN DER PUTTEN is assistant professor of Malay studies at the National University of Singapore. His publications comprise articles about traditional Malay writing, the advent of printing and identity, and include two books about private letters of two Malay authors in the nineteenth century: *In Everlasting Friendship: Letters from Raja Ali Haji* and *His Word Is the Truth: Haji Ibrahim's Letters and Other Writings*.

DAVID WILT, University of Maryland, specializes in the study of film and society, and in Mexican cinema. He is the author of *The Mexican Filmography 1916–2001* (2004) and *Hard-boiled in Hollywood* (1991), and the co-author of *Doing Their Bit: Wartime American Animated Films, 1939–1945* (second edition, 2004) and *Hollywood War Films, 1937–1945* (1996). He has also contributed to *The Columbia Companion to American History on Film* (2004), *Mondo Macabro* (1997), *Mexican Horror Cinema* (1999), as well as liner notes for various DVDs.

INDEX

	DATE DUE	